NO DEPOSIT—NO RETURN

Anthology of papers presented at
13th National Conference
of the U.S. National Commission for UNESCO
November 1969, San Francisco, California

▲▲▲ ADDISON-WESLEY PUBLISHING COMPANY

Edited by **HUEY D. JOHNSON**

NO DEPOSIT—NO RETURN

Man and His ENVIRONMENT:
A View Toward Survival

Reading, Massachusetts
Menlo Park, California • London • Don Mills, Ontario

It is understood that the statements made and opinions expressed are the authors'
and editor's and do not necessarily reflect the views of the U.S. National Commission for UNESCO.

GF
3
N 38
1969

Cover photograph by Bruce Anderson.

Barry Commoner, "The Ecological Facts of Life." Copyright © by Barry Commoner.
Huey Johnson, "Implementation for Goals." Copyright © by Huey Johnson.

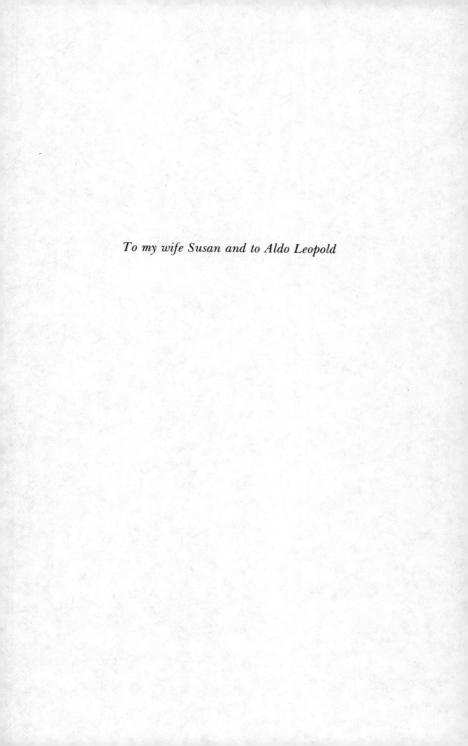

To my wife Susan and to Aldo Leopold

Foreword and Acknowledgments

"Man and His Environment: A View Toward Survival" was the title selected for the 13th National Conference of the U.S. National Commission for UNESCO dealing with man's environment. This book is an edited anthology of papers presented at the Conference.

The Committee's approach to the topic, considered controversial by some, was successful because of the latitude granted the Committee by the U.S. National Commission for UNESCO and, in particular, its Chairman, Dr. Alvin Eurich. The Commission staff—Dr. Arthur Minnich, Secretary, Miss Ann Jablonsky, Administrative Assistant, and Mr. Ray Kohn, Director of Public Relations—were essential to the success of the Conference.

Stanford University contracted the Conference and agreed to prepare it for the Commission. The competence of Stanford's administrators, its Office of University Relations with its Director, Lyle Nelson, his associate, Dixon Arnett, and their staff, was inspiring.

Dixon Arnett served as Conference Staff Director. His remarkable intelligence and ability were indispensable. His Conference paper, in the Government section of Part IIC, demonstrates his dedication.

The Planning Committee was comprised of well-known experts from diverse fields. They included Dr. Sterling Bunnell of San Francisco; Dr. William Catton, Jr., University of Washington, Seattle; Dr. Rolf Eliassen, Stanford University; Dr. Charles Foster, Harvard University; Mr. Lawrence Halprin of San Francisco; Mr. Alfred W. Heller, San Francisco; Dr. Richard H. Jahns, Stanford University; Dr. H. Thomas James, Stanford University; Mr. Joel Kuperberg, Naples, Florida; Mr. L. W. Lane, Jr., Publisher, Sunset Magazine; Mr. Aaron Levine, Honolulu; Dr. Paul Martin, University of Arizona; Dr. John McKee, Bowdoin College; Mr. Proctor Melquist, Sunset Magazine; Mr. Lyle M. Nelson,

Stanford University; Dr. Kenneth S. Pitzer, President of Stanford University; Dr. Thomas Tanner, Oregon State University; Dr. Frederick Wagner, Utah State University; Dr. William L. C. Wheaton, University of California, Berkeley. These men deserve praise and appreciation for the fine work they did in planning the Conference.

A special note of thanks is due Alfred Heller not only for his assistance in the planning but especially for his joining me for lunch one day, where in a flurry of inspired scribbles upon luncheon napkins, we outlined the basic Conference program.

Sunset Magazine's generosity included donating the Conference poster and aiding with printing material for the Conference. Stanford University Press was also instrumental in the preparation of the material. The comprehensive coverage of the Conference by KQED, the San Francisco based educational television station, was greatly appreciated.

Of course, many individuals contributed to the Conference and its success. I would like to thank: Melissa Shorrock, who served as assistant editor; Phil Wallin, Joan McIntyre, Keith Artz, who worked on exhibits; the staff of The Nature Conservancy's Western Regional Office, Keith Artz, Steve Steinhour, Si Foote, Dick Goodspeed, Gregory Archbald, Phil Wallin, Judy MacInnes, Diane Granger, Barbara Bush, and Amelia Garcia for assisting both at the Conference and for having taken on part of my work prior to it; and Thomas Richards, President of The Nature Conservancy, for allowing me the opportunity to work on the Conference.

There were many whose advice helped: Peter Behr, Charles Bordon, David Brower, Lynton Caldwell, Orlo Childs, LaMont Cole, George Collins, Richard Cooley, Bill Davoren, John DeWitt, Ray Fosberg, Harold Gilliam, Richard Goodwin, Walter Haas, Roger Hansen, Gordon Harrison, Sydney Howe, Bob Jasperson, Pennfield Jensen, Warren Lemmon, Doris Leonard, Norman Livermore, Congressman Paul McCloskey, Sylvia McLaughlin, Maya Miller, Richard Miller, Emil Mrak, Lyle Nelson, Dennis Reinhardt, Joan Rosen, Martin Rosen, Congressman James Scheurer, Paul Sears, Stephen Spurr, Rick Todd, Georg Treichel, Alan Wagar, Francea Welker, and others. To all of them go my thanks.

San Francisco   H. J.
May 1970

Contents

Part I

Introduction

This anthology is the result of a conference called "Man and His Environment—A View Toward Survival," sponsored by the United States National Commission for UNESCO. The papers are free statements by leading men in the interdisciplinary concern for the human environment. Together they provide an environmental overview encompassing many sectors, all of which interrelate to affect the environment.

As Program Chairman, I asked the contributors to prepare factual statements in terms that could be readily understood by the man in the street as well as by the representatives of more than 200 organizations who would attend the conference. I emphasized that many of the organizations in attendance were not active in, or particularly aware of, environmental problems, and that we would have an opportunity to alert new groups to the crisis.

Hundreds of hours were spent preparing the topical outline and selecting the speakers. Leading experts from such fields as biology, architecture, city planning, sociology, advertising, and psychiatry participated. The lions and the lambs sat down together, but no sides were chosen. The hope for survival was vital to everyone, regardless of his special interest, and lent a very positive cooperative tone. Obviously, we are all to blame for the mess, and each of us must now contribute to its solution if life is to go on.

In a situation as critical as the one we now face, survival of the individual, in fact, survival of society itself, begins with being informed. It then depends on doing something to correct what is wrong. This book is a primer for environmental awareness. It is meant for people who want to do something about survival. Its object is both to inform and to rouse people to act. Its success will be measured by what is accomplished by those who can apply these facts and viewpoints and get results along the broad front of environmental concern.

We have witnessed the building of highways through parks, proliferating pollution allowed by ineffective legislation, and destruction caused by mismanaged natural resources. All these are monuments to uninformed individuals and organizational failures —the result of man's failure to take an intelligent stand on environmental problems. Even when facts have shown the deleterious effects of our culture on the environment, those facts have not been marshaled and used. Selfish interests of countless small groups have won because of the apathy of the public.

Perhaps no one branch of technology believed that its individual activities would bring us all to the brink of environmental disaster. Exploitation of natural resources, the fantastic growth of technology, and the galloping increase in population have, nevertheless, compounded the abuse of our environment.

The public is at last beginning to realize that the words *environment* and *ecology* are directly related to the actual survival of humanity, and that man must start now to correct a deteriorating environment. The stark reality depicted by the authors in this book makes it clear that government and business will not, of their own accord, take the massive steps necessary to save man and the planet. Mankind may survive, but only if activist citizens are informed enough and are angry enough to demand action. Then the institutions will follow.

Knowledge and understanding are the nuts and bolts of succeeding at anything—growing crops, building machines, or winning elections. Information is especially important in matters of environmental concern. The uninformed response is one of emotion, frustration, and finally retreat to inner circles of kindred souls who complain to each other, while exploitation and disaster grow unchecked.

An individual knowledgeable in environmental matters may be better informed and have a better perspective than most politicians or even many experts who are so superspecialized that they are caught in narrow fields of interest. Every knowledgeable person can have a major impact by participating at public levels— supporting issues by speaking or writing. *Survival through environmental improvement must begin with concerned individuals.* We must reach a majority of men, particularly the decision-makers in our industries and institutions. They must become involved and accept the responsibility for decisions that will mean new cultural directions. It may be that the same technology which brought us these problems will now use its resources and ingenuity to conquer them.

Awareness of the dangers can bring improvement to technological processes. We can establish guidelines for future development.

There are some examples of environmental victories. Hawaii has planned development by zoning to maintain crop lands, Wisconsin has passed legislation to stop improper use of pesticides, California has made laws to upgrade water and air pollution controls, and many universities have responded to the need for a broad spectrum approach in dealing with environmental problems. The improvement is still scant, but it is enough to give us hope. The difference between improvement and exploitation can usually be traced to how well informed the people are in these sectors.

While the scope of this book is limited to environmental problems in the United States, the problems are worldwide. The place to begin is at home, and the way to progress is by example. We must first solve our own problems and then do our part as global citizens.

I am optimistic enough to believe that we will survive because of a little recognized phenomenon: The environmental dilemma offers us the first issue of universal appeal to everyone. Those involved in the conflicts of political left or right, or of racial black or white, will be forced to work together if they want to survive. No one escapes smog, and no one can live without clean water.

In addition to formulating educational objectives, the Conference set forth a number of action suggestions designed to save man from himself by ensuring a healthy environment. These are summarized in the last chapter. Because the life of every man's great-grandchild is at stake, I believe the time has come for us to adopt these and other action suggestions as urgent goals and to do our damnedest to achieve them. Survival demands our passionate commitment to meaningful action—now.

Part II
Facts

A. Introduction

These following statements cover some of a wide spectrum of environmental subjects. All require action if we are to survive. We must see what they contribute as individual areas of concern and then realize that they are all interrelated. We must gain a comprehensive grasp of the factors involved. Only then can we sense the complexity of an ecological perspective.

To cover one of these topics rigorously and definitely would require the lifetimes of many scholars. As yet, we do not have enough of these experts, in part because our priorities, such as military and space spending, haven't provided funds for their training and for research.

Each author is an expert in his field, a brilliant man who is willing to share his experience and training. Each man's conclusions are based on years of preparation—on a lifetime of passionate devotion to his work. As individuals, our first step toward action is to listen to what they have to say and be conversant in these and other areas of environmental concern.

1

A VIEW TOWARD SURVIVAL

ARTHUR GODFREY

Godfrey is the voice of the concerned citizen committed to action. He is listened to by many—industry, government, youth, and the general public. His was the opening keynote speech, calling for a "Pollution Pentagon." It brought the Conference to its feet in a thundering ovation and set the tone for what followed.

"Man is the only animal who blushes or has need to" is a bon mot attributed to Mark Twain. And he was right. We are blushing—or should be. Our faces should be scarlet with burning shame. Mine is fiery red all the time. Why? Because I am one of those guilty millions of us who have systematically wrought the ecological rape of this once beautiful planet. We have so badly fouled our environment that today many are fearful that the pollution has exceeded the capacity of nature to cleanse herself, and our little spaceship, Earth, has had it.

Like everyone else, I have contributed my share of crud in my time. Cigar and cigarette butts in the streets, on the floors of public buildings, out the car window; empty packages, boxes, cans, wrappings, bottles, newspapers, magazines. Ashes and smoke I have scattered in the breeze. Poisonous *persistent* pesticides on the farm. Hydrocarbons from my cars and boats and airplanes and househeating oil burners in the air and water. Rags, old rubber tires—yes, once I even left a battered heap of junk automobile on a side street back in 1929.

I have pumped raw sewage overboard in saltwater anchorages from my boat and, under cover of night, have even dumped trash over the side. Yes, until a few years ago, I was as big a slob with my "people droppings" as anyone and I've often wondered why.

I don't recall being particularly dirty as a youngster. Maybe I was, but I joined the Navy at 16 and damned soon learned to be clean. The Navy! Come to think of it, we always threw everything overboard. We kept the ship spic and span all right—but what a wake we must have left: raw sewage, bilge-pumpings, trash, garbage. Of course! The good old Navy "made a man of me" and taught me to love the sea as much as to respect her awesome power in storms; but I also acquired a badly exaggerated estimate of her ability to absorb human pollution, if indeed I ever thought about it at all. Which is probably the way it was: never thought about it at all. *Nobody* ever did until recently, and most people don't think much about it even now.

I remember when the first factory was built on the Saddle River in New Jersey not far from where I went to school in Hasbrouck Heights. We couldn't swim or fish in the river after that because it had become polluted with the factory wastes. We kids bitched about it some, but our elders didn't give a damn. In fact, they were glad because it was one less temptation for us to play hooky from school. Besides, lots of people got jobs in that factory. Saddle River Township was growing! This was progress. Yes, it was just about that time that the myth was established: prosperity means progress means people—the more people the more progress—the more prosperity. Too late we have seen that it also means more pollution, more filth, more death.

Little by little, I remember, the same thing happened to the Passaic River and the Hackensack and Berry's Creek. Of course, the Hudson had long since been ruined, even before Robert Fulton's time.

That's the way it all happened, I think. Nobody ever noticed except the kids and the folks downstream—who themselves sooner or later sold out to *progress* and joined the *growing economy*. Adding their own effluent to the mess, they shrugged: "What the hell: it's going out to sea! That's what rivers are for: to take the sewage and the garbage and the factory wastes out to sea! You can't pollute the ocean—it's too big, too vast!"

I can even remember when our elders taught us that water in a stream purifies itself every few hundred feet. All we had to do was go downstream a mile or so below town and we could drink the very water the town had flushed through the toilets. Typhoid fever played a big role in keeping the population down in those days.

Later, I remember "swimming call" aboard ship. In the early 20's I had served in two Navy destroyers stationed in Turkish waters. Often on balmy days, while riding at anchor in some harbor like Smyrna or Adalia or Beirut in the Mediterranean, or Samsoun or Trebizond or even Varna in the Black Sea, we sailors would dive happily overboard while the Quartermaster kept an eye out for sharks. We had very little trouble with sharks in those waters, but there was raw sewage in abundance. I remember one crusty old Boatswain's Mate in the USS Lawrence who, too smart to join us, used to delight in singing out: "Crud Ho!" Whereupon we'd all hastily but happily submerge like sea-turtles and swim away a few yards under water to avoid actual contact.

You see, just as landlubbers ashore believed fresh water in a stream purified itself every few yards (incredibly, many still think so!) an old sailor's faith in the antiseptic qualities of seawater was boundless. Since effluent floated on the surface, as was readily seen, all one had to do was find a "hole" in it and dive through. With arms outstretched ahead, one easily "swept" a clean spot for himself as he surfaced.

If that sounds too ridiculous, consider the urban apartment-dweller today who goes out for a walk around the block with her dog for a "breath of fresh air." Meekly, impassively, she steps over, around, between and often through the dog-do, oil smears, garbage, and trash without complaint. They even make bad jokes about it just as we old sailors did as we looked for holes in the harbor gook to dive through. It would be funny if it weren't so tragic. But it is tragic!

It becomes increasingly obvious that most people have become so accustomed to litter and effluent and flotsam and jetsam, foul air, and polluted water that they accept it nowadays as a way of life. Most young people, for instance, have never known anything else!

In St. Paul last August, at the Minnesota State Fair, despite the dozens of trash cans that were within easy reach of everyone, the fairgrounds were always ankle-deep in "people droppings."

I was there five days to fill an engagement at the stadium with my dressage horses. Twice each day, as I rode from the stables to the arena, my horse, having never seem such litter before, gingerly picked his way through fetlock-deep bottles (glass and plastic), paper cups, pie plates, half-eaten hamburger rolls, smouldering cigarette butts, and what-not.

The only bench along the route I followed twice each day was always occupied, usually by some young couple lost in mutual mesmerism. They would sit there holding hands, turning each other on, their feet completely buried in the trash around the bench. Occasionally a couple would look up as I approached astride my horse. Each time, as I returned their smiles, I would ask: "Doesn't that gook bother you folks?" The question always obviously took them by surprise. The way they'd glance around, sort of sheepishly, convinced me they hadn't even noticed the debris at all until I called it to their attention!

Why do I take time to speak of garbage and feces and litter? Let me try to explain. Forty years ago, in 1929, I learned to fly. Since then I have accumulated some 14,000 hours in almost every kind of aircraft: single and multiengine land and seaplanes, helicopters, and even blimps. The old barnstorming days we all loved are long gone, but nowadays endless pleasure is derived from precision-flying sleek little Lear jets on instruments. I feel safe and relaxed at 500 mph in thick weather because I've been trained to believe my instruments. I scan them constantly—looking for small changes—and making small corrections. Airspeed, power settings, temperatures, aircraft attitudes—a flicker of change gets a flicker of action. A big change gets proportionately big action. Always, when anything goes wrong, lights come on to indicate the trouble source.

Mainly, I think it's this training that led me to look at the indicators of this planet that I love and upon which I once felt safe and secure.

As a youth, the instrument panel read normal. I loved to walk through the woods and fields and swamps and early became steeped in woodlore. As a young flyer, I drank in the clean vistas, the commanding view of America from spacious skies. As the years passed, I began to observe I wasn't flying from town to town anymore but from smoky spot to smoky spot on the horizon. (Smog hadn't been invented then.) Gradually, during the last decade, smog has become a reality and an almost unbroken carpet over land and sea.

I have also been an ardent canoeist and a yachtsman most of my life. I remember how I used to enjoy taking a small boat up one of the inland waterways looking for quiet coves and marshes. After a time the coves were jammed with other boats everywhere and the marshes were filled in by developers.

I have always had a love for hunting, too, in the north woods, in the Rockies, and in Africa and India. I loved the solitudes of the wilderness and the lure of fine specimens. But the environments became restricted and the game too precious to shoot.

In a thousand ways the environmental instrument panel began to give me information: in the color of the atmosphere even far out over the Atlantic, in the harsh jam of a crowded street, in an oil slick, however tiny, in the surf at Waikiki. But no lights came on to identify the sources for me. I was confused and depressed because I felt so helpless.

Then I came across a marvelous book called "Moment in the Sun," by Robert and Leona Rienow, who had worked together for thirty years documenting their theories with facts.

When I finished the book, my environmental instrument panel lighted up like a Christmas tree. I knew, now, what was wrong—what was causing the trouble signs, and I began to react. First, I tried to control my own life and get my own wings level and then to suggest controls and guidelines to audiences everywhere.

There is more information available now, though, more and more every day—more and more lights are coming on all the time. Frankly, I'm scared, because the attitude gyros have tumbled and we're on our environmental backs. Now it's time for action and fast recovery or, my friends, we're going in!

What action do we take? That, of course, is the purpose of the UNESCO conference: to look at man and his environment and find a view toward survival.

I've read the background papers for the conference and was very much impressed. Especially by what the younger people have to say. To be honest, I didn't sympathize very much with agitation or rebellion until I read Pennfield Jensen's paper. Let me quote from it: "The naiveté, enthusiasm and idealism of young people is not a thing to be scorned, for it is the raw material of constructive growth. . . . We will stop the destruction of this planet even at the cost of our futures, careers and blood. The situation is simply like that. If you are not going to live for the Earth, what are you going to live for?"

That's good stuff. That's what it's going to take. But, frankly, I would feel better if the President's distinguished science advisor had said it last night.

Is there time for us to wait for our youth to become effective? Is there time for agitation or civil war? I don't think so. Dr. DuBridge rightly said that population control should be the "prime task" of every government. Also he said that as we proceed with this task, we must attend to our environment. But is there anyone here—anyone—who thinks that this administration, or the next, or the next will act with the kind of force that's necessary?

We are threatened by communism abroad and spend billions each month to counter that threat. Does anyone think that we will soon respond with billions to combat the causes of crowding and litter and smog at home?

What about action? What about a Department of Environmental Affairs? What about a "Pollution Pentagon?"

Paul Ehrlich is a man with the rare courage to voice the difficult truths. He says that the population of the United States must be cut back to 150 million. He says that to do this we must have an independent population commission empowered to act as a check on all government agencies. He says that parents should be taxed as parents, that instruction in birth control should be mandatory, antiabortion laws forbidden. And he suggests that sterilants be added to our water sources with only government-issued antidotes.

Ehrlich goes on. Frankly, a few years ago I would not have listened. Back then I was for small corrective actions. A few years ago it would have been good if the President had sent an urgent population message to Congress. It would have been timely to study the situation, timely to create councils, timely to allot a spare million from the highway program or the first space shot.

NO MORE.

It's time now to recognize that the only threat to civilization is civilization. It's time to use what little time is left.

It's time to use all of our brains, all of our courage, all of our resources to act . . . to recover.

It's time to survive—to volunteer for survival.

Good luck! Crud Ho!

2

THE EARTH'S NATURAL RESOURCES

PAUL B. SEARS

To work with Dr. Sears was a delight for me, for I have long treasured his philosophy. He expressed his strong feeling about resources as a cultural matter: "The creative genius of mankind is challenged in all its range to design a future, not only for survival, but for a kind of survival that has meaning."

Our planet, vast as it is in human terms, is finite. The age of exploration settled whatever doubts may have existed on that score. Jefferson understood this when he made the Louisiana Purchase, yet statesmen long after his time spoke of the limitless resources of North America. Much of our economic behavior and many of the ideas that defend it seem to be based on this kind of rosy assumption.

While circumnavigation showed earth's limits in terms of space, its unique qualities were made clear only much later. In a modest little volume, *The Fitness of the Environment,* Lowell Henderson drew upon information from geochemistry, energetics, and physiology, as well as astronomy, to show that ours was the one planet in our solar system fitted for life as we know it. He is said to have thought lightly of this work or even to have regretted writing it.

Perhaps he felt that he had taken valuable time merely to emphasize the obvious. If so, he greatly overestimated the level of understanding among his fellows, even among some who should know
better. One of the most valuable results of our exploration of
outer space has been the reminder to mankind of its good fortune
to be alive.

Among natural resources there are three—air, water, and food
—without which no animal, man included, can survive. As to those
three there is no choice; but whatever else becomes a resource—
materials for tools, shelter, clothing, energy, amenities, and luxur-
ies—is a cultural matter. Of all resources, air is the most uniformly
distributed in quantity and quality. But not even air remains unaffected by human use. Cultures may conserve resources or
dissipate them. So far as the basic physiological resources—air,
water, and soil (i.e., food)—are concerned, the most serious effect
of human activity has been to disrupt the great natural cycles that
regulate their quality and abundance.

And while the sun paints its energy with a broad brush, shift-
ing its band of pigments in obedience to celestial geometry, the
picture so created is modified by the irregular distribution of
water and land, as well as by the varying qualities and forms of the
latter. While stresses within our aging planet continue to reshape
its surface, wind and water, powered by the sun, share the task.
Yet, cushioning the violence of these changes in no small measure,
there is the life that has risen and flourished by virtue of a fraction
of the same energy that produces the stresses.

Uncounted forms of life have come and gone, giving rise to
highly organized communities in water and on land. By no means
changeless themselves, these communities are agents of constructive change, slowing the flux of endless physical forces. Stabilizing
the surface, regulating the economy of water, purifying the air,
and creating soil, they have not only maintained but enhanced the
capacity of the earth to sustain life.

Recently, in the scale of geological time, a new species has appeared. Endowed with grasping hands, binocular vision, erect
posture, the power of speech, and above all, an enlarged brain, it
has become the dominant organism and a major natural force. For
most of the more than a million years of man's existence in substantially his present form, his power to alter environment grew
very slowly. Communities of other forms of life continued to
maintain balance and heal the scars of fire and other human tools.

Little more than ten thousand years ago, the invention of
plant and animal husbandry increased both human leisure and

human numbers and thereby magnified man's impact on his environment. Natural communities, with their stabilizing effect, became his rivals for space as his own numbers increased and became more concentrated. As he intensified his efforts to produce food and fiber, more often than not he reversed the conserving and constructive processes of nature. The rise and fall of human cultures is witness to the resulting decay in the power of environment to regenerate itself.

It would seem reasonable to expect that increasing scientific knowledge would bring about a healthy relation of man to environment. Instead, his disruption of those conditions to which he owes his very existence has taken on new dimensions. His numbers are increasing exponentially. He has tapped vast reserves of energy built up during the geological past. Thus he has created a condition well known in physics—decreased freedom of the individual unit with increased numbers and energy within a finite space.

Currently there are six deaths per hour from automobile traffic. Mass fabrication, ranging far beyond the production of necessities, dissipates the reserves of minerals and taxes the power of soil, water, and air to recuperate. Industrial and municipal wastes pile up faster than they can be handled or even rendered innocuous, let alone reused.

Long ignored, these consequences are now causing sufficient discomfort and damage to receive attention. We hear increasing demands for more knowledge, new laws, or even new economic and political systems. Useful as such instruments may be, they are no better than the beliefs and accepted standards that give them force.

The creative genius of mankind is challenged in all its range to design a future, not only for survival, but for a kind of survival that has meaning. In its ultimate character this is not an operational but a philosophical problem. Behind the fact of life is the problem of its meaning. In the cold light of today's overwhelming mass of knowledge, whatever meaning life is to have must be the creation of man himself.

3

A VIEW OF THE PRESENT SITUATION

LAMONT COLE

An outspoken ecologist discusses the frightening realities created by man's exploitation, based on ignorance. "We have had an amazing run of dumb luck, but we should not count on it to continue."

A recurring theme in the conference has been the concept of Spaceship Earth. Undoubtedly a large percentage of the earth's people have recently seen pictures of the earth taken from the vicinity of the moon. It looks, as someone put it, like an "inviting blue fishbowl." Everyone can see that it's really round and really isolated—a spaceship, in fact, that can expect no commodities from outside other than the energy of sunlight to keep it functioning. And the message of the pictures is that the earth is an isolated, finite sphere on which an indefinitely expanding Gross National Product is complete nonsense.

I hope the space program will cause many such awakenings. People must realize that nature's way of dealing with what we call "wastes" is to reuse them, to "recycle" them. When we send astronauts to the moon, they carry with them all the water, oxygen, and food they will need for the mission. But for flights into deeper space this will be impracticable.

Water, for example, will have to be recycled, and this is not a trivial problem because distillation will not work under weightless conditions. As people become aware that this problem is giving a little trouble to the scientists and engineers, they may exclaim, "Gee, it's pretty good the way the earth recycles water all the time without our even thinking about it!"

When our space missions reach the point where oxygen also must be recycled, the problems will be a little more difficult. And when our spaceship reaches the point where it must recycle everything necessary to produce the astronauts' food, the public must come to realize that the problems of designing a life-support system that will function over a prolonged period are terribly difficult. Then will they not think, "Spaceship Earth has a marvelous life-support system that has functioned for millions of years, and we mustn't take any chances with it"? And then, when they look around at the desperate risks we are taking with that system, will they not insist on instant reform?

Few people as yet understand that our atmosphere is a biological product and would contain only traces of oxygen if it were not for green plants constantly giving off oxygen, and no nitrogen if it were not for denitrifying bacteria that reduce nitrates in soil and sediments. Even scientists have recently expressed surprise that they could not detect nitrogen in the atmosphere of Mars. This says something about the educational task ecologists face if even our scientific policy-makers are to gain a rudimentary understanding of how the biosphere functions.

We are now consuming fossil fuels—coal, petroleum, and natural gas—at an ever-accelerating rate. In burning these fossil fuels, we are extracting from the atmosphere oxygen equivalent to the amount that was put into the atmosphere back in geologic time when those fuels were formed. We must depend on green plants to compensate for the amount extracted—but not all green plants are equally efficient in this process.

A forest or a field of grass can produce a lot of oxygen, but when wood or grain decays or burns, it uses up as much oxygen as was released in its formation. So land plants, by and large, merely introduce a time lag into the oxygen cycle. The trick, in compensating for the oxygen used in burning fossil fuels, is to let green plants produce oxygen and then sequester the remains of the plants somewhere without their being oxidized. This can happen in the oxygen-free sediments of bogs and swamps and lakes, but the really important repository is in the marine sediments.

We are now imposing over a half-million different chemicals on the environment, and the number is increasing by several hundred each year; the sea is the ultimate sink for all of them. If some day one of those chemicals, or a combination of them, turns out to be a deadly poison for the marine phytoplankton, or for the organisms involved in the nitrogen cycle, or for any of a great many other types of organisms, the atmosphere will start running out of oxygen.

We have had an amazing run of dumb luck, but we should not count on it to continue. In an alarming recent paper, Charles Wurster reported results showing that DDT in concentrations as low as a tenth of a part per million does severely depress photosynthesis. If this turns out to be a general phenomenon, we may already be in trouble, because even if we stopped all use of DDT tomorrow, it would continue to wash into the oceans for several years—and the coastal regions where it will go are typically much more productive than the open oceans.

There has been talk about increasing the harvest of food from the seas. Yet Japan, which has been a leader in aquaculture, has had several recent outbreaks of fatal shellfish poisoning caused by industrial pollution of the seas. Furthermore, the domesticated seaweeds can no longer be cultivated in the polluted Sea of Japan, and these operations have been moved ashore. I have known since childhood that the San Francisco region is a frequent recipient of glass fishnet floats and other things drifting from Japan. How long will it be before her pollution becomes a contributor to the local problem? Our problems are not national—they are global.

What things are becoming extinct today that man might need tomorrow? If our ancestors had known how, they would probably have exterminated the mold *penicillium*. Are our pollutants wiping out equal potential wonders—perhaps in the seas—before we have even started to look for such things? If we should really ever become serious about farming the seas, our domestic herds might be manatees, dugongs, whales, or green turtles—if any of these now threatened species survives for us to use.

There is evidence from Africa that harvesting the native ungulates is a more efficient way of producing meat than is cattle-raising. Harvesting passenger pigeons, once the world's most abundant bird, might have been a very efficient way of obtaining protein—but we'll never know now.

Our trouble is that we make our decisions on the basis of short-term economic considerations. Factories and power plants don't have to discharge sulfur dioxide into the atmosphere, nor do nuclear plants have to discharge radionuclides into the environment. They do these things because it would cost them money not to. Furthermore, our legislature encourages them, and we pay the bill.

Present depletion allowances encourage mining with all its environmental effects. If our legislators would make it as expensive to mine and refine new ore as to reclaim used metals, the automobile graveyards would disappear, and empty beer cans would be less in sight. If our legislators were seriously thinking of the long-term welfare of the nation, then instead of restricting imports of foreign oil, they would be seeking means to obtain oil from anyone shortsighted enough to send us their nonrenewable natural resources.

The industrial exploitation of resources may mean wealth, but it is not progress. Every gallon of oil taken from the earth and burned leaves the earth a little poorer than it was before, with a little less potential to support the future. It may be, if man is lucky, that our descendants will curse us for squandering petroleum or generating power instead of leaving it as a raw material for their much more advanced technology. If, in fact, we have descendants several generations hence, I am fairly sure that they will curse us for the nuclear wastes we are now bequeathing them with the instructions that they must keep them from being dispersed into the environment for perhaps a thousand years—and perhaps with a heavy drain on their economy to keep replacing leaky containers.

Recall also the shock expressed last summer by Thor Heyerdahl at finding the mid-Atlantic so visibly polluted with globules of unknown composition that the men were reluctant to dip their toothbrushes in the water. In the Pacific some unknown factor has set off a population explosion of a formerly rare starfish that consumes reef-building corals. The corals of Guam are reported to be going at the rate of a half-mile per month, and the starfish is also at work on Australia's Great Barrier Reef and in the Indian Ocean. When the corals are killed, the fish rapidly disappear, and the land becomes very susceptible to erosion by wave action. So some islands may literally disappear as a result of whatever man did to start this process, for there is no doubt in my mind that man is responsible.

On August 10, 1969, the London Times reported that mustard gas that the British had disposed of in 1945 by dumping the containers in the Baltic had reappeared, injuring fishermen, endangering resorts in Sweden and Denmark, and causing the condemnation of thousands of tons of contaminated fish. Remember that we have dumped similar materials in the Atlantic even more recently. Recall also that when we were testing nuclear weapons in the Pacific, the Japanese were forced to condemn and bury thousands of tons of radioactive fish—and note that the Atomic Energy Commission is talking right now about using nuclear explosives to dig harbors and canals.

American industry is awakening to the fact that there is wealth other than seafood on the ocean floor. On October 30, 1969, a company that would like to mine manganese from the ocean bottoms sought assurance that the Navy would protect it from piracy and foreign invaders. Are we to have another colonial-type race for the ocean floors? All in all, man, as usual, is not acting like a rational creature bent on feeding itself.

Frederick Smith, a prominent ecologist at Harvard, recently estimated that the environment in this country is deteriorating at the rate of 30 billion dollars per year. This is an estimate of what it would cost us to allow it to get *no worse* each year—it does not include the cost of restoring a *better* environment. It now appears

__timate carrying capacity of the earth for human life may __nd less on its ability to produce food than on its ability to degrade wastes.

And in the midst of all this, our legislation even provides incentives for people to have more children. I've been publishing despairing papers on this subject for over 20 years—and Paul Sears and others were sounding the alarm before me. I'm tired of talking about the subject, but it is not even conceptually possible to solve our other problems if the population is going to continue to grow. It is time for a vigorous challenge to the fundamental precepts of our way of life.

4

THE ECOLOGICAL FACTS OF LIFE
BARRY COMMONER

Several months ago the people of the earth held their breath as a spaceship with three men nearly missed the planet and hurtled hopelessly into black space. The earth itself, now, is headed on a similar death tangent. Commoner, with great care, demonstrates why we must get the earth and her life systems back into a circular closed pattern.

To understand the content of this paper is to know the principles of ecology and to have the informational base for a survival ethic. Even though the paper is concise and suited to the layman, it may take several readings to digest. It is well worth it; one couldn't spend time better in laying a personal foundation for action.

The ecological facts of life are grim. The survival of all living things—including man—depends on the integrity of the complex web of biological processes which comprise the earth's ecosystem. However, what man is now doing on the earth violates this fundamental requisite of human existence. For modern technologies act on the ecosystem which supports us in ways that threaten its stability; with tragic perversity we have linked much of our productive economy to precisely those features of technology which are ecologically destructive.

These powerful, deeply entrenched relationships have locked us into a self-destructive course. If we are to break out of this suicidal track we must begin by learning the ecological facts of life. If we are to find the road to survival we must discover how to mold the technology to the necessities of nature, and learn how these constraints must temper the economic and social demands on technology. This, I believe, is the momentous task which now confronts mankind—a task for which this conference is intended to ready us.

It is the purpose of this contribution to provide some factual background to the foregoing assertions.

1. THE ORIGIN OF THE ECOSYSTEM

The global ecosystem in which we now live is the product of several billion years of evolutionary change in the composition of the planet's skin. Following a series of remarkable geochemical events, about two billion years ago there appeared a form of matter, composed of elements common on the earth's surface, but organized in a manner which set it sharply apart from its antecedents—life. Themselves the products of several billion years of slow geochemical processes, the first living things became, in turn, powerful agents of geochemical change.

To begin with, they depleted the earth's previously accumulated store of the organic products of geochemical evolution, for this was their food. Converting much of this food into carbon dioxide, the earth's early life forms sufficiently increased the carbon dioxide content of the planet's atmosphere to raise the average temperature—through the "greenhouse" effect—to tropical levels. Later there appeared the first photosynthetic organisms, which reconverted carbon dioxide into the organic substances that are essential to all living metabolism. The rapid proliferation of green plants in the tropical temperature of the early earth soon reduced the carbon dioxide concentration of the atmosphere, thereby lowering the earth's temperature and depositing a huge mass of organic carbon which became in time the store of fossil fuels. And with the photosynthetic cleavage of water, the earth for the first time acquired free oxygen in its atmosphere. By shielding the earth's surface from solar ultraviolet radiation (through the concurrent appearance of ozone), this event enabled life to emerge from the protection of an original underwater habitat. With free oxygen available, new, more efficient forms of living metabolism became possible and the great evolutionary outburst of proliferating species of plants and animals began to populate the planet. Meanwhile terrestrial plants and microorganisms converted the earth's early rocks into soil and developed within it a remarkably complex ecosystem; a similar system developed in surface waters. Taken together, these ecosystems control the composition of the soil, of surface waters and the air, and consequently regulate the weather.

There is an important lesson here. In the form in which it first appeared, the earth's life system had an inherently fatal fault: The energy it required was derived from the destruction of a non-renewable resource, the geochemical store of organic matter. The primeval life system became capable of continued existence only when, in the course of evolution, organisms appeared that converted carbon dioxide and inorganic salts to new organic matter—thus closing the loop and transforming what was a fatally linear process into a circular, self-perpetuating one. Here in its primitive form we see the grand scheme which has since been the basis of the remarkable continuity of life: the reciprocal interdependence of one life process on another.

In the course of further evolution the variety of living things proliferated; new interactions became possible, greatly enriching the network of events. Cycles were built on cycles, forming at last a vast and intricate web, replete with branches, interconnections and alternate pathways; these are the bonds that link together the fate of all the numerous animals, plants, and microorganisms that inhabit the earth. This is the global ecosystem. It is a closed web of physical, chemical and biological processes created by living things, maintained by living things, and through the marvelous reciprocities of biological and geochemical evolution, uniquely essential to the support of living things.

2. THE BASIC PROPERTIES OF THE ECOSYSTEM

We know enough about some parts of this vast system to delineate the fundamental properties of the whole. These properties define the requirements of any activity—including human society—which is to function successfully within the ecosystem of the earth.

a) Because they are fundamentally circular processes and subject to numerous feedback effects, ecosystems exhibit nonlinear responses to changes in the intensity of any single factor.

Consider, for example, the ecological processes which occur in surface waters, such as lakes and rivers. This is the cycle which links aquatic animals to their organic wastes; these wastes to the oxygen-requiring microorganisms that convert them into inorganic nitrate, phosphate and carbon dioxide; the inorganic nutrients to the algae which photosynthetically reconvert them into organic substances (thereby also adding to the oxygen content of the water and so providing support for the animals and the organisms of decay); and algal organic matter to the chain of animals which feed on it, thus completing the cycle.

Since it is a cyclical system with closed feedback loops, the kinetic properties of this ecosystem are strikingly nonlinear. If the load of organic waste imposed on the system becomes too great, the demand of the bacteria of decay for oxygen may exceed the limited oxygen content of the water. When the oxygen content falls to zero, the bacteria die, the biological cycle breaks down, and organic debris accumulates. A similar nonlinearity is observed in the growth of algae. If the nutrient level of the water becomes so great as to stimulate the rapid growth of algae, the dense algal population cannot be long sustained because of the intrinsic limitations of photosynthetic efficiency. As the thickness of the algal layer in the water increases, the light required for photosynthesis that can reach the lower parts of the algal layer becomes sharply diminished, so that any strong overgrowth of algae very quickly dies back, again releasing organic debris. These are relatively simple examples of the ubiquitous propensity of ecosystems for strongly nonlinear responses, for dramatic overgrowths and equally dramatic collapse.

b)   Because the chemical events that occur in an ecosystem are driven by the metabolism of living things, they are subject to the special constraints of biological chemistry.

One important characteristic is that the rate of chemical reactions in living cells, being determined by the catalytic action of enzymes, is subject to the considerable specificity of enzymes for their substrates. Another feature is a consequence of the long course of evolutionary selection which has been at work in living things. Living cells are capable of carrying out an enormous variety of particular chemical reactions. What is remarkable, however, is that the number of different biochemical substances which are actually synthesized in living cells is *very much smaller* than the number of substances which could, in theory, be formed—given the types of reactions which can occur. Thus conditions suitable for the separate chemical reactions which give rise to both *dextro* and *levo* amino acids are present in cells—but because of the stereospecificity of the relevant enzyme system, only the synthesis of the *levo* forms occurs at an appreciable rate. Because of similar constraints, cells produce many fatty acids with even-numbered carbon chain lengths, but no fatty acids with odd numbers of carbons. Similarly, organic compounds which contain NO groups are singularly lacking in living things.

Thus, living systems have had a long opportunity to, so to speak, try out the enormous variety of biochemical reactions that *could* take place in the cell. In effect, the biochemical constituents now found in living cells represent the survivors of this evolutionary trial, presumably selected for their compatibility with the essential features of the overall system of cellular metabolism. This situation is analogous to the tendency of genes found in current organisms to be maximally advantageous—i.e., nearly all mutations to alternative genes are lethal. Therefore, in the same sense we can expect that the entry into an ecosystem of an organic reagent not normally found in living systems is likely to have deleterious effects on some living organisms.

c)   The feedback characteristics of ecosystems result in amplification and intensification processes of considerable magnitude.

The fact that in food chains small organisms are eaten by bigger ones and the latter by still bigger ones inevitably results in the concentration of certain environmental constituents in the bodies of the largest organisms at the top of the food chain. Smaller organisms always exhibit much higher metabolic rates than larger ones, so that the amount of their food which is oxidized, relative to the amount incorporated into the body of the organism, is thereby greater. Consequently, an animal at the top of the food chain depends on the consumption of an enormously greater mass of the bodies of organisms lower down in the food chain. Therefore, any *non*metabolized material present in the lower organisms of this chain will become concentrated in the body of the top one.

d)   Because of the circularity of ecosystems and their complex branching patterns, the behavior of any given living member of the system is dependent on the behavior of many others.

The specific relationships are varied: One organism may provide food for another; one organism may parasitize and kill another; two organisms may cooperate so closely in their livelihood as to become totally dependent on each other. As a result of such relationships, a change in the population of any one organism is likely to have powerful effects on other populations. Because of these numerous interconnections, a single cause-and-effect relationship is rare. Instead, a given intrusion on an ecosystem is likely to have effects which spread out in an ever-widening circle from its original source, affecting organisms and parts of the environment often very remote from the initial point of intrusion.

e) The stability of an ecosystem is achieved by a complex network of dynamic equilibria which permits alternative relationships to develop when any particular link in the network becomes inoperative.

In a very simple form, this relationship is illustrated by a common farmyard practice. The farmer who wishes to maintain cats in order to control mice will provide for the cats an alternative source of food, a doorstep dish of milk. Otherwise, the cats might kill so many mice as to run out of food, and they would then leave the farm in search of richer fields. There is an increasing body of more sophisticated evidence to support the generalization that the stability of an ecosystem depends closely on its degree of complexity, on the fineness of the ecological web.

f) The cyclical processes of an ecosystem operate at an overall rate which is determined by the intricate coupling of the numerous separate events that constitute the whole.

One result is that the ecosystem web has a kind of natural resonance frequency which may become evident in periodic fluctuations in a particular population of organisms—for example, seven-year locusts. Similarly, an ecosystem seems to be characterized by a specific "relaxation time"—that is, a rate at which it can successfully respond to an external intrusion by means of internal readjustment. Hence, we can expect the system to maintain its integrity only so long as external intrusions impinge on it at a rate which is compatible with the natural time-constant of the cycle as a whole. Thus, an environmental change—for example, in temperature—which develops slowly may permit organisms to adapt or to evolve adaptive forms, and the system as a whole can persist. In contrast, a rapid, cataclysmic environmental change, such as that which trapped the arctic mastodons in fields of ice, can override the system's natural rate of adaptation and destroy it.

3. HUMAN INTRUSIONS ON THE ECOSYSTEM

This brief summary gives us a working knowledge of the system that constitutes the environment—a system generated by the evolution of the vast variety of living things on the earth. But among these living things is man, an organism which has learned how to manipulate natural forces with intensities that go far beyond those attainable by any other living thing. For example, human beings expend in bodily energy roughly 1,000 kilowatt hours per year. However, in a highly developed country such as the United States, the actual expenditure of energy per capita is between 10,000 and 15,000 kilowatt hours per year. This extension of the impact of human beings on the ecosphere is, of course, a consequence of technology. Prehistoric man withdrew from the atmosphere only the oxygen required for respiration, but technological man consumes a far greater amount of oxygen to support fires, power plants, and chemical processes. The carbon dioxide produced by technological processes has measurably altered the carbon dioxide concentration of the atmosphere. Technology has had effects on the ecosystem which approach the magnitude of the natural processes themselves. Technology has also introduced into the environment substances wholly new to it, such as synthetic pesticides, plastics, and man-made radioisotopes.

What we mean by environmental deterioration is the untoward effect of human activities, especially technology, on the quality of the environment and on the stability of the ecological processes which maintain it. Given the previous list of ecosystem properties it is illuminating to determine the degree to which our major technological activities are consistent with them. Such an inquiry reveals that much of our technology is, in its very success as a productive enterprise, a grave threat to the stability of the ecosystem. Some examples follow.

a) Sewage Treatment Technology

One of our best-developed technologies is sewage treatment, a technique intended to convert the noxious organic materials of human wastes into innocuous materials that can be assimilated into the aquatic ecosystem. This technology reflects an excellent understanding of *part* of the aquatic cycle: Given sufficient oxygen, aquatic microorganisms can convert organic matter to innocuous inorganic products which are readily carried off in surface waters. By domesticating such microorganisms in artificially aerated sewage plants, we can indeed convert nearly all of the organic matter of sewage into inorganic products and discharge them to rivers and lakes.

So far, so good; the fatal stress of an overburden of organic matter on the stability of the aquatic cycle is avoided. But given the circularity of the process, it is evident that now a new stress must appear, this time the impact of excessive inorganic nutrients on the growth of algae. And given the nonlinearity involved in the growth of dense algal populations, we ought to expect trouble at this point. And indeed the trouble has come—but it has been largely unexpected. Only in the last decade, when the effects of algal overgrowths had already largely destroyed the self-purifying capability of an ecosystem as massive as Lake Erie, was the phenomenon recognized as a serious limitation on the technology of sewage treatment. In effect, the modern system of sewage technology has failed in its stated aim of reducing the organic oxygen demand on surface waters because it did not take into account the circularity of the ecological system on which it intruded. Because of this circularity, the inorganic products of sewage treatment were themselves reconverted to organic nutrients by the algae, which on their death simply reimposed the oxygen demand that the treatment was supposed to remove on the lakes and rivers. This failure can be attributed, therefore, to a simple violation of a fundamental principle of ecology. The price that we pay for this defect is the nearly catastrophic pollution of our surface waters.

b) The Nitrogen Cycle

One of the great fundamental cycles in the ecosystem is that traversed by the element nitrogen. In this cycle the vast store of the element in the nitrogen gas of the air is converted to the organic materials of the soil and water; the latter is in turn transformed ultimately to nitrate, which is in turn the source of organic forms of nitrogen in plants and in the animals that feed on them. Finally, such organic matter is returned to the soil as waste, completing the cycle. The nitrogen cycle of the soil is of enormous importance in agricultural technology, being the basis for the yields of protein and other nitrogenous foods which it produces.

In natural soils nitrates are produced slowly in the soil by the action of microorganisms on humus. Once free in the soil, nitrate is quickly taken up by plant roots and converted to proteins. Most plants ordinarily contain little free nitrate, and in an efficient natural soil system nitrate production and removal are so dynamically balanced as to keep the nitrate level of the soil relatively low as well. As a result, little of it leaches into surface waters, so that the concentration of nitrate in surface waters is ordinarily only of the order of a few parts per million.

In the United States, as in most advanced countries, the nitrogen cycle has been subjected to major changes arising from new agricultural technology. One important change has been the development of a break in the physical continuity of the nitrogen cycle, especially in the Midwest. Originally, in the Midwest cattle were raised and fattened largely by grazing in pastures, from which they acquired their nutrition and to which they contributed organic wastes which maintained the natural fertility of the soil. As indicated earlier, in such a natural system the nitrogen cycle in the soil operates with low levels of soil nitrate, so that relatively little of the latter leaches into surface waters.

However, in recent years, a major change has taken place: most cattle are removed from the pasture for a considerable period of fattening in confined feedlots. Here, feed is brought to the animals and their wastes become heavily deposited in a local area. The natural rate of conversion of organic waste to humus is limited, so that in a feedlot most of the nitrogenous waste is converted to soluble forms (ammonia and nitrate). This material is rapidly evaporated or leached into ground water beneath the soil, or it may run directly into surface waters during rainstorms. This is responsible, in part, for the appearance of high nitrate levels in some rural wells supplied by ground water, and for serious pollution problems due to eutrophication in a number of streams in the Midwest. Where feedlot manure is allowed to reach surface water untreated, it imposes a heavy oxygen demand on streams already overloaded by municipal wastes.

A livestock animal produces much more waste than a human being, and the total waste produced by domestic animals in the United States is about ten times that produced by the human population. Much of this waste production is confined to feedlots. For example, in 1966 more than 10 million cattle were maintained in feedlots before slaughter, an increase of 66% over the preceding eight years. This represents about one-half the total United States cattle population. Because of the development of feedlot techniques, the United States is confronted with a huge wast disposal problem—considerably greater than the human sewage which we are attempting to handle with grossly inadequate treatment.

The physical separation of livestock from the soil is related to an even more complex chain of events, which again leads to severe ecological problems. When, as in much of the Midwest, the soil is used for intensive grain production rather than pasturage, the humus content is depleted; generally such soils now contain about one-half the humus present before intensive agriculture was introduced (i.e., ca. 1880). In order to maintain and increase crop productivity, farmers have resorted to increasingly heavy applications of inorganic fertilizer, especially of nitrogen. Since 1945 the annual use of inorganic nitrogen fertilizer in the United States has increased about 14-fold. This has yielded an appreciable increase in crop productivity. However, in a humus-depleted soil, porosity is reduced; as a result, plant roots are not adequately aerated, and their efficiency in withdrawing nutrient salts from the soil is diminished. In these conditions, the crop may be well nourished by using inorganic fertilizer to maintain a high nitrate level around the roots. However, since efficiency of nutrient uptake is low, a good deal of the nitrate is not taken up by the crop, but leaches into ground water or drains from the fields into lakes and streams. Where streams traverse heavily fertilized farmlands, for example, in Illinois, nitrate concentrations in excess of the levels which lead to algal overgrowths have been observed consistently in recent years. Nearly all the streams in Illinois are now polluted by algal overgrowths. When such streams are the source of municipal water supplies—as they are in some Illinois towns—there is a risk of infant methemoglobinemia, due to the conversion of excess nitrate to nitrate in the infant's digestive tract.

We see in the impact of modern agricultural technology on the nitrogen cycle gross violations of a number of basic ecological principles. Feedlot practice breaks the physical continuity of the cycle, transferring organic wastes from large soil areas, where they can be accommodated into the natural cycle, to confined places, or surface waters. Here the heavy, rapid influx of organic matter, or of its inorganic degradation products, stresses the natural system beyond its capacity to accommodate, and the cycle breaks down, destroying the self-purifying capacity of surface waters and introducing nitrates in toxic amounts into livestock and man. Reflected in this situation is the propensity for the multiplication and spread of ecological perturbations, and the inability of an ecosystem to accommodate a stress which is imposed at a rate which exceeds the system's natural rate of response.

The most serious long-term effect of modern agricultural technology on the nitrogen cycle may be due to its effects on the natural complexity—and therefore stability—of the soil ecosystem. For example, modern agricultural systems have increasingly reduced the use of legumes which, with their associated bacteria, are capable of restoring the organic nitrogen content of the soil through fixation of nitrogen taken from the air. Recent studies, especially of tropical areas, suggest strongly that microbial nitrogen fixation is far more important in maintaining the nitrogen cycle than was believed previously. There appear to be numerous bacteria, not only in legumes, but widely associated with many different species of plants, that are capable of rapid conversion of air nitrogen into useful soil materials. When this subject has been more fully investigated, it is likely to be found, I believe, that such widespread bacterial nitrogen fixation has been a major factor in maintaining the natural fertility of soil, not only in the tropics but in temperate regions as well.

What is particularly alarming is that this natural process of nitrogen fixation is seriously disrupted by inorganic nitrogen fertilizers. It has been known for some time from laboratory experiments that when nitrogen-fixing bacteria are exposed to excessive amounts of nitrate, the process of nitrogen fixation stops. Under these conditions nitrogen-fixing bacteria may not survive or, if they do, may mutate to nonfixing forms. It is probable, therefore, that the widespread use of inorganic nitrogen fertilizer is depleting the natural population of microbial nitrogen-fixers, upon which we do have to rely considerably in any program to restore the natural efficiency of the soil. Here then is an instance in which a new technology—intensive use of inorganic nitrogen fertilizer— cuts important strands in the web of ecosystem processes, thereby impoverishing the structure of the system, laying it open to collapse under the continued stress of the technology, and diminishing the opportunities for recovery.

c) Synthetic Detergents

The story of the nondegradable detergents introduced into the environment during the period 1945–1965 is now well known, but the lessons are worth recording here. This technological failure was again the result of a lack of concern with one of the distinctive features of natural biological systems—that their chemical events are governed by the extreme catalytic specificity of enzymes. The nondegradability of these detergents was due to the failure of the enzymes in the bacteria of decay to break down the carbon-carbon bonds in the organic backbone of the detergents, a process which these bacteria readily carry out on natural hydrocarbon chains, such as those of fatty acid soaps. The failure can be traced to the fact that the nondegradable detergents possessed a branched carbon skeleton, for it is quite characteristic of degradative enzymes to prefer unbranched chains over branched ones. For 50 years this specificity has been known to biologists and has, in fact, for a long time been employed in starch technology to produce highly branched residual dextrins from partial enzymatic degradation branched starches. Here again is the technological failure of a massive intrusion into the environment which resulted from a lack of concern with one of the fundamental principles of ecology —the extreme specificity of chemical events in natural biological systems.

The nondegradable detergents have now been largely replaced by straight-chain substances which are therefore accessible to the action of bacterial enzymes. But this change still fails to make modern detergent technology compatible with the demands of ecology, for the new detergents, like the old ones, contain considerable amounts of polyphosphate. The massive introduction of this material into the surface waters through municipal sewage (the phosphate released to surface waters from this source has increased about 27-fold since 1900) has sharply increased the nutrient available to algae and has therefore exacerbated the effect of sewage treatment technology on algal overgrowths. A good deal of the pollution due to algal overgrowths can be traced to phosphate imposed on surface waters by detergents in municipal wastes —again a failure to observe the ecological facts of life.

d) Insecticides

One important aspect of the biological capital on which agricultural productivity depends is the network of ecological relationships that relate insect pests to the plants on which they feed, and to the other insects and birds that, in turn, prey on the pests. These natural relations serve to keep pest populations in check. Pests which require a particular plant as food are kept in check by their inability to spread onto other plants; the other insects which parasitize and prey upon them exert important biological control over the pest population.

What has happened in attempts to control cotton pests— where the great bulk of synthetic insecticide is used in the United States—shows how we have broken down these natural relations and allowed the normal pest-regulating machinery to get out of hand. Here the massive use of the new insecticides has killed off some of the pests that once attacked cotton. But now the cotton plants are being attacked instead by new insects that were never previously known as pests of cotton. Moreover, the new pests are becoming increasingly resistant to insecticide, through the natural biological process of selection, in the course of inheritance, of resistant types. In the Texas cotton fields, for example, in 1963 it took 50 times as much DDT to control insect pests as it did in 1961. The tobacco budworm, which now attacks cotton, has been found to be nearly immune to methylparathion, the most powerful of the widely used modern insecticides.

In certain important cotton-growing areas the insecticides kill off insect predators and parasites, which are often more sensitive to the insecticide than the pest itself. The result: insecticide-induced outbreaks of pests. Finally, DDT affects liver enzymes which inactivate sex hormones; one result is that DDT causes abnormal shell formation in birds, which is the apparent cause of the sharp decline in the population of certain raptorial species.

If we continue to rely on such broad-spectrum insecticides, recovery of the natural forms of control will become increasingly difficult. Where restoration of natural biological control has been successful, it has depended on a natural reservoir of insects which are predatory or parasitic toward the pests; if, through widespread dissemination of insecticides, species that make up this natural reservoir are lost, biological control may be difficult to reestablish.

The ecological failures involved in the use of DDT and related insecticides are only too evident: the failure to anticipate that an unnatural substance such as DDT is likely to be incompatible with the evolution-tested system of cellular biochemistry; the failure to take into account the effect of food chains on the accumulation of DDT in the bodies of top carnivores, including man; the failure to appreciate the multiple relationships which regulate the population of a given insect; the failure to anticipate the nonlinear responses which cause massive insect outbreaks.

And again, this is an instance in which a new technology is destructive of the natural biological capital—the biological systems of control—upon which we must depend for stable agricultural productivity.

e) Some Other Examples

In further support of the generalization that we consistently fail to take into account basic ecosystem properties in our recent technological developments, certain other examples are worthy of brief note.

A long list of examples can be provided which show that the effects of amplification and biological interactions on substances newly introduced into the ecosphere have been ignored. Apart from the earlier example of DDT, these include: the accumulation of iodine 131 in the thyroids of animals and human beings following dissemination of this radioisotope from nuclear explosions and, more recently, from peaceful operation of nuclear reactors; the appearance of toxic levels of mercury, applied to seeds in the form of mercurial fungicides, and ultimately found in the eggs of hens fed on the grain produced on the plants grown from such seeds. A particularly striking example of such a failure to take into account ecological amplification effects in technological considerations was reported recently by Tamplin, relative to radioactive wastes from nuclear reactors. Starting from the radioactive materials, which according to AEC standards would be allowed to enter a typical river ecosystem during reactor operation, Tamplin has calculated the effects of amplification in the food chain. He shows that, following passage through the food chain, certain radioisotopes released into a river at allowable concentrations can become concentrated in fish at levels which exceed the maximum permissible concentrations if used as human food.

The multiple consequences of environmental intrusions have also been unanticipated by technological planners. Consider a proud example of modern technology, the Aswan High Dam on the Upper Nile River. The dam has already cut down the flow of nutrients to the Mediterranean, reducing the algal population and the productivity of the local fishing industry. At the same time, the dam and its attendant irrigation system are likely to cause a catastrophic increase of snail-borne schizosomiasis in the Egyptian population. Another example of such "ecological backlash" is the unexpected effect of a campaign to control malaria in remote mountain villages in Sarawak, Malaysia. The insecticides not only killed mosquitos, but also poisoned cockroaches as well; these were eaten by the village cats, which died. As a result, disease-bearing rodents—primarily controlled by the cats—invaded the villages and serious epidemics resulted. The natural balance was finally restored when the Royal Air Force organized a parachute drop of a force of fresh cats for the villages.

4. THE ECONOMIC BENEFITS AND ECOLOGICAL HAZARDS OF TECHNOLOGY

The technologies which are responsible for the environmental problems cited above were designed for, and have in fact achieved, important benefits to human welfare: increased food production through the intensive use of inorganic nitrogen fertilizer, and through improved cattle-feeding techniques; improved control of harmful insects through the use of insecticide sprays; improved crop yields due to the use of mercurial fungicides. Most of our major new pollutants are similarly connected to technological benefits. Photochemical smog is a consequence of the development of the efficient and widely used, modern high-compression gasoline engine. Due to their elevated operating temperatures, high-compression engines bring about the combination of nitrogen and oxygen in the air. And smog is the result of a complex chain of chemical events triggered by the release of nitrogen oxides. Similarly, nuclear reactors improve our power resources, but at the same time pollute the environment with man-made radioisotopes and with excessive heat.

These pollution problems arise not out of some minor inadequacies in the new technologies, but because of the very success of these technologies in accomplishing their designed aims. A modern sewage treatment plant causes algal overgrowths and resultant pollution *because* it produces, as it is designed to do, so much plant nutrient in its effluent. Modern, highly concentrated nitrogen fertilizers result in the drainage of nitrate pollutants into streams and lakes just *because* they succeed in the aim of raising the nutrient level of the soil. The modern high-compression gasoline engine contributes to smog and nitrate pollution *because* it successfully meets its design criterion—the development of a high level of power. Modern synthetic insecticides kill birds, fish, and useful insects just *because* they are successful in being absorbed by insects, and killing them, as they are intended to do.

Moreover, there are usually sound economic reasons for the specific technological design which leads to environmental deterioration. This is particularly evident in the case of the intensive use of inorganic nitrogen fertilizer. Since 1945 the cost of farm labor, land, and machinery in the United States has risen about 50–60%, but in that time the cost of fertilizer has *declined* about 25%. Moreover, intensive use of fertilizer, especially of nitrogen, provides a quick return on the farmer's investment; a fertilizer investment made in the spring is quickly reflected in the return obtained from the crop in the fall. As a result, intensive fertilizer use has become crucial to the farmer's economic success. Certain government policies have intensified this effect. For example, the establishment of the Land Bank system has encouraged farmers to grow more crops on less land. This can be accomplished by very intensive use of nitrogen fertilizer, which permits a marked increase in the number of crop plants grown per acre. Similarly, feedlot operations represent a more economically efficient use of agricultural investment than do purely grazing operations.

We can expect, therefore, that effort to reduce such environmental hazards will compete with the benefits available from the technological process, at least in economic terms. Thus, a nuclear power plant *can* be built in such a way as to reduce the resultant radioactive or thermal pollution. But this increases the cost of plant construction, raises the price of power, and reduces the plant's competitive position with respect to other types of power production. Similarly, it would be possible to reduce nitrate pollution from feedlots by requiring the installation of complete (i.e., including tertiary treatment) disposal systems for the resultant wastes, but this would reduce the economy of the feedlot operation, perhaps below that of old-fashioned pasture operation. Organic fertilizers could be reintroduced in place of inorganic nitrogen fertilizer, but since the latter are cheaper to obtain and to spread, crop production costs would rise.

Equally complex relationships encumber most of our major pollution problems. It is now apparent that urban pollution due to photochemical smog cannot be eliminated without replacing present individual use of gasoline-engine transport with electric-powered mass transit systems, or possibly by replacing them with steam-driven vehicles. The first of these actions would require a massive new economic burden on cities which are already unable to meet their social obligations; the second course would mean a serious disruption of one of the mainstays of our economy, the automobile industry. The construction of nuclear power plants is now governed by certain federal standards regarding allowable emission of radioactive wastes. These represent a distinct—if poorly evaluated—health hazard resulting, for example, from the accumulation of iodine 131 in the thyroid. If emission standards are made more rigorous, the added expense might render the nuclear power industry incapable of competing with fossil-fuel power plants. This would severely curtail a major, federally financed technological program, and would clearly require a serious political decision.

There is an important generalization to be derived from these observations: Part of the social value of new technological processes —their productivity and economic efficiency—depends on the *avoidance* of a reckoning with the important social costs represented by the ecological hazards which they cause. In effect, the social utility of such new technology is delicately balanced on a scale which can be readily tipped by actions designed to prevent their hazards to the environment. Such a corrective action becomes, thereby, a trigger which can readily set off major economic, social, and political sequelae.

In sum, environmental pollution is not to be regarded as an unfortunate, but incidental, by-product of the growth of population, the intensification of production, or of technological progress. It is, rather, an intrinsic feature of the very technology which we have developed to enhance productivity.   Our technology is enormously successful in producing material goods, but too often it is disastrously incompatible with the natural environmental systems that support not only human life, but technology itself. Moreover, these technologies are now so massively embedded in our system of industrial and agricultural production that any effort to make them conform to the demands of the environment will involve serious economic dislocations. If, as I believe, environmental pollution is a sign of major incompatibilities between our system of productivity and the environmental system that supports it, then, if we are to survive, we must successfully confront these economic obligations, however severe and challenging to our social concepts they may be.

5. WHAT IS TO BE DONE?

We are concerned, in this conference, with developing ways to mobilize the resources of this nation—and ultimately, if the 1972 United Nations Conference is to succeed—of the world for a momentous effort to restore the ecological stability of the planet. Some suggestions for the needed action are relevant here.

We ought to begin, I believe, by preparing a public declaration that there is now a clear and present danger to the integrity of the ecosphere and therefore to the survival of man. While some of us have made individual efforts in this direction, I believe that the public is entitled to hear from the scientific community as a whole, or at least some organized segment of it, that human survival is now at risk. Among the consequences of such a declaration should be the establishment, in the United States as well as in all the nations that expect to participate in the United Nations Conference, of large-scale efforts to evaluate the major ecological stresses that are now operative on the earth. We shall then need to define the ecological constraints within which each major technology must operate if it is to avoid a fatal stress on the stability of the ecosphere. Finally, we shall need to develop new types of technologies which can help to restore the broken strands in the earth's ecological web. If, as seems clear, the complexity of the ecological network is a prime source of the stability of the ecosphere, a major goal of science and technology ought to be the restoration of previously broken ecological links, and, if need be, the establishment of new ones.

This much is, I believe, the direct responsibility of the scientific and technological community. But we have one more duty.

The task of restoring the planet's ecological stability is vast, complex, and deeply rooted in economic, social, and political issues. The most grave social judgments must be made. This is a responsibility which belongs not in the hands of scientists and technologists, but to all the people. However, to make these judgments and to organize the vast restorative program, the public will need to have the relevant facts in understandable terms. Here, too, we in the scientific community have a responsibility. As the custodians of this knowledge, we owe it to our fellow citizens to help inform them about the crisis in the environment. Public judgment is essential for the action needed to restore the ecological balance of the earth; but such action can succeed only if it is guided by judgment which is *informed* by the facts.

This, I believe, is the task which is placed before us by the ecological facts of life: to organize the survival of man.

5

THE POPULATION EXPLOSION: FACTS AND FICTION

PAUL R. EHRLICH

I believe Ehrlich will be remembered in history for sounding the clarion call to control population, that loaded cannon pointed at our best endeavors. If he isn't, it will be because he failed, and history will no longer be recorded.

The facts of today's population crisis are appallingly simple. Mankind, at first gradually but recently with extreme rapidity, has intervened artificially to lower the death rate in the human population. Simultaneously we have not, repeat *have not*, intervened to lower the birth rate. Since people are unable to flee from our rather small planet, the inevitable result of the wide discrepancy between birth and death rates has been a rapid increase in the numbers of people crowded onto the Earth.

The growth of the population is now so rapid that the multitude of humans is doubling every 37 years. Even in developed countries, with growth rates typically around one percent per year, the population is doubling every two or three generations. This dramatic increase is "slow" only in comparison with the unprecedented situation in many underdeveloped countries, where the doubling time is 20 to 25 years. Think of what it means, for example, for the population of a country like Colombia to double in the next 22 years. Throughout its history the people of Colombia have managed to create a set of facilities, albeit inadequate, for the maintenance of human beings: buildings, roads, farms, water systems, sewage systems, hospitals, schools, churches, and so forth. Just to remain even, just to maintain today's level of misery, Colombia would have to duplicate all those facilities in the next 22 years. It would have to double its human resources as well—train enough doctors, lawyers, teachers, judges, and all the rest so that in 22 years the number of all these professionals would be twice that of today. Such a task would be impossible for a powerful, industrialized country with agricultural surpluses, a high literacy rate, fine schools, good communications, etc. The United States couldn't hope to accomplish it. For Colombia, with none of these things, with 30–40% of its population illiterate, with 47% of its population under 15 years of age, it is inconceivable.

Yes, it will be impossible for Colombia to maintain its present level of misery for the next 22 years—and misery it is. Death control did not reach Colombia until after World War II. Before it arrived, a woman could expect to have two or three children survive to reproductive age if she went through ten pregnancies. Now, in spite of malnutrition, medical technology keeps seven or eight alive. Each child adds to the impossible financial burden of the family and to the despair of the mother. According to Dr. Sumner M. Kalman, the average Colombian mother goes through a progression of attempts to limit the size of her family. She starts with ineffective native forms of contraception and moves on to quack abortion, infanticide, frigidity, and all too often to suicide. The average family in Colombia, after its last child is born, has to spend 80% of its income on food. And the per capita income of Colombians is $237 per year, less than one-tenth that of Americans. That's the kind of misery that's concealed behind the dry statistics on population doubling.

But, it seems highly unlikely that 22 years from now, in 1992, Colombia will have doubled its present population of 20 million and reached 40 million. The reason is quite simple. The Earth is a spaceship of limited carrying capacity. The three and a half billion people who now live on our globe can do so only at the expense of consuming some nonrenewable resources, especially coal and petroleum, and dispersing the rest—steel, nickel, phosphorus, and so forth. And our attempts to stretch still further the carrying capacity for man by ill-considered applications of technology (broad-spectrum pesticides, saturation levels of fertilizer use, massive water projects whose costs outweigh the benefits) are destabilizing the environmental systems on which all life depends. Indeed, it is unlikely that even the sorely needed, *enlightened* technology could support three and a half billion people for long at a decent level of living without irreversible harm to the environment.

We are, of course, doing a deplorable job today and looting the world's resources. Somewhere between one and two billion people are *today* undernourished (have too few calories) or malnourished (suffer from various deficiencies, especially protein deficiencies). Somewhere between 10 and 20 million of our fellow human beings will starve to death this year. Consider that the average person among some two billion Asians has an annual income of $128, a life expectancy at birth of only 50 years, and is illiterate. Look at the situation in India, where Professor Georg Borgstrom estimates that only about one person in fifty has an adequate diet. For the vast majority, the calorie supply "is not sufficient for sustaining a normal workday. Physical exhaustion and apathy [is] the rule." And while such misery envelops the underdeveloped world, overdeveloped countries such as the United States are making the dominant contribution to resource depletion and environmental destruction, in the pursuit of extravagant material affluence and empty economic growth.

No, we're not doing a very good job of taking care of the people we have in 1970. And the population of the Earth is increasing by 70 million people each year. Think of it—an equivalent of the 1970 population of the United States *added* to the world every three years! We have an inadequate loaf of bread to divide among today's multitudes, and we are quickly adding more billions to the bread line; already threatened with environmental disaster, particularly at the hands of the affluent, we are adding two million super-consumers and super-polluters per year in the United States alone.

As I said at the beginning, the facts are indeed simple. We are faced by a most elementary choice. Either we find a way to bring the birth rate down or the death rate will soon go back up. Make no mistake about it—mankind has not freed itself of the tyranny of arithmetic! Anyone who stands in the way of measures to bring down the birth rate is automatically working for a rise in the death rate.

The death rate could rise in several ways. Perhaps the most likely is through famine. The world has very nearly reached its maximum sustainable food production capacity—increases bought with massive use of pesticides, vulnerable monocultures of new crops, and depletion of finite groundwater supplies may be short-lived indeed. The most responsible proponents of the well-publicized "Green Revolution" admit that *at best* their enterprise might buy a few decades' time in which to control population growth. But the inertia built into the population age structure virtually guarantees that a birth-rate solution will take longer than this, which is one reason many of us are so pessimistic.

Plague presents another possibility for a "death rate solution" to the population problem. It is known that viruses may increase their virulence when they infect a large population. With viruses circulating in a weakened population of unprecedented size, and with modern transport capable of spreading infection to the far corners of the globe almost instantly, we could easily face an unparalleled epidemic. Indeed, if a man-made germ should escape from one of our biological warfare labs we might see the extinction of *Homo sapiens*. It is now theoretically possible to develop organisms against which man would have no resistance—indeed one Nobel laureate was so appalled at the possibility of an accidental escape that he quit research in this field.

Finally, of course, thermonuclear war could provide us with an instant death-rate solution. Nearly a billion people in China are pushing out of their biologically ruined country towards Siberia, India, and the Mekong rice bowl. The suffering millions of Latin America are moving towards revolution and Communist governments. An Arab population boom, especially among Palestinian refugees, adds to tensions. The competition to loot the sea of its fish creates international incidents. As more and more people have less and less, as the rich get richer and the poor poorer, the probability of war increases. The poor of the world know what we have, and they want it. They have what is known as rising expectations. For this reason alone a mere maintenance of current levels of living will be inadequate to maintain peace.

Unfortunately, we will not need to kill outright all human beings to drive mankind to extinction. Small groups of genetically and culturally impoverished survivors may well succumb to the inevitably harsh environment of a war-ravaged planet. War not only could end this population explosion, it has the potential for removing the possibility of any future propagation.

Faced with this dismal prospect, why haven't people, especially in an educated country like the United States, taken rational action to bring the birth rate down? Why haven't we led the way toward a world with an optimum population living in balance with its resources? Why indeed have most Americans remained unaware of the gravity of the entire problem? The answers to these questions are many and complex. In the rest of this paper I'd like to discuss one major reason why we have not managed to defuse the population bomb. This reason is the perpetuation of a series of fictions which tend to discount the problem or present fantasy solutions to it. These fictions are eagerly believed by many people who show an all-too-human wish to avoid facing unpleasant realities. Let's look at some of the fictions, and some of the unpleasant realities.

Fiction: The population explosion is over, at least in the United States, because the birth rate is at an all-time low.

Fact: Although the birth rate of the United States reached a record low (around 16 per thousand per year) for brief periods during 1968, it did not approach the death rate, which was and is down around 9 per thousand per year. Even at the record low rate (if it had continued) the population of the United States would double in about 100 years. But, as all knowledgeable parties predicted, the low birth rate has not persisted; it is now moving upward again because the large group of females born in the post-World War II baby boom are now moving into their peak reproductive period. In general, birth rates are subject to short-term fluctuations, according to the number of women in their reproductive years, the condition of the economy, the occurrence of wars, etc. Viewing a temporary decline of the birth rate as a sign of the end of the population explosion is like considering a warm December 26th as a sign of spring. The ballyhooing of the temporary decline of birth rate (with, if you recall, no mention of death rate) has done great harm to the cause of humanity.

Fiction: The United States has no population problem—it is a problem of the undeveloped countries.

Fact: Considering the problems of air and water pollution, poverty, clogged highways, overcrowded schools, inadequate courts and jails, urban blight, and so on, it is clear that the United States has more people than it can adequately maintain. Simply stopping population growth would not eliminate our other problems, of course—they must also be attacked directly and vigorously. But we cannot hope to catch up in even a few of the multitude of critical areas if population growth's drain on our social and economic resources and its aggravation of the problems themselves are allowed to persist.

Even if we were not overpopulated at home, we could not stand detached from the rest of the world. We are largely dependent on imports for our affluence. We use roughly one-third of all the raw materials consumed on the face of the Earth each year. We need the ferroalloys, tin, bauxite, petroleum, rubber, food, and other materials we import. We can afford to raise beef for our own use in protein-starved Asia. We can afford to take fish from protein-starved South America and feed it to our chickens. We can afford to buy protein-rich peanuts from protein-starved Africans. Even if we are not engulfed in world-wide plague or war we will suffer mightily as the "other world" slips into famine. We will suffer when they are no longer willing or able to supply our needs. It has been truly said that calling the population explosion a problem of undeveloped countries is like saying to a fellow passenger, "Your end of the boat is sinking."

Fiction: Much of the Earth is empty land which can be put under cultivation in order to supply food for the burgeoning population of the planet.

Fact: Virtually all the land which can be cultivated with known or easily foreseeable methods already is under cultivation. We would have to double our present agricultural production just to adequately feed today's billions—and the population of the Earth is growing, I repeat, by some *70 million* people per year. No conceivable expansion of arable land can take care of these needs.

Fiction: Although land agriculture cannot possibly take care of our food needs, we still have "unmeasurable" resources of the sea which can be tapped so that we can populate the Earth until people are jammed together like rabbits in a warren.

Fact: The resources of the sea have been measured and have been found wanting. Most of the sea is a biological desert. Our techniques for extracting what potential food there is in the sea are still very primitive. With a cessation of pollution, complete international cooperation, and ecologically intelligent management, we might manage to double our present yield from the sea or do even better on a sustained basis. But even such a miracle would be inadequate to meet the needs of the population growth. Food from the sea today provides only 3% of the world's calories and 20% of the protein. If we could manage a doubling of yield in the next thirty years, we would barely have kept pace with population, and the probability of doing even this well is diminishing fast. Indeed, there is increasing pollution of the sea with massive amounts of pesticides and other biologically active compounds. In addition, a no-holds-barred race to harvest the fish of the sea has developed among China, Japan, Russia, the United States, and others. This race is resulting in the kind of overexploitation which led to the decline of the whaling industry. All the signs point to a *reduction* of the food yield of the sea in the near future—not to a bonanza from the sea.

Fiction: Science (with a capital S) will find a new way to feed everyone—perhaps by making food synthetically.

Fact: Perhaps in the distant future some foods will be produced synthetically in large quantity, but not in time to help mankind through the crisis it now faces.   The most-discussed methods would involve the use of microorganisms and fossil fuels. Since fossil fuels are limited in supply, and much in demand for other uses, their use as a food source would be a temporary measure at best.   Direct synthesis, even should it eventually prove possible, would inevitably present problems of energy supply and materials supply—it would be no simple "food for nothing" system. But, I repeat, science holds no hope of finding a synthetic solution to the food problem at this time.

Fiction: We can solve the crowding problem on our planet by migrating to other planets.

Fact: No other planet of the solar system appears to be habitable. But, if all of them were, we would have to export to them 70 million people a year to keep our population constant. With our current technology and that foreseeable in the next few decades such an effort would be economically impossible.   Indeed the drain on our mineral resources and fossil fuels would be unbelievable. Suppose that we built rockets immeasurably larger than any in existence today—capable of carrying 100 people and their baggage to another planet. Almost 2000 of such monster ships would have to leave each day. The effects of their exhausts on the atmosphere would be spectacular to say the least. And what if through miracles, we did manage to export all those people and maintain them elsewhere in the solar system? In a mere 250 years the entire system would be populated to the same density as the Earth. Attempting to reach the planets of the stars raises the prospect of spaceships taking generations to reach their destinations. Since population explosions could not be permitted on the starships the passengers would have to be willing to practice strict birth control. In other words, the responsible people will have to be the ones to leave, with the irresponsible staying at home to breed.

Fiction: Family planning is the answer to the population explosion. It has worked in places like Japan; it will work in places like India.

Fact: No country, including Japan, has managed to bring its population under rational control. After World War II, Japan employed abortion to reduce its birth rate, but it did not stop its growth. Indeed, in 1966, with its birth rate at a temporary low because it was the "Year of the Fiery Horse" (considered inauspicious for births), Japan's population was still growing at a rate which would double it in 63 years. Japan is in desperate straits. Today it must import food equivalent to its entire agricultural production. In addition it depends heavily on its fisheries from which it gets food equivalent to more than one and a half times its agricultural production. Japan is so overpopulated that *even if her population growth stopped* she would succumb to disaster as her sources of food imports dry up and as her share of the yield from the sea shrinks. But, remember, grossly overpopulated Japan is continuing to grow at a rapid rate.

Family planning in India has had no discernible effect even though it has had government support for some 17 years. During those years the population has increased by more than one-half, and the growth rate itself has increased. The IUD (intrauterine device) was promoted by the professional optimists as the panacea for India, but the most recent news from that country indicates a recognition of the failure of the IUD campaign and a return to the promotion of condoms.

Most depressing of all is the point that family planning promotes the notion that people should have only the number of children they *want* and can support. It does not promote family sizes which will bring about population control. As Professor Kingsley Davis has often pointed out, people *want* too many children. Family planning has not controlled any population to date, and by itself it is not going to control *any* population.

These fictions are spread because of a wide variety of reasons. Some people have long-term emotional commitments to outmoded ideas such as population control through family planning. Others wish to disguise the failure of the government agencies they run. Still others have simple economic interests in the sale of food or agricultural chemicals and equipment. Almost all also have genuine humanitarian motives. Most of these people have at best an incomplete view of the problem. The less well-informed simply have no grasp of the magnitude of the problem—these are the ones who propose solutions in outer space or under the sea. More sophisticated are those who hold out great hopes for agricultural changes which will at least temporarily solve the problem. Such people are especially common in our government.

Many members of this sophisticated group are ignorant of elementary biology. Our desperate attempts to increase food yields are promoting soil deterioration and contributing to the poisoning of the ecological systems on which our very survival depends. It is a long and complex story, but the conclusion is simple —the more we strive to obtain increased yields by ill-considered means in the short run, the smaller the yields are likely to be in the long run. No attempt to increase food yields can solve the problem. How much, then, should we mortgage our future by such attempts?

I've concentrated, in my discussion, on the nature of the population explosion rather than attempting to detail ways of reaching a birth rate solution. That is because the first step towards any solution involves a realistic facing of the problem. We must, as that first step, get a majority of Americans to recognize the simple choice: *lower the birth rate or face a drastic rise in the death rate.* We must divert attention from the treatment of symptoms of the population explosion and start treating its cause. We have no more time; we must act now. Next year will not do. It is already too late for us and our environment to survive unscathed. Now we must make decisions designed to minimize the damage.

CONCLUSION

There are numerous possibilities for action for the United States. I have suggested before that we need changes in domestic policy both to preserve the quality of life for Americans and to set an example for the rest of the world. Reform at home is particularly vital because we, as the world's most prodigious consumers and polluters, pose the gravest threat to the long-term livability on the planet. We should immediately consider

1. The establishment of a powerful federal Department of Population and Environment, with primary missions in the areas of encouraging reproductive responsibility, and preventing environmental deterioration.

2. A revision of our tax laws so that they discourage, rather than encourage reproduction.

3. The passing of federal laws making birth control and instruction mandatory in all public schools; and securing the right of any woman to have an abortion if she desires one.

4. A change in the pattern of federal support of biomedical research, so that the majority of it goes into investigation of the broad areas of population regulation, environmental sciences,

human behavior, and related subjects, rather than into short-sighted programs on death control.

5. A fundamental change in economic philosophy. We must switch from the present "Cowboy Economy," emphasizing planned obsolescence, exploitation for short-term gain, and waste, to a "Spaceman Economy," emphasizing recycling and the preservation of the planetary life-support systems.

Solving the problems of the quantity of life must have priority. Only when those problems have been solved should we shift our major effort back to the important problems of quality. If we don't solve the quantity problem, the quality problem will no longer bother us.

In the area of foreign policy changes are also needed. Once we have demonstrated *by example* our own willingness to adopt a responsible attitude toward population and environment, we should

1. Make available to all interested countries massive aid in the technology of birth control.

2. Make available to all countries massive aid for increasing yield on land already under cultivation. The most important export of this area should be teachers, not pesticides. We need to establish centers in each country where people can be trained not only in agronomy, but also in ecology and sociology. Many barriers to increased yields are sociological, and all increases should be made in a manner which minimizes environmental deterioration.

3. Withhold all aid from any country with an expanding population unless that nation convinces us that it is doing everything possible to limit its population. We should accept the fact that if we can use our power to further goals, it can be used for the good of mankind as well. Extreme political and economic pressure should be brought on any country or international organization impeding a solution to the world's most pressing problem.

If some of these measures seem repressive, reflect on the alternatives—the still less palatable measures sure to be adopted in haste as the symptoms rapidly worsen, or the comprehensive death-rate "solution" which has always been nature's way of dealing with a species out of control.

6

WAR ON HUNGER: THE NEED FOR A STRATEGY

GEORG BORGSTROM

The author says, "Let us, therefore, for a moment rip away the embellishing veils that hide an ugly reality." Dr. Borgstrom explodes a few of our comforting fallacies, and his final plea is to see the world "as it is," not "as we believe it is." When I first read it, it brought back the shock I experienced walking on sidewalks covered with sleeping people my first night in Calcutta.

A surprising lack of awareness exists as to the gravity, magnitude, and nature of the current world crisis. Statistical data about the numbers of hungry, the shortage of resources, and the needs and requirements as to housing, water, and land swirl around almost daily in mass media. Yet our imagination seems to fail to realize their significance. A world in poverty and misery is out of focus and so badly blurred that it almost constitutes an unreal reality. In relative terms there is even less progress today than a decade ago. Statistics speak all too clearly.

Unquestionably, there are many good deeds to admire and register. There are innumerable accomplishments of merit. Nonetheless, the truth is that we have hidden much behind a mastery of rhetoric beautification. Let us, therefore, for a moment rip away the embellishing veils that hide an ugly reality. Let there be no misunderstanding as to the truth about our failure as a human race.

Failure Despite Impressive Advances

Despite our proficient performances and unprecedented advances in public health, agriculture, fisheries, and technology, resulting in impressive gains in food and fertilizer production, we are nevertheless losing the race. The backlog of hungry and malnourished now exceeds 2.5 billions. We have failed even to provide adequately for the one billion added since 1948. For instance, no less than 2700 million people are short of water and even the literacy campaign is slipping. The world adds 30 more millions each year to an already existing backlog of 750 million illiterate adults.

There are more than a billion children in the world, around 650 million of whom will never reach adulthood, largely because of direct or indirect effects of malnutrition. Most sick people of the world never see a doctor. Despite laudable efforts by WHO, more than 900 million people carry life-sapping hookworms. More than 500 million suffer from vision-depriving trachoma, due to eye infections sustained by lack of vitamins. Many successful campaigns have been launched against malaria, yet 250 to 300 million people suffer from this debilitating disease. More money would be needed to launch an effective campaign in Africa against this single disease than WHO's total budget for the fight against *all* maladies in this disease-ridden continent.

As ominous as the hunger-gap is, the poverty-gap is still greater, and is widening all the time and at an increasing rate. Social revolutions were initiated around the turn of the century for the redistribution of wealth to the mutual benefit of the entire society. The only alternatives that emerged in most of the world, however, were increased production, transfer of resources through taxation, or more revolutions. The alleged miracles of Mexico and Japan have not involved the total society. The chief beneficiaries are an emerging middle class of less than 10%. Averages are on the whole misleading both to experts and to laymen. Boosting average food intake by including tourist eating or by overlooking top consumption by a privileged minority blurs the true nutritional picture. In many instances, a major fraction of society does not earn money and as a consequence lacks the resources to purchase necessary food.

Double-talk

Our double standards are evident in a number of additional areas. We expend far more effort peddling weapons than we do in providing food. This country's military aid, for example, has far superseded constructive agricultural or economic aid.

We talk about education, yet we do not hesitate to lure experts in significant numbers from crucial areas such as India and Latin America. India provides the United States with a number of doctors each year amounting to the output of three major medical schools.

Aid loans through the World Bank and other institutions are considerably emaciated by the servicing of earlier loans. Currently, close to half the amount of new loans are earmarked for this purpose. In effect, the poor, hungry world is drowning in debts. In addition, in several countries, the outflow of funds through invested capital exceeds the amounts received through grants and loans.

Land reform has become the most misused word between the Rio Grande and the Strait of Magellan. Redistribution of agricultural land is trumpeted as a panacea from the skyscrapers of the capitals, and strongly advocated in development symposia on university campuses in Europe and the United States. Yet, most developing countries lack land for distribution, with the landless queues longer than ever before, and the members often counted in the millions. The fact is that in Latin America at least 40 or even 50 million people need to be relocated from their present lands as "ecologically displaced persons" currently on land that should never have been tilled.

Industrialization is another verbal panacea with little concern for the well-being of the pressing multitudes of unemployed. This remedy is advocated despite the glaring lack of investment capital, the nonexistence of basic resources such as water, food, metals, and so forth. Few countries, if any, have more than a fraction of the funds required for adequate investment to employ gainfully the youngsters who reach the labor force each year.

We take comfort in rapid changes, but fail to recognize their nature. In the decade from 1970 to 1980, 280 million more people will be added to the global labor market. Of these no less than 226 million will belong to the less well-developed areas of the world. The ideas proposed for coping with this dilemma fail on most counts. It is already too late to effect a cure or even to initiate remedial measures.

We recommend expanded trade with little attention to the needs and basic interests of the involved countries. Proposing to buy the produce of their soils or the resources of their mines or forests primarily to fill our own gaps is at best a highly questionable approach to their extensive needs. Paying for foreign exchange by depleting resources and extending malnutrition is a poor economic policy. More emphasis will have to be placed on health and nutrition as true assets. The human capital of a nation should be entered into the bookkeeping in equal balance with the investment value of machinery and equipment.

We advocate family planning, well knowing that rigorous birth control is what is needed. Many more examples could be brought forth to show the growing discrepancy between our words and our actions, between what we believe about the world crisis and its true nature and magnitude.

Technical Salvation Alone Impossible in an Overdeveloped World

A simplistic notion that the world needed merely a little technological oiling here and there took shape in the Technical Aid Program of postwar years. This was unfortunate. We are still stuck with this outlook, with a persistent emphasis on our superior technology, legendary thriftiness, famed ingenuity, unparalleled creativity, and unexcelled way of life. That other world is described in terms of its "atrocious backwardness," "notorious listlessness," and so forth. This kind of thinking entirely misses the vital causes and effects of the Hunger Gap.

Classifying the world on the other side of the Hunger Gap by the all-embracing designation of underdeveloped, and as one single backward world reflects two dangerous fallacies. Key parts of that hungry and malnourished world have borne most of the advanced civilizations prior to ours. They now stand out as seriously overpopulated as well as *over*developed. They are overextended in terms of water and soil. A majority of their people are extremely poor and diseased. Most of our programs, national and international, have for far too long failed to see the dimensions of their misery and the frightful rate of deterioration which is due primarily to their skyrocketing population.

Others of these so-called underdeveloped countries also show signs of overdevelopment notably by extensive deforestation, excessive ploughing, and overextended use of water. As a consequence, they are hampered by grave soil erosion, creeping salination, and serious overgrazing.

Our civilization with its tremendous wastefulness in water, energy, and metals simply cannot be copied on a global scale.

The Diversity

There is far too little recognition of the lack of uniformity within what we arbitrarily call the developing countries. By and large, this hungry and malnourished world comprises three major social categories: (1) The indigenous population still in the traditional societies of villages (India, Indonesia, Andean region, etc.), (2) the tradesmen and the emerging middle class, and (3) the exploding slums. The last are little aided by conventional industrialization. As mentioned, only a fraction of those who would like to enter the labor force of these countries gain employment. Unfortunate millions are squeezed from a countryside with no space left. This rural superpressure of added millions is clearly mirrored in the fact that most of the world no longer has "farms," only plots (1–2 acres), often further fragmented into subplots. Glib talk about land reforms poorly recognizes the fact that the number of landless can now be counted in the millions and there is no land to distribute. Dumping these people who will soon number 30 to 50 million, without work and without hope in cities is in itself an absurdity. Add to this the herculean task of feeding these rootless and homeless and you have the ingredients of mass epidemics and mass famine.

Evasive Verbalizing

Mankind desperately needs new ways of measuring economic progress. Not to include economic activities such as handicraft within the concept of GNP (gross national product) is misleading. It seems absurd to measure GNP by including the number and complexity of space vehicles or amount of military hardware produced. If these are a gauge of GNP, the figures certainly do not reflect human prosperity.

To retreat, like the economists do, into the dreamlands of "purchasing power" is to create another grand-scale deception. To recognize only those individuals who are in a position to dangle a dollar (or ruble or pound or franc) is too easy a way out from the rapidly expanding poorhouse of the world. More than half of the world's population lacks the means of buying the minimum amount of food it needs. The spectacle is completely absurd when seriously malnourished countries like Pakistan, India, South Africa, and Rhodesia report surpluses despite the notorious fact that available food falls far short of needs.

No Single Remedy

We are caught in an immense oversimplification of the issue. There is a glaring lack of coordination both in national and international endeavors. The grave nature of man's crisis is only vaguely recognized even by many professional groups, let alone the public. News media and general education have failed on almost all levels to convey a reasonably correct picture of the crisis.

Mankind lost more than twenty postwar years being almost brainwashed into accepting the naive notion that agriculture and technology could readily provide for the human family in almost any number. The entire discussion was one-dimensional, based simply on a question of producing more food. Only about five years ago the magnitude of our failure was recognized. Despite magnificent advances both in agriculture and fisheries, and impressive contributions by medicine and technology more people were short of food and water than ever before in human history. The discussion quickly shifted as the population dimension finally became universally acknowledged. Although this was a step forward, the debate was still dangerously eclipsed. Slogans about more food and fewer people now became the oversimplified approach to the problem.

Let us briefly review some neglected aspects. It is well recognized that shortage of food affects working capabilities and physical efficiency. Many people in poorer areas of the world have to operate a whole week on what an average person in the Western world consumes in one day. Modern nutritional science has, moreover, uncovered still more crucial relationships. Shortage of protein in the fetus and in infants produces irreversible damage to brain tissue. This hungry world is suffering losses of 30 to 75 percent on its crops through waste and spoilage, by rodents, insects, and microorganisms. Additional food for hundreds of millions of people could be obtained by improved storage, distribution, and other marketing facilities. The whole area of processing and marketing has been grossly neglected in most aid programs. These key links have either been taken for granted or simply vanished from consideration.

A Sick World

Furthermore, the poor, hungry world is by and large, despite our efforts, a thoroughly sick world. This not only applies to man himself but to his livestock and crops as well. Losses through pests and parasites are enormous. Despite potent chemicals and advanced technical devices even the well-fed world suffers considerable losses.

The Water Scandal

Another neglected dimension is that of water, which broadens into the need for appraisal of all basic resources. The water used in growing food for humans and feed for animals moves back into the hydrologic cycle. It is returned to the earth primarily by precipitation. This applies both to the cropping controlled by irrigation as well as to that on "natural" or nonirrigated fields. Despite the skyrocketing figure for human domestic use of water and the requirements of modern industry, more than nine-tenths of the water is used in the production of food. About 3500 gallons of water per person per day is used to provide the food for one American. Water available for crops on the globe does not allow such a nutritional standard for more than a thousand million people. An average of 475 gallons of water per person per day is used to provide the food for East Indians. A strict vegetarian may subsist on the product of 350 gallons per person per day.

These figures raise very serious questions and focus attention on the inexcusable water scandal of the globe. According to WHO, more than 2000 million people receive water which is both inadequate in supply and unacceptable in quality. Each year, 500 million fall victim to water-borne diseases. Tens of millions have to walk miles (not uncommonly three to seven miles) to pick up water daily. More people are serviced by water peddlers than by faucets. The fight for sanitation is a costly, futile battle.

The Green Revolution

We talk about the high-yielding strains of wheat and rice, forgetting that their productive capabilities can be realized only by using more water, more fertilizers, more spray material, expanded storage and processing, and vastly increased amounts of capital. In addition, we must consider the ecological dimension. Only in a very few instances do we know the result of these strains on the environment.

More significant, however, is the lack of awareness of nutritional realities. In the Third World Food Survey, FAO (Food and Agriculture Organization) established that the globe needed a 270% *increase* in meat production up to the year 2000, but preferably a 50% *reduction* in grain output. This report revealed how far astray man has gone by thinking only in terms of tonnage and calories, forgetting the far more fundamental C/N ratio. To pump in starch to the already heavily protein-deficient areas of tropical Asia seems less than prudent. Most of the high-yielding strains show little gain in protein but gains in starch, making a less tasty and far less nutritious food with a decline of 10 to 25% in relative protein content.

The Historical Perspective

Yet, there are far more fundamental factors. I will limit myself to two: the availability of resources and trade exchange. The white men who got control of the North American prairies received the greatest and richest booty ever gained by any group of men in history. Others grabbed the rich pampas of the South. We brought in manpower from Africa to use in taking care of overwhelming riches, and for a time we nibbled on Asia too. In the nineteenth century, Europe released the greatest migration in human history: 70 million people roamed to all corners of the globe. Such extraordinary measures cannot be duplicated. There are no new lands to which man can migrate. World trade will presumably have to abandon the patterns laid down in the past and be rearranged to provide for the new impact of human numbers.

Although the migration era came to an end after World War II, the white man still retains much economic power in many areas of the world, and acquires their resources to provide for himself. We in the United States not only have larger per capita resources in soil and water than the peoples in other parts of the world, but we depend on these transoceanic imports as well. In most commodities, the net flow is from the hungry world to the well-fed.

Trade and Aid

This absurdity more than anything else has undermined foreign aid activities. Climbing prices of capital goods, reflecting how the rich world persistently raises its standard, contrast with the almost equally persistent drop in commodity prices. This has undermined the relative value of foreign exchange and nullified much foreign aid. A five percent drop in commodity prices eats up half the aid contributions.

Most American foreign aid is neither foreign nor aid. Chief beneficiaries have been its own agriculture and industry. True investments aiding recipient countries constitute less than three percent of the total. Most investments have been made to take care of United States national interests or needs, such as the building of strategic roads, discovery and exploitation of oilfields, mines, and so forth. United States investments in Canada have as a rule been larger than the total placed in the so-called developing world.

Dangerous Omniscience

A dangerous notion is furthermore prevailing that the United States has all the needed expertise. This is best reflected in the recent Presidential Report on World Food Problems. No findings, opinions, or conclusions by non-American researchers or experts are registered, nor are any research findings by scientists in the involved countries reviewed. This gives the American people the false notion that only the United States cares or knows. It is hardly conducive to cooperation and constructive action or to the right kind of United States involvement by experts and educators.

The Global Crisis

As this world crisis takes on a more sinister nature, the foreign aid programs are shrinking and dwindling not only in the United States, but universally. This global aid crisis appears in one regard to be a healthy sign. After 25 years of almost euphoric rhetoric the necessity to face the truth has arrived. We now encounter an unsettled board-and-lodging burden for no less than 2.5 billion people plus an almost unbelievable additional load of one billion more in the next ten years. The discrepancy between talk and action is staggering—yet mankind is quickly reaching the most important crossroad in history. The road we choose into the future will forever determine mankind's fate.

The Gap Between Words and Action

The tragedy of our day is not primarily the Hunger Gap, but rather the growing gap between our words and our actions. There is a zooming inflation of conferences, symposia, meetings, and seminars *ad infinitum* in sovereign disregard for the fact that the catastrophe is already here. The hungry billions cannot wait. They have not the slightest interest in how many billions some professor might think the world could feed, nor in the warnings that a more serious analysis might express. The hungry pay attention only to what is done to save them or substantially relieve their suffering. Neither do they care whether the grain bowl offered to them is red, blue, or black.

Need for a Strategy

Our tragedy is basically a failure to formulate our goals and work out a strategy. We have been so impressed by the marvels of our means and techniques that we naively opined that by willing the means we should be able to banish hunger and poverty. We have been masterful at tactical maneuverings but we have failed miserably as strategists. A crash program is called for. In food terms, this means moving away from the prevailing simplistic notion that (1) producing more food and (2) limiting human numbers are in themselves sufficient. It has taken mankind nearly a quarter of a century to move from the one-dimensional thinking prevailing in post-war days that all that we needed was more food. This was precious time lost, and we can ill afford to lose another quarter of a century by getting stuck in a two-dimensional world. The paradox is that global endeavors are needed to fight waste and spoilage, to recognize nutritional needs, to stave off parasites and diseases, to process and market foods, to appraise available soil and water resources, and so on.

Outline of a Strategy

What then is needed? What kind of strategy? It is not within the capability of an individual researcher to outline a complete battle plan. As in all strategic planning, we may need alternative options. Some irrevocable conditions will, however, be presented. First, a great number of expert groups hitherto bypassed or only occasionally consulted need to be brought into this strategic planning. They are presently only operating on the fringes. They include, for example, entomologists, phytopathologists, ecologists, geographers, food scientists, marketing experts.

1. Some 10 to 20 emergency task forces, picked among experts around the globe, should be created to tackle crucial areas and formulate valid and realistic programs. Gadgets and toys are poor substitutes in a world of stark reality.

2. At least one to two million development extension agents need to be quickly trained in the respective regions.

3. Mass media need to be mobilized to convey information in depth about the crisis, its true nature and magnitude.

4. A coordination of the operational activities of all the specialized agencies of the United Nations is long overdue.

Despair and impotence easily become the feeling among those who realize the urgency and the imperative nature of the world's crisis. A defeatist attitude invites still greater disasters. Mankind's greatest moment may still lie ahead if we replace the current lethargy of complacency with the courage of immediate determination. Only then will man and civilization prevail. No young generation was ever faced with a more exciting challenge. But first the call goes to experts in international matters with an urgent plea to bridge the frightful veracity gap, the staggering discrepancy between the world *as it is* and *as we believe it is*.

7

SOLID WASTE MANAGEMENT

ROLF ELIASSEN

As a direct result of our standard of living, garbage threatens to bury us. It must be dealt with in terms of a whole system, on a regional basis. "Relationships between such factors as economics, public health, engineering, law, political science, city planning, geography, and demography are involved." The author clearly defines the problem and provides some answers.

The constant increase in per capita production of refuse, coupled with population growth and concentration in the urban areas, is a major consideration in management of solid wastes. The size of the problem as well as the practices or lack of practices used in its solution are responsible for the nation's crisis in solid waste management. It is estimated that over one billion pounds of urban solid wastes are generated in the nation each day, and that the costs of community collection and disposal already approximate four billion dollars a year.

The term "solid waste" describes that material which is normally solid, and which arises from animal or human life and activities and is discarded as useless or unwanted. Solid waste also includes deposited waste particulates, even when temporarily suspended in air or water. It refers to the heterogeneous mass of throwaways from the urban community as well as the homogeneous accumulations of agricultural, industrial, and mineral wastes.

The traditional view of solid wastes requires some reexamination. There is more to the problem than just handling and disposing of community or urban solid wastes, even though this is far from solution. Congress in the Solid Waste Disposal Act of 1965 defined solid waste as "garbage, refuse, and other discarded materials, including solid waste materials resulting from *industrial, commercial,* and *agricultural operations,* and from community activities." Disposal was defined to include the "collection, storage, treatment, utilization, processing, or final disposal of solid waste."

Implications for public health have been linked to mismanagement of solid wastes. As many as 22 diseases have been associated with mismanaged wastes. Open burning often results in air pollution. Many residues which cannot be eliminated are hazardous not only to human health but also to plant and animal well-being. The combined or synergistic effects of many contaminants are not yet known. Nature has shown a great capacity for degrading and disposing of unwanted residues, but the major concern now is that some species may be damaged so much that there is a shift in the ecological balance of the biosphere.

Practical problems in solid waste management have often been treated without the full use of available information. Short-range remedies have held sway over long-range solutions. Local decisions have prevailed over state or regional planning. Standards set may meet some objectives but fail others. Decisions may be made on the basis of cost analysis alone.

The trend for the future must include the development of solid waste management systems that permit progress without harmful side effects. The preservation of public health and the esthetics of the environment should be of paramount consideration.

Natural Resources

The earth's mineral and other resources are not unlimited. Man extracts metals and ores and transform them into products, but when these products have fulfilled their usefulness, and are classified as solid wastes, the valuable materials are often lost. A prime solution to the resource depletion problem created by the profligate use of metals would be to improve methods for recycling and reuse. The salvage industry has somewhat served this purpose, but the concept might well be much more widely applied. Present-day tailing dumps, landfills, and automobile graveyards may be looked on in the future as "mines" for minerals whose natural ores have been depleted beyond cost feasibility.

Economic Aspects

Implicit in public attitudes toward waste materials is the problem of economics. National concern must transcend both the concept of what the public can "afford" to pay and the question of why the expenditure of about four billion dollars each year for solid waste collection and disposal has not staved off the present mounting problems. The truth is that the national standard of living depends to a great degree upon processes leading to waste generation. Thus if wastes themselves could be salvaged, reworked, and recycled, there would be less to dispose of.

A system for managing solid wastes must be economically as well as technologically feasible. Many communities are unable or unwilling to pay for available disposal devices. In general, only large cities find incineration economically feasible and it may become even more costly as legislation requires increased investment to meet air quality standards, and as open space landfill becomes more scarce.

Three of the four billion dollars spent yearly for disposal is attributed to collection and transportation. Yet this has purchased only hit-or-miss collection systems in many cities. The other billion dollars, despite public objections, has been spent on the use of the open dump as the predominant disposal method.

It is apparent that even more money must be devoted to improving the management of solid wastes, more economic efficiency must be achieved, or both. Clearly, paying for waste disposal is a legitimate and necessary expense of living.

Technological Aspects

The problems of waste management are greatly influenced by industrial and market considerations. Planned obsolescence, for example, is a way of life. The consumer is urged to buy the new and trade in or throw away the old. The rise of the nonreturnable container, despite the fact that it costs the user more, is another example of the close relationship between market strategy and the generation of solid waste. Little thought is being devoted to the true disposability of the product. With the exception of the new biodegradable detergents and current efforts in the field of pesticides, there is virtually no instance in which product design consideration has included that of ultimate disposability. "Disposability" has been interpreted only in terms of user consideration.

Political Aspects

Cities throughout the world have traditionally dealt with wastes by transporting them beyond their own immediate confines and discarding them in the least expensive way the public might tolerate. No serious problems arose from this practice so long as the cities were separated by wide spaces. But today, urban sprawl is erasing spaces between cities. A major obstacle to organizing metropolitan refuse collection and disposal systems is the multitude of local government units, many of which are remnants from another era. Furthermore, many communities, particularly the smaller ones, have failed to combine with others in their efforts and financial resources for collection and disposal. Without cooperation, communities usually are not able to afford the best equipment, management personnel, or the most desirable disposal site.

Area-wide disposal service not only reduces unit costs, but also makes it possible to operate on a more sanitary and acceptable basis and to avoid duplication of investment. This regional approach to solid waste management usually provides the answer to the problem even when a region includes interstate areas. Failure to take the regional approach may be a matter of local pride or inertia, or there may be legal barriers to interjurisdictional cooperation. In either case, a more realistic legislative or administrative response is needed.

Operational planning is an important factor. In some communities and cities waste disposal is still not recognized as a collective need nor considered in basic community facility planning. Like other public services, solid waste management is related to population growth, density, and industrial and commercial zoning. Land is required. Planning calls for a long-range look at the total area involved. Communities are inclined to conceive of solid waste collection and disposal activities in terms of how to deal with community refuse for the next few years; they should think in terms of 25 or 50 or even 100 years.

Perhaps the basic political fact of solid waste management is citizen response to factors and solutions regarding the problem. The citizen, together with minicipal administrators and industrial executives, must be made aware of the need for a new concept of solid waste management.

SOURCES OF SOLID WASTE

Solid wastes fall into five major catagories: urban, including domestic, commercial, and municipal; industrial; agricultural; mineral; and those from federal establishments. The 1967 total as disclosed in the National Solid Waste Management Survey conducted by the U.S. Public Health Service was 3.65 billion tons, equivalent to 100 pounds per capita per day for a national population of 200 million. By 1980 this figure is expected to increase to 5 billion tons.

Urban Waste Sources

Traditionally, urban refuse disposal has been concerned only with wastes collected from households, mostly paper and garbage. This limited view of community responsibility was altered by the rapid expansion that followed World War II. Customary concepts of solid waste management are being revolutionized by the need for area-wide plans and for solutions beyond the capabilities of many of the myriad political jurisdictions of the modern community. Even when one city is nominally located at some distance from another, urbanization has progressed as satellite suburbs have flowed into the rural areas. With high land values and heavy investment in fixed installations for dairies, poultry and egg production, and animal feeding facilities, the traditional characteristics associated with rural areas have disappeared.

New materials, planned obsolescence, and a never-ending variety of new products from industry have also had their impact. Single-use containers and nonreturnable containers have affected the combustability and degradability of refuse.

What are urban wastes? Food wastes, garbage, paper, wood, bedding materials, tin cans, glass, crockery, dirt and ashes, dead cats and dogs, sweepings and leaves, abandoned cars and trucks, residue from demolition and new construction projects, such as lumber, masonry, metals, paints, and concrete, certain radioactive materials, explosives, pathologic wastes, and a myriad of similar materials from hotels, institutions, stores, and industries.

Industrial Waste Sources

Municipal incinerators, refuse dumps, sanitary landfills, and acres of old automobile hulks are a common manifestation of solid wastes. Less obvious, in warehouses and back lots of industrial properties, are industrial wastes, the piles and acres of sludges, slags, waste plastics, scrap metal, bales of rags and paper, drums of off-grade products. Solid wastes of industrial origin comprise a category of major magnitude. The magnitude of their disposal is compounded by the fact that industrial wastes are so diversified.

Industrial scrap metal is generated at a rate in excess of 15 million tons annually. The paper industry generates over 30 million tons of paper waste. Approximately 115 million tons of industrial solid wastes are being generated each year. Two factors influence the size of these "stored" inventories: adaptability to reprocessing or reuse and the cost of storage. Most of these wastes cannot be reintroduced into use. Manufacturers therefore are seeking new methods of coping with these wastes.

Agricultural Waste Sources

The principal agricultural and forestry wastes are animal manures, vineyard and orchard prunings, crop-harvesting residues, animal carcasses, greenhouse wastes, and pesticide containers. Domestic animals produce more than a billion tons of fecal wastes every year and over 400 million tons of liquid wastes. Used bedding, paunch manure, and dead carcasses make the total production of animal wastes close to 2 billion tons. As much as 50% of animal wastes is generated in concentrated growing operations close to urban areas. Large-scale animal raising operations have developed rapidly in the last 20 years. Production of farm animals has become a major business resulting in a yearly manure waste load of 1,562,721,000 tons.

Mineral Waste Sources

During the past 30 years, well over 20 billion tons of mineral solid wastes have been generated by the mineral and fossil fuel mining, milling, and processing industries. These wastes amount to about 1.1 billion tons per year, and increased waste generation can be expected in nearly every commodity area.

Although some 80 mineral industries generate wastes, 8 industries alone are responsible for 80% of the total. Of these, the copper industry contributes the largest tonnage, followed by the iron and steel, bituminous coal, phosphate rock, lead, zinc, alumina, and anthracite industries. Mineral mine wastes are, for the most part, barren over burden or submarginal grade ore from open-pit or surface mining. These mountains of waste, often hundreds of feet high and covering extensive land areas, accumulate over the landscape adjacent to the mining operations. Other mineral wastes include coal waste piles, vast accumulations of finely ground tailings, slag and smelter wastes, and wastes from the chemical processing of mineral concentrates. Dredging and strip mining also create large-scale pollution and destruction.

The breadth of the environmental effects of waste accumulations is evident from an inventory of the land disturbed by the mineral and fossil fuel mining and processing industries. Prior to 1965, 7000 square miles were either covered with unsightly mineral and solid fossil fuel mine and processing waste, or so devastated by operations as to be not only useless and ugly, but in some cases a hazard to human life and property. Currently, about 20,000 active surface and strip mining operations are carving into the landscape at about 153,000 acres a year. By 1980, it is expected that more than 5 million acres will have been defaced by these operations.

MANAGEMENT OF SOLID WASTES

The System Concept

Solid waste management is a concept of a whole system. Relationships between such factors as economics, public health, engineering, law, political science, city planning, geography, and demography are involved. The urban-suburban-rural complex must be seen as a single system. We need comprehensive planning and the application of engineering and technological advances. The goal is the most efficient and economic system possible under the constraints imposed by private industry and local government. Research, development, and demonstration of new improved concepts for one waste source may likewise be applicable to another. A unified approach will also avoid duplication of research, development, and demonstration efforts. Let us examine the subsystems in this system.

Collection and Transport

For many Americans, solid waste can be disposed of in the can outside the back door. But many others must transport their wastes to a disposal site, and still others dispose of their waste on their own property. The great variety of community approaches is further evidence of the need for planning in this field, particularly when collection and handling represents about 80% of the waste disposal costs. About half of 6300 communities surveyed make no comprehensive plans at all. Some 53% of all these communities exercise no control over on-site storage of household garbage. The degree of control over other kinds and sources of refuse is even less.

Even the present grossly inadequate disposal systems account for a major portion of community expenditures, budgeted or unbudgeted. The millions of cans of household refuse, the street sweepings, litter, and all the other urban solid wastes added together cost the public for collection and disposal services about four billion dollars. Among city public services, only the costs for schools, roads, and welfare exceed it.

In public facilities, the cost of storing refuse before it is collected is significant. The most inexpensive and feasible means is in lightweight, galvanized steel or plastic containers. The most expensive means of storage is disposable paper refuse bags. For large or multiple-unit facilities, the least expensive way is by using a movable bin-type container. Collection and transport account for 75% of the $4 billion annual cost of urban solid waste management.

Processing

The technology of urban solid waste management is developing, but more data is needed on the logistic, economic, and technological aspects of processing the heterogeneous mixtures in urban wastes. The wide cost range in unit processing reflects both the technical sophistication of the equipment and the wide variations in the kinds of waste treated. The following are the most commonly used techniques at the present.

Incineration

Combustion is one of the oldest methods of dealing with the organic fraction of urban solid wastes. It has advanced through the years from simple open poles or pits to highly mechanized and carefully engineered systems. The best incinerators can reduce the volume of organic matter by 90%. The combustion products include gases, particulates, and fly ash and residue, which may be sterile gases in particular. At its best, with care, air pollution control can be achieved. At its worst, it creates objectionable air pollution from fly ash, and leaves a residue of as much as 40% of the original volume.

A modern incinerator is costly. It requires land for disposal of residues, bulky and oversized wastes, and any unburnable wastes. More than half a dozen municipal incinerators in Los Angeles were closed down for economic reasons when stringent regulations were enacted for control of air pollution. About 96% of surveyed incinerators are publicly owned and operated. They are usually located in areas zoned for industry and on the average process about 8% of collected solid wastes in the country.

Composting

Although anaerobic decomposition of waste materials has been practiced to produce soil additives in Asia for centuries, and aerobic composting has been practiced in Europe for years, these techniques cannot be applied to composting in the United States because of differences in the composition of waste.

Most studies of the process have been toward producing a soil conditioner marketable for agricultural use, but the simple reduction of the volume of the material has not been overlooked. The existing orientation of agriculture to the use of commercial chemical fertilizers and other related factors have made the large-scale marketing of the final product difficult. No special merit, however, is given to one method of processing over another. Composting is given preference only when it is the most economical system or when society is willing to pay for returning wastes that are compatible with the environment.

Despite hopes for the method, only 1 of the 15 composting plants in the United States in the last 17 years has operated for a period long enough to indicate success. Most of the plants that have closed were operated by businessmen who expected a profit. The main difficulty is the unsuitability of much of city refuse for composting use. Another is location; there is an odor from compost plants, especially in warm, humid weather.

Utilization and Salvage

Diverting some of the overall waste materials from a waste stream to the basic and natural resources of the nation is an example of "direct recycling" or "salvage." The term has been used rather loosely in practice to include both residues, such as scrap metal which was recycled within an industry for utilization and hence never really part of the community waste stream, and materials which are segregated from mixed refuse and sold. In this latter category are such items as rags, bottles, paper, nonferrous metals, and metal cans, which are destined for landfill unless sorted out and reclaimed. Salvaging is an essential part of the economy; if it were not for the utilization of scrap materials, there would not be sufficient materials at an acceptable price to meet the needs of basic industries.

The ideal of solid waste management would be the disposal of wastes by reuse or recycling, and the disposition of the irreducible residue without insult and perhaps even with enhancement to the environment. Direct recycling is most readily carried out in situations in which the waste is relatively homogeneous and high in value, as in commercial and industrial operations. When reusable material is mixed with garbage, its reclamation is economically unfeasible. As a result, salvage in municipal operations is relatively limited and sporadic. This difficult fraction cannot be ignored, however, because it represents a sizeable portion of the nation's waste.

Disposal

Disposal is the ultimate step in a solid waste management system. All solid wastes, whether raw refuse, sewage sludge, incinerator fly ash and residue, or compost, must be utilized in some way or given final disposal. The major categories of disposal are open dumping, open burning, ocean disposal, mulching, land spreading, animal feeding, and sanitary landfills.

Open dumping has been and is the simplest and most widely used means of urban waste disposal. By and large, the most advanced method of ultimate disposal for urban areas is the sanitary landfill. It disposes of refuse on land without creating nuisances or hazard to public health or safety by utilizing the principles of engineering to confine the refuse to the smallest practicable area, to reduce it to the smallest practical volume, and to cover it with a layer of earth at the conclusion of each day's operation or at such more frequent intervals as may be necessary.

Communities vary widely in their approach to wastes. Land disposal sites provide by far the predominent disposal method in use by American communities. But in an investigation of over 6000 sites, most publicly operated, only 14% of the sites were adjudged to be sanitary landfills. Though it is a highly recommended method, the public has yet to accept it.

Mineral Waste Disposal

The minerals industry generally has lacked any long-range plan for wastes. Because of the cost of transportation, its solution has been local. The solid wastes are deposited near the mining or processing operation. No systems concept of management to include a flow of materials from generation to disposal has been developed.

SUMMARY

Many citizen and conservation groups have begun to recognize solid waste as posing a costly and pressing national problem that can seriously menace health and welfare in this country. There are only three repositories for all waste materials: the earth, its waters, and its atmosphere. One result of poor waste management is pollution of these. New technologies are required for the disposal, or more importantly, the recycling, of the new and nearly indestructible materials. There is, moreover, a great shortage of qualified and well-trained personnel to design and administer the processing, collection, and disposal of waste. The present national solid waste practices are immensely costly when all environmental factors are considered, including the waste of valuable resources. Reducing these costs is a major goal of solid waste management.

I would submit these recommendations:

1. A broadly expanded research, development, and demonstration program in solid waste management to be adopted by the federal government with the goals of cost reduction, recycling of solid waste for refuse, protection of the environment, and better service.

2. Establishment of educational programs at universities for engineers, planners, economists, public administrators, public

health administrators, and those in other disciplines confronted in the course of their professional service with the problems of waste management.

3. Establishment of training programs for public officials and employees and information services for the public.

4. Designation within the federal government of an inter-agency group chaired and possibly staffed by HEW, to establish goals, set priorities, and coordinate all federal solid waste research and development, and demonstration activities.

5. An inter-agency group to develop a comprehensive five-year plan for research, development, and demonstration programs. This plan, to be revised annually, would cover the agreed-upon tasks to be included by all the participating federal departments and agencies in their budgets, and would serve as the basis for submission to Congress of a coordinated program funding request.

6. Preparation of an annual report to the President and the Congress by HEW with the assistance of the inter-agency group, reporting progress made on the plan and on the status of overall national efforts.

7. Provision for continuing federal support to responsible state agencies which complete state plans, so that they can continue research, development, and demonstration programs on solid waste management.

8. Encouragement of private industry to develop and demonstrate new technologies.

9. Recognition by federal installations of a special obligation to develop the best solid waste technology and to undertake research, development, and demonstration projects with the goal of minimizing the impact of solid wastes from these sources upon the environment.

10. Convening of a National Conference on Solid Waste Management to correlate information in the solid waste field and to stimulate further research, development, and demonstration. Attendees of the conference would include representatives from all levels of government, industry, universities, and other groups with an interest in solid waste management.

11. Amendment of the Solid Waste Disposal Act of 1965 with title to read: Solid Waste Management Act, which should reflect a total and systematic approach to the solid waste problem.

8

ENVIRONMENTAL PROBLEMS ARISING
FROM NEW TECHNOLOGIES

KENNETH S. PITZER

This discussion questions "the net effect of the result of science and tech-nology on the quality of human life." Its recommendations for improve-ment are illuminated by the author's personal commitment.

For twenty years after the close of the Second World War, science received unprecedented and often unquestioned support in this country. During that period, research and development expendi-tures contributed significantly to our national economic progress and prosperity, but that period has ended. The net effect of the results of science and technology on the quality of human life is now being questioned.

For an even longer period of time in world history, we have held a sort of laissez-faire theory that scientific knowledge would automatically yield economic and social progress. To a consider-able extent this has been true. But just as economic laissez-faire was found to be unsatisfactory because of boom-bust instability, so also scientists are coming to realize more fully that some practi-cal applications can be extremely dangerous to the world.

The atomic bomb is a shattering example. Concern about the seismic safety of large underground nuclear tests has recently intensified—and for good reason. But I am not a geophysicist, and therefore my concern does not arise from an exact estimate of earthquake hazard. My concern arises from a more basic human reaction to the need for open discussion and public examination of the Atomic Energy Commission's evaluation. There was and is no real need for secrecy in discussing this problem; the details of explosive devices are irrelevant. I hope that the subject is now being examined by scientists who have no affiliation with AEC and that their findings will be submitted to extensive public hearing.

The proposed supersonic transport airplane is another ex-ample of a growing number of decisions, made principally by the Executive Branch, which have caused almost irreversible commit-ment of high priority to a project which would clearly cause sonic annoyance to a majority of the people if overland flight is allowed.

Those are spectacular examples. But we are now observing that the cumulative degradation of our environment from many less spectacular causes can, in the end, be even more serious. Most major new technologies are already influenced or regulated by the government in some way. It would not necessarily extend the range of government control to ask that the influence on, or regulation of, new technologies be more sensitive to humanistic factors.

The extremists tell us to stop all scientific work, but I doubt that they really mean it. I am sure that most people want to retain the advantages of science and technology, and basic science must move ahead substantially, as at present.

I would distinguish between basic science and the applications of technology. It is really impossible to predict the applications of basic research. It will not be easy to foresee all of the possible damaging effects of a new product or machine, but we should try to do so. In the past we have usually assumed that deleterious side effects of a new technology would be negligible or could be remedied by subsequent action. In many cases that assumption was correct, but when it was not correct, the problems became severe. Once the new technology is established, there is a strong pressure for its continuation. It is far harder to stop an operation than not to start it at all. Furthermore, a modified technology may be possible which accomplishes the purpose and avoids the damage, but the change is a lot easier at the design stage than after the plant is built.

André Malraux says that "the most basic problem of our civilization is that it is a civilization of machines." Some intellectuals charge that science alone is at fault. If we are to avoid a damaging emotional reaction against science, scientists must help guide technology in the true service of all mankind. As soon as a technology is conceived, one should ask not only "Is it possible?" but also "Is it desirable?" and scientists must play a major role in this judgment process.

A central group close to the President might well promote this view throughout the government. In 1969 a task force of the National Academy of Sciences tendered a report to the Committee on Science and Astronautics of the House of Representatives. The report, entitled "Technology: Processes of Assessment and Choice," affirms that the federal government should take the lead. It suggests a general plan and several alternatives for evaluative processes. Further, it emphasizes three major guidelines. First, it notes that technology is pluralistic and that assessment efforts can encourage the many existing mechanisms while new ones are being added. Second, it suggests that assessment should remain independent, though close to the President and Congress, objective, and open to the public. Third, it urges caution, so that many viewpoints, including those of the poorly organized elements of society, would be weighed.

I endorse the broad guidelines and the spirit of those who rendered that report. But there must be a popular demand if that spirit is to be brought into action. I would favor some type of committee, within the Executive Office of the President, which would concern itself with environmental problems only and have no other responsibility. One section should forecast the effects of new technologies while other sections are dealing with already recognized problems. Professional organizations and university professionals, including scientists, engineers, lawyers, and humanists, must express the need for such a program and be willing to back it up by their own commitment, institutional and personal. I, for one, am willing to do so.

9

CHALLENGE IN OUR TIME

LEE A. DUBRIDGE

Speaking for the administration, the Director of the President's Committee on Science and Technology discusses some directions for improvement. Feasibilities, needed research, and a balance between extremes of cost and quality controls are included.

Caring for our environment is an enormous task, and to accomplish it we first need to recognize the nature of the task. Let us first separate the problem into two major components: (1) reducing pollution of air, water, and land, and (2) enhancing the beauty and pleasantness of the places where we live, work, and play.

Pollution, in its broadest sense, results from the fact that all forms of life by their very nature must live in their environment, and thereby change it in some ways. Life processes use materials from the environment, chemically converting them into materials which are eventually returned to the environment. The chemical processes are those which sustain life. The product materials are called waste. The waste materials produced by one life form may be taken up and used by another form—as the carbon dioxide produced as waste by animals is a necessary source of sustenance for the green plants. But other waste products serve only to pollute the environment to which they are returned.

Man—especially industrialized man—is the greatest of all consumers of the materials of his environment, and is therefore the greatest of all producers of waste products. Some of the materials man consumes, such as coal, oil, and natural gas, are the waste products of the life of bygone ages. Others, such as iron, copper, aluminum, and other metals, as well as water and oxygen, are the natural constituents of the primeval earth. Still other products come from naturally occurring plant and animal life—forests, crops, food, animals—which man sometimes depletes and sometimes seeks to replenish.

But all of these materials are converted eventually into other kinds of materials. Most of them are not readily reusable and so are waste products which still, of course, remain in the environment. There is no place else for them to go.

Pollution of the environment, then, results from the conversion of large quantities of natural products into corresponding quantities of waste products. If civilized man is to survive, and especially if he is to continually try to live better, there is no way he can avoid the production of waste products.

Our problem then is threefold:

1. To adopt procedures to ensure that harmful waste products are converted to harmless forms before they are returned to the environment. Dangerous bacteria and obnoxious or poisonous chemicals must be removed at the source.

2. Other materials—dirt, smoke, trash, junk, garbage—must be disposed of in ways that do not dirty the air or water or deface the land.

3. Greater care must be exercised in allowing the marketing of new products—food additives, insecticides or herbicides, household chemicals—to ensure that they are not harmful to humans or fish and wildlife.

These three tasks are straightforward ones, but not necessarily cheap or easy. The necessary technology is available in some cases, but not in others.

Further research on techniques for these measures are responsibilities which must be borne by local, state, and federal governments and by international agencies.

1. Regulations must be developed and enforced to protect the public interest, and they must be imposed in such a way as to provide an equitable distribution of the cost involved.

2. Research must be fostered by many agencies—private, public, and international—to determine where health hazards exist and to develop technologies for safer and more considerate disposal of waste products.

3. Since absolutely pure air and pure water are unattainable in this modern world except at prohibitive cost, research must be fostered to determine tolerance levels of various impurities —levels below which hazardous or obnoxious effects will be negligible. *Zero* tolerances are both unnecessary and impractical.

4. A broad educational program must be established to inform the average citizen that (a) his actions may degrade the environment and (b) he must be willing to share the costs of environmental improvement through higher taxes or higher costs for the products he buys.

As we turn from the subject of pollution to that of enhancement of the environment our task becomes more difficult. A new power plant in a given region may be essential to meeting the electric power needs of the people and the avoidance of power failures or disastrous blackouts. But such a facility, even if non-polluting, is bound to be an unwelcome sight to nearby residents, or it will occupy recreation areas or make unwelcome noise. If the plant is forced into the country it may still be an intrusion (though to fewer people), and the necessary transmission lines will occupy space and offend the senses. Promoting the public welfare and protecting the rights of citizens may often prove incompatible, and imaginative new solutions will be needed.

Factories and power stations do not exist primarily to make a profit. They exist to provide a product or a service which the public needs or demands. They attempt, in a competitive economy, to produce those goods and services at the lowest possible costs. If they must spend more money to protect the environment, their products must cost more. The consumer must pay these costs willingly.

The consumer, as a taxpayer, must be willing to pay higher taxes to provide funds to city, state, and federal governments to beautify our cities, dispose of wastes, create new parks, develop better plans for the location of homes, factories, streets, highways, public transportation, and all the rest.

Miracles cannot happen overnight. One hundred million automobiles cannot be replaced with smogless machines tomorrow. The multibillion dollar industrial plant of the United States, so essential to our everyday lives, cannot be shut down. The problem is a huge one. It involves nothing less than changing the habits of billions of people and adopting wholly new attitudes and very expensive new technologies by our whole world-wide industrial system.

But we have begun. We can turn the tide. And we can all help.

10

GROWTH AND THE QUALITY OF THE AMERICAN ENVIRONMENT

ROGER REVELLE

Our concern for natural resources as material utilities has been replaced during recent years by a rising realization that we must think about the whole environment as a resource that can be depleted or worsened by misuse. We are becoming increasingly aware that our happiness and our health are being jeopardized, our fulfillment as human beings limited, by destructive changes in our environment. Unless we can find remedies, the quality of life for our own and future generations will be dulled and diminished.

It is tempting to say, because it is partly true, that continuing population growth has caused the degradation of our surroundings which has become so evident during the past 25 years. Yet a good case can be made that equally important villains are the increase in Gross National Product and the changing patterns of our lives. Our growing affluence has had several effects. Each of us uses a larger quantity of materials, and thus there is more to throw away, and we can all better afford to throw away than retain or return. Our habits of consumption have changed toward using materials and doing things that are especially destructive to our environment. As the primary wants of the great majority have become satiated, we have become more concerned with the quality of life and the effects of our own actions in demeaning it.

Pollution and environmental deterioration certainly existed before World War II, but their greater, more pervasive prevalence today may indicate that a kind of quantum jump has occurred. The capacity of air, water, and land to absorb abuse without much visible change is very large; yet if enough pressure is exerted, the system may break down. Accelerating, every more obvious change then spreads rapidly through the environment. An alternative explanation is that our destructive capacity had grown to a level where it is on the same scale as many natural processes in the environment. We do not have enough evidence to decide which of these explanations is correct, or whether both are true.

During the 25 years from 1940 to 1965 the population of the United States increased by 46%, but the Gross National Product, in terms of constant dollars, nearly tripled, and the product per capita almost doubled. The number of passenger automobiles and the amount of gasoline burned in their engines kept pace with prosperity. There was one private automobile in use for about five Americans in 1940. By 1965 there were almost two for every five persons. Each automobile burned a little more gasoline with the passage of time—590 gallons in 1940; 650 in 1965.

As our affluence grew, our use of polluting materials grew even faster. The average American used about 250 pounds of paper in 1940. By 1965 his paper consumption had more than doubled, rising to 510 pounds a year.

Electric utilites consumed 54 million tons of coal and fuel oil, containing about a million tons of sulphur, in 1940. By 1965 this industry was using 263 million tons of coal and oil and releasing over 10 million tons of sulphur oxides into the air.

Production of plastics nearly doubled in those 25 years, from 34 to 60 pounds per person, while the population was growing by 46%. Plastic materials were increasingly used as containers which, like our enormous production of paper, quickly became waste products. Unlike paper, however, they were virtually indestructible and simply accumulated in our environment.

Longer vacations, rising incomes, and shorter travel times were clearly the major causes of the slumlike crowding of our national parks. Between 1940 and 1965, the number of visits in the national parks went from 19 million to 121 million, an increase of 550%, and per capita visits rose by nearly 350%.

The lack of any simple correlation between environmental deterioration and population growth can be demonstrated by calculating the size of population in the United States which, with the same per capita income and dirty habits as the average U.S. citizen in 1965, would have produced no more pollution than the country experienced in 1940. Other things being equal, the number of automobiles and the amounts of gasoline and paper consumed would have remained about constant over the quarter century if the population had declined from 133 million to 67 million. To maintain a constant flow of sulphur dioxide into the air from electric power plants, the population should have decreased to 40 million. The national parks would have remained as uncrowded in 1965 as they were in 1940 if our population during the interval had gone down to 30 million souls.

These speculations emphasize the uncertainties of the relationships between population, Gross National Product, and the quality of life of which environmental deterioration is one aspect. Almost surely our national productivity would not have risen, and indeed the country would be in the grip of a depression if any such declines in population had occurred. Conversely, it is widely believed, especially by businessmen, that a growing population is a strong stimulus to economic growth. If this is correct, then the increase in Gross National Product per person and the accompanying changes in patterns of consumption, which we have indicated as major factors in the destruction of environmental values during the past 25 years, may reflect the growth of population over the quarter century, at least to the extent that population growth is a necessary, if not a sufficient condition, for continuing prosperity. There is very little evidence, however, that there is much connection in modern industrial societies between population growth and economic development.

One must not go too far, of course, in discounting the role of population growth. Even conceding the important roles of per capita economic growth and changes in consumption, it is still clear that population changes have also been significant factors in the degradation of our environment. About one-third the increase in Gross National Product, numbers of automobiles, and gasoline and paper consumption can be accounted for by our increasing numbers.

The effects of the great migration to the cities and the coasts have been destructive also. In the countryside they are revealed by rotting farmhouses, decaying towns, dismal second-growth brush, and untended piles of trash; in the cities by the boarded-up windows and rat-infested buildings, the dirt and despair of the ghettos.

Nor can one view with much complacency the future increase in the number of Americans. We live in a generous land, and by comparison with many European countries, it is still a sparsely filled one. Of its nearly 2,300 million acres 1,800 million are in crops, range, pasture, or forests. Fewer than 60 million acres consist of urban and other built-up areas, including highways and airports. But the semiarid western half of our country has a delicate ecology that is highly vulnerable to the destructive actions of man, and even in the eastern half, the difficulties of maintaining a quiet harmony with the world of nature will increase with increasing numbers of people.

Nevertheless, the demonstration that our environmental problems are in large part caused by our behavior, as well as by our numbers, is of fundamental importance. It points strongly to the conclusion that maintaining and improving the quality of life requires changes of values and priorities, from private goods and individual consumption to public goods and cooperative action, from production of material things to preservation of our natural heritage.

In the past, our growing affluence has led to environmental destruction. In the future, it can give us far greater opportunities, both to perceive and to protect the quality of life and the diversity, beauty, and wonder of our land. As long as we were preoccuped with the struggle for existence, we could give little thought and less energy to cherishing our surroundings. Now the situation has changed radically. We must assume new responsibilities and take up new causes, both to serve our fellowmen and to become faithful stewards of our planet Earth.

11

COMPREHENSIVE PLANNING: WHERE IS IT?

ALFRED HELLER

The gadfly efforts of the independent conservation movement are not effective enough; the independent sector's energies are used up battling a government that should be on its side. To change this we need a "comprehensive governmental policy" with a master plan that would put government on the side of the public interest in survival.

Our deteriorating environment is the product of extremely powerful social and economic forces. We cannot successfully meet these forces by fighting local battles, no matter how fiercely. Nor can we do so at the state and national levels by advancing one big cause at the expense of another.

This paper has been substituted by the author for the one presented at the conference.

If I am right, then the traditional and accepted methods and concerns of the conservation movement come into serious question.

Consider the following: Major conservation organizations in this nation devoted their finest energies over a period of more than a decade to the creation of a Redwood National Park, which finally came into being in 1968. The legislation creating the park resulted in the protection by the public of about 30,000 acres of redwood lands not previously protected. Yet every three or four months the State of California loses 30,000 acres to urban use—30,000 acres of other land, scenic and fertile, important land.

In other words, we are fighting what we regard as big battles, but in fact they are tiny battles, and we are losing the war. Therefore, to be effective in a substantial way, conservationists will have to take on programs of much greater scope than they have in the past—that is, programs which will actually be adequate to meet our environmental needs.

If it is true that our environmental predicament is going to require large-scale programs to counter the forces creating it, then we must look for leadership to the entities which have the resources for providing that leadership, namely state government or the federal government. Local government hasn't the strength or the will. It is sacred only to those who indulge in it or are indulged by it. Private enterprise is out to make money first and save the world second, or third, or not at all. Regional government, although desperately needed, doesn't exist. State government is the best regional government we have around, unless you prefer Washington.

Nevertheless, we need not deceive ourselves that the state and federal governments meet their responsibilities. Most of the planning conducted by the state and federal action agencies remains narrowly single-interest, and our legislatures continue to pay for these single-interest plans and for carrying them out. In the current fiscal year my state, California, will funnel well over $1 billion to road-building activities. Comparable state expenditures for transit-type forms of transportation will not total 1/100th of this. The highway planners continue to set the course for California, along with the water planners, who persist in constructing the environmentally destructive California Water Plan. According to what vision of our future are all the single-agency planners controlled and directed? To my knowledge, none has been declared for my smoggy state, nor, for that matter, for the nation or the oasis, earth. In this age of eco-rhetoric it turns out that the need is as great as it always has been for a comprehensive approach to our environmental problems, guided by responsible government and sustained by massive public financing. At this late date California has no discernible plan for its future, nor really does any other state, with the doubtful exception of Hawaii, nor indeed does the United States of America. No plans—and no program and budget priorities for carrying out the plans.

In their way, conservationists form a mirror image of the governmental pattern of single-interest activity—everybody doing his own thing (and often doing it very well) but none troubling to ask what it all adds up to. We are too busy, it seems, making our insistent loose-leaf demands for getting oil out or reducing the population or cleaning up the air or preserving the wilderness, to recognize that none of them will be met, as all of them must be, without a comprehensive strategy and program for survival advanced by our senior governments. Therefore we would all do well to tithe a portion of our energy toward achieving this kind of comprehensive planning and administration. I do not suggest that we abandon our own special interests. On the contrary, the strength of this movement is in the genius of individuals and independent organizations finely aware of the hum and buzz in the local air. What I am saying is that the *lack of comprehensive governmental policy* is what relegates us to fighting these hundreds of impossible, losing, energy-draining environmental battles. Why shouldn't the state and federal governments be on our side one hundred percent? Let's demand that they be!

12

PLANNING THE EARTH'S SURFACE

HENRY CAULFIELD

The author's experience as a Department of Interior official gives him a realistic understanding of government planning programs. He describes the need to revise planning concepts on the basis of a fundamental survival ethic, namely, the "substantial accommodation of mankind within his natural environment, earth."

The 1960's will become known to history, I suspect, as the decade in which popular awareness of environmental degradation in the United States and recognition of the need for common action to achieve livable environments began to take hold.

Insight and concern with respect to natural environments and the need to maintain compatibility between man and nature have long been a part of our heritage. Within the decade of the sixties, intellectual awareness of our environmental plight has achieved new dimensions of concern. Ecology is becoming a part of the general vocabulary. Popular reaction is manifest to a variety of environmental pollutants, to the depredation of specific areas of wild and scenic beauty, and to the claustrophobia of urban life without open spaces. A New Conservation, as a public philosophy and guide to political life, is in the beginning stages of development. That we as a nation should be concerned with our total environment, not just with the quantity of our material production but also with the quality of our environment, is the main policy thrust of the New Conservation. Its widespread and general acceptance in principle seems to have been achieved.

Most, but not all, action to date at local, state, and national and international levels has been a reaction to clear and present dangers—pollution of air, water, and the whole biological environment by atomic wastes, pesticides, and other contaminants; loss to development of specific natural areas; deterioration or loss of historic sites or areas, or of beautiful vistas; and extinction of specific species of fish or wildlife. Public reaction to the prospect of population explosion, on the other hand, involves a public vision of more long-term future consequences. This is also true of support, generally, of all antipollution activities, of a system of wild and scenic rivers, and of other major strategic actions.

Only in the most inchoate form, however, does it appear that this public vision reflects knowledge of the basic insight of scientific ecology. Thus ecological policy concern (i.e., sustainable accommodation of mankind within his natural environment on this earth) is not yet the foundation of a new sense of community of man in which the enhancement of environmental quality pervades all decision.

Hence, planning comprehensively the environment of, say, 1976, 2000, 2050, and 2100 is not undertaken anywhere in the world. Comprehensive, multipurpose river-basins planning, as conducted today in the United States by federal, state, and local agencies under the Water Resources Planning Act of 1965, comes as close to comprehensive planning as any in existence today. Moreover, "The Nation's Water Resources," the first national assessment of the Water Resources Council, published in November 1968, comes as close to a national environmental assessment as any today.[1]* But support for these efforts is found among those concerned more with development than with environmental quality.

The several Environmental Quality Acts now under consideration by the Congress provide for periodic national environmental assessments. But none of them comes to grips with the organizational problems of planning all the public-sector activities, including environmental quality planning, and of the relative roles therein of federal, state, and local governments. The plethora of uncoordinated "councils" now surrounding the President is not considered either.[2]

A much more fundamental problem, one with which an environmental quality act now could not hope to cope, lies in the implicit policies of the United States and most other countries in favor of ever-increasing population and national income per capita. President Nixon has followed up on the proposal of former Secretary of the Interior Udall with respect to the establishment of a Population Policy Commission.[3] Presumably the Commission will consider the need for stability of population at some time in the future and the means that might be viewed as appropriate to its achievement.

Man's environment on this earth involves finite space composed of finite environmental areas of differing natural capability in support of man and other life. Thus, clearly, infinite expansion of population and material production is incompatible with man's situation. At some point growth in population and material production are going to have to stop. The reason may not be "an early running out of resources" as leaders of our traditional con-

---

*   Raised numbers are keyed to the references at the end of this article.

servation movement and Malthus feared. Scientific and technological advances may continue for many years without increasing real cost. But what of the quality of life, the livability of the earth?

The President's new Council on Environmental Quality obviously cannot avoid these issues, and one hopes that it will not try to do so indefinitely. Without policies calling for stabilization of population and national income per capita, detailed efforts in government, with the help of an alert and informed citizenry, to plan now and in the future for environmental quality will be of no avail. The first national environmental assessment should recognize these fundamental issues and begin to deal with them. Incidentally, the President's Council of Economic Advisors, on the basis of present theory and methods of managing our economic life at full employment and with large areas of freedom of private decision-making, may have more difficulty confronting these issues than will his Council on Environmental Quality.

The Council on Environmental Quality is plagued by another problem, the poverty of solid, detailed scientific knowledge of ecological relationships and their tolerances of external intrusions. Ecology today is strong on concept but weak on solid knowledge. This knowledge is basic to the preparation of practical plans for environmental quality. A very substantial national and worldwide program of ecological research and survey is vitally needed.

"Planning the earth's surface" involves, as a first step, facing these three major issues: population growth, ever-expanding material production, and the present dearth of scientific ecological knowledge. I need hardly add that a cultural revolution, worldwide, is implicit in all of this.

REFERENCES

1. "The Nation's Water Resources, the First National Assessment of the Water Resources Council," for sale by the Superintendent of Documents, U.S. Government Printing Office, Washington, D.C. 20402; full report $4.25; summary, 65 cents. Library of Congress Catalogue Card Number: 68–62779.

2. See "Environmental Management: Water and Related Land," written by the author when Executive Director of the Water Resources Council, Washington, D.C., *Public Administrative Review,* Vol. XXVIII, No. 4, July–August 1968, pp. 306–311.

3. Stewart L. Udall, *1976—Agenda for Tomorrow,* Harcourt, Brace and World, New York, 1968, p. 124. Library of Congress Catalogue Card Number: 68–28819.

13

URBAN DESIGN

NATHANIEL A. OWINGS

Successful enough to be blunt, Owings deals with practical problems in ideal terms. In his summary for understanding urban design he makes these points: Place must have priority over mobility .... The highways are destroying the places .... Open space is the heart of this organism .... A man can't live in a city where a tree won't grow .... Man is gregarious and a pedestrian .... Our cars are not basically for transportation .... [The car] will pass—our cities will not .... All the great cities throughout history have been multileveled. Ours must be also.

Design means "to plan, to make preliminary sketches, to advance ideas; a working out by plan." *Urban* means citified as opposed to rural. Under these definitions there is no such thing as urban design in the United States today. Nor has there been any since the creation of Washington, D.C., Indianapolis, Indiana, and Buffalo, New York, as new cities long ago.

Cities—that is, the existing ones in the United States and particularly the principal ones—are natural phenomena and as much a part of the scene where one finds them as the bays, the harbors, the inlets, the river crossings, and the mountain passes. These existing cities are man's ecological unit, just as the watershed, the estuary, the plain, and the High Sierras combine to form the ecological unit for deer, elk, mountain lion, or sea otter.

So-called new towns are destined for failure in a culture such as Americans pursue. If we cannot govern our existing cities, how can we do better with new ones? To cite our new towns as a solution to the urban design problem of the United States is a tragic misrepresentation. The natural places for cities, where the desire lines of people and things cross, are already preempted, and the only thing new cities can do in this huge complex country is to further intrude on the open space so needed in the total scheme of things.

Urban design is applicable where subcity patterns can be influenced, or at least guided, in their normal processes of evolution. In other words, it can be a guidance program for easing our growing pains during our adolescent period. We haven't grown up yet. We are still playing house, and we are not living in the house we will build when we grow up.

In the early stage where we are now, we are suffering from the irrationality of early forms of urban systems, which affected disastrously, in some cases, the relationship between *mobility* and *place*. Things have been happening at climactic speed. This will bring the city crisis to a head sooner—at the present speed of evolution, in only years instead of centuries. But we Americans do not take our troubles seriously. For instance, we have the technological know-how to solve the Manhattan traffic problems overnight by simply adding another level to the existing one—by spanning certain streets in Manhattan with a second level. Then we would have instant pedestrian walkways, malls, traffic separation. Another solution, simple but unacceptable: eliminate the use of cars, taxis, and buses in Manhattan.

But people don't want perfect cities any more than they want perfect heaven. Hell, they say, is much more fun. Mayors can't run cities. Police don't police them. Cities, in fact, are the fluid state of a glacier-like substance that is self-perpetuating.

There are a few—very few—basic elements necessary to an understanding of urban-design problems in this country.

First, place must have priority over mobility. Although in the late 1800's the railroads helped to make the places, the opposite is now true. The highways are destroying the places.

Second, the plaza, the open space, the square, the piazza is the heart of this organism. We reestablished this principle in the Lever and the Chase Manhattan Bank buildings in New York, and in the Crown Zellerbach and the Bank of America buildings in San Francisco. A man can't live in a city where a tree won't grow.

Third, man is gregarious and a pedestrian. A ten-million-year-old fact hasn't disappeared in the 75 years that the automobile has been around. Our cars are not basically for transportation but are an economic pterodactyl on whose flesh we are temporarily feasting—and it is poisoning us. It will pass—our cities will not.

Finally, all the great cities throughout history have been multileveled. Ours must be also.

14

HOUSING AND THE ENVIRONMENT

WILLIAM C. WHEATON

Housing is basic to every man's idea of a quality existence. To gain the support of a majority of mankind, including residents of Peking, Paris, or Brooklyn, for a survival effort, we need to solve the problem of housing, a giant among all our problems. The author emphasizes this point by saying, "The housing condition of lower-income families . . . remains one of the most disastrous circumstances of our civilization." To provide needed housing, at least in the United States, would require "a mere fraction of what we spend annually for highways or space exploration."

The United States has become an overwhelmingly urban nation with 80% of its population in urban or metropolitan areas. In the other Western developed areas, the proportion of urban population may be even higher. In many of the developing nations migration from rural to urban areas is at rates which suggest that a similar condition may be reached in the next generation. Thus we face a future in which people will live in cities rather than in or near a natural environment. The conditions which men build into cities become the determinants of the quality of life, its productivity, and its longevity.

Housing is an overwhelmingly dominant requirement of the urban environment; it is a necessity along with food and clothing. Housing it is the largest single expense—or the second largest, after food—for most of the world's population, and it fills 40–50% of the land in urban areas. The pattern of housing dictates the form of the city, the journey to work, transportation modes, child-rearing patterns, educational possibilities, and many other critical determinants of life.

The United States is blessed with the highest standard of living in the world. Yet despite the affluence and comfort in which three-fourths of its people live, the distribution patterns of housing, especially scattered suburban growth, impose real burdens on the middle and upper classes, and they have been criticized by scores of writers for failing to provide the richness and variety of urban life that are possible. The housing condition of lower-income families, who constitute 15–25% of our population, remains one of the most disastrous circumstances of our civilization. About 15% of the population live in substandard housing, often under conditions which American farmers would not tolerate for domestic animals. Crowded slum dwellings, infested with crime, situated in areas characterized by low standards of education, low standards of health services, and inaccessibility to employment opportunities are simply intolerable under any standard of justice or equity.

In the past two years, four different national commissions reached essentially similar conclusions: The United States has failed to provide a decent home in a suitable living environment for every American family, thus reneging on a promise made as a matter of national policy by the Housing Act of 1949. That measure has actually increased the housing shortage for the poor by not entirely replacing the more than half million dwellings inhabited by 30 to 40 million people, and another 5 to 10 million dwellings are located in substandard areas.

Thirty-five years ago we adopted our first housing legislation. But we have made efforts only on a token scale. The Kaiser Commission has set forth the reasons with clarity and candor. To house low-income families properly, we should be building 500,000 new units a year with some sort of federal subsidy. Instead we have been building fewer than 100,000. Some of the needed units must be in public housing for families of the lowest income. However, many can and should be built by nonprofit housing corporations, cooperatives, church groups, and similar private groups, with federal subsidies to hold down mortgage interest rates or rents. Providing these 500,000 homes would cost much more than we have been spending on housing, but the cost would be a mere fraction of what we spend annually for highways or space exploration, perhaps less than 2% of the prospective 1978 national budget.

But there is another critical pressure—population growth. Our expanding population will need as many as $2\frac{1}{2}$ million units of housing per year during the 1970's. The average number of units built yearly during the last decade was $1\frac{1}{2}$ million. This expansion will put serious inflationary pressure on our limited supply of building materials, skilled man power, savings resources, governmental service institutions, and land within metropolitan areas. We need a rapid evolution in our existing practices in order to come anywhere near our goals. We must make substantive changes in building technology, for instance, in order to reduce costs and increase production without increasing stress on the national economy. We need a considerable expansion of savings and mortgage-lending institutions. We need reforms in local government regulation; we need improvements in our capacity to provide schools, health facilities, streets, utilities, and other public services to urban areas.

Conservationists, in particular, are fond of jeremiads about urban land uses intruding into rural land—the destruction of the agricultural land supply by suburban sprawl. In fact, such claims are greatly overrated. A generation from now, not more than 5% of the land supply of the United States will be in urban use. Of course, there are serious problems of scatteration in the environs of the cities. But increasing concentration of people in the metropolitan areas will reduce the population load on the remaining 95% of the land area. We may actually, if agricultural production continues to increase, need less farm and forest land to keep us in food and fiber. The problem is not any gross shortage of land but the distribution and location of urban growth.

In the developing countries of the world, of course, housing conditions are even worse—to an incredible extent. Half the urban population in many South American cities live in self-help shacks, in areas almost totally lacking in streets, sewers, water, schools, or health facilities. In Calcutta, a half million people live on the streets or sidewalks with no homes at all, and other millions live in bustees built on swamps and cesspools, in shacks made of rags, mud, sticks, and tin cans, with no access to sanitary water and without any sewer system at all. And it is forecast that the population of Calcutta will grow to 25 million in the next generation.

At the same time, however, some parts of the developing world offer examples for us. In Singapore and Hong Kong nearly half the population now live in high-rise apartments at densities of 2,000 people per acre, or more than a million per square mile. At such densities they are happy, productive, and reasonably healthy. The Western illusion that people cannot tolerate ultra-high density is clearly destroyed by this living fact. How parochial and culture-bound many of our Western preconceptions about cities and density may be!

Nevertheless, housing conditions in the developing world are far more precarious than any we know. In spite of the fact that we have a United Nations Committee on Housing, we have utterly failed to develop international programs of technical or material assistance which would in any way alter the prospects for humanity in those regions.

Perhaps we can fulfill our responsibilities to that larger mankind only after we have done so at home. To date we have failed; we have launched token programs that promise much but deliver little. We can change the situation by allocating an additional 1% a year of our Gross National Product to housing. If we want decent homes in suitable environments for all Americans, we can have them. We have merely failed to demand them. How long can we tolerate major misallocations of monies—to programs like the supersonic transport. In the name of justice, can a society which does so be worthy of being called civilized?

Preserving nature, trees and grass, land and open space, are tremendously important topics. The cumulative effect, however, is to create the impression that trees are more important than people, and rabbits more important than children. Indeed, at times the more strident appeal for population control begins to sound like the opening of a campaign to stamp out people. I hold, to the contrary, that we have ample resources to accommodate our future population fairly, equitably, and with greater amenity than we do today. Indeed, until we undertake that task, I wonder whether we can undertake any other?

15

TRANSPORTATION

WILFRED OWEN

Transportation is an immediate test of good environmental management. So long as we need to move by devices that pollute and cause social blight, we are not on a survival course. Says Wilfred Owen: "Instead of improving transportation to accommodate congestion, we should use transportation as a developmental tool to bring about new urban settlement . . . providing the environmental quality that science and affluence now make possible."

Transportation as well as the lack of it is helping to make the urban environment unacceptable and increasingly uninhabitable. Yet transportation more than anything else could help redevelop the cities and create the new urban settlements we want.

The Negative Impacts of Transport

The undesirable side effects of urban transport are everywhere obvious:

The crowding, confusion, and congestion of motorized traffic in a setting never designed for mechanized movement.

The pollution of the atmosphere—60 percent from internal combustion engines.

Tens of thousands killed and injured by mixing machines with pedestrians.

The excessive noise of buses, trucks, and airplanes that shatters the quiet of the community.

The endless rows of parked cars that have converted the streets into garages.

The miles of dismal asphalt streets—one-fourth of the area of the city—lined with billboards, filling stations, garish eating places, poles and wires—the linear slums of the automotive age.

The elevated expressways disrupting neighborhoods and arching over the slums to conceal them from the public conscience.

The easy access to suburbia, providing an escape from the center and from civic responsibilities, helping to divide society into separate enclaves of black and white.

The crowded buses, the noises and dirt of the subways, and for many citizens the lack of transport to get to a job or to enjoy the economical and cultural advantages of the city.

The growing distances from recreation and from the countryside, and the increasing time and frustration of getting from one city to another.

The Inherited Environment

Today we either live very much the same as in the past, huddled into overcrowded cities, or we are spread out across municipal boundaries in a planless dispersion that is a dormitory rather than a community and ends up transporting slums to the suburbs. Transportation is not being used to help accomplish the new and satisfying urban environment that new technology and the growth of national income make possible. Yet transportation can be a powerful tool for redesigning old cities and building the new settlements that another hundred million urbanites will require in this century.

The transportation revolution of the past two decades has completely changed the urban future. When urban industrial growth began in this country, transportation determined the character of cities. Cities had to be located next to waterways, and compressed into a space small enough for walking to work or riding a streetcar. That made them densely packed and short on open space and amenities. The speed of urban growth and the relative poverty of the times made cities planless, tasteless, and esthetically hapless.

Today urban settlements are freed from these constraints by highways, motor vehicles, airplanes, and telecommunications, combined with affluence and the shift from an industrial environment to a service environment. Most Americans can live anywhere, work anywhere, and go anywhere. But moving better does not necessarily mean living better. The challenge is to visualize the kinds of living we want, and to use transportation to help achieve them.

Solving transportation problems and improving the environment will never be possible until we stop to ask what kind of community we want—what are the goals? Obviously goals start with a decent home for everyone, in an acceptable environment. The United States must build one new dwelling unit every 27 seconds between now and the year 2000. What kind of a setting will there be for these homes? Will there be fresh air, nearby recreation, easy access to schools and to shopping services? The possibilities of an affirmative answer lie to an important degree in redesigning the transport system of existing cities and in building new transport links to entirely new cities.

A Transport Program to Redesign the Cities

The gridiron of streets that gives form to the city needs to be redesigned to make way for new housing and community facilities. The first step is to revise the Federal aid highway program. After half a century, it is time for this program to focus on the urban areas:

Eliminate street mileage to create super-blocks for campus-type housing, shopping centers, and industrial estates. Use the streets to delineate commercial centers and insulate neighborhoods.

Convert selected streets to pedestrian walkways and neighborhood shopping malls by paving from curb to curb, barring automobiles, and renovating buildings.

Convert other streets to playgrounds and neighborhood parks by removing the pavement and introducing grass and other plantings.

Remove all parked cars from the streets and provide esthetically attractive off-street parking facilities at frequent intervals as part of the transportation system.

Extend the rural landscaping programs of the state highway departments to the cities. Remove utility poles and wires, plant trees and shrubs, use vacant lots for streetside rest areas and scenic overlooks, and regulate the size, location, and frequency of advertising signs to make them attractive and readable.

Make use of tunnels to get traffic on major streets underground in strategic areas, thus eliminating the nuisance and hazards of through traffic.

Set aside the downtown area for the exclusive use of traffic on foot, with selected routes for taxi and free minibus service. Provide off-street parking on the periphery of downtown areas and under or around other clusters of activity reserved for people.

Remodel the streets by installing attractive lighting standards, flower beds, benches, book stalls, kiosks, sidewalk cafes, commercial displays, and other exhibits, to make local streets perform nontransport as well as transport functions.

Introduce aids and supplements to walking—covered sidewalks, escalators and elevators, moving sidewalks with air conditioning, self-propelled electric vehicles, minitrains, free electric buses.

Connect all parts of the city by appropriate mass transit. This may include frequent service by small buses that respond to passenger demand by telephone call or other signal, and which are routed by computer programming to provide door-to-door service. In large cities, underground transit in tunnels will be needed, by bus, rail, or wheelless vehicles.

Transportation to Help Develop New Cities

Redesigning old cities to loosen the fabric and improve the environment will increase the need for space. So will the overall growth of population. Fortunately there is space available: urban America still uses less than 2 percent of the nation's area to accommodate 70 percent of its people.

But using more of the space on the fringes of today's cities in a continuation of unplanned sprawl is likely to add to environmental deterioration faster than existing ills can be remedied. Moreover, this course will compound all our urban problems by simply making cities bigger.

In many parts of the world, planned new cities with a high-quality environment have proved to be feasible because transportation and communications have overcome isolation and made relatively remote locations economically desirable. Transportation investments by road, rail, and air should be located and timed to support new cities in the United States. A joint Federal-state program combining the acquisition of new city sites with public investment programs, including transportation, can create planned cities that could be either remote from existing centers or serve as satellites of an established metropolis. This is the sensible alternative to the present unnecessary build-up of a polluted urban environment.

Instead of improving transportation to accommodate congestion, we should use transportation as a developmental tool to bring about new urban settlements and new designs within established cities, both providing the environmental quality that science and affluence now make possible.

16

COMMUNITY

MARGARET MEAD

A needed national sense of community based on values shared by everyone including industry and individuals would help stop our present negative, fragmentary social trend. Doctor Mead's point sounds unworkably idealistic; however, when the public realizes the alternatives involved, I believe her concept will bloom. For now it is awaiting the leadership of a new Theodore Roosevelt, someone who sees survival as a crusade rather than an issue.

Another point made, that of seeing the earth as an island rather than a spaceship, focuses on the traditional success of primitive island dwelling in handling population and resources.

The image of the spaceship has been widely used recently to describe the perilously limited nature of the closed biological system we call Earth. I think it is being overused. It is a very good symbol of man's power over his environment, a good symbol to describe the fact that we are going to have to recycle our resources, and for many people, it is a good symbol of hazard. I would like to suggest, however, that this image of what man has made is not going to enlist a great portion of the people we need to enlist. For many think of this earth in its natural form, as part of what man was given and not what man has built. These people are concerned with man's relationship to his natural environment, whether God-given or as the result of the process of natural evolution. They think that at the moment man is making a mess of it.

I think an island is a more appropriate figure of speech. We are all living on a planet that we can now know as men once knew small islands. And we can make the kinds of provisions for population control, for the use of land, for buildings, for the conservation of resources that island dwellers have had to make and were able to understand in the past. The only people in the past who have ever understood self-limiting situations have been people who have lived on islands. Japan is an outstanding example, in understanding what population control meant.

We cut our country up into fragments at every point, and we fragment man himself as the recipient of hundreds of fragmented services. We expect the directors of industry to be demons of self-interest during the week, and then to sit on a board and give the money away again after they have made it. We never expect industry to be capable of taking responsibility for a community. Industry is actually just as capable as anyone else. We decide that it isn't industry after all, that it is city hall that is doing the polluting, and we hate city hall. Then we discover that the federal government hasn't done the job it was supposed to, and we hate it too. Now we have all the demons we need, and we do not have to do anything but demonology. We will never get together this way.

My title is community. Whether it is the little community that has to deal with its local problems in order to understand state, regional, national, and international problems, or whether it is the world community we have to understand in order to protect the small community, we have to get away from demonizing everyone else. We have to move to some kind of genuine community of interest.

At the local level the small town conservation group hates the gas station, and hates the company that built it. But it was only very recently that it occurred to one of these community groups to ask the gas station people if they would be willing to save the trees they were going to cut down, and to build a decent gas station. The gas station people didn't object to building a decent gas station, and they are now using it in national advertising, showing how beautifully they have built their stations under stately trees. This is the sort of thing that can happen if we do not continually blame some other group in society.

Furthermore, we have never accepted the fact that we are part of other people's views. We are always trying to save our view, to find a house where there is nothing unpleasant for us to look at. We never think of ourselves as part of other people's view. To me this is extraordinarily one-sided. We need a national and international movement in which everybody will be involved, in which the basic values will be accepted by all the different aspects of our economy. We need to prevent setting small communities against the state, the state against the region, the region against the federal government, government against industry, noble activities against both government and industry. This is what we are doing to the present in almost every respect.

We will have to have values well enough grounded, well enough understood, so that everyone can accept and work for them. This can be done; we do it once in a while in this country. But to do this we must recognize that every segment of society has a few good intentions. Ever since the New Deal, we have been insisting that people only do good things for bad reasons. This is the way we appeal to Congress. We never ask Congress, do you believe in children? We talk instead about the disposal of agricultural commodities in schools' lunches.

So that is our major job—to create a set of shared values, one that can admit timber and oil companies, and paper companies and road builders and developers. It is not to the interest of industry to have all the towns and cities go to pieces. We have to put this together in one package.

Also if we are going to survive we are going to have to do quite a lot of work. Because we are faced with difficulties we have never handled before, difficulties we do not know how to handle, it is going to be a struggle. And we are only going to get people to work to survive if they think the quality of life in the future will be worth living. Just as soon as they decide the world of the future is going to be impossible, their willingness to work on the survival problem is weakened. Our young people are demanding that life be human and livable. They are a crucial component in our capabilities as a people. But unless we can use imagery that involves everybody in this country and ultimately everybody in the world, unless we can use both the notion of a spaceship and the notion of an island, both what man has made and what he has received as a precious heritage from nature, unless we can put these things together we will again fragment ourselves and again have people fighting with one another instead of working together toward a common goal—to protect the earth and its people.

17

ENVIRONMENTAL HEALTH

CHARLES C. JOHNSON, JR.

Health applies to the total environment: resources, diet, open space, housing, recreation, medicine and others. That the United States, with the world's highest standard of living, in 1968 was fourteenth in the list of 25 countries with the lowest infant mortality rates* offers another target for change in our evaluation of quality.

A suitable environment is the first requirement of all living things. And human health is dependent, first of all, on the maintenance of an environment which is compatible with the basic needs of the human organism.

The modern environment, which is increasingly artificial and man-made, poses a twofold threat to human health: In the first place, it contains elements which are outright noxious; second, it is undergoing rapid, drastic, and often irreversible changes which more and more endanger the delicate balance of the ecological system and outrun human capability for adaptation.

Man is required to use to his own advantage the limited resources of the earth, and is, in fact, the only species capable of creatively cooperating with nature to ensure his own progress and survival. Yet, for most of his time on earth, he appears to have believed that he could exploit, contaminate, and alter the world about him without endangering the environmental milieu on which his own life depends.

Recent history, and increased population pressures, now demonstrate the shortsightedness of such a view. Almost incredible advances in science and technology have given man a new and awesome power to alter—or even destroy—his environment. His skill and ingenuity in manipulating the environment have produced tremendous benefits to human life. But, more and more, these benefits have been accompanied by frightening, and sometimes irreversible, changes in the ecological system of which he is an integral part. Man has seriously depleted the world's natural resources, and devastated much of the earth's surface. The waste products

---

*   This figure is limited to countries with more than 2.5 million population in the year 1965. This does not include Norway, Sweden, Denmark, Canada, Belgium, and Ireland. (From Myron E. Wegman, "Annual Summary of Vital Statistics," *Pediatrics* **44,** 6, 1034, December 1969.)

of his technology and of his own biological processes have grossly polluted the land, air, and water. Moreover, 20th century man is beginning to discover that his basic social and psychological drives are increasingly frustrated by pressures of the artificial, urbanized world which he himself has constructed.

The bacteriological, chemical, physiological, and psychological insults which man has injected into his environment are clearly associated with the rising toll of chronic disease throughout our society, while the effect on future generations is the subject of anxious scientific speculation. Even therapeutic drugs, with their manifest benefits, pose subtle threats when considered as part of the total chemical assault sustained by modern man. And thousands of consumer products, from foods to television sets, offer potential hazard to human health and safety. These too constitute part of modern man's total environment.

Certainly our progress in meeting human needs has been great, but it has been uneven. In our failure to come to grips with our consumer and environmental problems, we have now reached, or at the very least are rapidly approaching, a critical point.

It has become clear that if we are to maintain an environment that is conducive to human health and well being, while continuing to enjoy the benefits of modern science and technology, we must recognize the interrelationship and interdependence of all factors in the ecosystem of which man is a part. The effects of environmental manipulation are far-reaching and interacting. For example, pesticides are now present throughout the environment, polluting our water, concentrating in the "food chain," threatening extinction of beneficial species of wildlife, and building up in the fatty tissues of human beings. Furthermore, the effect of single environmental insults on man can only be fully understood in the context of their total, combined, and often synergistic impact on human health. Chemicals, for example, are ingested with the air we breathe and the water we drink, as part of medical formulations, in the form of food additives or traces of veterinary drugs, as pesticide residues on foods; they have the dangerous potential of interaction and intensification of effect.

Our efforts to maintain a healthful environment in the past have largely ignored these interrelationships and have too often failed to view man as part of the ecosystem.

We need now to reexamine and reassess traditional ways of doing things to ensure that all the systems and subsystems which we devise to maintain ourselves on the planet truly contribute to the total health and well-being of those they were designed to serve.

18

FOOD AND FOOD PRODUCTS

EMIL M. MRAK

If we have an unquestioning confidence in our ability to feed ourselves, we may be ignoring factors beyond the new technological advances in food production: distribution, culture, supplies of basic resources, and even political and financial structures of the country and the world.

The relation of food to the quality of existence is a world-wide problem, whether we are in an affluent country or an impoverished one. The reasons may be different, but there are problems that relate to what I would include in the term "the quality of life."

In the more affluent countries, the diet may be adequate; but even when we include gourmet dinners, there is sometimes a lack of wise nutrition. Abundance is not necessarily an indication of adequate nutrition and healthy diets, for there may be too many calories, too much fat, a lack of vitamins, a lack of minerals, and so on. In our country, where there should be enough food for all, all do not get an adequate supply of food. Dr. Arnold Schaefer's observations showed a definite deficiency of certain vitamins, iodine, and so on in a specific population in Texas. Often the problem is one of culture. How do we change a culture? How do we induce mothers who cannot speak English to serve an adequate diet?

Our farmers have increased their efficiency greatly, so that the number of man hours required to produce food for one individual has been reduced over the years from more than 20 down to about 4. But we need to direct more of our energies toward the production and the manufacture of better foods, a lower cost of production, and above all, better distribution, particularly in the urban areas and among ethnic groups in the poverty areas. Reapportionment has not, and will not, help these situations for years to come, for the legislators from the urban areas are more concerned with other matters. Perhaps it will take a catastrophe before they are brought to realize the importance of these aspects.

But what about the rest of the world? Europe perhaps has plenty, but Africa, Asia, South American, and Central America definitely have populations that show food deficiencies. A large number suffer from caloric, protein, vitamin, and other deficiencies. There is evidence today that inadequate nutrition during the prenatal period, and even during the early stages of the postnatal period, can affect the mentality, growth, and work ability of an individual. It can relate to the occurrence of illness, and to the amount of energy and drive. A quality existence in many of these areas which I have seen firsthand just doesn't exist. When people live on a meager diet of beans, corn, rice, and plantains, they do not have a quality existence.

There is adequate land to produce all the food we need. In Brazil alone there are 200 million acres of land that might be brought into production by the application of fertilizers, particularly nitrogen, potassium, and phosphate. But the matter is not that simple. There are no nitrate factories in Brazil, and if there were, the question of transportation would come into the picture. If the fertilizers could be transported to the land, then comes the matter of political aspects: Who owns the land, who distributes the products, etc. This situation exists throughout South and Central America. Moreover, it takes wealth to produce. To start farming 10, 20, or 30, acres, or even 50 acres, requires capital. Today loans for the small farmer are just not available, and a change in this situation is not imminent.

In recent years, with our encouragement, South Americans have tried to diversify and have had a good degree of success in producing cattle. It was their hope that they might export substantial amounts of beef to the U.S., but this has been limited by quotas that we have imposed on these countries. The ironic part of it all is that the people in the country could well utilize the meat produced there, to improve their own nutrition and conditions of life; but the political and financial structures of the countries and even the world do not seem to make this possible. How this could be done is beyond my understanding, unless the wealthier nations pour millions of dollars into these countries to help them utilize their own products.

Great hope has been placed in the fantastic developments of the Rockefeller and Ford foundations in Mexico, the Philippines, and India. These developments are dramatic, and great credit belongs to these private foundations that have done what our government with its millions has not been able to do. They have employed good scientists, trained local people, and exercised patience and perseverance. They have been free of politics and bureaucracy. They have studied the cultures of the countries and learned how to work with the people, and have done a magnificent job. Much has been said about the increased crop yields in Mexico, the increased rice yields in the Philippines, the increased wheat production in India.

In an article entitled "The Green Revolution: Cornucopia or Pandora's Box?" in the April 1969 issue of *Foreign Affairs*, Clifton R. Wharton, Jr., states that some now believe that the race between food and population is over and that the new agricultural technology constitutes a cornucopia for the developing world. It remains to be seen whether the development of this technology may open a Pandora's box, and whether its very success will produce new problems which are far more subtle and difficult than those faced before the development of the new technology.

Wharton points out that it will not be easy to achieve the potential increased production offered by the new technology, particularly when it involves millions of diverse farms and farmers scattered over the countryside. Will the new varieties of crops spread as quickly as they should? And what problems will the new technology bring with it? New varieties, for example, will require irrigation, with a revision of irrigation systems, and new irrigation management, all of which are costly.

There are also doubts about the ability of the existing markets to handle increased products, since there is an inadequate system for transporting and storing agricultural products, and so on.

Wharton believes that the new technology is likely to be much slower where the crop is a basic food staple, grown by a farmer for family consumption. Such farmers are reluctant to experiment with the very survival of their families. This is the same observation made by Borlaug in Mexico. Thus far, spectacular results have been achieved primarily among relatively large commercial farmers, but the semi-subsistence farmers have gone the new way very slowly. Farmers must learn that planting several varieties of a given crop can produce 2 or 3 crops a year instead of one. This multiple cropping, of course, is good, but there are many difficulties if the new harvest comes during the wet season, particularly if there are no dryers for handling the crop. Finally, the harvest may very well come during the religious or other holidays, which will cause problems. In other words, the very psychology of an impoverished people must be changed to alter their production of food.

The agricultural situation in the savannahs in Africa involves driving herds of low-yield milk cows over many miles, so that the tribe accompanying the herd will have milk and perhaps blood to live on. Changing this custom would require years of research to determine how to use the soils that exist in these savannahs.

In India, if waste and losses resulting from insects, mold, bacteria, enzymes, chemical deterioration, and rodents could be eliminated, the food production would be adequate to take care of the population. Eliminating waste may not sound dramatic, but it is extremely important.

There are some people who think that one of the key factors in food production is energy. Dr. Stout, of the University of California at Davis, believes that food sufficiency can be achieved and maintained in India if adequate sources of low-cost energy can be established. Power must be made available to pump water out of the ground for irrigation, and to manufacture fertilizer. These energy-consuming farm inputs would enable Indian farmers to grow high-yield cereal and grains during the winter's dry season on good lands, lands that unfortunately now lie idle.

The simple facts of plant nutrition, however, dictate that any shift into modern intensive cultivation and high agricultural productivity must be supported by nonfarm energy in large amounts, energy that is required principally for the manufacture of fertilizer and for irrigation. In developed countries such as our own, fossil sources—cheap natural gas, petroleum, and coal— supply energy for producing mineralized atmospheric nitrogen, for processing rock phosphate, and for moving water; they also provide a multitude of nonfarm energy inputs which have been incorporated in our food-producing operations. We in developed countries are in effect ingesting calories obtained by our liberal use of fossil fuels in our agricultural industry.

Food is an all-important factor to the quality of existence. Inadequate diet is related to production, to distribution, to culture, to knowledge of foods, and so on. But in the end, it is all related to the political and financial structure of the country and the world. We cannot separate these factors. We cannot expect to have a world-wide high-quality existence without adequate food. And we cannot expect to walk in a land of abundance—any more than we were able to take a few steps on the moon—without spending billions of dollars. Perhaps we need to reassess our values.

19

AN INTERNATIONAL CONSENSUS

MICHEL BATISSE

This French scientist's statement of the ideal is framed by the realities of our value system as seen in his shoestring budget limiting biosphere studies and preparations for the coming United Nations Conference.

Survival "... requires a complete reassessment of many values which will affect economic theory, social structures, political institutions as well as individual freedom."

I would like to stress two or three issues which appear important to me. The first one is that we are terribly emotional about the environment. This is good. Nothing great is ever done without passion and enthusiasm. But, at the same time, the implications of what we are talking about are such that we had better have our facts straight. The truth of the matter is that we do not. We do not like air pollution, but we are not so certain about what it really does. We talk of ecosystems—a nice word—but we are not so certain of what they are, where they are, and how they work. We fear major climatic changes because of CO_2 or air turbidity, but we do not know in which direction. We feel things are going bad, but we do not measure how fast they do. We need systematic studies and worldwide monitoring for all this.

This is precisely the main objective of the proposed program on *Man and the Biosphere*, which is at present being formulated by the UNESCO Secretariat. This interdisciplinary program is to be a follow-up and an extension, at the intergovernmental level, of the International Biological Program. Five working groups have met in Paris, with scientists from 31 different countries and from other UN agencies, to define the content of this new program, which will be submitted to the UNESCO General Conference next October. The objectives of this program are scientific. It will aim at establishing the facts of the world's environmental situation. It will also aim at pooling scientific talent to measure and understand the changes which are threatening us, and define rational ways toward either remedy or prevention. The program will also be *educational*. It will aim at building up adequate manpower and developing appropriate attitudes through the promoting of "environmental education." Unless these attitudes are developed among children and adults all over the world, many people will not even see that they create an environmental crisis.

The second point I would like to stress is that we are—quite naturally—very parochial about environment. In being so, we fail to see some major problems and do not necessarily get our priorities right. In this great country of yours, America, the problems are enormous. But they relate to a rich, educated, affluent, industrialized, and selfish society, which wants everything it has plus everything else, such as clear skies and trout fishing. This is legitimate. But the problems are far more enormous if you consider the whole world. And you have to consider it. For you cannot just keep America beautiful and clean, and let the rest of the world sink into overcrowding, pollution, erosion . . . and frustration. You can no longer isolate yourselves from the global situation.

So what are the problems in the rest of the world? This is a long story, but we can make it short. Western civilization has practiced the greatest ecological rape ever seen. It has raped all other civilizations. In doing so, it has increased population there and created formidable needs. It does not matter to know whether we thought our civilization was so wonderful that it should be exported—the good missionary spirit—or whether, more simply, we wanted to sell refrigerators. Now developing countries want to follow our road. They want industry. And as an African delegate put it at the Biosphere Conference, they want pollution. Because pollution means industry. The price of this ecological rape by *homo occidentalis*—including the subspecies *homo occidentalis sovieticus*—is that the whole world wants development, that is, penicillin, beer cans, and automobiles. Can you picture the world once every Indian and every Chinese family will have three automobiles? And why shouldn't they have them when you have them?

So it is very nice to discuss here what is desirable for the happy few. But we should not lose sight of what is essential for the rest of the world: food, shelter, education, hospitals, consumer goods, export goods, jobs—that is what is called development. And all this will not be done without deterioration, or at least major changes of the environment of the entire planet. All we can do in the developing countries is to try to minimize deterioration and to prevent some of the mistakes we have made. But do not tell them they should not "develop."

My third remark is related to *action*. We have to know the facts. We have to educate people; we have to define our goals. But we have also to *do* something. And there happens to be a lot of knowledge which is just *not applied*. Why is that? We come here to the main objectives of the 1972 United Nations Conference on the Problems of the Human Environment. This Conference will take stock of the overall world situation and the various programs and activities—such as those of UNESCO—which are intended to meet specific objectives. It will not be a scientific or a technical conference, but a conference at the policy-making level, a conference focusing on *problems of concrete action* by public authorities at all levels, to deal with the planning, the management, and the control of the human environment.

From the overall scene on this planet, it appears today that man is a *threatened species*—just like the whooping crane. But unlike the whooping crane, he is only threatened by himself, by his own proliferation, by his fatal pride to conquer and dominate, by his greed and his carelessness, by his inability to plan his collective needs and to cope with his own wastes. The trouble is that the problems of man's own conservation are unfortunately not commensurate with those of the conservation of the whooping crane.

These problems are formidable. It is not only a question of laws, of regulations of gadgets and dollars. It requires a will, a collective will of all nations. It requires a new philosophy of the relationship of man with nature, accepted by all. It requires a new ethic based on ecological principles. It requires a complete reassessment of the many values which will affect economic theory, social structure, political institutions as well as individual freedom. It will hurt and is not going to be accepted lightly.

To me, the fact that so many eminent people of all age groups, with so many different professional interests, have come here a is a most encouraging sign that this change in attitudes is taking place in America. This is fine.

But what are we going to do now? As far as I am concerned, I am going back to my office in Paris, where at the moment one person and a half is trying to formulate the UNESCO intergovernmental program on *Man and the Biosphere.* I shall also spend some time in New York, where at present half a person is preparing the 1972 United Nations Conference. The fact is that we talk a lot about the environment in international affairs, but so far we operate on a shoestring!

My question to you, therefore, is this: Are we going to be consistent? Are we going to do something serious about the world environmental crisis?

B. Natural resources

Achieving a policy governing the nation's natural resources is crucial. At present our nation's policy on natural resources might be compared to a ship at sea without a helmsman; from time to time, special interests come on deck to steer through the storm of the moment. Then the ship is left to founder until the next (unrelated) interest steers a bit. As a result the ship is following an unpredictable course that is bringing us closer and closer to the reefs of destruction. For the long-time good of man and the world, we must steer a straight course. We can't afford the time, energy, or social and economic cost of mismanaging our resources any longer.

"The basic facts about the world's natural resources are that, though they are vast, they are finite in amount and their prudent use is an ethical obligation of all mankind." (Sears, in *Discussions*)

20

DEVELOPING A NATURAL RESOURCE MANAGEMENT POLICY

STEPHEN H. SPURR

Stephen Spurr, asked to summarize the conference papers on resources, produced an analysis which combined the pivotal suggestions of each author in so cohesive a way that it is distinctively Dr. Spurr's analysis as well. Equally important, he captured the enthusiasm of youth and the seriousness of the discussions which resulted from the challenges from the floor.

The overwhelming impression I got from the three seminar sessions at the Conference on the Development of a Natural Resource Management Policy is that time is running out. We are creating new people faster than we can take care of them. We are despoiling the environment faster than our democratic processes can come up with deterrents.

I can summarize the seminar sessions which dealt with the development of a natural resource management policy with four connected conclusions. *First,* our present natural resource management policy is hopelessly inadequate when judged by the continuing rapid deterioration of our human environment. *Second,* the only defensible management policy is one that will not only stop further deterioration, but will build a better environment for the future. *Third,* such a policy will require strong public agencies at all levels, not only to manage public resources but also to regulate human influences on our planet. *Fourth,* we shall not be able to achieve these goals unless we can mobilize an angry and determined majority.

The speakers at this conference have amply documented the deteriorating state of our environment and the minimal effect of our past public effort to stem the tide of deterioration. Rolf Eliassen points out that the combined budgets of state, local, and regional agencies for air pollution control amounted to a negligible $47 million in 1969. The scale of our national efforts to reduce water pollution, conserve open space, maintain natural resources, and improve the urban environment is correspondingly low.

At the international level, the situation is even worse. Taylor Pryor's discussion of the ocean and Michael Batisse's contribution as seminar chairman remind us that the ecological system is worldwide rather than nationwide, and must be approached as such.

Yet Ray Dasmann points out that the entire budget of the United Nations is less than that spent by New York City to dump its garbage into the Atlantic Ocean. And this at a time when the quality of our human environment is deteriorating before our very eyes! One can justifiably draw the conclusion that our natural resource management policy is hopelessly inadequate.

Our only defensible management policy is one that will not only stop further deterioration, but will lead to constructive steps to repair the damage, or at least to create a better environment. This is a truism, of course, and the real problem is how to achieve the millennium. Some progress is being made. Last year's congressional white paper on a national policy for the environment speaks of the need of and support for a formal legal national commitment:

> It is the policy of the United States that:
>
> • Environmental quality and productivity shall be considered in a worldwide context, extending in time from the present to the long-term future.
>
> • Purposeful, intelligent management to recognize and accommodate the conflicting uses of the environment shall be a national responsibility.
>
> • Information required for systematic management shall be provided in a complete and timely manner.
>
> • Education shall develop a basis of individual citizen understanding and appreciation of environmental relationships and participation in decision-making on these issues.
>
> • Science and technology shall provide management with increased options and capabilities for enhanced productivity and constructive use of the environment.

I do not think we should underestimate the importance of this kind of explicit policy statement.

A growing number of congressional leaders have called on the scientific community to make their views and expertise available to Congress as it struggles with formulating environment-related policies and legislation. The day has long since passed when anyone can responsibly shun involvement in such matters or sit back waiting to be summoned to offer testimony. Our environmental policy must be ecologically based. We need first to know much more about ecological relationships and second to express this knowledge in plain English. The ecologist must become the working partner of the Congressman as well as of the environmentally involved executive. Both are of crucial importance.

It is encouraging that the legislative reference service of the Library of Congress has recently created a central research and evaluation unit on environmental affairs. Such activities will surely help congressional committees obtain better information on the environment. We must now work to ensure that environmental considerations are a central part of all decisions which might affect the environment.

At the judicial level, we can take heart from the case of Storm King Mountain, on the Hudson River, in which the courts have held that citizens indeed have "standing to sue," to come to the defense of the environment and to seek legal recourse to prevent environmental degradation. This is an important precedent in that it opens the doors for judicial help in protecting environmental interests from ill-considered, hasty, and unnecessary destruction.

Yes, we are doing a little. The trouble is that we are not doing enough. We are certainly not doing it fast enough. It is all very well to set up a Board of Environmental Quality Advisors to study and analyze, to periodically review and appraise, and to assist and advise—but little will actually be accomplished until our governmental agencies can manage, regulate, and enforce. And what is more, we should be managing, regulating, and enforcing today— not ten years from now.

Congressman Scheuer made the point that individual action is not sufficient. We have to change institutions. At the very least we have to improve our public institutions. We must also ensure that the interests of the human community are reflected in the decisions of private institutions. If we are to achieve a quality environment, we must use every device available to us.

Norman Livermore has pointed out that it is easy to point out environmental problems, but it is a lot harder to implement solutions. This shouldn't keep us from trying. The tools of our trade are familiar; through research, education, and dissemination of information, we can influence the public and the political process. Through our governmental agencies, we can make grants-in-aid, and we can provide tax and other incentives. More than that, we can and should regulate. Several at the UNESCO conference made concrete proposals worthy of further consideration, and I would like to add a few of my own.

First and foremost, we need a central agency at the Federal level which draws its support from the people as a whole rather than from regional or special interests, and which is charged with establishing national standards for our environmental quality and with enforcing regulations established through congressional action. There is much merit in Senator Moss's suggestion to establish a Department of Natural Resources and Environment—what Arthur Godfrey calls a Pollution Pentagon. What to put into it and what to leave out of it, however, constitute difficult questions. Certainly, much of what is now in the Department of the Interior belongs in such an agency. Equally, however, much of what is now in the Department of Agriculture belongs here too. In any event, the civilian functions of the Corps of Engineers must be included.

Second, putting such a department together is only the first part of the job. The functions and services provided by the individual agencies must be reconsidered and in many cases redistributed. As Joe Moore recommended, both Congress and the executive branch should realign their structures and working patterns to consolidate consideration of natural resource programs.

Third, I support Gordon Harrison's view that we should systematically review all our public programs in terms of the effects they are having on our environment. We should include our grants-in-aid programs in housing, highway development, and indeed all public works. We should include our system of incentives, especially those embedded in our tax structure. And we should include our regulatory programs, such as those entrusted to the Federal Power Commission. Periodic national reassessments of where we stand on the road to survival will help us to focus on our surroundings and what we can do about them.

Each agency dealing with resources should have a defined role and place in our governmental structure, a place in which it has the best chance of obtaining the political and financial support for fulfilling its functions. Regulating agencies should not at the same time be management agencies. Agencies responsible for the production of usable natural resources should not also be responsible for their protection. Different uses, often conflicting, require different policies and different personnel with different training and outlook if they are to be properly served.

Fourth, we must develop more sophisticated and economically sound bases for decision-making. As Murray Gell-Mann put it recently, "technological renunciation" is a real alternative to public works. Because we can fly to the moon doesn't mean we have to do it often. Because we can build a dam doesn't mean that we ought to. Cost-benefit ratios have fallen into disrepute because they have too often been manipulated to justify a project which is wanted for political reasons. I submit, though, that the principle is sound—provided, first, that the intangible values to mankind are properly introduced into the formula, and second, that all alternatives, including technological renunciation, are objectively compared so that we can judge which alternative is the best to follow. Joe Moore has warned us of the dangers of blind acceptance of the pseudo-precise cost-benefit ratio. The rationale behind such ratios is false when the benefits are computed on one time horizon and for one geographic entity, while the costs are computed on a different time horizon. For example, in the case of scenic wonders: Once they are destroyed, they are destroyed in perpetuity. Decisions about them should be made as objectively as possible, and in the interests of the public at large.

Fifth, urban and regional planning can achieve much if the plans are codified by law and put into effect by the combined efforts of public and private agencies. I am intrigued by Rolf Eliassen's proposal that water supply be used as control to prevent the overdevelopment and overpopulation of cities. His answer that we should create new cities away from current metropolitan centers should be taken most seriously.

Sixth, education is a must. Attention is being paid to the need for making environmental training and sensitization as basic a part of education as the three R's. But we cannot afford the time lag of waiting for a new crop of right-thinking and acting adults. We cannot give up the present generation. If we recall the success of the land grant institutions in creating and spreading the knowledge and techniques of sound land and animal husbandry, we can see the potential for our universities and colleges today to serve a similar function with regard to the quality of the environment. In fact, a recent staff report from the White House office of science and technology suggests that we establish schools of human environment. Congressman Scheuer's proposed Environmental Quality Education Act, properly funded, would provide a giant step in this direction. Orlo Childs has decried the reluctance of young men and women to enter university programs leading to careers in engineering and technology. I suggest that if we provide the right programs, we shall be overwhelmed by student demand! But perhaps we should also borrow from the successful Agricultural Extension Service and utilize such a framework to get the message out to the present adult population. Certainly a more informed citizenry can help in the formulation and implementation of better management policies.

Seventh, our youth need collective opportunities to serve society, opportunities that are better than fighting in Viet Nam. The Civilian Conservation Corps served a vital need in my generation. The Peace Corps put organized youth activity on a firm basis of altruism and service. How about a Survival Corps, dedicated to bringing about an environmental renaissance?

Eighth, we can accomplish much more with incentives to industry than we can accomplish with penalties against industry. For example, our tax structure could incorporate an environmental appreciation allowance to encourage private compliance with national standards. The oil depletion and timber depletion allowances have had enormous effects on our natural resource development. Why not use the same principle to stimulate environmental development? Charles Foster has pointed out that we need a preferential tax system which will encourage people not to develop land; Richard Taber has demonstrated that public incentives are needed to persuade landowners to develop the wildlife and fish resources on private land.

Lastly, those who do not choose to comply should be forced to do so. Despoiling land, water, and air constitutes a crime against the human race, and should be punishable by fine, imprisonment, and expropriation. We should hold city councilmen, company directors, and all others in authority individually and collectively liable for crimes against our planet committed by the organizations for which they are responsible.

Am I too adamant? I think not, when we consider the alternatives of continuing degradation of the human habitat. Can we carry through major reforms leading to an effective natural resources management policy? I think yes, provided that we can mobilize scientific, technical, and popular efforts to demonstrate that a good life is compatible with good business and good public policy.

How do we accomplish our objectives? How do we cut the time lag and make democracy work? I am not a political activist myself, but I see no effective means other than political activism. Harvey Wheeler put it succinctly when he said we need a politics of ecology, combining the scientific contributions of the scientists with the new politics of youthful radicalism. If we are to achieve an environmental renaissance, we must convert the silent majority to putting a common interest in survival above our individual selfish interest as taxpayers, automobile owners, shareholders, and landowners. We need to adapt the tactics of the civil rights and the peace movements to the urgent need of environmental quality. We need demonstrations, teach-ins, marches, and the all-out efforts of the dedicated. Only if we can shock the silent majority into sharing our sense of urgency can we effectively control our air, our water, and our land.

21

ECOLOGICAL DIVERSITY
RAYMOND F. DASMANN

A recurring conference theme was the need to preserve diversity, both biological and cultural. Says Dasmann, "... I believe that if we fail to rise to the challenge of ecological diversity, there will be no humans on earth." About the small amount of money provided for this ecological diversity compared to the amount provided for developing the SST, he says "... I think we are begging for extinction."

The greatest challenge to humanity during the remaining years of the twentieth century is the challenge of understanding, preserving, and learning to manage diversity: the ecological diversity of the natural world, and the cultural diversity of the manmade world. Perhaps the most valuable quality that remains in the human environment is the quality of diversity, the knowledge that one can leave the place where he happens to be and find some other place that is different. The differences may be small; they may be those of different neighborhoods built into a different plan; they may be only the woods and hills outside of town. They may be more major, as great as those between Chicago and Baghdad. Or they may be an entirely different scheme of things, the differences between a bushman's hunting camp in the Kalahari and a church meeting in the Maryland suburbs. I have been in places in recent years where I had to say, "Either this is real and the United States doesn't exist, or the United States is real and this doesn't exist. They can't both be on the same planet." But they do exist, and this is the wonder of the world we still have. We still have diversity, in peoples, places, and in the natural world.

The value of such diversity is immeasurable. The existence of places and people that are different gives to any individual that needs it the opportunity for a new start. It gives to others the chance to see their normal existence in new perspective. It gives an opportunity for recreation, in the sense of re-creation, a chance to renew and perhaps reshape one's existence. Think for awhile what life would be like if there were no outside, if everywhere life was shaped in the same mold by the same man-made environment, in the same universal, world-embracing human monoculture. Yet this is a danger we face, and a direction in which we have been heading. Lewis Mumford said it very well at a conference in 1965 when he stated:

> When we rally to preserve the remaining redwood forests or to protect the whooping crane, we are rallying to preserve ourselves, we are trying to keep in existence the organic variety, the whole span of natural resources upon which our own future development will be based. If we surrender this variety too easily in one place, we shall lose it everywhere; and we shall find ourselves enclosed in a technological prison, without even the hope that sustains a prisoner in jail—that someday we may get out. Should organic variety disappear, there will be no "out."

Man came into existence in a world that was, from a geologic point of view, probably more diverse than it has been at any previous time in its history. It was a world of high mountains and deep valleys, of plateaus and coastal plains, of lakes and rivers, of swamps and deserts, of ice floes and Arctic barrens, as well as humid tropical lowlands and tropical mountains that reached up into glacial climates. In this world, over the millions of years of evolution, forms of animal and plant life had evolved that could occupy most of the ecological niches, the places in the environment that the geologic world had to offer, and they in turn provided shelter, or food, or a proper substrate in which countless other forms of animals and plants could live—new and different ecological niches. Lichens evolved that could occupy the barren rocks of the Arctic, fishes evolved that could live in the equally barren depths of the ocean, parasites adapted to life within other animals.

The world in which man developed and spent most of his history was a world of incredible biotic diversity developed in response to the existence of geologic and climatic diversity. It permitted not only the survival of man, but also the evolution of all the different kinds of people and different ways of life that characterized the world up until the present century. Man's survival depended in turn on his own cultural diversity. If any particular human group happened to follow a course leading to disaster, as many did, there remained other groups in other places, living in different ways.

Life in general is favored by climates that are not marked by extremes. This means that the humid tropics are most favorable to plant and animal life, and the climatic extremes of the earth—the deserts, high mountains, Arctic and Antarctic—are the least favorable. The greatest biotic diversity is therefore in the tropics; the least, in the deserts and the colder parts of the earth.

Such diversity in the tropics is characterized by a dynamic balance, stability, resistance to deformation by natural forces, and also significantly by high productivity. All the chemical elements needed for life are flowing through the various living systems. Maximum advantage is taken of the sun's energy to produce new life or to break down and rechannel the elements from those things that are dead.

By contrast, the simplified ecological systems of the dry and cold areas are characterized by a high degree of instability, by great fluctuations in numbers, by fragility in the face of disturbing factors, by low rates of turnover of chemical elements, high losses of solar energy, and low productivity.

Labrador, for example, has about 80 species of breeding birds, the continent of Europe about 250 species of breeding land birds. But the one tropical country of Colombia has about 1400 species. Throughout the entire subarctic region of Canada you can find no more than half a dozen species of dominant trees, and one or two species dominate over hundreds or thousands of square miles. In Malaya, a small country, you can find at least 2000 species of trees. In all of California there were never more than half a dozen species of native wild ungulates: deer, elk, antelope, mountain sheep. In a ten-square-mile area of tropical Africa, you can find three times that many.

Diversity has always favored man's survival, but man has progressed by simplifying the complex. A cornfield dominated by a single species was substituted for a prairie with dozens of species sharing the solar energy and soil chemicals. By such simplification, mankind channeled the productive forces of nature into pathways of his own choosing.

Initially this process was benign. A cornfield added diversity to the prairie region; a patch of sugar cane subtracted nothing from the diversity of the rain forest. But then human numbers increased, and there were cornfields everywhere and no prairie; sugar cane, coffee, or bananas, but little rain forest. With the new power of our technology, we are eliminating diversity wherever we can. With the new pressures of population, we are demanding that more and more of the energy reaching the earth in sunlight and the chemicals of the world's soils be channeled into pathways of our own choosing. We are reaching the end of the line.

If we were all knowing and all wise, we could substitute for natural diversity, with all of its built-in checks and balances, new factors that we ourselves controlled. But we really know very little. In simplifying the complex systems of nature, we set in motion all the forces of instability, fragility, and erratic fluctuations that characterize the simple ecological systems of the earth.

In an effort to dampen or control these effects, we draw upon our chemical arsenal and come up with pesticides and biocides that serve for temporary alleviation, but in the long run aggravate the problem by eliminating more wild species, more natural checks and balances, and set in motion wilder fluctuations.

It is a matter of no little concern, since the atmosphere that we breathe, the water we drink, the soils that grow our food, have been maintained by the once-enormous variety of species on the earth. As we simplify, reduce, or eliminate natural diversity, we reduce our chances for survival.

We have since 1600 A.D. eliminated through extinction more than 350 species and races of birds and mammals. More than 800 species and races of birds and mammals are now known to be endangered. We do not even know how many kinds of animals of other groups, or how many species of plants, have been eliminated or are now endangered. We do not have a good guess about how important to our survival these species may be. We persist in breaking up the earth's systems and throwing away various— perhaps essential—parts. Thus far we have been lucky. Or so we think.

What can we do about this situation? We could begin by preserving natural diversity, through parks and reserves and the protection of wild species, through good management and rational use of our productive lands, by cutting down on and hopefully eliminating the various poisons we are now dispersing around our landscapes. We could go beyond this in a program to protect and preserve human diversity, to build or modify our cities, settlements, and economy so as to favor the maximum range of ways of life, human cultures, human individuals. We could. We have a wide range of experts able and willing to tell us how it should be done. We could experiment, build pilot systems, model communities. Why don't we undertake a major world program along these lines?

The choice is really crucial, since I believe that if we fail to rise to the challenge of ecological diversity, there will be no humans on earth. Perhaps we shall get what we deserve, and if our past record is evidence of that, we probably deserve to become extinct. It is really up to us, up to you and your organizations and your friends and relations to make this decision. The decision involves not resolutions or hopes or prayers, but money, and we must be willing to pay for it.

There is one organization—of a nongovernmental nature— engaged in an international effort to preserve the world's wild species, wild places, and natural resources; in other words, life-support systems: the International Union for the Conservation of Nature. The budget of the International Union is so inadequate that I hesitate to state it. Suffice it to say that its president, an American, has to plead each month for a few thousand dollars to make possible the preservation of a species or of certain unique natural places around the world. A few thousand dollars to keep the world alive, while we can spend billions on an SST! I think that we are really begging for extinction.

22

WATER

JOSEPH G. MOORE, JR.

Water is a primary need of life. This paper discusses the chaos of our present water management, examines the reasons, and proposes ways to improve the situation. We could apply the same outline approach to air, housing, transportation, and similar areas of resource management.

There was a time when man's activities were controlled by his physical surroundings and by the availability of resources for his needs. Today, more and more, man goes where he wills and expects to tailor his environment to suit his comfort. There was a time when man could not congregate where there was little or no water. Now man settles where he pleases and expects his government to bring water to him. Government has become the people's water boy. If the flow of a stream is erratic, fluctuating between flood and drought, dam it up to provide a sustainable supply. If sustained flow is too shallow for navigation, dredge a channel. If all other factors except rainfall are favorable to agriculture, provide water for irrigation. And above all, construct the dams, waterworks, and distribution systems to maximize recreational opportunities and enhance fishery resources. Then come those who urge that we hang the "Do not disturb" sign on more and more of our watercourses. Add to this the rising chorus of esthetic demands and of demands for higher water quality, and we have a maze of conflicting interests, pressures, and counterpressures, all competing to gain ascendancy.

I propose the following assumptions to help us proceed toward a national and international policy for the management of water resources.

1. Decisions about the development of water resources are more likely to be made in the light of political rather than economic or engineering considerations.

2. Since water projects have traditionally been viewed as "public works" and therefore subject to political trade-offs, an effective policy will require restraint and a change in the psychology of water development.

3. The promoters who are the most aggressive, and who can secure the most political support, currently have more impact on the priority ranking of projects—and therefore on the course of development—than any rational selection system.

4. Existing yardsticks for evaluation, such as the cost-benefit ratio, are imperfect tools that appear inflexible, but tend to become flexible under strong and sustained pressure.

5. The present government screening process for individual water projects in the United States serves more to reward the persistent interest group than to produce a rational pattern of development.

6. Institutional forms for the development of water supplies encourage conflicting proposals, produce competition and duplication, and therefore fragmented development, but are so entrenched in legislative and executive organizations in the United States as to make change difficult.

7. Water resource policy involves a choice between alternatives and thus a balancing of diverse interests. In our burst of concern for environmental protection, we should take care that "conservation" does not become "stagnation" or "deprivation" for some of our people. The tyranny of a minority must be avoided—whether that minority are "exploiters" or "protectionists."

8. The availability of water will not alone assure prosperity for a city, state, or nation. There must be other resources as well.

9. Water has shifted from a matter of purely local interest to a forum of interstate, regional, and national attention. Increasingly the development of water resources can proceed only as an international undertaking.

Although these assumptions may sound pessimistic, we must be realistic if we are to progress. Some constructive steps might be:

1. An announcement should be made now that both Congress and the executive branch will realign their structures and working patterns to consolidate programs for the protection and development of natural resources in as few organizational units as possible. We could then hope that other nations would follow suit and establish rational patterns of development.

2. We should make a national inventory and assessment of water projects at all levels of government, and continue to do so frequently for the next 50 years.

3. We should try to arrange known and potential water uses in some scale of national priorities; i.e. industrial, agricultural, navigational, recreational, etc.

4. We should state the general level of water quality we wish to attain, and give some indication of how it can be achieved.

5. Preparation, review, and approval of individual water projects would make possible simultaneous consideration by local, state, Federal, and other national governments, with maximum public information and participation.

6. Individual water resource projects should be considered in the context of long-range regional, national, and international plans.

7. Variations for "people reasons" from plans and policies that are sound from the standpoint of economics or engineering should be possible, since water use is intended for the people's benefit.

8. International considerations will receive attention only after national priorities have been attended to.

9. National priorities should be modified wherever neighboring nations' priorities are in conflict.

10. The area in most urgent need of international attention and cooperation is data-collecting and research. Particularly in the fields of desalination, weather modification, and water quality should there be full disclosure and exchange.

23

THE SEA

TAYLOR A. PRYOR

Any successful use of the sea for survival will need the teamwork of science, business, and politics.   Says the author, a rare generalist with technical background, "All of our terrestrial [and marine] experience . . . suggests . . . [that the use of] marine resources will be destructive.   It need not be." He recommends massive use of science and technology, with ecological guidelines, to gain positive results.

"The end of the ocean came late in the summer of 1979 and it came even more rapidly than the biologists had expected." I am indebted to Dr. Paul Ehrlich for that one-liner which introduced his persuasive fable on the future of the ocean titled *Eco-Catastrophe.* Previously, I'd been concentrating on the promise of oceanic resources; but I am disturbed by his threat.   He imagined a techno-political trend ending in a global disaster.   Other disastrous trends, global and local, are possible.   These visions of threat rival the visions of promise.   A perspective of both would be useful.
the known, the partly known, and the unknown resources of the ocean.   The known resources are those nearest at hand in our coastal regions.   Here at the land–water interface, the highest-valued commodity is access.   The coast is where we dump our wastes, where we load for transport and travel.   It's where we play, dipping as a civilization into our Cambrian home.   It's where we get esthetic nourishment from varied seascapes.   It is the boundary for national defense, the nursery for offshore fishes, the mother lode of shellfish, the nesting ground of sea birds, and, in North America, it is a day's travel from the residence of 150 million humans.

A lot different—and only partly known—is the continental shelf zone a few miles out.   Traversed but rarely entered, it averages 600 feet of depth and is easy enough to chart and sample, but hard to visualize.   Out to modest depths it has yielded oil and gas, not easily but economically.   Long drowned and not precisely continental in character, it must contain a wealth of minerals, but they may be deeply embedded and not readily accessible.   Production of fish resources of the continental shelf is a different story, though.   Once abundant and available, the commercial species are inevitably decimated by over-harvest, sometimes to be replaced by other species, which are again decimated.

Technology now promises to reduce the difference between the coastal and shelf zones and eventually to make them one in terms of human access. Sea-floor and subsurface habitats with high-pressure, mixed-gas life-support systems now allow men to live and work routinely, at commercially reasonable costs, to 600 feet. With interior arrangements similar to luxury trailer homes, these habitats will soon be in use around the shelf, allowing skilled work crews to move their quarters with their job, like early railroad gangs, freely entering the environment and returning after work for rest and relaxation. There is no shortage of applicants ready to be trained to use the new subsea systems.

Offshore harbors—large facilities—are being designed which can be created where no inshore harbor exists or where the old harbors are no longer adequate due to such obstacles as municipal congestion and shallow tunnels which limit dredging for deep-draft vessels. Free of topographic limitations, the offshore harbors can sprawl out in any direction, connected back to shore cities by tunnels, air-cargo systems, and perhaps bridging. Similar facilities can also replace the congested onshore airports. Nearly every major U.S. coastal city must consider this use of the continental shelf in this century.

The continental shelf is suited to multiple use. Is the open sea, then, useless? Academicians often call it too deep for mineral or petroleum production, too distant for facilities, too sterile for aquaculture, too remote for reality. However, admirals and Sunday editors use words like "vast" and "unlimited" for this area and are fond of quantifying the amount of the planet that it covers, indicating by suggestion great wonders to come which are then not specified. The fact is that when it comes to the open sea, we don't know what uses we shall find, or when.

Soon, however, deep-submersibles on Apollo-like missions will begin to cruise at all depths, returning with elaborate records of the environment, including photographs and rock samples. Fisheries experts who spurn the idea of sea farming, of animal husbandry in the open ocean, will have an opportunity to examine new data next year, information which suggests that millions of acres of open sea pasture can be provided through placement of devices such as plastic, floating growing surfaces where grazing herbivores can be introduced, raised and harvested by techniques now in prototype. When more nutrients are needed they can be brought up from the sea-floor ooze to support the diatomaceous pasturage. Maintenance stations and hatcheries can be built on concrete stable ocean platforms. Should sea lanes cross, they can be routed and controlled as canals are elsewhere. Even sea state may be flattened by the volume of acreage possible.

Ehrlich has called food from the sea a "red herring" and again, in the long run of population growth, he is right. If open-sea aquaculture is possible, it could provide enormous tonnage of low-cost protein. It could therefore delay the date when famine outruns production again, the date when there is no further capability to expand production offshore or on. Delay looks good, however. Men must adapt to the planet because it will not change to suit them. Time will be needed to make that adaptation. If in this decade we recognize that we must adapt, the sea could give us food, space, and access to resources, while the shore-side changes are attempted. The sea as it now exists could do this, but contaminated and altered it could not.

All three zones are threatened. Even without pollution, continuing removal of marshlands by filling and dredging has already permanently limited the coastal zone's capability of supporting marine bird and aquatic life, not only through direct loss of nesting and nursery areas but also by altering tidal flow and silt transport. Further destruction may not just further limit; it may push whole ecological systems permanently out of whack. Then even the carefully preserved areas go too. This of course is the global concern. All goes well until a threshold is reached, then suddenly all goes badly.

Much has been said about coastal-zone pollution. The effects are becoming obvious to children, legislators, and industrialists. We register concern. We establish controls. However, while we locate and limit sources of recognized pollution such as raw sewage and factory waste, we add new contaminants such as the run-off of inorganic fertilizers which introduce massive amounts of the wrong kind of nitrates into confined coastal areas. Once acceptable in occasional traces, these unnatural nutrients, in ever-increasing quantities, are now exponentially hastening the aging process of estuaries, bays and sounds, encouraging rapid algal growth from Lake Erie to Tampa Bay. Standing near a condemned beach, one Ohio resident said, "It may be algae, but to us it looks and smells like crap."

The threats to the coastal environment go on and on: Oil spillage in Santa Barbara, hot-water effluence in the Connecticut River, waste salt from desalinization in the California gulf. Each is a product of well-intentioned, highly skilled technology honestly motivated by profit and progress. Similar good intentions will eventually have their effect on the continental shelves. Who can read of the AEC Amchitka Island testing without pause? There one agency, working in secrecy, has fired a nuclear underground calibration shot and states publicly that this proves that far larger shots will not cause earthquakes, start tsunamis, or disturb the fragile animal populations in the wilderness preserve where the shots are centered. If we write these off as the local concerns of Alaska, Hawaii, and wildlife lovers, we must still wonder what would happen if an unexpected fissure caused a large amount of sea water to pick up radioactive contamination. The water body would slowly move south with the California current, walking along as a massive unit exposing every organism on the continental shelf for as long as the water was passing on its way toward the equator. Eventually it would slide off the shelf into the nearly motionless depths of the open sea, affecting all the creatures that might pass through.

All the Arctic is a part of the continental shelf. Known to us as a harsh land that has been forbidding to penetration, it is now being conquered and may turn out to be one of the most fragile environments of all. When the winter ice of the St. Lawrence seaway was first cracked and held open for year-round passage, it was a demanding task for the icebreakers. Now large areas of water there remain open without human effort. Should the northern passage through the Arctic pack ice respond similarly, it will be a boon to our petroleum and shipping requirements. But open bodies of water absorb the sun's heat, while ice largely reflects it. A slight rise in temperature could force more melting, and further melting from an oil spillage, if spread to substantial areas of the ice pack, could cause large changes. Large open areas of water in the Arctic would alter the entire global weather system.

One investigator cannot find an uncontaminated sample of surface sea water within three hundred miles of the California coast. Tetraethyl lead, carried in the atmosphere from auto exhaust, reaches that far. Farther yet is the reach of DDT. Antarctic penguins carry an increasing load of this hydrocarbon and can eventually be considered candidates for extinction, along with the brown pelican. Since marine organisms seem to concentrate DDT in large amounts as they move up the food chain, the predators on top of the chain are trapped. Already the Atlantic bottlenose porpoise of the Florida coast carries 800 ppm of DDT in blubber, while the Department of Agriculture permits 5 to 10 ppm in salable meat. But for once the great whales may have a break, with their reservoirs of fat for ready absorption. Not so for the sea birds. It is hard to say yet, but they may all be doomed now. Most of the DDT ever used is still active in the atmosphere, or locked in soils, ready to be removed by evaporation or by run-off into the sea. With a 10- to 50-year half-life remaining, what effects will follow? How much sea food will human predators be able to consume?

The end of the ocean in 1979 was postulated assuming a series of technological and political events which encouraged much-increased dumping of DDT and similar chlorinated hydrocarbons, thereby altering the planktonic ecosystem and causing poisonous diatom blooms in the open sea. Other events with different chronologies can also be contemplated. Most of the mixing process at sea seems to occur above the thermocline, especially at the air–sea interface. Most marine plants live as phytoplankton in this mixing area, and most of our oxygen in the atmosphere is derived from these plants. While terrestrial forests contribute, that contribution is largely balanced, since the eventual decay of trees returns their stored carbon dioxide to the atmosphere and use oxygen in the combustion process. Marine plants, however, sink to the depths and decay in the still darkness below the thermocline. Since pesticides are known to slow the photosynthetic process in those marine plants, it is the contamination of the open seas which could eventually alter the global life-support system for good.

The sea is the machine which drives the global atmosphere. We can put energy, nutrients, and toxics into it and they will return. Some of the return effects will be delayed a long time, but eventually they will come back. The sea literally washes all shores, mixing the bath water into itself and into the atmosphere. We want to gain beneficial use of the sea, but before saying that anything that benefits us will not harm the sea we have to view that thing as a cosmic ecologist might. This is a very urgent cause for research. The urgency is clear from the threats, but is multiplied by the promise and by our needs for that promise. Recreation, food, minerals, petroleum, transport, sciences, exploration, art, and defense: They all call us to the sea. Add only residence to the list and it is the entire community of terrestrial activity. All are possible. Massive application of science and technology is necessary. Massive results will follow.

All our terrestrial experience and more that is marine so far suggests that our effort to utilize marine resources will be destructive. It need not be. Scientific applications and technology have rarely been guided ecologically, let alone used to implement ecological standards. Certainly now is the time and the ocean is the place to try. Although threatened, the ocean is still in a primitive state and the past errors made in the sea are largely retrievable. Moving carefully, we can contemplate a productive distribution of nutrients, perhaps leaching them out at rates matched to the absorption rate of harvestable materials. With knowledge we can exploit natural populations forever, even going far deeper to the huge schools of squid and shrimp for our protein, but never over-cropping as we go.

If we learn to reuse and preserve the ores and to reuse hydro-carbons in favor of burning them, we can certainly learn to extract them without harm. Wastes must be controlled, but surely any population of a given size can learn to control its waste.   The trouble comes when the population grows faster than its waste controls. The trouble too is that too often we are irreversible our-selves. We must be able to stop erring once the error becomes apparent.

We need not be negative about our future. This earth has the possibility of being a paradise. We don't have to go along forever living in the present like the rest of the animals. We can use our technology to do otherwise. The ocean gives us a chance to use technology correctly. It may be both the first and last chance. Using the best efforts of world politics and world economic systems, we can let the successful development of the ocean be a model for redevelopment of our terrestrial planet. There is no better time to start. There may be no time again.

Perhaps another fable would be useful: In 1979, United Na-tions ecologists had convinced the General Assembly that the ex-tinction of any species was symptomatic of an ecosystem imbalance. By then it was obvious to all nations that with the loss and pending loss of so much of nature, not even human life could be sustained. With no alternative, the nations voted to re-establish civilization at sea.

Floating ocean platforms were designed and tested. Geneticists cultured new seaweeds which grew thickly and deeply, surround-ing the platforms with solid stable turf; building on buoyant pil-ings, new structures rose from the new green masses. Engineers designed whole communities, elegant for their emphasis as closed systems.   Marine ecologists determined that not more than one-third of the open ocean could be occupied, along with a similar volume beneath. Apartments were inverted to use the extra space in the ocean depths. Social scientists determined that if the world's population would level at 6 billion by 2000, the new communities could provide for them with an increasingly improved standard of living during the next century. In the new communities, arts and crafts were encouraged and they flourished; materialism gave way to peace of mind.

The terrestrial three-tenths of the earth was largely returned to natural park. Aboriginal people were encouraged to remain ashore. High-yield grain areas were kept in production. Many buildings and parts of some freeways were left as archeological wonders. Carefully selected populations of people were trained as terrestrial wardens. Transportation systems were limited to the needs of the wardens and the many tourists who enjoyed cruising the wild continents on leave from their oceanic communities.

By 2100 some legislators agitated for a return to the good old days on shore, but the ecological computer which had supreme veto power refused permission. Besides, no one had volunteered.

24

THE SEA: SHOULD WE NOW WRITE IT OFF AS A FUTURE GARBAGE PIT?

ROBERT W. RISEBOROUGH

For those who don't as yet believe that the sea is dying, this is ample proof. For those who do, it is further documentation. Risebrough discusses the seas' productivity, their pollution, and our vital dependence on living and healthy seas.

Should we now prepare to write off the sea as the inevitable garbage pit of a future terrestrial technology? Of the various roles the sea has played for man's benefit, the most useful in the long run might be its function as the receptacle for waste materials that cannot be reclaimed or recycled. Even though the sea might then become irreversibly polluted, the environment on land could be better managed and controlled for the well-being of man.

At first hearing, this proposal is clearly unacceptable. We have assumed that farming of the sea will provide the essential food for expanding populations, that recreational use will continue to expand, and that the sea could also provide essential living space. The sea could not therefore be permitted to become polluted. The arguments in favor of the proposition, however, are surprisingly strong. They are equivalent to the argument that pollution of the air is inevitable in a technological society, or that large tracts of virgin forest are an expensive luxury if a significant fraction of the population has no land. They are also equivalent to the proposal that we should continue our present ways of producing and disposing of waste.

The arguments in favor can be summarized briefly. Productivity of the sea is finite and, far from being large in the scale of human activity, is no greater than the total amount of waste material now being released by man into his environment. At best, the sea can now provide food for only a fraction of the world's present population, and as population increases the sea will become increasingly less important as a source of nourishment. Some marine organisms already contain higher concentrations of both agricultural and industrial pollutants than their terrestrial counterparts, and we are only at the beginning of our technological revolution. Increasing outputs of wastes, on a global scale, will increase by many times the rate at which pollutants enter the sea. Pollution has already begun to destroy a portion of the sea's productivity. Synthetic foods are becoming much easier to manufacture on land. Should we not admit, therefore, that our present activities are already making the sea into a garbage dump, and that this might be its most sensible future use?

These arguments are powerful and very likely will prevail if population growth proceeds unchecked. Destruction of the marine environment as an ecologically healthy entity entails, however, the destruction of the ecological integrity of the total planetary environment. We can hardly afford to permit the degradation of the environmental checks and balances that have developed over several billion years of planetary evolution. Scientific, practical, economic, moral, and esthetic reasons require that the sea *not* be used as a garbage dump.

Pollution ecology is a relatively new field, multidisciplinary in nature, and with an orientation somewhat different from the disinterested approach of traditional science. Its goal is to determine the causes of environmental degradation and to document the effects of the input wastes. The scientist working in this field has an additional responsibility. In order to preserve the ecological integrity of the environment as a suitable habitat for man and his fellow species, the relevant facts and scientific judgments must be transmitted to those who formulate policy. Strictly political and economic factors have so far dominated the decision-making process. As our global environment becomes smaller in relation to the scale of our own activities, we must now also consider environmental factors.

I shall attempt here to review the scientific arguments that the integrity of the sea must be preserved. Although scientific opinions frequently evolve or are otherwise modified, the knowledge now available should convince anyone that the problem is already with us. We must learn to reduce and control the levels of marine pollution and of planetary pollution in general.

The Productivity of the Sea

It is a popular misconception that the resources of the sea are infinite. The ocean "supports more photosynthesis and plant food production than can be readily imagined or than a much vaster human population than that presently living could eat."[1]* Is this realistic in implying that the potential food resources of the sea are practically infinite?

Dr. John Ryther of the Woods Hole Oceanographic Institution has summarized the results of his research in this field in an article in *Science*.[2] He relates that the primary event in the production of organic matter in the sea is the absorption of light energy by microscopic one-celled plants in the top 100 meters of the sea. The total productivity of the sea can be estimated by calculating the amount of the energy that is transferred into organic material by all the plants of the sea. This is done by measuring the amount of radioactive carbon dioxide that is incorporated during photosynthesis into phytoplankton collected at known depths and from various areas of the sea at different times of the year.

What factors other than sunlight limit the amount of organic material that can be synthesized by plants in the sea? We are all now aware that release of a combination of phosphates and nitrates into fresh-water lakes may produce a proliferation of algae growth. The lower amounts of these nutrients under normal conditions limit the growth of algae in the lakes. In the sea also, the growth of phytoplankton is limited by the low concentrations of these same nutrients.

Over the vast expanse of open ocean, which comprises 90% of the total sea area, the amount of sunlight does not limit the growth of plankton during the daylight hours, but the low concentrations of phosphates and nitrates permit only a relatively small amount of organic matter to be synthesized.

Coastal areas are more fertile. A combination of factors brings some of the deeper waters, which contain higher concentrations of the nutrients, up to the top 100 meters which also have sunlight.

---

*   Raised numbers are keyed to the references at the end of this article.

These coastal areas, and several offshore regions, where winds and currents also combine to bring deeper waters to the surface, comprise most of the remaining 10% of the sea surface area. Along the coasts of California, Peru, and parts of Africa and Arabia, surface waters are diverted offshore and the richer, deeper waters rise to take their place. Nutrients are therefore present in these areas in much greater supply, and a larger amount of organic matter is available for marine animals, so that the total biomass of animals and plants combined is comparatively high. These few upwelling areas comprise only 0.1% of the sea area, but they are the most productive fishing grounds of the world.

The amount of carbon incorporated into phytoplankton through photosynthesis is about 10,000 pounds per year for each person now living, but will be only 1000 per person when the population reaches 30 billion. This potential food exists, however, as microscopic particles in huge volumes of water. The energy required to harvest them would be considerably greater than the energy harvested as food. In order to preserve the ecological integrity of the sea, moreover, most of the phytoplankton must be eaten by small animals which in turn constitute the food of larger species.

The present yield of fish from the sea is about 60 million tons.[3] Almost all this is from the upwelling and other coastal regions; a comparatively small proportion is from the open ocean that comprises 90% of the sea surface. Could the yield from the open sea be increased? Food chains in this area of the sea progress from phytoplankton to small zooplankton to small fish and finally to larger fish that can be harvested. At each level about 90% of the energy is lost through metabolism and excretion.[2] At most, only 10 pounds of fish per year per person now living could be harvested from the open sea. Unless a technology develops that would produce artificial upwelling, the open ocean is not a source of unlimited amounts of food to feed the future generations.

The coastal regions and the upwelling zones, then, are much more productive than the open sea. An area as large as California produces about half the world's fish supply. In these regions the fish used by man frequently feed directly upon the phytoplankton, which tend to be larger than the species in the open sea. A much smaller fraction of the primary productivity is therefore lost in the intermediate levels of the food chains, and more is available to man. Not all of it is available, though, since some fish must remain to replenish the stocks and to provide food for other predators. M. B. Schaefer[4] has estimated that the total potential harvest of the sea, including species lower in the food chains, could amount to three times the present yield—150 pounds of fish and other sea food per person at the present time, but only 15 pounds at a population level of 30 billion. We might anticipate radical innovations in marine technology, but it would appear that we must rely on terrestrial sources to supply the balance of the anticipated food requirements.

And if pollution of the sea is the necessary price to pay for the increased productivity on land, should we not now plan to write off the sea?

There are several answers to this question. The first is that if the resources of the ocean are finite, so also is the capacity of the land. Photosynthesis on land might be more efficiently utilized for man's benefit than marine photosynthesis. The available space, however, no matter how efficiently used, is finite. A continuously expanding population cannot be indefinitely sustained.[5]

Fisheries Resources

The marine fisheries industry is expanding at a rate faster than the rate of population growth, but the capacity for future growth is both limited and finite.[2] Already the fisheries for cod, herring, ocean perch, plaice, and other species in many areas of the North Atlantic are either operating at full capacity or are now over-exploited. Increased effort no longer yields an increased catch.

The nutritional value of fish derives from its protein content. Most plant proteins are deficient in several amino acids and alone do not constitute an adequate diet. The protein composition of fish, however, is essentially identical to human protein. The daily protein requirement is about one gram of protein for each kilogram of body weight. But at least one-third of the daily protein intake should be animal protein. Three quarters of the world's population do not get this minimal amount. Per capita consumption of animal protein, however, is very high in the United States and Canada.[6]

The age group most severely affected by protein-deficient diets is clearly the children who have just been weaned from milk and who must subsist on rice or maize. Malnutrition at this age may produce both physical and mental retardation. Since the problem is most acute in the developing countries, a greater proportion of children in these countries can be expected to suffer from some form of permanent brain damage.

The marine fisheries resources, although finite, can fill this gap and provide an adequate diet for all the world's children. The buying power of the average person in the developed countries is so much greater than that of his counterpart in the underdeveloped countries, however, that animal protein or high-protein plant products such as soybeans are now exported from these countries.[6] Great advances have been made in the technology of fish-meal production. A protein-rich fish meal could be manufactured in sufficient quantities to correct the protein-deficient diets of children. It is clearly in the vital interest of the underdeveloped countries to develop available fishery resources for the benefit of their own peoples and to work on an international level to prevent the sea from becoming polluted so that it can continue to be a source of protein-rich food.

A Future Technology

Significant advances are being made in the field of mariculture. Oysters, other shellfish, and edible algae can be artificially cultivated in productive estuarine waters.[7] The protein yield per acre of artificially grown oysters can be many times higher than the beef protein obtained from the world's lushest grasslands. A technology could perhaps be developed to bring the nutrient-rich deeper waters to the surface so that productivity would be further increased. The contribution to the world's protein supply could thus become essential and irreplaceable within a few years. It might be irresponsible, therefore, to assume that the oceans can be used indefinitely as a garbage pit.

Marine Fish and Pollutants

In 1969 fish from the sea were found to be unfit for human consumption because of pollutant contamination. Shipments of jack mackerel from the Pacific Ocean off Southern California were seized and condemned by the Food and Drug Administration because they contained twice as much of the DDT compounds in their flesh as the maximum amount permitted in interstate commerce. The fishery was subsequently closed.

The publicity given to the pollution problems caused by the DDT compounds in the environment has tended to minimize the threat of other environmental pollutants. DDT is produced in smaller quantities than many industrial products, some of which have the capacity to become persistent wastes. The most abundant synthetic pollutants in the environment after the DDT compounds may be a class of chemicals called polychlorinated biphenyls, or PCB. They are used in such vast amounts in industry that they can be purchased in railway-car quantities.[8] They are found in many plastics, rubbers, paints, hydraulic fluids, and in countless other industrial products.[8] They are now also found worldwide in marine fish and birds[9, 10, 11, 13] and in human mother's milk.[12] In some species, such as the peregrine falcon in North America[11] or the white-tailed eagle in Sweden,[9] the concentrations may be one or two hundred parts per million in fresh tissue; in mother's milk the concentrations are equivalent to those of the DDT compounds.[12]

The usefulness of the PCB compounds to industry derives to a large part from their chemical stability and their miscibility with oil and other nonpolar substances. The same properties ensure that they will not dissolve in water, that they will readily enter biological systems and be concentrated in food chains, and that they can be degraded, if at all, only with great difficulty by biological systems.

The high concentrations of PCB recorded in marine fish[9, 10] suggest that fish are a major source of PCB in the human diet. Tolerance limits for these compounds have not been established, and the tests for carcinogenicity, effects upon reproduction, etc., have not yet been made.

Within the past two years, therefore, we have become aware of the existence in our planetary environment of a whole new class of pollutants. What would happen if these substances were shown to be carcinogens? The damage to human lives and the harm to wildlife would be the major effects, but also, overnight, the world's marine fisheries would be wiped out.

Pollutants in Marine Fish

Among the American states, California uses a large fraction of the pesticides applied in the United States. Fresh-water fish in California might therefore be expected to accumulate higher residues of the DDT compounds than fresh-water fish in most other areas of the world. The averages of the total concentrations generally fall between 0.2 ppm and 2.0 ppm. Most of the DDT values so far recorded in Pacific marine fish also fall between 0.2 and 2.0 ppm. Additional evidence from Sweden[9] also suggests that DDT concentrations in marine fish are now as high as or higher than those in fresh-water fish.

In the California coastal waters, the highest concentrations were not found in San Francisco Bay, which receives the drainage waters from the principal agricultural areas of California, but in the area near Los Angeles, where no major river enters the sea.[14] A considerable amount of various kinds of evidence has shown that aerial transport of DDT throughout the world is more important than water transport.[10]   DDT is but poorly soluble in water, but eventually becomes a gas and leaves the areas where it is used, especially if it is applied to water. The high concentrations in the sea near Los Angeles might therefore have originated anywhere in the world.

Contaminated Sea Birds

Sea birds are now in general more contaminated with agricultural and industrial pollutants than are land birds. Of all the bird species of the world, the Wilson's petrel and the sooty shearwater could be the two most abundant. Both are sea birds and spend their entire lives at sea, where they feed on small organisms at the surface. Petrels and shearwaters contain especially high concentrations of both the DDT and PCB compounds. All regions of the world are now evidently affected, although the data collected suggest that regional fallout patterns exist.[11]

Impaired Reproduction

Few events in environmental biology have attracted as much attention as the rapid decline, beginning in the 1950's, of several species of raptorial and fish-eating birds. Among the species that prey on marine fish, the bald eagle and osprey have shown reproductive failures in areas along the East Coast of the United States. The causes have been found to include abnormally low production of young per nesting attempt, which in turn has been correlated with a deficiency of calcium carbonate in the eggshell.[15,16,17] Thin-shelled eggs have now been shown in controlled experiments to be caused by one or more of the DDT compounds, alone or in combination with dieldrin, in a species of hawk and a species of duck.[16,17]

The most spectacular event linking eggshell thinning and reproductive failure of a marine bird occurred this year in California. Scientists, bird-watchers, and the general public had noticed a decline in the numbers of brown pelicans. These large-beaked birds have long been familiar to fishermen and seashore enthusiasts in California. Several years ago, the pelicans suddenly disappeared in Louisiana and are no longer found there as breeding birds, although Louisiana was once known as the Pelican State. The cause of the California decline became obvious to scientists who visited the breeding grounds on Anacapa Island this year. The pelicans were laying eggs, but they were so thin-shelled that they promptly broke when the parent birds began to incubate. Of about 1200 nesting attempts, at most five eggs survived the incubation period and hatched. The species will undoubtedly soon become extinct as a breeding bird in the state.[18] The brown pelicans on the Coronados Islands near San Diego also laid thin-shelled eggs in 1969, eggs that did not survive incubation.[19] Elsewhere, in Mexico and in Florida, the shells were weaker than normal, but strong enough to permit the young pelican to hatch.[19]

The brown pelicans feed only on marine fish, which are contaminated with both the DDT and PCB compounds. Three other species of birds at the tops of food chains—the peregrine falcon, the bald eagle, and the osprey—have already disappeared from the coastal ecosystem of Southern California. The double-crested cormorant of Anacapa also failed to produce young in 1969 because of egg breakage. Symptoms of shell-thinning were also found in other marine species.

Oil the Pollutant

In 1966, 700 million tons of oil were shipped across the sea.[20] Of this amount, between 1 and 100 million tons entered the ocean through spillage and waste.[21] This amount is only three orders of magnitude less than the productivity of the sea. A loss on the order of a million gallons of oil, such as occurred in Santa Barbara, would represent an input into the sea of considerably less than 1% of the yearly input from all sources. A very spectacular local event was therefore but a small part of what is occurring on a worldwide basis continually through dumpings, accidents, and waste.

Production of petroleum and natural gas from the continental shelves now has a value of about $4 billion, representing about a fifth of the world's total production.[22] By 1980 the output from the ocean may increase by as much as four times.[23] The use of huge tankers to transport oil across the sea will further increase the chances of accident.

Oil spillages have an immediate and drastic effect on sea birds, but the long-term effects on other marine life are now impossible to predict. Oil is a complex mixture of compounds, some of which are readily degradable by the bacteria of the sea. Others are more persistent and may be changed into compounds that have biological action.

Like DDT and PCB, the hydrocarbons found in oil are poorly soluble in water and can be expected to enter biological systems and to be concentrated by food chains in the sea. 3,4–benzopyrene, a carcinogen to man, has been found in bottom sediment of the Mediterranean, and was presumably derived from waste oils.[20] A vast amount of research must now be begun in order to determine which of the compounds found in oil—or which of the derivatives of these compounds—enter biological systems in the sea, are accumulated in food chains, and exert a biological effect.

Abundant Carbon Dioxide

Not only is carbon dioxide a product of our own metabolic activities, but it is also formed when any of the conventional fuels—wood, coal, petroleum, natural gas—are burned. Coal, petroleum, and the other fossil fuels derive from vast amounts of plant and animal material that were once deposited in swamps, lakes, and seas during the history of our planet. A significant amount of carbon was therefore withdrawn from active circulation. During the photosynthetic process that produced this organic material, the oxygen that now sustains animal life on earth was released into the atmosphere. Today we are rapidly reversing this process in using oxygen to burn vast amounts of carbon-containing fuels that enter the atmosphere as carbon dioxide.

A certain amount of evidence indicates that the amount of carbon dioxide in the atmosphere is increasing as a result of the burning of the fossil fuels.[24] A significant increase would produce a warming effect on the planet, since the carbon dioxide tends to absorb the heat radiation emitted by the earth, heat radiation that would otherwise be lost in space. A greenhouse effect would develop. Precisely the opposite effect—colder climates—would result from an increasing amount of particulate material in the air. The particulate material, frequently conspicuous in the air over cities, is yet another waste product of our daily activities. These particles absorb incoming radiation, so that the earth receives less heat energy from the sun. It is by no means clear which process will eventually dominate.

Oxygen Production and Carbon Dioxide Storage

It is evident that nations like Canada and the Soviet Union must rely on imported oxygen over a large part of the year after photosynthesis stops in autumn. This has never posed much of a problem for these countries, since the global wind circulation distributes the oxygen produced by distant jungles and by the photoplankton of the sea.[25] Terrestrial and marine plants each contribute about half of the oxygen supply. The long-term future of our planet requires that neither source be damaged.

Pollutants may produce environmental effects that could never be predicted. The most conspicuous example in 1969 was the thin eggshells resulting from the DDT compounds in several species of birds. What else is now going on in the environment that will someday approach a critical level? In the year 2000 it will undoubtedly be said, "If we had only known in 1969 . . ." Release into the environment of large amounts of any persistent pollutant which has biological effects constitutes an experiment with unpredictable results. Some of the results of the experiment with the brown pelican are in.

The discovery that photosynthesis by marine phytoplankton could be impaired by one of the DDT compounds has aroused considerable popular interest.[26] Marine oxygen production is evidently one of the processes that should not be subject to experiment. It must be emphasized, however, that there are no reasons for fearing that oxygen production in the sea is threatened by any one of the DDT compounds. The effects on photosynthesis of the most abundant DDT compound—p,p′–DDE—have not yet been determined, but from a knowledge of the distributions of these compounds among the various components of a marine community we can confidently predict that concentrations will never reach the levels that produced the effects in the laboratory experiments. The global oxygen supply is not therefore threatened by DDT, but the possibility exists that in local areas where concentrations of the DDT compounds are high, the composition of the phytoplankton community could be adversely affected.

The sea also plays an important role as a reservoir of carbon dioxide. Many marine animals and some phytoplankton have shells or skeletons of calcium carbonate, of which the carbonate half is derived from dissolved carbon dioxide. The increase in atmospheric carbon dioxide[24] suggests that the rate of equilibration of carbon dioxide between air and sea is not sufficiently fast to remove the carbon dioxide from the air into the water as fast as it enters the air.

Other Pollutants

Large amounts of mercury and lead are released into the environment by industry and agriculture, and may have harmful effects on biological systems. In Japan a nervous disease among the residents of the Minimata Bay region was traced to the eating of fish and shellfish in which there was an accumulation of mercury.[27]

Other industrial chemicals, so far undetected, might also be pollutants that are present in significant quantities in the sea. To be of ecological significance, a potential pollutant would have to have several but not necessarily all, of the following characteristics: (1) It would have to be chemically relatively stable. (2) It would have to be nonpolar in nature; i.e., it would have to dissolve poorly in water but readily in fatlike materials. (3) It would have to have the capacity to be accumulated by organisms. (4) It would have to be mobile, moving from sites of application through air or water. (5) It would have to be biologically active. (6) World production would have to be in quantities greater than 10^{10} grams per year. Many plastics are now being produced in quantities of 10^{12} grams or more a year. Have some of their ingredients become pollutants?

A Small World

The high concentrations of both the DDT and PCB compounds in marine birds and fish suggest that the amounts of these materials in the biosphere constitute a biologically significant fraction of the total biomass. We have traditionally believed that Nature is vast. Our global environment is surely now more like Los Angeles than a jungle forest of Ecuador. When we look at estimates of waste material inputs into our atmosphere, the striking conclusion emerges that the total is close to the primary productivity figure, which has an order of magnitude of 10^{16} grams. A population of 30 billion, producing per capita as much waste material as the present American population, would put between two and three orders of magnitude more waste material into the environment, swamping the capacity of Nature to absorb them by at least one order of magnitude.

There is as yet no evidence that DDE, the principal DDT compound in the environment, is degraded to other compounds in the sea at any significant rate. At the present time there is no evidence that it degrades at all in the sea. If its half-life is nevertheless assumed to be about ten years, and since yearly production figures are about 10^{11} grams, the amount of DDE in the global environment would be on the order of 10^{12} grams, only four orders of magnitude less than the amount of primary production. We could therefore predict from a knowledge of the production figures and of the physical and chemical properties of the DDT compounds that marine organisms would be heavily contaminated. We might do the same with PCB, were not the production figures a trade secret.

The Sea A Garbage Pit?

The answer to this question must be a resounding "No!" Already we have reason to believe that increasing pollution could interfere with the utilization of food from the sea, and that fundamental ecological processes could be disturbed. Several species that have evolved on this planet with man are already facing extinction because of environmental pollution, and many more will follow. The handwriting on the wall could hardly be written in larger script.

Is pollution of the sea an inevitable result of the advance of technology? Not necessarily. Relatively minor shifts in technology to produce biodegradable waste products could reduce and eventually eliminate each instance of persistent pollution. A global commitment to create a technology that would produce only waste materials that can be recycled and used over and over again has now become essential. DDT is already becoming obsolete, as insects develop resistance and as better insecticides are discovered and developed. We have just become aware of the existence of PCB in the environment and do not as yet know what effects it has on biological systems. Surely substitutes with no environmental side effects could be found.

The technology that has produced the environmental degradation that we see today has developed rapidly—too rapidly to permit the inclusion of environmental values in the planning scheme. A new technology devoted to a recycling process is essential if man is to continue to breathe, live, and survive, but it would also permit the brown pelican to continue to flap and sail in long lines along our coasts, and the white herons to fish in lagoons.

And Population . . .

More people inevitably produce more pollution. The sea is clearly not the unlimited source of food some people have imagined. Let me repeat part of the resolution passed by the U.S. National Committee of the XIth International Botanical Congress in Seattle, Washington, in 1969:

> In spite of the progress which has been made in maintaining food resources to keep up with the world's increasing population, the members of the XI International Botanical Congress, conscious of their responsibility as biologists, consider that there is no solution to the final problem unless population control is achieved. Therefore we urge governments to adopt such policies, while at the same time ensuring an adequate standard of living for their people, particularly by encouraging increased food production commensurate with proper land use.[28]

An International Care

Like the radioactivity released by atomic explosions, DDT, PCB, other chlorinated hydrocarbons, and other waste materials travel across national boundaries and may exert effects thousands of miles from their respective sources. It is only realistic to anticipate that the problem will become much worse. It is not premature, therefore, to establish the machinery that might cope with it.

Research on the identity of pollutants, their movements through ecosystems, and their effects on organisms and on the total environment must be expanded and given high national priorities. Dissemination and distribution of the results and conclusions of this research to the member governments of the United Nations would be a natural extension of educational and scientific activities already carried out by UNESCO.

It has now become essential to monitor both the input and the accumulation of several pollutants in the global environment. Categories of recognized and potential pollutants might be established by international agreement. Production and use figures might then be submitted to UNESCO by the member governments for annual compilation, just as fishery and health statistics are compiled by the Food and Agricultural Organization and the World Health Organization. This would be an invaluable contribution to the scientific effort to keep track of such pollutants and to assign research priorities.

UNESCO might also make an invaluable contribution to the efforts being made to establish international monitoring programs to determine the extent to which the recognized pollutants are accumulating in the global environment. The existing national programs have looked at only very small segments of local ecosystems.

In its commitment to educational, scientific, and cultural values, UNESCO has already made a distinguished contribution to the cause of wildlife conservation. By supporting the efforts to reduce planetary pollution, it could make an invaluable contribution to the cause of preserving our total environment.

REFERENCES

1. W. K. Chapman, "Potential Resources of the Ocean," Van Camp Sea Food Company, Long Beach, Cal., 1965

2. J. H. Ryther, "Photosynthesis and Fish Production in the Sea," Science 166, 72–76 (1969)

3. FAO Yearbook of Fishery Statistics 25 (1967)

4. M. B. Schaefer, "The Potential Harvest of the Sea," *Trans. Am. Fish. Soc.* **94**, 123–128 (1965)

5. P. R. Ehrlich, *The Population Bomb,* New York: Ballantine Books, 1968

6. C. L. Rasmussen, "Man and His Food: 2000 A.D.," *Food Technology* **23**, 56–74 (1969)

7. S. J. Holt, "The Food Resources of the Ocean," *Sci. Am.* **221**, 178–194 (1969)

8. Monsanto Chemical Company, Technical Bulletin O/PL-306

9. S. Jensen, A. G. Johnels, M. Olsson, and G. Otterlind, "DDT and PCB in Marine Animals from Swedish Waters," *Nature* **224**, 247–250 (1969)

10. R. W. Risebrough, "Chlorinated Hydrocarbons in Marine Ecosystems," in *Chemical Fallout,* M. W. Miller and G. G. Berg, editors. Springfield, Ill.: C. C. Thomas, (1969)

11. R. W. Risebrough, R. Reiche, D. B. Peakall, S. G. Herman, and M. N. Kirven, "Polychlorinated Biphenyls in the Global Ecosystem," *Nature* **220**, 1098–1102 (1968)

12. R. W. Risebrough, J. D. Davis, F. Beland, J. Enderson, and R. Anastasia, "Polychlorinated Biphenyls in Mother's Milk," manuscript in preparation (1970)

13. J. H. Keoman, M. C. Ten Noever de Brauw, and R. H. De Vos, "Chlorinated Biphenyls in Fish, Mussels, and Birds from the River Rhine and the Netherlands Coastal Area," *Nature* **221**, 1126–1128 (1969)

14. R. W. Risebrough, D. B. Menzel, J. D. Martin, and H. S. Olcott, "DDT Residues in Pacific Marine Fish," manuscript in preparation, (1969)

15. J. J. Hickey and D. W. Anderson, "Chlorinated Hydrocarbons and Eggshell Changes in Raptorial and Fish-Eating Birds," *Science* **162**, 271–273 (1968)

16. R. D. Porter and S. N. Wiemeyer, "Dieldrin and DDT: Effects on Sparrow Hawk Eggshells and Reproduction," *Science* **165**, 199–200 (1969)

17. R. G. Heath, J. W. Spann, and J. F. Kreitzer, "Marked DDE Impairment of Mallard Duck Reproduction in Controlled Studies," *Nature* **224**, 47–48 (1969)

18. R. W. Risebrough, F. C. Sibley, and M. N. Kirven, unpublished observations

19. J. Jehl, unpublished observations; R. W. Risebrough, J. D. Davis, D. W. Anderson, R. W. Schreiber, and F. C. Sibley, unpublished observations

20. R. W. Holcomb, "Oil in the Ecosystem," *Science* **166**, 204–206 (1969)

21. M. Blumer, quoted in Holcomb (20)

22. K. O. Emery, "The Continental Shelves," *Sci. Am.* **221**, 107–122 (1969)

23. E. Wenk, "The Physical Resources of the Ocean," *Sci. Am.* **221,** 167–176 (1969)

24. B. Bolin and E. Eriksson, "Changes in the Carbon Dioxide Content of the Atmosphere and Sea Due to Fossil Fuel Consumption," in: *The Atmosphere and the Sea in Motion,* edited by B. Bolin. New York: The Rockefeller Institute Press, 1959

25. L. Cole, "Can the World be Saved?" *Bioscience* **18,** 679–684 (1968)

26. C. F. Wurster, Jr., "DDT Reduces Photosynthesis by Marine Phytoplankton," *Science* **159,** 1474–1475 (1968)

27. K. Irukayama, "The Pollution of Minamata Bay and Minamata Disease," *Advance Water Pollution Res.* **3,** 153–180 (1966)

28. H. G. Baker, letter in *Science* **166,** 312–313 (1969)

25

CONSERVATION OF OPEN SPACE

GORDON HARRISON

Here open space is defined, the multiple factors affecting it are described and realistic solutions are suggested. "The critical importance of open-space preservation may be that, as a community good, it is a measure of how much a community is in control of its own welfare." Harrison's experience is based on his role as a member of a foundation which is deluged with impossible requests for open-space aid.

Open space is undeveloped land that serves human needs with which buildings would interfere. Open space is a human resource and it is meaningful only in an obverse or complementary relationship to building. Open space is land that might be built upon but by choice is not.

Saving open space does not mean reserving land from use. It does not mean a hopeless rearguard action to try to save the country from the encroachments of the city. It means rather the recognition that open space lands are as integral to urban development as buildings and streets; a city is not fit for human habitation that does not provide space for such human needs as recreation, esthetic satisfaction, freedom from crowding, opportunities for quiet, and a modicum of privacy.

Viewed another way, open space is the context within which building takes place. A city may be land entirely covered with houses and shops, paved with concrete, in which there is nothing to look at and no place to play. Or it may be clusters of high density housing and business interspersed with parks, squares, places to stroll, to sit, to relax and expand. From that perspective open space is a community asset that should be provided by collective community action. An individual citizen may plan a shopping center and make it attractive or ugly, a boon or a curse to neighbors. But a city whose construction is left solely to individuals has to come out looking the way our cities look now: they reflect in planless chaos the anarchic processes by which they have been constructed.

Public authority is nothing more than the mechanism by which people can collectively satisfy their collective needs. The fact that we have so far done so badly in building our cities and suburbs, especially in ignoring the need for open space, means that people have so far not recognized their collective interest. Private efforts to save open space have therefore been very important. They do not and cannot substitute for public action. They do complement, educate, and goad governments in several effective ways.

Wealthy individuals and foundations may purchase land and donate it to the public for parks or nature reserves. This has been significant, from spectacular gifts such as the Rockefeller donations to the nation, to hundred of estates deeded to counties or municipalities or to private organizations who hold them in trust for the public. In the New York area a nonprofit group called the Open Space Institute for six years has been proselyting among local land-owners to persuade them to preserve their open-space lands and make them enduring assets to the community. But the opportunities to use private money to buy land and convey it to the public are closing down because of the prohibitive costs. The open space that would best serve a community is more often than not prime land for building.

Groups like the Nature Conservancy use interim purchase of lands to hold them for later public acquisition. Open space has been preserved by including it in a development plan from the beginning, by persuading a commercial developer that the resulting amenity values can return him extra profits. So-called planned unit development involving clusters of houses is a well-known device tried out with some economic success and some worthwhile gains in open space. Unfortunately, conditions favorable to holding open large areas are likely only on a relatively few "difficult" tracts that can be developed for relatively expensive housing.

One may also come in by the other door as a nonprofit group with the object of preserving open space by developing only so much of a given tract as is needed to defray the costs of the whole. But these private efforts can never amount to more than palliatives or prods. So far public authority has failed dismally to rise to the challenge. I mean not only that federal and state programs such as the open-space matching grants of HUD and Interior's Land and Water Conservation Fund have been regularly starved for appropriations. Also and perhaps more critically, localities still tend to regard open land as waste land and building of whatever character or place equivalent to growth. As always, politicians and bureaucrats lag behing public opinion. The record of popular approval of park and open-space bond issues in metropolitan areas suggests that there is a lively public appreciation of the need and a refreshingly realistic willingness to pay.

The two critical questions are how to get public action and what kinds of action are likely to be effective. William Whyte concludes that a variety of needs for many different political and economic situations requires a variety of responses, from the exercise of zoning to acquisition of fee rights.

As to the second question, I think the critical need now is not for fresh inventiveness in legal or fiscal gimmickry, but for local education and organization to get communities to act collectively. That is not easy. Firmly on guard against change is a mistaken but strongly held view of private property as monolithic and absolute. The current notion that land is a commodity to be freely owned and traded derives from the Western world's 19th century free-market economic system. Yet it has come to seem to many as derived from the charter of human nature if not from the divine constitution.

We need to be reminded that the ownership of land is not a single indivisible right. It is a bundle of rights each conferred by society, and protected by law. There are rights of use: to take produce, to occupy, and to build upon it. There are rights of exclusion: to prevent trespass, to fence, to charge rent. And finally there are rights of disposal. None of these rights is inalienable and all are more or less independent of each other. An owner may have the right to sell land without having the right to build on it or to build on it without the right to take the minerals beneath it. In fact, many of the rights in land are routinely restricted. Taxes limit financial gain; trespass may be modified by rights of way; zoning may restrict building, and so forth. Society confers rights in land in different mixes that accord to prevailing social needs and customs.

The flowering in our time of city and regional planning testifies that the community recognizes a material interest in how it looks and functions as a community. This interest, however, cannot be served without some kind of overview of the development process and some community control over it. Ironically, planning has been tolerated in this country because although it is quite meaningless without community authority to back it up, it has almost never had that backing. Plans have proliferated as exercises in rational piety, not as guides for action. Perhaps we collectively expiate our sin of exploitation of the land by turning now and then from the actual mess on the ground to our nicely organized dreams in the file cases. In that way we can have our greed and reason too.

What makes our situation new today and requires new constraints on the private uses of land is the three-headed cancer we call growth: more people, more money, and more technology. This synergistic trio has pushed us into a new world in which the old rules don't apply. One old rule that is not working is that each man should be free to do what he pleases with his own land. In our crowded communities there is now very little that one man can do to his property without materially impairing the freedom of his neighbor. Hence there is a growing need for the community to find which interests are common and mutual.

Open space will be provided in sufficient quantity and quality only in those communities that resolve to put such public need ahead of private profits and organize to do so. Whatever the method, society must first reassert the fact that land and the uses of land are the physical basis for community. It is therefore unreasonable and finally catastrophic for any community to surrender its right to order land use for those who live on it. If the physical basis of the community is anarchic, the community itself will be ungovernable, subject increasingly to violence and frustration. The critical importance of open space preservation may be that, as a community good, it is a measure of how much a community is in control of its own welfare.

26

AGRICULTURE, FORESTRY, AND WILDLANDS

CHARLES H. W. FOSTER

Dr. Foster defines policy to include objectives and attainment of objectives within a time framework. Then a direction is outlined: "... policy must be directed towards maintenance of ... options for an uncertain future." He speaks of monitoring quality, intense management, and public participation.

The determination of a national policy for agriculture, forestry and wildlands is a staggering assignment for any mortal! First, just what *is* national policy? I would submit the following in response to the question:

1. a set of objectives, sound in principle and acceptable in practice;

2. a program to attain these objectives derived from a known set of facts and a projected series of alternatives;

3. a time framework sensitive to the temporal but anticipatory of the eventual.

In short, the need is to know what we have, where we should be going, and how we are going to get there.

In the case of agriculture, the United States' 336 million acres of cropland currently support its 200 million citizens with seeming food and fiber to spare. Although total population has increased 32% since 1950, farm production has risen 42% during the same period of time. Of the nation's more than 600 million acres of potential cropland, barely half is now in agricultural usage. Discounting even further increases in yields through technological advances, the United States should suffer no major shortages of food and fiber at least to the turn of the century.

Despite our intensive agricultural development, one out of every three acres is still in forest growth. My own state of Massachusetts, for example, the third most densely populated state in the nation, is by proportion of land area in woodland more heavily forested than the states of Washington and Oregon!

More than 500 million acres nationally are currently classified as commercial forest land. Nearly three quarters is in private ownership. Disregarding regional and species imbalances, the net annual growth of timber exceeded our domestic production by almost 60% in 1962. Despite a projected need for some 17 billion cubic feet of timber products by 1980, annual forest "income" should supply these needs comfortably provided growing stock remains undepleted and forest management attains the desired intensities.

But there is more to a national land resource than mere commodity products. Undisturbed reserves of land can serve as havens for vanishing species, preserve samples of natural areas for scientific study, and furnish recreational opportunities for the increasingly harassed urban dweller. The need for a *quality* experience in human life is the essential mission of a third category, wildlands.

By the close of the celebrated Alaska Purchase in 1867, nearly 1.8 of the 2.3 billion U.S. continental acres had entered the public domain. National policy had enunciated two primary goals: the settlement of the west, and the raising of revenues for the new national government. Less than a century later, this extensive public domain had been eroded by land grants to a mere shadow of its former self. Half of the remaining 700 million acres lay in a single state, Alaska, and a full sixth of this land would be selected by the state for eventual sale to private parties.

Yet by 1964, Congress had determined that a reserve of wildlands, "an area where the earth and its community of life are untrammeled by man," was urgently needed. A national wilderness system, a national wild rivers program, and a network of national trails were authorized. Ironically, the intangible qualities of wildland entered the fabric of national policy only after much of the paramount wilderness has succumbed to civilization.

What then do these brief accounts tell us about national natural resources policy? Policy usually consists of conflicting or competitive objectives, program approaches that generally lack cohesion, and a sense of direction that rarely remains relevant over time.

If these factors continue to prevail, the central thrust of policy must be directed toward the maintenance of the maximum number of options for an uncertain future. Preserving the most productive lands, for example, through private initiative and action or, as a last resort, public ownership is one such example. Increased interlinkage of the world resources community, a fundamental goal of UNESCO, is yet another.

Some type of impact assessment process, with human environmental quality as its central theme, would seem another essential ingredient of national policy. Intergovernmental checks and balances, or a system of periodic overview by disinterested private citizens, would help countervail the impending holocaust of resource development consequences that many responsible scientists now predict.

Yet more intensive physical management of land and resources should not be ignored as a national goal if the finite commodity needs of the future are to be met. Energy requirements are doubling on the average every decade. Urban uses of land will require at least 10 million new acres by the year 1980. The nation's water consumption is predicted to increase at least 150% by the turn of the century. In addition to better management, our waste materials will have to be recycled back into productive use if these future needs are to be met.

Finally, a high degree of public participation in resource decision making should be the cornerstone of national policy. This would produce thoughtful and timely decisions on increasingly complex matters and insure the high degree of flexibility required to meet changing conditions in the future. In this regard, Pericles' admonition to his fellow Athenians more than two thousand years ago seems equally appropriate today: "We alone regard a man who takes no interest in public affairs, not as harmless, but as a useless character; and, if few of us are originators, we are all sound judges of a policy."

27

THE CONSERVATION OF FISH AND WILDLIFE
RICHARD D. TABER, RICHARD A. COOLEY, AND WILLIAM F. ROYCE

The wildlife inhabiting a parcel of land is a good measure of its health. Since man's survival is related to the land's quality, this measure should be heeded.

Recently I walked along Montana's Missouri River, a headwater for the Mississippi, and marvelled at the diverse life forms, including trout, blue-birds, and wild mountain sheep. A few days later I stood on the Mississippi Delta and was appalled at the oil-slicked, trash-laden brown waters. It was sad, but not surprising, to learn that Louisiana's state symbol, the pelican, is now extinct.

This brief survey deals with wild populations of animals—fish and wildlife—as a natural resource used by citizens of the United States, and the mechanisms through which this resource is administered and perpetuated.

The status of fish and wildlife as a natural resource is equivocal, since some species are abundant and important, some are abundant but unimportant, and others are so rare as to be almost extinct, with every shade of variation between these extremes. But since events may make the common rare, and the rare more abundant, we will take all fish and wildlife species together as a natural resource of at least potential significance.

We believe that there are four interrelated problems in the use of fish and wildlife as natural resources in the United States: ownership, habitat, cropping, and husbandry.

OWNERSHIP

Our present pattern of fish and wildlife ownership has its roots in the distant past, in the preliterate state of human culture when men were organized in bands and fish and wildlife constituted primary and essential resources. Generally, under such conditions, the band hunted or fished over a rather definite territory. This territory and the fish and wildlife to be found on it were considered to belong equally to the members of the band. This concept, that the resource was in common ownership, remained entrenched in human cultures in northern Europe even after the rise of agriculture.   As rulers grew stronger, they claimed ownership of *ferae naturae*, and enforced this claim forcibly against the common man's tendency to act as though fish and wildlife were still a common resource.

As human populations increased, with attendant pressures on wildlife habitat, there was also a gradual development of the concept that those who owned land were rightfully the owners of the fish and wildlife that sheltered upon it. In England, for example, the lawyers would argue thus:

> . . . a wild animal is practically the property of no one, though theoretically it may be deemed that of the crown; but when any individual exercises the right of ownership over it by curtailing its natural freedom, supplementing its food supply, or protecting it from the ravages of its natural foes, he establishes a title to it which converts it into more or less of a domestic creature.*

These sentiments found no great sympathy among the common folk, who kept right on taking fish and wildlife when they could get away with it, in spite of penalties designed to chill their blood. This difference of opinion between the privileged and the common classes naturally became a political issue.   When Wat Tyler led a rebellion of English peasants in 1381, for example, he

> . . . insisted on the total repeal of the forest and game laws. All warrens, woods, waters, and parks were to be common, and the poor as well as the rich were to have rights of venison, vert, piscary, and hawking.*

They hung him, of course, but these demands reflect the conviction that fish and wildlife are, or should be, common property.

When King George reigned over the original thirteen colonies, he claimed a sovereign right over the fish and wildlife in his domain, and in some of the southern colonies there were real efforts to tie the right to use these resources to land ownership. But when these same colonies had successfully broken away from British dominion, each colony took unto its citizens the former sovereign rights of the King, and fish and wildlife came to be owned in common, once again, by the citizens of the state where they were found.

---

*   Russel M. Garnier, *Annals of British Peasantry.* Swan Sonnenschein & Co., London, 1895.

As each new state was added to the United States, this same legal provision was repeated, and so it stands today—the citizens of each state own in common all fish and wildlife residing in that state.

This public ownership of the fish and wildlife resources becomes private ownership when some private person gains possession of the animals. With a virgin continent before him, the American went with a characteristic zest into the business of turning this public property to his private account. As settlers increased, as railway lines were pushed across the country, as firearms became more efficient, and as markets grew in the industrial cities, the exploitation of fish and wildlife for commercial profit intensified. The decades following the Civil War saw a rapidly mounting pressure on these resources, both by the widespread population existing on subsistence agriculture and by commercial hunters. The tremendous fish and wildlife wealth of the new continent could not stand this strain, and most of the exploited species went into a sharp decline. Law upon law was passed to provide protection, but since these were not enforced, the pressure on the resource grew.

By the 1880's the buffalo were almost gone, by the 90's the passenger pigeon was virtually extinct, and many other exploited animals were in similar straits.

Shortly after the turn of the century a wave of reaction from uncontrolled exploitation permitted the establishment of an effective system of administration for fish and wildlife resources.

On the level of state government, the sportsmen were for the first time charged a fee for the hunting or fishing license. This provided a source of earmarked revenue for the state departments of fish and game. One consequence was that funds were now available to hire full-time officers to enforce protective regulations. These regulations had two main aims—to prevent over-harvesting, and to equalize opportunity among the harvesters. Another consequence was that the sportsmen came to act as stock-holders in a corporation. Since the sportsman paid the cost, fish and wildlife resources should be managed for his benefit. And since state departments of fish and game were dependent for income on license sales, they were quite responsive to the sportsmen, devoting their attention primarily to those species of interest to sportsmen, and to the preservation and increase of the sportsmen themselves. Meanwhile, the citizens of each state, legal owners of all the free living fish and wildlife in the state, support this resource with virtually nothing from the general funds.

As part of the protection provided for the sportsmen, most species of game fish and wildlife were removed entirely from commercial markets.

Commercial fishing was regulated separately. But even here the thrust of the regulations was the same—to prevent over-harvesting and to equalize opportunity among the harvesters.

The administration by state departments of fish and game, described above, is only partially effective as a means of administering fish and wildlife resources. There is little interest in the multitude of species which are not important for game or commerce. There is little interest in the control of pest situations involving fish and wildlife. There is no effective means for dealing with populations which pass in migration from state to state, or nation to nation, or which are found in international waters. All of these aspects of administration of the fish and wildlife resource, which were largely excluded from the conservation activities of the states, were gradually taken over by the federal government.

These federal activities have been supported partly from the sportsmen—through taxes on sporting equipment, through the "duck stamp," and partly through general appropriations. The federal fish and wildlife conservation structure, then, is not tied quite so tightly to the sportsman's interest as is the state.

HABITAT

Fish and wildlife populations, when reduced, will rapidly increase again to fill their habitat. But habitats can change and become less suitable for animal species, which thereupon decline.

There has been an ever-increasing spectrum and intensity of uses by man of the lands and waters of the North American continent. These uses have changed fish and wildlife habitat, often for the worse.

On any particular piece of the landscape, there will be some use which will yield a tangible and immediate reward to a definite group of human beings. At the same time, its value as fish or wildlife habitat is spread over an indefinite period of time during which it will yield fish and wildlife benefits of unknown magnitude to the citizens as a whole, present and future.

Privately owned land is private property. Wildlife living on that land, in the United States, is public property. Access to this public property—that is, to the wild animals—might be considered a common right of ownership—that is, of citizenship.

The land owner, though theoretically protected by trespass laws, is in reality faced with an army of sportsmen and a state agency devoted to the welfare of these sportsmen. The effects are several. The landowner is inhibited by his own cultural attitudes from charging fees for use of his lands by sportsmen; and state government has long reinforced this cultural inhibition by promoting free use.

The results are clear: the land owner makes his land management decisions with little regard for fish and wildlife. Since these do not provide him with any income, they are not part of his profit-making decisions. Considerations far removed from the perpetuation of the fish and wildlife resource are fed into his calculations. His fields become larger as more powerful farm implements become available to him; irregularities and obstructions are eliminated from his fields; he no longer needs a woodlot for fuel and posts; weeding and insect control through pesticides are suited to his increasingly mechanical system of husbandry. As a result of these improvements in the efficiency of agriculture the quality of wildlife habitat, and consequently population of wildlife, declines.

To date all the efforts made in the United States to overcome the consequences of this system—mainly through the purchase and management of wildlife lands and the improvement of wildlife habitat on private lands with state funds—have failed to counterbalance the steady deterioration of wildlife habitat on private lands. Consequently the states, in licensing hunters, are selling them the right to pursue an ever-dwindling resource. Hunters resist governmental efforts to charge more for this scarce resource, and eventually some of them give up these sports altogether. The result is that the state has, at best, a static income from sportsmen, with no prospects for this income to increase. If this trend continues, the services offered by the state can only decline.

There is one exception to this general pattern which provides some food for thought. The State of Texas has exceptionally rigorous trespass laws, and little public land. This has permitted the land owner to charge fees for entry to hunt. The wildlife resource upon his land has thus become a source of revenue for him. The consequence is that many Texas landowners protect and improve wildlife habitat as part of their overall business-management plan. The actual changes in land-management practices which would enhance rather than destroy wildlife habitat are often not difficult or expensive to achieve, so the landowner has the potential to realize a rather good return upon his managerial investment in wildlife resource.

The lesson is clear. If the wildlife resource means income to the landowner, he will consider it along with his other sources of income. And although the sportsman is reluctant to pay the state substantial fees, he will, if necessary, pay the landowner.

A different pattern has emerged for most of the fish habitat. A major part of the sport fishery has always been pursued in the public waters of the sea, the estuaries, the large rivers, and the lakes. Recently a large expansion of the public fish habitat has occurred in the multipurpose reservoirs that are being built in all sections of the country. But even though habitat and fish are both clearly under public control, other uses of the water create problems.

Of increasing importance is the problem of pollution. Pollution has many forms, among which we instantly think of waste materials dumped into waters, pesticides widely spread through all our ecosystems, and the results of such industrial accidents as oil or chemical spills. These are private acts diminishing public values. If there were clear evidence of the responsibility for these acts and their detailed effects upon fish and wildlife biology, and if we knew the resultant losses in public property, the effective remedies, and their costs—if we had knowledge of all of these things the problem would be largely solved, because the polluters could be held financially responsible for their acts. But the polluters and their pollutants are many, the effects of pollution are often subtle and only partially understood, and remedies, if such exist, are not yet found.

Finally, fish and wildlife habitats are suffering from the massive ecological changes connected with our expanding population with its even more rapidly expanding demands for space and power. Everywhere we turn marshes are being filled, streams are being straightened, estuaries are being dredged, strip-mines are operating, suburbia is spreading into the forest, and new highways, new dams, and new subdivisions are on the drawing board. Losses of wild animals are sometimes spectacular, as in the case of the migratory fish of the Columbia or the resident wildlife of the Everglades. Even more important, on a continental scale one can see the summation of the many small changes continually going forward—particularly changes in streams, which are becoming increasingly channelized, with a greater high-low water differential, and small ponds and marshes, which are continually being filled to provide a base for construction. These losses are greater than the gains, and we have a problem. Solution lies in a realistic evaluation of both the gains and the losses. Our ability to evaluate fish and wildlife resources, particularly in any terms other than pounds of meat or quantity of furs, is still rudimentary.

CROPPING

There are values in fish and wildlife resources alive and free, and there are values in harvesting an annual crop. The magnitude of this crop must obviously be controlled if excessive exploitation is to be avoided. Controlling the magnitude of the crop is one major objective in administration of fish and wildlife resources. At the same time, it will be recalled, we here in the United States strive for maximum participation in the cropping process, and equality of opportunity among the participants. Both state and federal administrators, then, are forced to control cropping by indirect means, through regulation of seasons and equipment. The present wide participation in fish and wildlife cropping, described above, does not lend itself well to attaining a close control over cropping magnitude.

It would not be far from the truth to say that a goodly share of the time of fish and wildlife conservation agencies is devoted to determining what the annual crop should be, and tinkering around with the regulations to achieve a harvest which approximates, but does not exceed, this allowable crop. The tendency, since control is uncertain, is to err on the conservative side, and under-crop. This is often of little practical consequence, but under certain circumstances it leads to trouble. Principal among these is the case in which there is some population of fish or wildlife which is involved in a pest situation. The population, often, should be reduced. However, the species involved is usually dear to the heart of some group of consumers. One familiar example is the great increase in populations of white-tailed deer over the past half-century, the damage often done by excessively heavy populations to forest and farm crops, and the public resistance to effective measures for deer population control. There has been similar opposition to needed control of many other populations of native animals.

This focus on harvesting an annual crop by the regulatory agencies, and saving the lives of individual animals by the sympathetic public, tends to distract attention from the need for fish and wildlife husbandry: the protection, maintenance, and enhancement of this renewable resource.

HUSBANDRY

Fish and wildlife resources can be husbanded most successfully if the habitat is controlled.

There are two sorts of lands or waters on which fish and wildlife husbandry is seriously attempted. One consists of publicly owned landscape units such as major waters and national forest and range lands. The other consists of those relatively small units of private land on which fish and wildlife are intensively managed for private benefit. Over most of our private lands and waters, which cover the most productive regions of the United States, husbandry of fish and wildlife resources is minimal, to say the least.

In the case of the many species of fish and wildlife which are adapted to life on publicly owned lands (usually forest, range and recreational lands) minor adjustments in management can perpetuate at least fair habitat. Then there are the species of fish and wildlife which have habitat requirements which are not met in this way; the numerous species of waterbirds provide a good example. For these there must be special habitat preserved, or else created and maintained. Since our system has discouraged us from attempting to preserve habitat on private lands, we have left ourselves with only one alternative; buy up the needed lands with public money and manage them to provide habitat for those species which would otherwise have none.

One result of this policy is our national system of waterfowl refuges. Another is our system of sanctuaries for species threatened with extinction.

But the national system of waterfowl refuges is only half established because of a shortage of funds, and as more and more species become threatened with extinction, can we expect to obtain larger and larger sums of money to establish sanctuaries for them?

The prospects of accommodating all the fish resources we would like to have in the United States in public waters seem reasonably good. The prospects of accommodating all the wildlife resources we would like to have in the United States on public lands seem poor indeed.

RECOMMENDATIONS

From this review of the administration of fish and wildlife resources in the United States, we can draw the following conclusions

1. The state departments of fish and game need a broader base of responsibility and the appropriate public funding to free them from their present dependence on the sportsmen.

2. Both state and federal fish and wildlife resource agencies need a substantial increase in research support and improved means of feeding research findings into husbandry.

3. Means should be devised to reverse the deterioration of wildlife habitat on private lands, probably through income from the sportsman to the landowner for this service.

4. Pollution of fish and wildlife habitats should be fought at both state and federal levels with increased research funding and more effective regulation.

5. Although this brief review has been intentionally limited to the United States, it must be recognized that the problems of ownership, habitat, cropping, and husbandry present serious international complications. These can be expected to greatly intensify in the years ahead, and their equitable resolution will require much more effective international cooperation and control than presently exists.

6. Finally, and most important, none of these recommendations will be practical if we continue to pack more and more of mankind and his works into the landscape of North America. The control of human populations is the first necessity if the multitude of populations of other forms of life is to survive.

28

MINERAL RESOURCES AND HUMAN ECOLOGY

RICHARD H. JAHNS

Mineral resources, iron ore, and coal aren't renewable as are forests that yield a new crop. So the gentle philosophy associated with growing things is rare in the mineral field. Dollars torn from land left harsh and infertile have been an American tradition. The following ecologically sensitive statement fortunately suggests that that tradition is passing.

To judge from the principal thrusts of this conference, we are in serious, even deadly, trouble with many elements of our environment. And what thoughtful person could disagree? Our vast earth, we are beginning more to appreciate, is essentially a closed system in many important respects, and some of its inescapable limitations are now beginning to attract the kinds of attention they should have received long ago. That natural resources, for example, cannot be expected to accommodate endless or mindless uses by man is a hard and basic fact of life. Perhaps this message has not been fully understood by those either preoccupied with "conquering nature" or unconcerned about the future of their own species, but it is coming through in stronger and stronger terms as the demands of a burgeoning population draw ever more heavily upon some of our resources and lead to alarming deterioration of others.

This country is properly reckoned as affluent in terms of current abundance, riches, gross national product, and standard of living. The considerable costs for achieving so pleasant a state of affairs have been offset in substantial measure by benefits gained, but we cannot ignore a critical residue that promises to grow with time. This debit can be put in the form of two general questions for the future: (1) For how long and by what means can we satisfy our demands for nonrenewable resources? (2) In the context of such demands, can we learn to live harmoniously within the boundary conditions of our natural system rather than assaulting its constraints in tragic tests of their reality? These questions are fundamentally interlocked, and favorable responses to both must be realized if the earth is to remain a reasonably decent place for human residence. Further, it should be self-evident by now that the very best of long-term responses may turn out to be little more than exercises in futility unless real progress is made toward effective control of human population during the next two decades.

Problems of mineral supply have repeatedly drawn the attention of experts, particularly during wartime periods of intensified industrial production and waste, and their careful analyses have ranged in tone from cautiously optimistic to deeply gloomy. Such nonrenewable resources as mineral fuels, metals, and industrial minerals and rocks must be of grave concern to all of us, as pointed out in this Conference by Orlo Childs; some of them already are in seriously short supply, and known reserves of others will be exhausted within two or three decades. Common sense dictates that sharpened efforts be directed toward discovery of additional sources, development of satisfactory substitutes, and general improvement in mineral-management policies. For these tasks we shall need the interest and the talents of many more qualified people than appear on the horizon at the present time.

Man already has demonstrated high degrees of ingenuity and dedication in finding new mineral deposits, in extracting desirable substances from leaner and leaner ground, in processing raw materials with increasing efficiency, and in reusing many kinds of scarce commodities. He can be expected to improve upon these performances—indeed, he will have to! Undoubtedly he will move into many areas not long ago considered inaccessible, including the ocean floors, and he also will learn to process commercially some of the earth's more common rocks in substitution for richer mineral concentrations no longer available. Yet the sum of all moves he can make must have its ultimate limitations. In the words of the National Academy of Sciences, National Research Council Committee on Resources and Man, "If population and demand level off at some reasonable plateau, and if resources are used wisely, industrial society can endure for centuries or perhaps millennia. But technological and economic brilliance alone cannot create the essential raw materials whose enhancement in value through beneficiation, fabrication, and exchange constitutes the basic material fabric of such a society."

If man has been ingenious and dedicated in winning useful substances from the ground, he also has made some terrible mistakes. His efforts have left a growing legacy of scarred slopes and debris-filled valleys, soils no longer capable of sustaining plant life, burning coal mines and waste piles, chemically polluted surface and subsurface waters, caving or subsiding ground that is unsafe to build upon, and air that is a challenge to breathe. Too often the process of extraction seemingly has reflected a "get in, get it out, and get out" philosophy, with the natural environment emerging as the big loser.

It is true that nature often struggles back, and that the surface disfigurations of many abandoned mine workings have now become so overgrown with vegetation within a few decades that they are all but obliterated from view. But the process can be agonizingly slow in other areas, such as the southwestern desert, where a single wheel track may be clearly preserved for half a century or more. And for how many generations will the hills remain bare from past effects of copper smelting at Ducktown, Tennessee? Or lengthy reaches of acid-laden streams in Pennsylvania remain free of trout? These and other undesirable environmental changes may well be with us for a long, long time, and a few of the least pleasant ones could reflect processes that for all practical purposes are irreversible.

To mourn such examples of unfortunate mistakes is hardly enough to repair them or to forestall future occurrences, nor is it proper to level blanket accusations of reprehensible behavior at the mineral-producing industries. Not only must we all share parts of the blame with each individual or company engaged in fouling our natural system, but we also must look with imagination, vigor, and reason for avenues to solution of the problem. Sensitivity to deleterious environmental effects already has been shown in many ways by industrial organizations, and a great deal of money has been put on the line. Actions have ranged from the elimination of stack pollution at smelters to the planting of trees on tailings piles for dust abatement, and from control of subsiding ground to general rehabilitation of strip-mine areas. Whether or not such efforts have been made in terms of "enlightened self-interest," it should be noted that the basic problem is one of dollars and cents in highly competitive situations, and that where no applicable governmental regulations have been in force, conservation often has come out second best.

Increasing public awareness of the need for improved environmental control has been long overdue, and the hour already is very late. Many of those engaged in supplying the resources demanded by this same public share much of the same concern, but to date there has been little meeting of the minds. Public statements have been characterized more by recriminations than by thoughtful proposals, and private discussions more by heat than by light. Too little effort has been aimed at joint solutions of the basic technical and financial problems as various protagonists have struggled along lines seemingly dictated by their respective kinds of tunnel vision. Thus a concerned citizen may insist upon foreclosing a producer activity without evident interest in consequences or alternatives, and a producer, with equal vigor, may insist upon his established legal rights with little or no regard to side effects of his activity.

What can be done about this dilemma? Here I must admit to sharing the faith expressed by Stephen Spurr in the principle of the cost-benefit ratio. Even though some of its past applications have reflected improper assumptions, incomplete input, or questionable motivation, we cannot afford to abandon this principle in favor of concepts that do not include all pertinent factors. It stands as the ultimate practical necessity for wise decision-making in areas that involve mineral resources and human ecology. Markedly differing kinds of costs and values must be assessed, to be sure, but isn't this really the name of the game? It will be formidably difficult to appraise and compare the entries in each column, for the long term and for all areas and peoples concerned, but in what other way can the present confusion of purposes and interests be resolved?

For a running start, we need a complete inventory of mineral resources, known and inferred, and corresponding inventories of all other significant elements of our natural environment. Here much of great value already has been done by the U. S. Department of the Interior, and there are encouraging indications that much more is to follow soon. As these appraisals grow more complete, it should be possible to achieve better match-ups among competing factors. Thus some ground of relatively low mineral potential could be given high priority for designation as wilderness areas, military reserves with mineral promise could be opened to prospecting, and producing facilities could be designed more in harmony with their physical situation.

Futher basic research on the interplay of production activities and the complex natural processes of the environment also will be necessary for wise cost-benefit analyses and "best-use" decisions. Right now there is much too much that we simply don't know. What environmental standards should be adopted? What shifts in producing, trading, and use-patterns should be encouraged or mandated? What incentives can be offered to industry for making improvements identified as desirable or necessary? To what extent are we all willing to trim our environmental demands, or our demands for mineral resources? In what ways will we *have* to?

These are questions for which we must have complete answers, answers that will be very expensive to obtain and to translate into action. I suggest that we should be willing to put some of our monies where our mouths are, and that we should continuingly insist upon decisions deriving from sound, objective analyses. We have much going for us, perhaps more than we realize, in terms of lessons already learned. If we start putting the puzzle together, with what I am convinced can be the solid and enthusiastic help of our deeply concerned young people, we shall be well on our way. We cannot expect instant answers, but, in the words of Preston Cloud, "The goal should be to avert the thoughtless foreclosure of options."

29

QUALITY MANAGEMENT OF OUR AIR ENVIRONMENT

ROLF ELIASSEN

One suggestion voiced by Dr. Eliassen and others at the Conference was that we create new cities with logical bases. At present, we tend illogically to juggle resources to fit political pressures: bringing water to accommodate a larger Los Angeles when the city is already out of air.

"Quality management of our air is feasible . . . but we have a long way to go before we can achieve successful management."

Urbanization is taking place at an alarming rate all over the world. At the beginning of the 21st century the United States will be an overwhelmingly urbanized society, with over 75% of its population of about 340 million living in metropolitan areas. In order to be able to live under these conditions, control of the pollution of the air–water–land environment is an essential feature of the natural-resource management policies of all levels of government.

Dr. Lee A. DuBridge, Science Adviser to President Nixon, has stated the basic policy for management of our air–water–land environment: "To ask human beings to stop altering their environment or using it, would be to ask them to cease living. Human beings evolved because of the earth's environment, they live off the environment, and in living they inevitably change it. The question, therefore, is not how shall we cease to use or change our environment, but how can we avoid despoiling and degrading it, and how can we reverse those habits and procedures which now contaminate our air, our water, and our landscape."

The Air Environment

Air pollution is considered one of the most serious threats to man's environment. Air knows no state or national boundary, nor can the effects of contaminated air be limited to the source itself. People must breathe the mixture of air as it comes to them—35 pounds for the average person each day. Into the air over the United States is being poured over 200 million tons of pollutants each year from motor vehicles, industries, power plants, the heating of buildings, and the burning of solid wastes. And the amount is increasing each year at an alarming rate! Physical, chemical, and biological damages from air pollution lead to social costs measured in billions of dollars yearly. Damage to agriculture, to structures and materials, the obscuration of sunlight and other esthetic effects, and the shortening of the life-span of man through emphysema, bronchitis, lung cancer and other diseases should be signals to the populace that constructive action must be taken on a national scale.

Former President Johnson suggested a path to a resource management policy when he declared: "Air pollution is the inevitable consequence of neglect. It *can* be controlled when that neglect is no longer tolerated. It *will* be controlled when the people of America, through their elected representatives, *demand* the right to air that they and their children can breathe without fear."

Current Air Pollution Control Legislation

The Congress has reacted to the demands of citizens and political leaders.

Senator Edmund S. Muskie, Chairman of the Senate Subcommittee on Air and Water Pollution, was one of the principal sponsors of the Air Quality Act of 1967. In his words: "The federal government supplies leadership and creative resources, as well as research finding . . . . Federal law provides a framework around which the states can organize their pollution control efforts and mechanisms by which their goals can be implemented."

The Air Quality Act provides for matching-grants to state and local control agencies. This has permitted an increase in air pollution control budgets of state, local and regional agencies from $9.3 million in 1961 to $47.3 million in 1969. About 43% of the latter represented federal funds, indicating the increased financial support from nonfederal agencies. Other funds are allotted for research and development aimed at achieving more effective control processes for many sources of pollution. This includes assistance in financing cooperative research projects on the part of industry and government.

In the field of actual management of air resources by control and regulatory agencies, the Department of Health, Education, and Welfare has been given the authority to designate specific air quality control regions in those areas of the country where air pollution constitutes a serious threat to health and welfare. A total of 57 air quality control regions has been established to incorporate areas which involve most of the urban populations of the 50 states.

Dr. John T. Middleton, Commissioner of the National Air Pollution Control Administration of the Consumer Protection and Environmental Health Service of the Department of HEW, has stated that "these regions will be designated on the basis of factors which suggest that a group of communities should be treated as a unit for the purpose of setting and implementing *air quality standards*. Factors to be considered include meteorological, topographical, social, and political considerations, jurisdictional boundaries, the extent of urban-industrial concentrations, and the nature and location of air pollution sources."

The National Air Pollution Control Administration is responsible for the development of air pollution *criteria*—the degree to which each pollutant will be injurious to health or property, and the techniques available for preventing and controlling their emission to the environment. Criteria for two major pollutants, particulate matter and sulfur oxides, have already been developed. Many more criteria are under consideration. As these are published, the individual states in the various regions will develop air quality *standards* and plan for their achievement and enforcement. Public hearings will emphasize air quality goals for the protection of public health, the current status of atmospheric contamination in a region, and the need for enhancement of air quality. Citizens, industries and municipalities will thus have a voice in establishing air quality standards and in determining a time schedule for their achievement. These standards will then be subject to review and approval by the U.S. Department of HEW.

Pending Legislation

Legislation for a National Environmental Policy Act was introduced into the 91st Congress in 1969 by Senator Henry M. Jackson and all of his colleagues on the Senate Interior and Insular Affairs Committee. S. 1075 is entitled "A bill to establish a national policy for the environment; to authorize studies, surveys, and research relating to systems, natural resources, and the quality of the human environment; and to establish a Board of Environmental Quality Advisers." As of September 23, 1969, both the Senate and House had passed versions of this bill and the differences in the two bills were to be resolved in a conference committee.

The Environmental Quality Council is composed of three members appointed by the President and serves in the Executive Office of the President. A staff serves with the Council. Section 302 of the Act states that "(a) the primary function of the Boa ᵈ shall be to study and analyze environmental trends and the factors that affect these trends, relating each area of study and analysis to the conservation, social, economic, and health goals of the Nation; (b) the Board shall periodically review and appraise Federal programs, projects, activities, and policies which affect the quality of the environment and make recommendations thereon to the President; and (c) it shall be the duty and function of the board to assist and advise the President in the preparation of the annual environmental quality report . . . to the Congress."

Progress in the State and Local Agencies

When the Clean Air Act of 1967 was enacted, half of the states were lacking in air pollution control authorities. At the beginning of 1969, 46 states had passed air pollution control laws, with the others to follow soon. Earlier laws have also been strengthened. The degrees of adoption of regulations and the types of regulations for combustion processes, industrial plants, space heating, and motor vehicles vary greatly from state to state. Regulations on visible emissions have been adopted by 22 states. However, an average of 90% of air pollution is from invisible emissions; regulation of these will take a longer time. Many are based on criteria and standards not yet promulgated.

Over 100 local and regional air pollution control agencies have been formed. Some, like the Los Angeles Air Pollution Control District, have been effective for many years. Others will await the promotion of their activities in the 57 newly established air quality control regions. There is hope for progress in combatting air pollution and this hope lies with local and regional air resource management boards, supported by state and Federal funds and activities, both cooperative and regulatory.

Some Factors in the Future

It must be emphasized that although the industries, utilities and municipalities have already spent many billions of dollars for air pollution control, progress is not fast enough. Former President Johnson emphasized this in a special message to Congress in 1967 when he said: "We are not even controlling today's level of pollution. Ten years from now, when industrial production and waste disposal have increased and the number of automobiles on our streets and highways exceeds 110 million, we will have lost the battle for clean air unless we strengthen our research and regulatory activities now."

Many other factors enter into the control of air pollution. Automotive engines must be redesigned as these are the principal cause of smog in many areas. Other sessions of this conference will stress the need for birth control. The increase of air pollution is an exponential function of population growth. So is expansion of the power industry. Total electric generating capacity in the United States in 1969 is close to 300 million kilowatts. In the year 2000, it will have increased more than five times to approximately 1600 million kilowatts. The Joint Committee on Atomic Energy of the U.S. Congress has published an estimate of $5\frac{1}{2}$ billion tons of carbon dioxide and 9 billion tons of oxides of sulfur to be discharged in the year 2000 if all of this power were generated in fossil fuel plants. We cannot afford this atmospheric insult. Therefore, it behooves conservationists to encourage the use of nuclear power plants which discharge less bio-effective radioactivity than coal-fired plants because of the radioactivity in coal. If half of the 1600 million kilowatts of generating capacity in the year 2000 were in nuclear plants, air pollution from the oxides of carbon and sulfur could be cut in half. Conservationists have a great role to play in persuading power companies, and so many other industries, to consider all alternatives in order that an optimum quality of the air environment may be achieved.

A Broader Perspective

Consideration of resource constraints must govern the decision-making of the physical, economic, social, and political planners of urban areas. Air is not limitless in real time. Therefore, the population capacity of any particular air quality region is not limitless; the numbers of people must be controlled. To be specific: there is not enough air for all of the people and their associated activities in the Los Angeles Basin now. How can the current population be reduced to match the ecological constraints placed upon them by limited air resources? This raises the question of a natural resources management policy, which is difficult to achieve in a democracy.

Water may be the key to population control in specific areas where it is a limiting resource, as in Southern California. However, civil engineers have built structures and facilities to transport water many hundreds of miles from the Owens River Valley, the Colorado River, and now from far up in Northern California so that more industries could support more people in the Los Angeles Basin. A more rational approach to planning for living in a limited air environment would have been to restrict the development of new water supplies and thus restrict population. Who would have the courage to do this?

Demographers are predicting that four immense metropolitan regions will exist by the year 2000, the outgrowth and coalescence of cities along the North Atlantic Seaboard, the Lower Great Lakes, Florida, and California. It is further predicted that although these regions will occupy only 7 to 8% of the land area of the United States, 60% of the population—about 200 million people—will be living in these megalopolitan areas. Surely there must be a choice for the future to live somewhere else than Megalopolis!

The answer lies in the creation of *new cities* away from current metropolitan centers. These cities must take into account the availability of adequate air resources and provide policies for the management of all natural resources. Many political, economic, social and land-planning problems could be solved by modern computer-based design-making principles such as operations research and systems analysis. It would be necessary for state and federal governments to aid in the conception, planning, financing and construction of these new cities, and in providing for water, transportation, and other utilities. Private industry should be encouraged to establish research, production, and commercial facilities in order to create employment for the residents. Many other features such as providing for educational and cultural centers, recreation facilities, and the other intangibles which make up the "good life" must be included in the planning of these new cities. This includes the control of all sources of air pollution—from industry, commerce, transportation, municipal, and residential activities.

As one flies from San Francisco to Chicago, he observes very little habitation for 2,000 miles. Vast areas of land are available for the potential development of new cities. Of course, there are deserts, but cities on the desert are more than a remote possibility. Look at Las Vegas—a small railroad town only 30 years ago. Look at Tucson and Phoenix! The consulting civil engineer can provide water anywhere—at a price—and also transportation and other necessities for urban development. Engineers talk about transporting excess water from the Columbia River to the Colorado River so that the Southwest can support more people. Would it not be wiser to establish new cities in Oregon and Washington and thus move the people to where the water is, and where there are adequate resources of air and land? The Texas Water Plan, recently turned down by the voters, contemplates taking water from the Mississippi River and transporting it to the megalopolitan complex of Dallas–Ft. Worth–Houston. Would it not be wiser to use this water in the Mississippi Valley, to build new cities and industries in Alabama, Louisiana, and Mississippi and thus put a halt to the migration of their present rural inhabitants to the slums of so many over-populated and impoverished cities in the Northeast, Midwest, and Southwest?

These are questions which must be asked—and answered—in the rational development of a natural resources management policy for a nation. This applies not only to the United States, but to so many countries of South America where new cities are desperately needed, and to other countries as well.

Conclusions

Quality management of our air environment is feasible. Control legislation is being enacted at all levels of government in the United States. The technology of air pollution control is well established and is being developed to a higher degree through cooperative industrial–government research. The public must be willing to pay the price; they must continue pressure on their elected governmental officials; they must learn to adopt new industrial processes and modes of transportation which engineers can design to reduce air pollution; they must learn to control their own numbers and to build new cities within the constraints of the air–water–land environment. The resources of the earth are not limitless; natural resources in some areas of this country have been used to excess; others not enough. There is hope in this country as natural resource management policies are being developed on a rational basis. But we have a long way to go before we can achieve successful management of our air environment.

30

THE ATMOSPHERE

THOMAS F. MALONE

Weather prediction, planned modification, unplanned modification (CO_2 and greenhouse effect are an example), dangers of air pollution, and research needs are some subjects discussed. Survival will require international cooperation. Smog-laden winds from Los Angeles polluting Arizona today are a domestic problem. Tomorrow the problem can become an international one, for these winds may deposit Asia's industrial pollutants on Los Angeles.

A PERSPECTIVE

The solar system had its origin some 10 billion years ago. Spaceship Earth first appeared about 5 billion years ago. Life originated about 3 billion years ago and evidence of human life goes back at least 3 million years. Modern man emerged between 50 to 100 thousand years ago. It should be possible—barring man-made catastrophes—to sustain life on our planet for at least 3 million more years.

In short, we are about half way "there"—if we survive.

Earth was probably without a primordial atmosphere and what we now think of as "the broth of life" surrounding our planet rose from secondary sources such as local heating, volcanic action, and photochemical processes.

Actually, we have plenty of air—between 5 and 6 quadrillion tons. About half of it is concentrated in the lowest 18,000 feet; the part we use and re-use is restricted to the first few thousand feet, and we draw most heavily on that in the lowest ten feet. The air we breathe contains about 20% oxygen, 80% nitrogen, and traces of other gases, including water vapor. The last ingredient—the "junk" liquid, gaseous, and solid waste products—would amount to only about 1.5 parts per million if all the pollutants were released and distributed simultaneously. Of course, they are not, and the air is also constantly being cleansed by precipitation. Even so, since nearly half the pollution is released in less than 1% of the United States, where 50% of the population lives, the concentrations are much higher.

We are sensitively dependent upon that particular one-fifth of the air which is composed of oxygen. Man cannot survive for much more than six minutes without it. How did oxygen originate? Isaac Asimov (*A New Intelligent Man's Guide to Science*) hypothesizes:

> The most dramatic suggestion is that it arose through the activity of life. As the result of photosynthesis, the process by which green plants use the energy of sunlight to convert water and carbon dioxide into the carbon-containing compounds which make up living tissue, the plants liberate oxygen. Thus they steadily increase the atmosphere's oxygen and soak up its carbon dioxide. In this way a carbon-dioxide and nitrogen atmosphere might be converted into an oxygen and nitrogen atmosphere. Photosynthesis could also transform an ammonia and methane atmosphere into the one we have now, but by a more complicated process.

> In all events, it seems likely that the earth's oxygen-filled atmosphere (which is unique in the solar system) is a modern development that has been in existence for only 10 percent or so of the earth's lifetime.

THE SCIENTIFIC PROBLEM

The atmosphere is a complex physical system in which movement of air, changes in temperature, and transformation of water through the liquid, solid, and gaseous phases are all taking place in response to certain forces or processes. Although the atmosphere is far from being a tidy little deterministic system, in principal, we can cast those processes in quantitative form and relate a given state of the atmosphere to a subsequent state. This is the basis for weather prediction. When there is intervention either conscious or inadvertent, there is weather modification.

Weather modification and weather prediction, however, are complicated problems. The earth's atmosphere is affected not only by the motion of the earth, but moreover by the forces arising from energy variables. These variables depend on the distribution of shortwave solar radiation, the flux of outgoing long-wave radiation, the latent heat involved in the change in phase of water, the transfer of heat between the atmosphere and the earth's surface, and finally, the air motion itself. The kinetic energy of air motion exists in an array of scale sizes that extend from planetary wave systems down to molecular movement.

Atmospheric conditions also tend to change with amazing rapidity, puffy clouds growing into towering thunderstorms in hours. This is a frustration to weather predictions, but a hopeful sign to weather modification. We are just beginning to understand many of these phenomena.

It may be that there is an upward progression of instability of energy through the size spectrum; if this is of significant degree, there may be a possibility of great effect from modest but selective human intervention. We could break the eggs rather than slay the dragon. There is reason to believe that this process, small tendencies causing large effects, may have created several radical climatic alterations.

From the data gathered from the new global perspective we have had in this century, and from fragmentary and scattered studies on the fundamental physics of atmospheric processes, there has begun to emerge, during the past 20 or 30 years, a picture of the scientific problem to be solved in the lower portion of the atmosphere. The fact that elements of the problem can even be formulated is perhaps the most exciting development in meteorology over the past 3,000 years.

Five developments of recent years have opened up new dimensions of scientific research and given special relevance to the exploration of new patterns of international cooperation.

First, the physical processes occurring in the atmosphere are now understood well enough to be expressed in equations that constitute mathematical models. These models permit simulation of natural processes useful both in the perfection and prediction techniques and in the assessment of the consequences of human intervention in these natural processes. Although crude and over-simplified relative to the actual processes, useful models have been constructed of atmospheric phenomena that range in size from a single cloud to circulation of air over an entire hemisphere. There is almost unlimited potential for extension and refinement.

Second, the advent of electronic computers has hastened the promise of being able to integrate the nonlinear partial differential equations expressing atmospheric motions. Computers, in turn, provide a powerful new tool for understanding atmospheric processes by analysis of the relevant mathematical equations.

Third, there are expanding capabilities of making the atmospheric observations and measurements that specify the initial and final conditions that must be reconciled by the computerized atmospheric models if they are to be meaningful.

Fourth, computer-based simulation experiments strongly suggest that weather predictions for two weeks or more in advance—and distinctly superior to any now available—are likely to become possible during the 1970's. This possibility, coupled with the modern statistical decision theory predictions, for predictions in weather-sensitive operations such as food production, construction, transportation, commerce and trade, hold promise of great benefit.

Fifth, it is becoming increasingly clear that the problem of weather modification, conscious or inadvertent, is passing from an era of intellectually undisciplined speculation to an era of rational, organized inquiry. In a decade or so, it will become possible to explore, through simulation techniques, an array of deliberate interventions in natural atmospheric processes, and to assess possibilities and limitations. These studies will inevitably lead to specific requirements for meteorological measurements that will deepen our understanding of natural processes. Mathematical models of the atmosphere have already been used in a preliminary way to assess the consequences of the inadvertent intervention of increased atmospheric carbon dioxide. Models may yet be used to define the tolerable limits to large-scale geophysical experiments than man is undertaking.

INADVERTENT WEATHER MODIFICATION

Let me quote at this point the summary of the principal air pollutants as stated by the United States Department of Health, Education, and Welfare Publication No. 1555.

> At levels frequently found in heavy traffic, carbon monoxide produces headache, loss of visual acuity, and decreased muscular coordination.

> Sulfur oxides, found wherever coal and oil are the common fuels, corrode metal and stone, and at concentrations frequently found in our larger cities, reduce visibility, injure vegetation, and contribute to the incidence of respiratory diseases and to premature death.

> Besides their contribution to photochemical smog, described below, nitrogen oxides are responsible for the whisky-brown haze that not only destroys the view in some of our cities, but endangers the takeoff and landing of planes. At concentrations higher than those usually experienced, these oxides can interfere with respiratory function and, it is suspected, contribute to respiratory disease. They are formed in the combustion of all types of fuel.

> Hydrocarbons are a very large class of chemicals, some of which, in particle form, have produced cancer in laboratory animals, and others of which, discharged chiefly by the automobile, play a major role in the formation of photochemical smog.

> Photochemical smog is a complex mixture of gases and particles manufactured by sunlight out of the raw materials—nitrogen oxides and hydrocarbons—discharged to the atmosphere chiefly by the auto-

mobile. Smog, whose effects have been observed in every region of the United States, can severely damage crops and trees, deteriorate rubber and other materials, reduce visibility, cause the eyes to smart and the throat to sting, and, it is thought, reduce resistance to respiratory disease.

Particulate matter not only soils our clothes, shows up on our windowsills, and scatters light to blur the image of what we see, it acts as a catalyst in the formation of other pollutants, it contributes to the corrosion of metals, and in proper particle size can carry into our lungs irritant gases which might otherwise have been harmlessly dissipated in the upper respiratory tract. Some particulates contain poisons whose effects on man are gradual, often the result of the accumulation of years.

Moreover, population and productivity per man hour are doubling every 30 to 50 years and their combined effect is certain to aggravate the situation. Some idea of the dimensions of the problems of the future is provided by the estimate that given "severe but realistic controls," the sulfur oxide emissions will increase 75% by 1980 and another 75% by the year 2000. Even under the assumption of "control of the maximum anticipated technology will be able to achieve," it is estimated that there will be a 20% increase by 1980, but then a 20% decrease from that level in 2000.

If it is assumed that by the year 2000 automobile registration will double, clearly air-pollution control for automobiles will have to be accelerated, or radically new means of transportation developed.

Apart from considerations of health, there are strong economic incentives for clean air. For around $3 billion a year, air pollution, which exacts an annual economic toll of $11 billion in property damage, could be reduced by about one third.

There is a special class of inadvertent atmospheric modification that deserves particular attention. These are the short-term and long-term influences on the behaviour of the atmosphere because of man's activity. For example, the carbon-dioxide content of the atmosphere is increasing, and because of the particular absorptive characteristics of CO_2 to radiate energy leaving the earth, there is a tendency toward rising temperatures. The possibility cannot be dismissed that this process could eventually alter the sea level. On the other hand, pollution by particulate matter tends to alter the transparency of the atmosphere, which would reduce the temperature near the surface and could, over years, start us back toward an ice age. Most short-term effects, the SST or DDT issues for example, are poorly understood and even controversial.

Finally, among the long-term effects is the possibility that the man-generated energy of the surface of the earth could equal the amount of radiant energy received from the sun within a century or two.

CONSCIOUS WEATHER—PRESENT STATUS AND PROSPECTS

At the risk of oversimplification, I have summarized our present position and some future possibilities for conscious weather modification.

1. Field results have demonstrated unequivocally that several cubic miles of supercooled clouds can be transformed into ice-crystal clouds by seeding with appropriate chemicals. The technology for this kind of modification will be perfected in a decade.

2. Dissipation of supercooled fog over an airfield runway is now feasible and has been used by the United States and other countries.

3. Recent experiments in clearing certain types of "warm" fog (droplets at temperatures above freezing) over airports is beginning to produce modestly encouraging results, and dissipation of warm fog may be practicable in several years.

4. Little attention has been given to conscious interference in the process between the atmosphere and the earth's surface beyond demonstrating that it is possible to inhibit evaporation from water surfaces and vegetation. If, as it now appears, these processes turn out to be important to large-scale modification of the climate, technology could go through explosive development during the period from 1975 to 1995.

5. Persuasive, though by no means conclusive, evidence suggests that rainfall can be increased through cloud seeding by 5 to 20%. The unknowns will be worked out by 1975, and by 1980 naturally occurring rainfall will probably be augmented or diminished locally by proven techniques. By 1990 rainfall will be controlled several hundred miles from the operations.

6. There are indications that the Soviet scientists have succeeded in reducing hail damage by a factor of 3 to 5 by introducing silver iodide directly into the clouds. This form of weather modification will probably always remain local, but will develop rapidly over the next decade and may be widely used by 1980.

7. Physically reasonable approaches to the suppression of light-ning have been tried with mixed but, on balance, promising results. Operational techniques might be available by the late 1980's.

8. Cloud-seeding techniques that are of sufficient merit to war-rant field experiments have been advanced for the modifica-tion of hurricanes. This approach should be pursued vigor-ously, but the probabilities of success are not high: perhaps 50%. It seems unreasonable to expect much before 1990, but there are good prospects for a proven technique by 2000.

9. No technique for consciously influencing large-scale weather patterns yet exists, and not much progress can be expected for another decade, when the scientific results of a recently approved global atmospheric research program begin to be available. The probability of success in broad climate modifi-cation is likely to exceed 50% by the year 2018!

It is distinctly possible that there will be large-scale *inadver-tent* climate modification before conscious modification is achieved. It should be possible by 1980 to predict with precision the effects on the atmosphere in 2018 of the likely rate at which carbonif-erous fuel is being consumed. There is a small probability that the effects will not be tolerable. Air pollution may have already ex-tended its influence beyond the urban domain. Contamination of the upper atmosphere by rocket exhaust is a problem that may be of practical importance sooner than we realize. Finally, agri-cultural cultivation and urbanization are transforming the earth's surface on a large-scale basis, with possible important consequences that we should be able to assess during the 1980's.

IMPLICATIONS FOR INTERNATIONAL COOPERATION

We must recognize the wisdom and prudence of fostering inter-national cooperation while the problem of weather control is a purely scientific one of uncertain outcome. Should the outcome be affirmative, a Pandora's box of political problems would be opened. Forging links between scientists and nations would better prepare us for the stresses and strains to come.

To a world scientific community often concerned over the uses of its knowledge, to the nations of the world seeking a unity in humanitarian objectives, to the people of the world who would benefit from a deeper understanding and more effective use of our environment, could one present a more magnificent challenge than the scientific problem of the atmosphere?

A modest affirmative step might be taken by assembling under the auspices of the International Council of Scientific Unions (ICSU), a small permanent, full-time working group charged with the responsibility of exploring in depth the scientific and other aspects of this matter and reporting findings and recommendations to the world community. Membership should include physical scientists with experience in the atmospheric sciences, oceanography, natural resource analysis, physics, mathematics, and chemistry. It should also involve life scientists with special interests in ecosystems, social scientists with special interests in economics and international relations, and legal scholars with particular interest in international law. Adequate and stable support should be assured for at least 10 years by voluntary national contributions or through an agency such as UNESCO.

Imaginative statesmanship, as well as imaginative science, will be required to explore the new dimension of international cooperation that the space age has opened up in this field. Justification for the effort is found in some wise words of Werner Heisenberg in his book *Physics and Philosophy*:*

> It is especially one feature of science which makes it more than anything else suited for establishing the first strong connection between different cultural traditions. This is the fact that the ultimate decisions about the value of a special scientific work, about what is correct or wrong in the work, do not depend on any human authority. It may sometimes take many years before one knows the solution to a problem, before one can distinguish between truth and error; but finally the questions will be decided, and the decisions are made not by any group of scientists but by nature itself.

---

* Werner Heisenberg, *Physics and Philosophy*.

C. Institutions and the environment

Several facts are central to the environmental importance of institutions. Institutions are composed of people, and to a great degree they determine the patterns of the lives of these people. Institutions tend to be self-perpetuating and resistant to change. Yet a constant theme at this Conference was that institutions are outmoded and must be changed.

One way to do it within our system is to bring public policy to bear on behavior which affects the environment.

31

OUR LAGGING INSTITUTIONS

HENRY L. DIAMOND

Mr. Diamond focuses on the issue of change: "Public pressure is the heart which makes the large institutions move." He points to a mode of achieving the pressure: the zealous new activists ". . . will keep the revolution going, and they will fire up the major institutions."

We are in the midst of an environmental revolution. The people of this country are really sick of the degradation of their environment, and they are demanding that their leaders and their institutions take action.

Not surprisingly, our broadly based institutions are not set up to respond as quickly and as aggressively as the people want. In the past, environmental concern has been a very minor theme of our society. It was in the province of the little old ladies in sneakers and the dotty brothers-in-law in tweeds. Our institutions simply did not have to deal with this issue.

Now they must.

Let me list the state of our institutions with regard to their concern for environment quality:

Government.   Government at all levels, but particularly the federal, has been literally unable to pull itself together to face the rising environmental aspirations of the American people. This year the President by Executive Order, and the Congress by legislation, are trying new ways. There are problems, but a start is being made.

The Courts.   Environment has not been a subject of litigation, but this is rapidly changing. The law may be the new frontier of environmental action. Half a dozen organizations are springing up to help people take their environmental grievances to court. The preliminary indications are that the courts are responsive, and we may be seeing a whole new body of law in the making.

The Press.   For many years reporting the environment consisted chiefly of stories on how the trouts were running. But now good newspapers are springing top reporters for environment and printing their stuff. And if TIME now has an Environment section, can NEWSWEEK be far behind?

The Church.   The Church has approached the environment chiefly from the point of the use of leisure time. Sloth being one of the first-order sins, the Church has worried about good, wholesome outdoor recreation for people when they are not working. Increasingly, however, the Church is becoming concerned with environment and "Thou shalt not throw crap untreated into the river" may become a pretty serious sort of commandment.

Education. A number of school systems have begun to teach environmental awareness with programs financed by the Education Act of 1965. New college courses, departments, and programs seem to be proliferating.

Unions. Some larger and more sophisticated unions have established departments to worry about the environment. Understandably the union position on any given issue is likely to be determined by whether jobs are created or not, but there is a trend toward environmental awareness. The UAW's redoubtable Olga Madar is an excellent example.

Business. There is a growing awareness of the importance of environmental quality in the corporate board rooms. Business is finding that the public reaction to what they want to do to the environment may become an important factor. Business is learning that what was once regarded as only a lunatic fringe is now a formidable opponent armed with lawyers, public relations men, and even voting stock.

Foundations. Five years ago one could name on the fingers of one hand the foundations that cared anything about the environment. Since then, Ford has come onto the scene in a big way, and scores of smaller foundations have an awakened interest.

I believe that this trend toward greater involvement in environmental affairs by our major institutions will continue. I am sanguine for a very basic reason. Years ago Mr. Dooley noted that the Supreme Court followed the election returns pretty well. Well, the same is true of our institutions. The bureaucrats, the businessmen, the churchmen, the foundation people, the publishers, all those who make policy for our institutions, keep their fingers pretty close to the public pulse. They watch not only the election returns but the polls, the buying patterns, the letters to the editors, and the hell-raisers.

And anyone who's doing any watching at all today should be able to discern that environment is "in." It has taken its place as a new, major concern of the American people.

In my view the real institutional lag—the most crucial one—is among the environmental organizations themselves. These institutions should be in the first wave of the environmental revolution. Public pressure is the heart which makes the larger institutions move. The environmental organizations must carefully ignite, fan, and direct the brush fires into white hot issues. But the existing organizations have been caught unaware and unprepared.

In the first place, there were no real environmental organizations. There were a number of highly specialized groups in the fields of conservation, outdoor recreation, natural resources, and city betterment, but none really had the scope of the entire environment. Traditionally these organizations have appealed to a limited membership. They existed to provide more birds as shotgun·fodder—not to build a broad environmental coalition. Secondly, these organizations commanded relatively few resources—money and staff have been spread pitifully thin. Thirdly, the existing organizations are not attuned to the new scene. The people who are generating environmental revolution are a whole new constituency—young, involved, politically committed, scientifically aware, and anxious for action. Nothing will turn them off faster than a dusty, old organization worried more about book sales and bird lists than clobbering the bad guys.

Some of these organizations are trying to broaden their base —to catch up in this environmental lag. Some are coming in from the wilderness, and some are coming out from the city, to cover the full range of the environment.

It may be, however, that we need a reshuffling of our environmental organizations. The most effective and most alive organizations are the new ones springing up at local levels. Quite often people have come together over a single issue and stayed together to fight other battles. These *ad hoc* groups have a vitality and a drive which has been lacking. They often are made up of politically involved people who know how to use campaign techniques. They are where the action is.

At present, I do not see any national environmental organizations able to serve these new action people across the country. It is these new, zealous converts who will keep the environmental revolution going, and they will fire up the major institutions.

Caldwell's opening comment states the theme that present government is inadequate for achieving environmental quality. Proof is everywhere around us, since governmental bodies are major polluters themselves. Oil spills, Navy ships polluting our bays and seas, and even cities like New York and San Francisco polluting their surrounding waters, with no true plan for improvement, are examples.

Somehow government must manage environmental affairs. It is too colossal a problem to approach any other way. The magnitude and complexity of the threat require that such quality management will have to come from higher levels of government.

Several other authors suggest that government isn't doing the job because of resource use traditions which have grown with and are supported by strong special interests. This real pressure is so intense that even a well-meaning President will have difficulty fulfilling needs.

One answer, of course, is to have those interested in survival become a special interest.

Another is the establishment of a super environmental agency of cabinet status, with accompanying Congressional changes to make it effective.

32

POLITICS OF ECOLOGY

HARVEY WHEELER

The author points to an exciting new direction: a new politics of ecology based on a liaison between alarmed public, especially youth, and the radical scientists as an information source. It is one that works within our system and yet can bring the necessary institutional changes for survival.

There is a need for a new politics of ecology. An older politics of conservation dates back to revered figures such as Gifford Pinchot, who used conservation issues as a lever to political success. The Sierra Club uses its considerable clout in specific issues. Some states are now considered "conservation-minded," but the state that wants to "Save Washington's Water" really wants to keep it away from California rather than to preserve its quality. Yet these efforts, whether sincere or cynical, are piecemeal approaches.

Congress now has a conservation coalition of 126 members. A new bill by Ottinger and others defines man's inalienable right to a healthful environment. While this is still the style of old pressure-group politics, it does point to the existence of a new constituency.

But our present party system and legislative system are not succeeding in handling the situation, nor can they. New ones are needed. Our legislators are chosen to represent territories. This assumes that their major problems come from the clash of local problems. We need new policy-forming institutions, based on a different kind of representation, eventually producing new parties devoted to the politics of ecology.

In a recent portent of the future, the politically powerful Sierra Club split. The more activist minority announced the formation of an ecology-based political party. This group, and others, continually re-armed by the advancing biological sciences, promise to be the wave of the future. Future legislatures, founded on ecological concerns, could be better suited to cope with the new problems posed by the technological and biological revolutions.

33

STREAMLINING ENVIRONMENTAL MANAGEMENT

SENATOR FRANK E. MOSS

It was an unforgettable experience to watch Senator Moss describe, to a room packed with federal resource-agency officials, his plan to reorganize those very agencies. He said, "I know you fellows are too well organized to have my bill passed this year, but I'll keep at it." And he has. Now some of those who were in that room hope such a bill is soon enacted.

The people of this nation are rapidly becoming aware of the ecological damage we are wreaking on the earth. But while we are becoming more aware of the problem, we still lack the machinery to deal with it. The governmental agencies established to help us preserve our national resources, maintain our environment, combat pollution, and do the other things necessary to keep our nation and planet livable, are scattered throughout numerous departments.

To unify our efforts, I have proposed the creation of a new cabinet-level department in the federal government, to be called the Department of Natural Resources and Environment. Very simply, this bill would center all government agencies which deal with natural resources and environment in one department.

I first introduced legislation to create this department five years ago, during the 89th Congress. I reintroduced it in the 90th and this year in the 91st. During the hearing conducted by Senator Ribicoff, we were not surprised to learn from the testimony of senators and agency officials, that most agencies would rather stay put. The hearing indicated the extent to which interests competing for the use of our natural resources would be ready to block all development and protection plans. But the choices we make in the coming years will affect the beauty and utility of our land for uncounted generations to come. We *must* develop a comprehensive management of our interrelated natural resources.

The bill would abolish the Department of the Interior, by transferring its agencies either to the new Department of Natural Resources and Environment or to other agencies. The Department of the Interior was conceived in 1849 as a "Home Department" for a young nation—a repository for numerous federal activities, many only tenuously related. It came to be chiefly concerned with management—of timber, forage, water, minerals, and so forth, and the marketing of power, and the promotion of out-

door recreation.   But the Forest Service still managed soil conservation and the Army Corps of Engineers dealt with their array
of water-resource activities.   A new department could concentrate all these misdistributed resource concerns in one agency.

To illustrate the urgency of this need, let us look at the present
state of affairs in water-resource management. We face a twofold
task in developing overall planning of our water resources. We
must find, and quickly, much more clean water. And we must
manage with far more wisdom than we have until now, the supplies
we now have. Total management, moreover, involves a variety of
functions, among them watershed protection, flood control, river
and harbor improvement, irrigation, fish and wildlife, recreation,
desalination, and prevention of pollution. We must plan for entire
river basins, from their sources to their mouths, and we must place
all basins under one authority. Precipitation, pollution, and water
use in one basin can vitally affect the others. Coordination in their
development and management is essential. Ideally, we should
have a national long-range plan for management which would be
the basis for individual river-basin plans.

At present, each water-resource agency strives to maximize its
use of water, which results in wasting and pollution. Moreover,
independent agencies jealously carve out their jurisdictions and
powers. We now have three cabinet-level departments—Defense,
Agriculture, and Interior, as well as the Federal Power Commission, and a Pandora's box of lesser agencies—the Bureau of Reclamation, three power-marketing agencies, the Bureau of Indian
Affairs, the Bureau of Fish and Wildlife, the Bureau of Mines, and
many more. We have no overall policy whatsoever.

A similar situation exists in public-lands management. At
present, the Bureau of Land Management and the Forest Service,
under Agriculture, share responsibility for public lands with the
National Park Service, the Bureau of Indian Affairs, and others.
Land is managed for multiple use, and many agency functions
overlap.

I would suggest, in the proposed department, an Assistant
Secretary for Oceanography. Many have commented on our inadequate national attention to our marine program. Senator
Muskie has pointed out the need for the improvement of our
merchant-marine fleet, the exploration of our continental shelf,
and the development of our fisheries products. In addition, we
need a review of our interests in the law of the sea and a study of
the possible import restrictions on those nations practicing poor

conservation techniques in our adjacent waters.   Our natural-resources program must recognize the rich resources of the oceans.

Administratively, the bill would provide for a Secretary of Natural Resources and a Deputy Secretary.   It would provide for two Undersecretaries, one for water, and one for land.   The first would supervise Assistant Secretaries for 1) reclamation, 2) flood control, 3) water supply, 4) water purification and 5) oceanography; and the second, Assistant Secretaries for 1) land resources, 2) recreation and wildlife, 3) minerals and fuels, and 4) air pollution abatement.   The functions now scattered throughout many federal agencies would be gathered under these jurisdictions.

The adoption of this proposal is long overdue.   The task of protecting and wisely utilizing the land, the water, and the forest is one task.   All these resources are interdependent and all require management on a national basis.   I intend to pursue this great need with all my energy.

34
PLANNING, THE LAW, AND A QUALITY ENVIRONMENT
JOSEPH E. BODOVITZ

Several times in the Conference discussions people said, "What about implementation?   We can't attain what we know should be done now." This paper describes a regional plan that was implemented and is working —one of the few that are.   For the first time planners were given legal teeth and a freedom to implement their plans.   It's a good example to demonstrate that we can work through the system for survival.

When the architects of America got together for their 1969 convention, they didn't just talk about houses and skyscrapers.

In words as crisp and clean as a Mies van der Rohe building, they said what they thought about the needs of the United States at the beginning of the 1970's:

> We call upon our leaders, at all levels of government, to recognize that an efficient and humane environment is basic to the maintenance of a harmonious and prosperous society and that the skills to produce it are well within our grasp.   At the same time, we wish to remind our representatives that neither hope, time, nor technology will solve the

problems that presently make urban life a dirty, difficult, and dangerous experience. Only a wholehearted commitment of will and money will enable us to apply the skills needed to erase the shame of urban America.

It's not just architects who are worried about the American environment. Some Americans appear anesthetized to bourbon-colored air, the noise of jets, and the smell of polluted waters, but plenty of others get mad at the destruction of America's livability.

Even Roger Blough of United States Steel Corporation has qualms about what industrial progress has done to the American environment. Here's what he said to a conference of the world's leading industrialists in San Francisco last fall:

> Would we not have been better advised during this century to have worked on our clean-air and clean-water problem as we created it, rather than to have left the problem largely unresolved until it built itself into a grand-scale, costly mountain of a problem—one to be removed, hopefully, in the next two decades?

Suppose, then, that many Americans are ready to make a wholehearted commitment to a humane environment. What do we do next?

We're apt to have trouble at once with the very words we use to discuss the problem. Conservation, for example. The dictionary defines conservation as "planned management of a natural resource to prevent exploitation, destruction, or neglect." But until recently, the word had somehow become debased, so that its advocates were derided as bird-watchers and posy-pluckers, little old ladies opposed to "progress."

Now, however, more and more people are coming to recognize the wisdom of George Bernard Shaw's comment that "in an ugly and unhappy world the richest man can purchase nothing but ugliness and unhappiness." Conservation is becoming synonymous with survival—with man's ability to manage the limited resources of the planet Earth so that man's children and grandchildren can have something more than a bleak and dreary future.

Then there's the word development. "Until recently, developing land meant civilizing it, not barbarizing it," said developer D. C. Marek in testimony before a California legislative commission in 1964. "The much admired landscape of France is an example of what development can mean. Through the centuries it has been tended and tailored, manicured and manipulated—*developed,* in fact, from nature's grand but chaotic order into an artful rearrangement implicitly suggesting that man and natural process need not be antagonists but can become partners."

True enough, but the problem comes with the implication that nature's "grand order" is always chaotic and it must be changed to be useful. Land and water in their natural, undeveloped, state may also be useful. San Francisco Bay, for example, need not be developed, i.e., turned into land, to be useful. The Bay as a body of water is useful in many ways—to provide fish, for example, which are in turn used by man for food (a use, incidentally, that may become increasingly important in helping to feed the world's sky-rocketing population), and to man directly, because the broad expanse of water helps to maintain the pleasant climate of surrounding areas and to combat air pollution.

What's needed in the 1970's, therefore, is recognition that both conservation and development are going to be required in the physical environment of the United States, and that the hard questions are how much of each, and where, and, perhaps hardest of all, who should decide and on what basis. Or, to put this another way, how can the American political system of checks and balances and representative government solve the difficult and unprecedented economic and environmental problems that we face in the 1970's?

One pioneering answer has been provided by the work of the San Francisco Bay Conservation and Development Commission, which has been wrestling with questions of this sort since it was created by the California Legislature four years ago. (The name of the Commission was suggested in a 1963 report, "The Future of San Francisco Bay," by University of California researcher Mel Scott; the most important word in the Commission's name may well be the conjunction, not the nouns—it's the conservation *and* development commission, not conservation *or* development.) The BCDC Plan for San Francisco Bay has drawn nation-wide praise, and the work of the Commission has been used as a model for legislation introduced in several other states for management of coastal waters.

The BCDC came into existence through the unlikely combination of a powerful state senator, the wife of the then-president of the University of California, a disk-jockey, and thousands·of letter-writing, telegram-sending Californians. Their campaign proved once again that, as the Connecticut essayist and editor Charles Dudley Warner wrote almost a century ago, "public opinion is stronger than the legislature, and nearly as strong as the ten commandments."

The university president's wife, Mrs. Clark Kerr, was driving across the Bay Bridge from Oakland to San Francisco one day in the early 1960's with Mrs. Donald McLaughlin, whose husband was then chairman of the university's board of regents. The two women were discussing the just-announced plans of the city of Berkeley to enlarge itself by filling in some 2,000 acres of the Bay. "The Bay is certainly beautiful today," said Mrs. McLaughlin, looking at the miles of blue water. "Well," said Mrs. Kerr, "it won't even be a bay if every city does what Berkeley wants to do."

Both women were suddenly struck by the prospect of dozens of dredges, dumptrucks, and bulldozers at the water's edge, filling the shallow margins of the Bay with dirt and sand and debris, and thus greatly shrinking the Bay. Could this really happen? Was the Bay in danger? How much of it could be filled? Mrs. Kerr, Mrs. McLaughlin, and a third university wife, Mrs. Charles Gulick, decided to find out.

They learned to their surprise that almost one-third of the Bay as nature created it had already been diked off or filled in, and that more than one-half of the remaining Bay was shallow enough to be economically fillable over the next half-century—"susceptible of reclamation" was how the Army Corps of Engineers had put it in a detailed study. And they learned that a rising population in the Bay Area (from 4.5 million in 1969 to a predicted 11 million in 50 years) would mean increasing pressures to fill more of the Bay for the same purposes for which it had been filled in the past —factories, homesites, garbage dumps, roadways, and all the other needs of urban civilization.

Furthermore, nobody seemed to know the consequences of so much filling, and with 32 cities and 9 counties each having parts of the Bay within their boundaries, nobody was really responsible for looking at the Bay as the single body of water it is.

The three women, unsure of what they could do as citizens in so complex a matter, recruited a few friends and formed the Save San Francisco Bay Association. They immediately began trying to interest governmental officials at all levels in doing something to protect the Bay. They badgered legislators in Sacramento to stop the piecemeal filling. And they began to find success: an Oakland assemblyman, Nicholas Petris, introduced a bill in 1964 that would have stopped the filling while a plan for the Bay was prepared. But Petris (who is now a state senator and still a leader in the fight for wise use of the Bay) found little support, and his bill was emasculated by the first committee to which it was sent.

Then the women sought the help of Senator J. Eugene Mc-Ateer of San Francisco, a member of the powerful "old guard" in the state senate, a lawmaker with a reputation for getting things done, but not for any great interest in conservation. He listened and said he would help; but he said the first step was to make the Legislature aware of the threat to the Bay so that a strong bill could be passed in a later year. McAteer therefore proposed a legislative study commission, to analyze the issues affecting the Bay and report to the following year's session with specific recommendations.

The McAteer bill was passed, and the senator was named chairman of the Bay study commission. As chairman, McAteer scheduled a whirlwind series of 12 weekly public hearings in all parts of the Bay Area, with statements sought from experts and ordinary citizens alike. Some witnesses testified eloquently as to the dangers of unrestricted filling, and others testified with equal eloquence for increased development of the Bay, meaning filling, because of the economic benefits the Bay provides. (Along the way, Berkeley gave up its massive fill plans.)

In slightly less than four months the McAteer commission had agreed on what it would recommend—establishment of a successor commission to:

1. make a more detailed study of the Bay than the McAteer commission had had time for,

2. use the results of that study to prepare a plan "for the conservation of the waters of the Bay and the development of its shoreline," and

3. of great importance, protect the Bay from further piecemeal filling while the plan was being completed; the new commission would thus have veto power over new filling and dredging for a three-year planning period.

"San Francisco Bay is the greatest single natural asset of the region," said the McAteer commission in its report to his fellow legislators. "The public interest requires creation of a governmental mechanism to balance competing interests in the Bay, and to weigh all the alternatives in making choices relative to the Bay."

Could any legislator—even as skilled a legislator as McAteer—steer such a bill through the California legislature, which had shown only sporadic interest in planning and conservation? McAteer vowed to try. The Save San Francisco Bay Association, the

League of Women Voters, and many other citizens' groups pledged their help.

And then a disk jockey named Don Sherwood, whose 6–9-a.m. radio program was one of the most popular in the Bay Area, joined the fight. "Write your legislators and tell them what the Bay means to you," said Sherwood to his morning audience, and write his listeners did. Telegrams and letters by the sackful arrived on the desks of surprised legislators, more mail than was sent on any other subject in the 1965 Legislature. Some citizens did more than write—they bombarded legislators who were thought to be hostile to the McAteer bill with sacks of sand that carried notes reading, "You'll wonder where the water went if you fill the Bay with sediment."

McAteer and the citizens prevailed. The Bay Conservation and Development Commission came into existence in late 1965 with the three assignments McAteer had fought for: to make studies of the Bay, to plan for the Bay, and to protect the Bay from unnecessary filling while the plan was being prepared. The legislature thus specified that any individual or any governmental agency wanting to place fill in the Bay or to dredge in the Bay had to first obtain a permit from the BCDC, and that the BCDC was to hold public hearings before deciding whether to grant a permit. Further, the legislature specified that permits could be granted for only two reasons: that a project was necessary to the health, safety, and welfare of the public in the entire Bay Area, or that a project would not adversely affect the Bay plan being prepared. (During the past four years, the BCDC has held hearings on 84 applications for fill and dredging permits, granting 60 and denying 14; 10 were withdrawn before a vote was taken. During this period the BCDC authorized 380 acres of fill; about $\frac{3}{4}$ of this amount was for expansion of airports around the Bay, and all the remainder was for waterfront parks, marinas, beaches, and other public recreational developments.)

The BCDC was unusual not only because it had legal powers to regulate development, but because of its size. Its 27 members were chosen to represent the many and sometimes conflicting interests in the Bay, which McAteer believed had to be represented if the BCDC's planning was to be successful. BCDC thus consists of representatives of federal agencies, state agencies, and cities and counties, and in addition the general public is represented through appointments made by the Governor and each house of the Legislature.

Is 27 too large? Some would say so. But McAteer believed that wide representation in planning is more important than the presumed greater efficiency of a smaller agency. Furthermore, BCDC showed that a 27-member body need not be unwieldy, particularly if it has an effective chairman. The chairman of BCDC from its beginning has been Melvin B. Lane, executive vice-president of the Sunset magazine and book company, a Republican who was first appointed chairman by Democratic Governor Edmund G. Brown and then reappointed by Republican Governor Ronald Reagan. As the BCDC work proceeded, Lane devoted countless hours to his unsalaried job as chairman, presided at meetings in a fair-minded manner that prevented polarization of BCDC into factions, and quietly kept BCDC on schedule so that decisions were made on time and the plan completed before its deadline.

In 1965, then, BCDC was born, with considerable public support but with no clear idea of how to proceed. How do you plan for something as complex and involved as the Bay? Had anything like this been done elsewhere in the country? Can 27 people together prepare a plan, or is planning a talent exercised by individuals who work in private and then try to sell their ideas to often-skeptical laymen? Could 27 people, particularly chosen to represent conflicting points of view, ever arrive at a consensus? Should BCDC divide into committees to explore various aspects of the Bay?

The first decisions were quickly made: There were insufficient planning precedents to follow; BCDC would have to develop its own procedures. BCDC would not turn its planning responsibilities over to private planning consultants, but would do its own work. BCDC would not divide into committees because committees could too easily turn into groups of specialists fighting for particular causes; instead, BCDC needed to meet as a whole to hammer out policy decisions—commission members concerned with development needed to hear the arguments of biologists, and conservation-minded commissioners needed to hear the needs of port development. In short, the commission would learn about the Bay, debate about it, and then construct a plan like a builder constructing a house, sometimes slowly, sometimes painfully, but from the foundation up, one step at a time.

The BCDC plan would have to be a collection of policy decisions about the Bay: for what purposes (if any) should further filling be allowed? How could the Bay be made more usable to the public? What benefits should the Bay provide? The goal was a plan for the Bay similar to a charter for a city or a constitution for a nation. Only then could plan maps be prepared, applying these policies to the Bay and shoreline.

Furthermore, and of great importance, the public support that had been so important to the creation of the commission had to be maintained; the public had to be kept involved in the planning as it progressed, so that a consensus of public opinion could be achieved.

This meant that the complex subject of San Francisco Bay had to be divided into manageable chunks. The BCDC therefore instructed its small staff and a group of outside specialists to prepare reports on 25 different aspects of the Bay, ranging from the importance of marshlands in nurturing fish and wildlife to the importance of waterfront industry in providing jobs.

The reports contained factual information, and often controversial opinions. The most important parts of each report—the parts most essential to establishing policies for the future of the Bay—were summarized by the staff in reports of 5 to 20 pages, concise enough for quick reading and understanding, with the complete report available for anyone wishing it. The reports were circulated widely as each was completed, and public reaction was vigorously sought.

Each report was considered at a separate BCDC meeting, and public comments were welcomed. The BCDC did not vote on whether to approve each report in its entirety, but rather on proposed findings and policies drawn from each report; these policies were then made the foundation of the BCDC Bay Plan. Examples of the policies:

1. Marshes and mudflats around the Bay should be maintained to the fullest possible extent to conserve fish and wildlife, to combat water pollution, and to abate air pollution.

2. Filling and diking that eliminate marshes and mudflats should therefore be allowed only for purposes providing substantial public benefits and only if there is no reasonable alternative.

3. San Francisco Bay is one of the world's great harbors, and maritime commerce is of primary importance to the entire economy of the Bay Area.

4. Some filling and dredging will be required to provide for necessary port expansion, but any permitted fill or dredging should be in accord with overall regional needs.

5. Housing should be encouraged in many dry-land areas fronting on the Bay, houseboats should be encouraged in some

areas, but no new filling should be allowed for housing, because even with a rapidly rising population, enough land will
be available for housing in the Bay Area so that the Bay need
not be sacrificed for this purpose.

The BCDC sought information from many disciplines: Would
Bay filling affect the climate of the Bay Area? (It would; meteorol-
ogists estimated that turning as much as 25 per cent of the present
water surface into land would cause noticeable increases in temperature in surrounding areas, and would increase smog.) How
would filled land respond to the complex forces of an earthquake?
(The Bay Area's leading geologists and soil engineers prepared
reports pointing out that filled land is more vulnerable than solid
rock to earthquake damage, but that sound engineering of the
fills and of buildings on the fills can reduce the risks to acceptable
proportions.) What sort of governmental organization is needed
to carry out a Bay Plan? (BCDC recommended that only a regional
agency, able to deal with the entire Bay, would suffice, and suggested this could best be established as part of a governmental
agency having limited but specific responsibilities in several areas of
regional concern such as controlling air and water pollution and
establishing regional transportation policy; BCDC also recommended that the governing body of such an agency be partly
elected directly by the Bay Area public and partly appointed by
Bay Area city and county officials.)
    Questions of law also received great attention. Almost from
the first day of statehood in 1850, California began parceling out
the Bay in small fragments; by 1879, when a new state constitution
put a stop to the sales, about 22 per cent of the bottom of the Bay
had passed into private hands; the sales were sometimes for as
little as $1 an acre, and were sometimes based on fraudulent docu-
ments. In later years, the state gave another quarter of the Bay,
free, to cities and counties, generally to fill, but subject to many
limitations. Many legal questions thus surround the various holdings of Bay property: Do owners have an unlimited right to turn
water into land? If the public wishes to prevent the filling of privately claimed property in the Bay, must the public buy it back?
What is the meaning of the provisions of the California constitution that the public has the right to use the navigable waters of the
state for commerce, fishing, and navigation—how can filling be
consistent with rights of the public to fish?
    Experts on the staff of the California Attorney General, the
State Lands Commission, and the Boalt Hall law school of the
University of California responded to the BCDC's requests for

legal help. As a result, BCDC strongly recommended speedy court determination of the rights of the private property claimants vs. the rights of the public regarding Bay fill. A test case seeking court answers has now been filed by the State Attorney General.

After the BCDC's policies had been tentatively adopted over a two-year period of debate, they were combined into a preliminary plan, and this was submitted to public hearings in different parts of the Bay Area. Unquestionably the most eloquent testimony at the hearings came from a leader of the black community in the industrial city of Richmond, who pointed out that North Richmond, like most of the black ghettoes of the Bay Area, is near the shores of the Bay but fenced off from it—and that these areas, desperately short of parks and other recreational opportunities, would benefit greatly if the BCDC could succeed in its efforts to open more of the Bayfront for public enjoyment.

When the day came for the dramatic final vote on the Bay Plan, the BCDC commissioners voted in favor of it with a unanimity that would scarcely have been thought possible three years earlier; the single dissent was from a county representative objecting to regulations that would reserve shoreline property in his area for specific industrial purposes.

The BCDC summed up its recommendations this way:

> San Francisco Bay is an irreplaceable gift of nature that man can either abuse and ultimately destroy—or improve and protect for future generations.
>
> The Bay can serve human needs to a much greater degree than it does today. The Bay can play an increasing role as a major world port. Around its shores, many job-producing new industries can be developed. And new parks, marinas, beaches, and fishing piers can provide close-to-home recreation for the Bay Area's increasing population.
>
> But the Bay must be protected from needless and gradual destruction. The Bay should no longer be treated as ordinary real estate, available to be filled with sand or dirt to create new land. Rather, the Bay should be regarded as the most valuable natural asset of the entire Bay region, a body of water that benefits the residents not only of the Bay Area but of all California and indeed the nation.

Harold Gilliam, environmental writer for the San Francisco Chronicle, described the Bay Plan as "a Magna Carta for the Bay —a declaration of the Bay's right to live." And the Bay Plan, together with BCDC's methods of public involvement in the planning, won a top merit award from the American Institute of Planners.

Under the original McAteer law, BCDC was scheduled to go out of existence in late 1969, after the Legislature had debated—and hopefully approved—the BCDC recommendations. The 1969 California Legislature thus became the scene of a major battle over the Bay.

The citizens' groups were even more vigorous in 1969 than in 1965; money had been raised by the Planning and Conservation League, the Sierra Club, and other groups to support a full-time lobbyist in the State Capitol. Bright blue and green bumper stickers reading "Save Our Bay" appeared by the thousands on Bay Area cars. Don Sherwood again urged his listeners to write. And although Senator McAteer had died of a heart attack in 1967, other legislators took up the cause and introduced bills to carry out the BCDC recommendations.

But strong opposition developed too. Newspapers reported that lobbyists in Sacramento were spending more money to defeat the Bay bills than on any other 1969 legislative campaign. Nobody was advocating that the entire Bay be filled; each governmental agency or private developer seeking to weaken the bills simply wanted a law weak enough to permit his particular filling to proceed. The advocates of each fill project argued—correctly—that no one project of one acre, 10 acres, or even 1,000 acres would of itself destroy the Bay. But the Bay Plan pointed out that the danger is not from individual projects so much as from a steady nibbling at a Bay that is as large now as it is ever likely to be.

Governor Reagan, in his January "state of the state" message to the Legislature, sounded the alarm over Bay filling, warning that unless a strong bill were passed, BCDC would go out of existence and unrestricted Bay filling could resume. Legislative leadership was provided by Republican and Democratic lawmakers alike, from all parts of the Bay Area. Citizens continued to write letters, send telegrams, and arrive in Sacramento by the busload for the many legislative committee hearings. Finally, in the last hours of the 1969 legislative session, a bill was passed that contained almost all of the measures recommended in the BCDC Bay Plan. The bill was signed into law by Governor Reagan; its author was Assemblyman John Knox of Richmond, a liberal Democrat. .

The bill continued BCDC in existence, and gave it the duty of continuing to regulate Bay filling and dredging in accordance with the policies of the BCDC Bay Plan. In addition, BCDC was given the responsibility of regulating limited aspects of development on the shoreline immediately surrounding the Bay, for two reasons: to try to ensure more public access to the Bay, and to try to ensure that existing land around the Bay is used wisely, to minimize the pressures for Bay filling.

Despite the 1969 legislative success, however, Assemblyman Knox has continued to warn that the pressures to fill will not abate. "Eternal vigilance is the price of conservation," he has repeatedly advised his conservationist supporters.

Why do so many people so highly value the Bay? The answer is more complicated than enjoyment of views, or protection of fish and wildlife, or simply preservation of a body of water that is, after all, only valuable, not sacred. Rather, the Bay has become to many people a symbol of the environmental questions faced everywhere in America: Do we of the present generation have the right to shrink this magnificent Bay into a river, and thus forever deprive future generations of the right to enjoy its broad expanse of water? If we can't manage to protect this irreplaceable Bay, how can we manage to solve the other and more difficult problems of modern America? And, perhaps most important of all, can ordinary citizens, working through the American political system, make their voices heard and thus manage to achieve a healthy environment in which to live?

"We must stop adding to the environmental casualty lists," said Sydney Howe, president of the Conservation Foundation, "and San Francisco Bay is a good place to draw the line."

35

A REGIONAL APPROACH

LIEUTENANT GOVERNOR THOMAS GILL

Presently Hawaii may have the nation's best environmental management program. Even when regional government and land rezoning are accomplished, problems remain. This is a candid discussion of that situation by Hawaii's Lieutenant Governor.

The Islands of Hawaii have a history of deliberate exploitation of the land, as indeed do most areas of the United States. It started long ago in Hawaii, in the early 1800's, when the chiefs and the king discovered that sandalwood was in great demand in China, and today our native forests are stripped of this fragrant wood.

When goats and cattle were brought in, there was a taboo placed on them so they would multiply. Multiply they did, and they destroyed a good part of the native flora.

Our greatest present-day version of land exploitation is the tourist industry. One would think that the tourist industry, dependent as it is upon selling scenery and good living conditions, would be highly conscious of environmental impact. But its main drive has been toward high-rise hotel construction and land speculation. One aspect of tourism has been the rapid growth of population in all our islands at the rate of 6% a year, twice the national average. Many of these are newcomers, adding fuel to the already overheated island economy and greater pressure for more housing, roads, cars, and all of the other items by which modern civilization contributes to pollution and general environmental destruction. Honolulu is now developing a serious smog problem caused by the concentration of automobiles, and is facing rising sewage and waste-disposal costs.

I think it is easy to see that our salvation lies in carefully planned use of our land, air, and water so that we do not completely destroy the delicate ecological balances peculiar to our islands. It is also easy to see that the forces of economics and those whose interest is basically exploitative will make this salvation extremely difficult. We have some tools, however: the statewide zoning or land-use law, and the concept of a statewide general plan, for example. We do have a growing level of public concern with environment.

Some steps are necessary at the outset. First, our control of urban sprawl can be strengthened. Our land-use law, which was the first in the nation, is meant to give a statewide pattern to land use. It needs both administrative and legal revamping. Its intention was to put all land in the state into four categories: conservation, agricultural, rural, and urban; to review the boundaries of these use areas every five years; and to readjust them only when there was a demonstrated need. This purpose has been largely lost by the practice of continually readjusting boundaries between review periods, and by granting special-use permits. This reduces the agency which should give us a major land-use pattern to the status of a minor zoning board, spending most of its time considering and granting variances.

Among the additional legal tools needed is the power to allow rezoning on a conditional or incremental basis. This means that both the Land Use Commission and the county zoning boards need the power to hold developers to the plans which they originally submit to gain rezoning permits. This is one of the biggest jokes in the zoning business: the plan looks gorgeous but the execution is incredible. They should have the power to refuse further rezoning of subsequent increments of the plan or even to revoke zoning where there is a bad-faith change of original plans or gross failure to perform as promised.

These amendments should also include the requirement that rezoning of agricultural or conservation land which results in substantial increases of land value, as it always does, should only be granted if the recipient of the rezoning donates some measure of this unearned increment to the public in the form of money or land. If land jumps from 5000 dollars to 40 or 50 thousand dollars an acre with the mere act of rezoning, there is obviously an unearned increment. Half at least of the increment might be donated. I think this might partially solve the problem of the government's having to acquire high-priced land for open-space recreation and other public uses, after such land has its value increased by rezoning.

A third tool might be the coordination of the real property system more closely with land-use zoning. The current tendency is to jump over or disregard land-use boundaries and to tax abutting agricultural land at discounted urban rates. This happens across the mainland. This not only helps destroy the effectiveness of the zoning process, but also gives the owner a good argument for rezoning on the basis of the taxes he faces. If we allow the recovery, on rezoning, of a major portion of the unearned increment of value, much of the reason for tax pressure on such land is eliminated. Further, the drive for rezoning is reduced.

Under our system of diffused governmental power, it is necessary to find economic tools to help direct and shape urban growth. Traditional tools of zoning and taxation are too easily blunted or turned aside. A very different but major step needed in the urban center of Honolulu is the development of efficient mass transit. Until we can transfer the bulk of our commuter traffic from cars to electrically-powered trains, we will never be able to control air pollution. Nor will we be able to channel our housing and commercial developments and lessen the evils of urban sprawl. The existence of a mass-transit corridor means giving higher-density zoning along it, and makes possible new-city type urban concentrations surrounded by adequate green belts. The automobile is central to the pollution problem of this nation. It is the devil in our modern-day morality play. It is also the implement which destroys our planning. Of course, it is difficult for us in Hawaii, or any other state, to handle this beast alone.

The new transit alternatives require a national effort. A few hundred million dollars put into development of alternatives to the internal-combustion engine would be well spent.

The matching formula on mass transit should be comparable to that in the Defense Highway Act, that is, 9 to 1. The federal money should be gathered in a trust fund so we will know it is there.

The federal housing effort for years has been concentrated through the Federal Housing Administration on detached houses in the suburbs; this emphasizes sprawl, and needs redirection.

These are some of the federal tools which will make regional and state environmental planning feasible. And through all of this runs the need for better urban design.

Our prime tool is public understanding and active support. Conservation is not for the few. It requires an effective constituency. We have to bring together all of those with a common concern, and weld them into a viable political force. Some of the legislation that has come out of Congress recently indicates a high level of concern across the nation. There is good reason to believe that in some of our coming elections the voice of the environmentalist will be heard in our land. This is the rock on which our temple will be built.

36

CLEARING OBSTACLES AND GETTING RESULTS AT THE LOCAL LEVEL

THOMAS W. RICHARDS

Mr. Richards is an effective implementer who, in a political role, stopped planning for planning's sake and started planning to accomplish a result. His strategy is described, using open space as an example.

I would like to share with you the experience of one former public official in attempting to improve the environment of his local community. It is probably far easier to get results at a local level than at any other level of government. Citizens and public officials can have a direct influence upon their environment by active participation in the environmental decision-making process. I shall use Arlington County, Virginia, as an example, and specifically the open-space and recreational-land acquisition program of the Arlington County Board, though many of the techniques can be applied in the area of social planning, fighting air pollution, and transportation planning.

The setting is Arlington County, Virginia, 1960. The County is immediately south of the Potomac River from the nation's capitol. In 1960, it had a population of 166,000 people. Of its 25 square miles, 20% was federally owned. Of the remaining lands, 93% were developed. An inventory of County parks and recreational lands available for public use indicated only 320 acres. The County, because of its close-in location, was beginning to feel development pressures for high-rise and apartment use. The community feared development and had a latent concern for the preservation of park land and open space. This concern, however, had not yet reached the ballot box—a $500,000 bond referendum for parks had just failed.

The community had been in the throes of a planning effort that had begun six years earlier. The bookshelves were full of plans, but there had been no attempt to implement the major planning recommendations. The planners were frustrated, the citizens were restless, and the political leadership was distressed. For some elements, planning had become an end in itself.

The political leadership, concerned with the inaction of the planners and without a solid base of support, jumped into the open-space planning process. They developed a plan that included an expansion of park facilities, acquisition of more recreation lands, and cooperative open-space endeavors on a state and regional basis. As a result of their endeavors, by 1968 the community had acquired 400 more acres of park land and open space, had participated in a regional program that purchased over 3,000 acres of recreational lands, and had developed a solid base of public support for the program. Let us examine some of their techniques.

Planning

As a first step, the County Board constructed a comprehensive park and recreation open-space plan to develop a broad base of support. The plan was needed to serve as an acquisition guideline, to meet the legal requirements for condemnation, and to qualify for state and federal matching grants. It had to be simple and concise.

Many plans had already been prepared in Arlington, and the planning function had become an end in itself. After discharging one planner and severing relationships with a number of planning consultants, the County Board jumped directly into planning by assigning one of its members the coordinating role. The Board was now part of the planning process, and political judgements were built into the plan. As a result, a program was developed that could realistically be accomplished.

Regional Cooperation

The County Board soon found that there were insufficient lands within its boundary to meet the needs of the population. To find such lands, the community needed to cooperate with sister jurisdictions. The Arlington County Board, working with the Washington Metropolitan Council of Governments, initiated an open-space program for the entire metropolitan area. Existing resources were inventoried, needs projected, and high-priority acquisitions identified. This regional plan was accomplished in 18 months, accepted by the jurisdictions, and became the basis for the successful applications to the federal government for first 20%, then 30%, and now 50% open-space acquisition monies. The plan for Northern Virginia was absorbed into the Virginia Outdoor Recreation program and allowed the immediate acquisition of over 2,000 acres of land. This is important, for the communities of Northern Virginia alone could not have provided sufficient funds.

In order to have enough land, the County worked with sister jurisdictions in the Northern Virginia Park Authority to acquire less expensive, more rural land. Three major park holdings of over 4,000 acres were purchased. This regional cooperation stretched the local dollar by adding the funds of sister jurisdictions. These dollars were then matched by the State of Virginia and, in turn, the total sum was matched by a federal grant. No one jurisdiction could have afforded the entire cost.

Program Funding

Local governments have great pressures on them for available funds. Traditionally, park-land and open-space purchase has had a low priority. Land acquisition programs, therefore, must be budgeted in association with other needs. Capital needs must be projected on a three- or five-year basis to plan sources of funds and demands. Available federal and state matching funds must be calculated. Realistic, defensible programs should result. Arlington did this on a three-year and a five-year basis.

Acquisition Strategy

The County developed a land acquisition strategy. Land values were increasing dramatically, and syndicates were trying to put together blocks throughout the County, several in areas earmarked for open-space purchase. The County acquired key tracts within the blocks, destroying overall development potential and cutting the heart out of speculative value. This checkerboarding technique on two occasions saved desirable in-town acreages from development.

The County also chose carefully between the possible agencies through which it could condemn the earmarked land. The speed with which an agency could act was critical because of rising values. In one case, the choice of the regional park agency over the County authority saved at least $70,000.

Grantsmanship

Securing funds from state and federal agencies is a skill. Local jurisdictions should know in detail the programs that can assist them. They should cultivate personal relationships with the officials responsible for processing grants. They should develop political tactics—finding Congressional support or encouraging key citizen contact with officials, for example. If grantsmanship is well practiced, local dollars can be matched up to 3 to 1.

Working with Private Conservation Groups

The County, working with the Northern Virginia Regional Park Authority, had identified a major acquisition—Mason Neck, below Mount Vernon on the Potomac. The State of Virginia, the Bureau of Sport Fisheries and Wildlife, and the Northern Virginia Regional Park Authority all wanted a portion of the area. No one of these three organizations had the financial resources immediately available.

All three requested The Nature Conservancy—a private, nonprofit, land-conserving organization—to step in and try to buy the heart of the tract. The Conservancy was able to acquire options and contracts tying down 2,600 acres valued at $5,600,000.

These lands formed a barrier which removed some very valuable land from development and blocked other potential development, allowing the park agencies to acquire additional acres as they came on the market.

By working with a private, nonprofit group, the state and regional agencies saved themselves massive severance damages that would result through condemnation by a single organization. And by taking the land off the market immediately, the agencies saved themselves rising value costs.   Finally, development was forestalled on 3,000 other acres.

Private conservation groups such as The Nature Conservancy also assist governmental agencies by participating in crisis purchases.   On several occasions the Conservancy has been able to buy and hold land for government agencies where the properties marked for purchase, but as yet unfunded, were facing immediate sale.

Private conservation agencies can also arrange advantageous sales and gift/purchases.   These agencies work with the seller to write off portions of his capital gain as a gift in the transaction. The Conservancy, working in Northern Virginia, has been able to arrange significant gift/purchases that have saved the government jurisdictions over $200,000.

It would be pleasant to leave you with the impression that all open-space needs of Northern Virginia and Arlington County have been met.   Unfortunately this is not only not the case, but an even greater tragedy is developing.   Many of the lands acquired in the program are now threatened by interstate highway development.   There is not a natural area, park, playground, historic site, or building that is safe today from the onslaught of highways. Near Washington, D.C., for example, the Three Sisters Bridge and its attendant highways is being built despite the protests of citizens and political leaders.   Its construction will wreck the beauty of a stretch of the Potomac which is much as it was when explorer John Smith saw it in the 1600's.   Our most successful open-space planning and acquisition efforts seem to be of no avail in the face of highway planners and bulldozers.   We must find the means of controlling this menace before our environment is irreparably damaged.

37

GOVERNMENT AND ENVIRONMENTAL QUALITY

LYNTON CALDWELL

As long as our government fails to serve our environmental needs, the chances for survival aren't bright. It is good to see the problem defined and some major directions for action given.

It is difficult to explain how and why government organizations fail to serve the environmental needs of man. What changes in governmental organizations are necessary for the wise use of the human environment? How are these changes to be obtained?

Basic to a discussion of governmental responsibility for the environment is man's relationship to the natural world. This relationship is complex and varied. No two men have precisely the same environment and they do not interact with their environment in precisely the same way. But there are certain generalities that hold true for all men in relation to all environments. These generalities comprise the environmental parameters for human health, happiness, and survival. They are mankind's planetary life-support system.

The elements of man's natural life-support system are familiar, but their relationship to one another and to man's well-being is not adequately understood. The major elements are air, water, soil, sunlight, and other living things. Man's parameters include his adaptive capabilities and his range of tolerance for temperature, noise, light, crowding, and isolation. Man needs to understand these interrelationships better, for he is now altering the state of all the elements of his environment, and the consequences of his action are proving to be disastrous.

Scientific knowledge and technology have enabled man to change his environment, but as yet they have been of little help in using the environment wisely and safely. He has also tended to take his environment for granted, to assume the biosphere to be a gift of God or nature. But by the beginning of the 20th century, the relationship of human society to the natural world was radically changed. It is this changed relationship that is basic to the question of the adequacy of governmental organization for the management of man's environmental relationships.

THE VULNERABILITY OF NATIONS

My thesis that government organization is inadequate rests on the following premise. Through scientific knowledge and technology, human impact on the planetary life-support system or biosphere is being stressed beyond the point of safety. The quality of man's natural environment is being steadily and rapidly impaired. The major factors are mobility of people and the impact of their technology. The Earth, which was once limitless in relation to the numbers and needs of man, has suddenly become limited and increasingly small in relation to the demands of man. When the world seemed limitless, and its capacity for self-renewal vast, man busied himself occupying the Earth and subduing it to his purposes. Organized governments not only maintained civil society, but helped man get what he wanted from nature. Modern man came to perceive the world as a limitless storehouse of natural wealth, or "natural resources." The concept of the biosphere was neither articulated nor understood.

Preoccupied with farming, mining, lumbering, city building, and disposing of waste residues, human society paid little attention to the resulting transformation of its own environmental condition. But not so long ago came a day when perceptive men looked around them and discovered that they had changed the open-space world of all past history into the closed-space world of the spaceship. The spaceship image, articulated by Adlai Stevenson, is equally valid for nations and for the world as a whole. It symbolizes the finite character of the world and its resources, and the necessity for protecting and maintaining its regenerative capacities as an unavoidable price for human survival. Implicit in the spaceship metaphor are concepts of carrying capacity, recycling of resources, articulation of subsystems and total system, and continuous system maintenance.

These are not concepts that governmental or international organizations have been designed to implement. The structures of law and public institutions have evolved on the basis of assumptions and objectives that, whatever their validity in the past, cannot be relied on to cope with the environmental problems of the present and future. Because man has not recognized a problem in the relationship of society to its total environment, he has not organized his public institutions to deal with it. On the contrary, his tendency to concentrate on immediate material objectives and to ignore the broader context of action has led to a structuring of government that actually hinders a good environmental policy.

The rules by which men use natural resources have been made by government through national states and are now supplemented by international agencies. National jurisdiction has been largely geographically defined. Now, however, human mobility and technology impacts upon the total terrestrial biosphere are altering the conditions of the planet beyond the unilateral control of governments. Nations cannot protect their people from the effects of global ecological disasters. Popular awareness of this has led to the nuclear test ban treaty, the treaty for the peaceful use of outer space, and growing worldwide concern over pesticides, the pollution of the oceans, manipulation of climatic conditions, and the destruction of the varied flora, fauna, and landscapes of the natural world. People are now calling for international action to safeguard the biosphere. At national levels, environmental quality is becoming a major political issue. At all political levels the condition and management of the environment has become controversial. Dissatisfaction grows with the declining quality of the environment, but consensus on remedial measures has been slow to develop.

The machinery of government was intended to assist in the exploitation of discrete resources with little regard to the full range of environmental relationships. The impact of science and technology on the environment has increasingly stressed its capacities for renewal and led to ecosystems and species extinction and to ecological degradation. In response to these threats, perceptive men have called for a new set of national and international policies for the protection and management of the environment.

But traditional assumptions still widely prevail. To men to whom Spaceship Earth is merely a poetic abstraction, and whose faith is placed in the unlimited beneficence of nature and the technological ingenuity of man, there is no environmental crisis. To men whose economic interests depend upon the exploitation of the environment, the prospect of public intervention on behalf of long-range ecological considerations is threatening. The present structure of public affairs favors traditional policies toward the environment. Organized blocks of resource users and economic development interests resist new policies of restraint.

There are then, 1) those users of the environment who would proceed along traditional lines, to use technology to offset the impairment of nature, and 2) the advocates of the political economy of Spaceship Earth. This new outlook sees the need for qualitative goals and for new types of organization, national and international, that can serve man's material needs without endangering his health, happiness, and survival on Earth.

ORGANIZATION AND PUBLIC POLICY

In government as in nature, form follows function. But government forms often prove resistant and restrain the exercise of new functions. The traditional structure of the American government, although malleable and adaptable in its broad constitutional outline, has become obsolete in detail. Some changes—such as the Hahn plan for restructuring local government in Virginia along regional lines—moves toward a more rational and realistic organization of public affairs. Yet, for the most part, reform lags far behind events. A crisis of institutional inadequacy is upon us, but few people understand its seriousness.

Because of public apathy and the entrenched interests of governmental agencies and their clients in Congress and throughout the country, fundamental administrative reorganization is very difficult to obtain. Even though the general interest may no longer be served by a narrowly programmed government agency, its beneficiaries are alert to the defense of their special interests. The natural resources use-and-development interests of the country are not generally satisfied with the present state of government organization. They may be critical of public policies that restrict their use of resources, but they would be even more displeased at the prospect of a reorganization in which the agency that administered their particular resource was replaced by or subordinated to an agency oriented primarily to environmental and ecological considerations. The present organization of government, as it relates to the natural environment, was created largely by and for the natural resources industry, including agriculture. Efforts to reorganize government for environmental quality purposes, therefore, encounter a phalanx of opposition from well-organized economic interests whose past influence with Congress and federal executives is a matter of record.

For more than a half century, conservationists have been making appeals for a more coherent and coordinated administration of natural resources policy. The argument for new approaches to public responsibility for the environment also believes that responsible and effective public administration requires a more coherent organization. But the environmental quality appeal has two great advantages over its conservationist predecessors.

First, the environmental quality movement is evolving an organizing concept and philosophy. Conservationists found great difficulty in articulating a positive, substantive goal. The goal of environmental quality was only latent in their arguments, while they actually worked to eliminate competition duplication, and cross-purpose action in the agencies. The politically sterile "economy and efficiency" objective had little public appeal. The specific problems of management were so dissimilar that coordinating them was impossible. In contrast, the environmental issue, with its Spaceship Earth image, has a more coherent view of society from which public policies might be deduced.

The *second* advantage of the environmental quality movement is that the complex and often synergistic character of many environmental problems is forcing new forms of administrative action. For example, the problems of pollution and waste disposal are linked in many ways. Initial efforts to deal with these problems as if they were discrete have followed traditional approaches to natural-resources problems, and they have been hardly more successful. It is becoming even more apparent that new public agencies must be invented. Total systems for the management of water and waste residues in urban communities are being considered. Aerospace technology is being applied to the planning of new approaches to the problem. Many new approaches will involve partnerships among governmental, quasigovernmental, and nongovernmental agencies working together in coordinated systems that are "total." But before this can happen, some fundamental changes in the popular attitudes and political behavior of Americans must occur. These changes, however, may be forced by a crisis in urban ecology.

The greatest immediate need now is for an explicit national policy for the environment and a high-level advocate of it. To this end, more than 35 bills have been introduced into the 91st Congress. Bills have been passed in the Senate and the House, but as of this writing, none have been enacted. These bills, and particularly Title 1 of Senate Bill 1075, declare a national commitment to a policy of environmental quality. The enactment of one of these bills would mark a first step toward the establishment of environmental administration as a major responsibility of government. A strong bill will not easily be enacted unless some sudden, alarming, critical event in the environment stampedes the Congress into action. Even after enactment, implementation will be rugged. A high-level national council on the environment is needed not only to encourage public awareness, but also to enable the United States to cooperate with rapidly developing international efforts to cope with growing threats to the world environment.

ORGANIZATION FOR INTERNATIONAL CONTROL

In a world governed by nations, there are still a great many things that nations cannot do. This has always been true, but today there are areas beyond the reach of national jurisdiction in which the survival of nations and of human society itself are at stake. No nation controls the oceans or the atmosphere. Limited multinational cooperative intentions have often proved ineffectual. Treaties to protect migratory wildlife or unique ecosystems have frequently proved unenforceable. A classic case is the failure of international agreement to prevent the overkill of Antarctic whales. The impact of technology and population pressure on the global environment has led to calls for international action to handle for all mankind those problems that nations cannot handle for their people alone.

The traditional approach to international efforts on environmental issues had been through treaties and conferences. A series of world meetings sponsored by the United Nations and its affiliated organizations has contributed to a foundation for worldwide environment policy in three ways. First, they have made natural resources and environmental issues visible; second, they have helped to marshal relevant scientific and technical information; and third, they have helped nations to become used to working together with minimal nationalistic and ideological considerations. An understanding of what these conferences have accomplished or failed to accomplish would be instructive for the productive outcome of the United Nations Conference on the Problems of the Human Environment to be held in 1972. These are some of the most important conferences held in the last two decades:

1949—United Nations Conference on the Conservation and Utilization of Resources. Lake Success, New York

1955—International Technical Conference on the Conservation of the Living Resources of the Sea. Rome

1963—Conference on Application of Science and Technology for the Benefit of Less Developed Areas. Geneva

1968—UNESCO intergovernmental conference of experts on the scientific basis for rational use and conservation of the resources of the biosphere. Paris.

With the exception of the Biosphere Conference of 1968, these meetings tended toward a technical rather than an ecological orientation, and they did not provide adequate or realistic follow-up.

Worldwide environmental issues also have been considered by the Conservation of Nature and Natural Resources. The IUCN was established in 1948 following an international conference sponsored by UNESCO and the government of France. It is the only international organization specifically and primarily concerned with the protection of the biosphere and the plants, animals, and ecosystems that bring variety, stability, and enrichment to the living world. There is an urgent need for its functions to be greatly enlarged and expanded.

Our evolutionary and environmental heritage cannot be protected through scientific findings or international resolutions. We must provide institutions to ensure that man does not impair the quality or viability of his environmental base by pursuing his immediate objectives. The foundation for these institutions is a coherent set of policies. Both institutions and policies must be developed simultaneously. Neither can be effective without the other. We must make a sincere effort to relate policies to institutions in order to bring about a rational, ecologically sound control of our environment.

38

THE ONE-TERM POLITICAL LEADER

DIXON ARNETT

It isn't the system; it is the shortcomings of elected leaders that cause the problem. There are young politicians with the potential to be a Theodore Roosevelt. Will we be wise enough to support them?

People have often asked me "Why on earth do you run for office and subject yourself to all that abuse and harrassment?" My stock reply is that "while the task may have unpleasant aspects, it is rewarding to be part of planning for the great future that belongs to my community." This seems to satisfy my questioner; it does not satisfy me!

It is immensely frustrating for the person who is result-oriented to serve in public office. Political wranglings for the bene-

fit of the press hinder decision-making. Pride in political author-
ship prevents legislators from acting forcefully on issues suggested
by their colleagues or by members of the opposition party. Personal considerations often supplant a true motivation for common
purpose.

Hundreds of thousands of Americans, young and old, are just
as frustrated now, wondering what our priorities have been over
the last 20 years and why, in God's name, we have not met our
problems head-on. Some youthful protestors would have us believe that the system is at fault, and that at any cost we must
overturn the system—immature nonsense! But what the protestor
reflects accurately is a growing criticism of the people who run
the system—not the system itself. And in this sense, I myself am
among the front ranks of the protestors.

Man's environment, indeed his basic need to survive, is one of
the bleakest of our known problems, getting worse by leaps and
bounds while shortsighted political leaders sit by grinding their
personal axes as they preside over the demise of quality living.
Their golden political rule seems to be that before they can take
action to solve a problem, they must wait until sufficient demand
for a solution builds up among their constituents. This, I suggest,
is only part of the political leader's job, and the lesser part, too.
Waiting for the public demand (which all too often means special-
interest demand in this day) is simply being responsive, the easiest
thing in the world to do. Anybody can be elected to do that.

A public official must not only be responsive; he must be responsible! That means having the perception to recognize problems and potential problems, being willing to meet them head-on,
and having the guts to come to a timely, yet deliberate decision.

Decisions about problems of the environment are especially
difficult and need forthright and comprehensive purpose. Environmental affairs cover the complex relation of man's physical
surroundings to his social needs. When a public official takes an
action opting for the preservation of open space, he may be affecting the need for housing in his area. When he opts for a transportation corridor, he may be affecting open space, and so on. There
is no magic in any single-purpose approach. A political leader has
to be willing to risk the anger of everyone or he will neither accomplish anything nor gain the appreciation of anyone.

The San Francisco Bay is one of the nation's best examples
of opportunity and one of the worst examples of political leadership failure as a result of political sluggishness. We seem to have
made a little progress through single-purpose regional agencies.
We have plans—beautiful plans. We have progress toward an

inclusive regional governmental agency—if that doesn't get too diffused by local politicians who think that regional rule is happening for the first time. But we have never had anyone forthrightly introduce legislation for anything but temporary, interim types of solutions. No state legislators had the foresight to introduce a bill to provide the funds to acquire for the public in perpetuity the tidelands and shorelines of the San Francisco Bay. That would be effective decision-making—investing in the future within the traditions of our private-property legal ethic.

These problems are all similar to other areas of our nation. The southern California coastline, Lake Erie, the Potomac River, Lake Tahoe, the entire multistate length of the Mississippi River, and others—all are areas which demand responsible political leadership. We need more political leaders who, when elected or appointed, need to think, talk, and act as though their present term were going to be their only term in office, and they didn't have to worry about the so-called first rule of politicians about being reelected.

I believe that if we had more political leaders with this kind of independence, they might be reelected on demand!

Industry

Technological exploitation may be "profitable" in 1970, but if the result is catastrophe in 1980, who profits? We all breathe smog. We all eat contaminated food. What can be done to balance our industrial production with a quality environment?

One answer is for business to formulate an economic design for environmental quality that provides profit but includes social costs such as pollution control.

Business has had a dual role. On the negative side, its use of ecologically unplanned technology is, to a considerable degree, responsible for our environmental problems. On the positive side, it is the cornucopia that gives man material comfort and, more importantly, provides the wealth and energy to clean up the problems we face.

Then, in the middle, is the individual. No person is really separate from industry for, as consumers, we all share in its effects on the environment—both good and bad—individually and or-ganizationally, nationally and internationally. We're all part of the problem; and a realistic solution to survival will require coopera-tion between all sectors.

It's certain that business must have a positive means of cooper-ating before it will help achieve a healthy environment. Any solution to environmental problems must include the financial aspect: how is it all going to be paid for? Taxes are one way. An-other is the application of environmental improvement costs directly to products, or to producers and consumers. Ultimately such action of higher taxes and higher prices could check limitless consumption.

Fortunately, there are economists who now argue that we don't need population growth to have a healthy economy; in fact, a reversal would be healthy.* It may well be that a business sector committed to quality production in a total sense rather than to growth only can be our salvation.

---

* See John G. Welles, "The Economy Doesn't Need More People," *The Wall Street Journal*, April 22, 1970.

39

ADVERTISING: AFFORDING THE MESSAGE

JERRY MANDER

Dr. Paul Ehrlich states that being proud of the gross national product is like a cancer patient being proud of his cancer. In this widely qoted paper, an advertising executive challenges the myth that economic growth is a social necessity.

It has occurred to me that I am employed in a dying industry.

Advertising is not dying out for any of the usually advocated reasons—immoral or distasteful behavior in the marketplace. Perhaps it should be killed for those reasons but it will not be necessary.

Advertising is a critical element encouraging an economic system committed to growth. Expanding technology is a by-word of political and economic rhetoric, and the country's economic health is judged by the rate at which Gross National Product increases, year by year.

The advertising business—based on a commission system—is particularly tied to the expanding economy. As long as expansion continues, ad revenues increase and so things would seem to be going along just fine for everyone. After all, as David Ogilvy, a well known ad man has pointed out, "Clients are hogs with all four feet in the trough."

However, there is only so much getting bigger possible.

That should have been evident, of course, the moment our astronauts flashed us pictures of the Earth and we noted it was round. The idea of an infinitely expanding Gross National Product on an isolated sphere, a finite system, an island in space, is complete nonsense, to put it as lightly as possible, or, to put it the way I personally perceive it, may be, together with population growth, the most dangerous tendency in the world today.

You simply may not have a continually expanding economy within a finite system: Earth. At least not if the economy is based upon anything approaching technological exploitation and production as we now know it. On a round ball, there is only so much of anything. Minerals. Food. Air. Water. Space . . . and things *they* need to stay in balance. An economy which feeds on itself can't keep on eating forever. Or, as Edward Abbey put it, "growth for the sake of growth is the ideology of the cancer cell."

Yet just the other day Mr. Nixon reaffirmed his faith in American industry's abilities to continue its "healthy" growth rate. And the President of U.S. Steel said he doesn't believe in "clean water for its own sake."

The first remark tells us that the patient hasn't yet noticed he's near collapse, and the second tells us that the cancer hasn't noticed it's running out of digestibles.

It will not of course be possible to ignore the disease much longer . . . not when whole bodies of water are dead, when species of fish and wildlife are disappearing, and now when forests are dying because of air pollution, with the oceans next on the list.

There *are* some hopeful stirrings in industry and we shouldn't be too surprised at that. After all, even a board chairman of a power company—no matter his politics and faith in the virtues of uncontrolled free enterprise—will feel some personal distress together with the rest of us when he finds that his weekend fishing isn't what it used to be. Dead fish.

So far, however, the response has remained very feeble and cynical at best, and destructive at worst. For the most part industry still sees pollution as primarily a public relations problem, duly assigned to P.R. and advertising men who are placed in charge of repairing the *image* rather than the cause. And so the company will contribute funds to conservation purposes . . . a tenth of one percent of net profits, for example, which is to go towards fixing up the damage, one supposes, or else it's an incipient "stop me before I kill" phenomenon.

Or, the public is treated to the sort of ads that oil companies are now placing, explaining how their rigs in swamps actually preserve the wildlife and plantlife there by preventing other worse encroachment. Another oil company tells us in ads of research having to do with the throwing of old cars into the oceans. It does wonders for the fish, say the ads, who use the rusting hulks as new homes. No reefs necessary.

Well, even fish will make the best of a bad situation of course, as exemplified by the fact that in the dead waters of Lake Erie, there was recently discovered a new strange mutant of carp, which actually lives off the poisons in the water. Not good for eating by man yet, however.

We also see vast advertising expenditures for spectacular technological antidotes, appearing everywhere. The hottest growth industry is in the field of antipollutants, air cleaners, water cleaners . . . or high yield chemicals to get the soil to produce more than it naturally would . . . all of which in my own view, have the effect of reinforcing an already suicidal tendency in a society dazzled by technology's feats to believe that technology will itself cure its own self-invented sickness.

I am prepared to believe it can in some isolated cases, such as in capture of polluting wastes in some industries, but in general, I doubt that the answer lies with more technological innovation.

All this industrial hustle to fix things up by more and better gadgets and chemicals is just one more example of man forever bringing rabbits to Australia, as Dave Brower has described it.

The cure always causes a new scourge of its own.

Take antibiotics. According to some people, they will soon kill off enough of the weaker bacteria to leave us with only a killer virus.

Or high yield wheat strains. Though they do keep some people fed for a bit, what else do they do? To the soil. To the wheat. To the people who eat it and to the plant life around it. We don't know, but I'm afraid we'll find out soon enough.

And now we find hundreds of thousands of advertising dollars being spent by companies girding themselves for the big gold rush in the oceans. The ads proclaim how everything in the world is just fine because of the "infinite" resources in the oceans . . . food and mineral wealth. They don't recognize, yet, that there is no such thing as infinity, and even if there were, industry's other hand is busily pulling infinity back in this direction by killing off the ocean's resources with DDT and garbage and a hundred other creations at a rate which is increasing faster than population.

I am prepared to bet that the ultimate answer to ecological problems is not cleverer technology. It will probably be less technology, at least of a certain sort, and I never would have thought five years ago that I'd be coming out on the side of the Luddites today.

Unlike them, however, I am not saying we should tear down factories, or that there should be no technology. Naturally. But I am saying there should probably be a lot less of it, and less people to be served by it of course, but most important, *less emphasis on increase, starting now.* Less emphasis on acquisition and material wealth as any measure of anything good.

Beginning now, national preparations toward a no-growth economy.

Not *no* cars. We are too far gone for that. But no new roads, say, starting today. And the beginnings of a national effort to de-glamorize automobiles and their so-called advantages. Eventually, I predict, we will have national control of auto manufacture

. . . no *new* cars unless one is turned in simultaneously somewhere else. Like New York taxi medallions. Or liquor licenses. It seems as sure to me as that the Earth is round. And I believe we'll have a ban on auto company advertising, or at least that portion of it that encourages the sale of new cars or that has the effect of increasing production.

If I judge the developing public mood correctly, we are nearer to that necessity than most of us would have believed a few years ago. Maybe we will continue to have *some* legal auto advertising, but it will be strictly informative in nature—WE HAVE THESE FORDS HERE TODAY—or, if there is a God, it will be something like the World War II slogan, IS THIS TRIP NECESSARY? It could happen, especially if auto companies purged themselves of all thoughts of annual style change—which encourages the more, more, more kind of thinking in society—and went for one high quality, expensive, very long lasting non-polluting model. And stabilized their production level. Either voluntarily, or because of government action.

The auto industry will of course not be the only industry to feel the bite when it finally gets through that Gross National Product is going to be stabilized, eventually, no matter what. All industry will feel it, but I believe the more polluting and exploiting industries will be the first to have their expansion curtailed.

It is not so important really that a computer manufacturer stabilize his production right now, but it does seem important that oil company expansion should be controlled, as well as power company expansion. Not no power, you understand, but no promotion of power and hopefully the beginnings of a mentality in the public mind of a stabilization of power levels towards a no-growth system. Even if power supply does not keep up with temporarily rising demand. The consequences of uncontrolled population growth and industrial expansion might then be brought home, literally; less power for everyone.

I think we will soon see public outcry against pushing of certain chemicals and detergents and certainly against all pesticides. I am already aware of movements to ban the ads of airlines and airplane companies. (It is certainly true that people who need to get from here to there will still manage to do so.) Similar movements are underway to ban ads of products which are sold in non-biodegradable containers, like glass; to ban the advertising of lumber company products and mining company products; and, in another vein, the advertising of furs of endangered species.

It seems to me that the trend got started with cigarette advertising, although cigarette advertising is demonstrably much less of a menace to society's survival and well being than lumber company advertising or chemical company ads. Cigarettes are only a menace to an individual person. Doubling of power, say, doubles pollution and thereby affects everyone, and we've no choice in the matter besides.

Lest it seem I am advocating the loss of a lot of good advertising talent, may I suggest that there may be *some* new growth industries to ease the strain. When power company ad dollars drop, perhaps the ad agency can keep going by a great big government subsidized campaign on behalf of the contraceptive industry. And the agency that had handled the Dow Chemical account could have the pornographic products campaign. And if the commercial media refuse to carry those sorts of ads, despite the fact that promoting for pleasure in sex rather than procreation might just help the population crisis, then may I suggest that free air time be offered by NET for that sort of commercial.

Despite the inherent logic of all this to me, I do not expect many advertising people to come rallying round at the end of this panel to discuss how they might encourage a no-growth mentality. My late partner, Howard Gossage, in his last speech, put it this way: "Public service advertising as it is advocated and performed by the ad industry, is willing to innovate and alarm and cause controversy, but only within those elements of society who are *for* cancer or *against* safe driving."

Someone *will* come rallying round after this speech to tell me that my observations are idiotic, for the following reasons: (1) The economy will fall apart if we begin to slow down certain industries starting now, eventually striving towards a no-growth system, and (2) it is impractical, because the masses of people would never go for it. They "want" the fruits of technology even if it's poisoned fruit.

I have some answers, insufficient though they may be.

One. As I've said, I do not see the elimination of industry any more than one sees the elimination of North American Rockwell Corp. at the end of a wartime period. There may well be other things North American Rockwell can do besides making armaments but if not there are other companies which can.

Likewise, there are plenty of companies engaged profitably in non-polluting or exploiting industry, or at least not seriously so. Let *them* do the brunt of whatever growing is still left, until things finally level off.

Also, it should be said, I am no economist and it will take an economist or a few thousand of them to figure out what this imminent no-growth system means—and I do mean it is imminent whether we like it or not, if you accept that the earth is round. While I don't know personally all the economic details, I do understand the consequences of *not* pulling back. You don't proceed over a bridge that will fall from your weight just for lack of another one in sight. The consequences of a short-run reduction in power, while population growth gets stabilized, which may mean that all of us will live with 20% dimmer light bulbs, strikes me as infinitely more desirable than no life in the rivers, or no oxygen in the air.

One more point in this area. I believe that the economic hardships which may accrue to society because U.S. Steel does not expand anymore, will only be hardships if (A) population and the work force continues to grow, and (B) if society refuses to redistribute available capital and material to those who are currently deprived.

Two. Impracticality. These ideas are impractical only in the sense that it's impractical to remove one cancerous kidney before it proceeds to the other. It's a painful and dangerous operation, but consider the alternatives.

Preparing the public for the changing facts of life is of course the major effort and requires every bit of media understanding and cooperation. And it requires every bit of professional advertising and public relations talent and a government commitment to use the talent for an effort on a par with, or greater than, the preparation of society to the end of a wartime economy, and I hereby volunteer my own office to undertake the ad campaign for the government, free, whether it's contraceptives or reduced power, if the government would only be willing to recognize the importance of both.

I don't think the communications problem is insurmountable. Great things were achieved during the Second World War when another sort of rationing became the absolute requirement. There are whole societies in the world who are very relaxed about enforced limits and it could be shown that they seem to be doing just fine.

I am speaking of people who have been born on and live on islands. I have just returned from the tiny islands in Micronesia and I can tell you that the natives there don't have any problem at all about understanding limits, or rationing of resources, or a no-growth system.

Micronesian "out-islanders" in particular—that is, those who live across a hundred miles or more of sea from any neighboring islands, and whose contact with the rest of the world is limited to a few souls who arrive on the eighty foot government boat every six months—simply don't think about infinity, or to put it more accurately, the idea that everything is possible.

In order to survive out there by themselves, they've had to gain a pretty good feeling for pacing the breadfruit production and the coconut eating. In some of those places the highest crime is cutting down a coconut tree without communal permission.

And on the islands surrounding Yap—where a culture thrives that is as nearly untouched by non-island ideas as any in the world —there is a very rigid birth control which works this way: Everyone gets married very late—late twenties or early thirties. While there is no particular emphasis on virginity until then, there is plenty of emphasis and sanctions against illegitimate children.

No man will ever marry a woman who has given birth first, and consequently the ladies have devised an intrauterine device made of hibiscus bark which works as well as the plastic ones and I'll bet doesn't cause cancer.

All the things we've been raised to worship—Man's limitless power, the ever-giving nature of Mother Earth—all those infinite possibilities are now beginning to seem less infinite. I'm suggesting that perhaps it's time to take as a model for our future survival-thinking and propaganda the way islanders have managed to do things, because that's what we're on, it's round, and there's only so much of everything and in general people haven't realized that.

At this moment we are totally unprepared emotionally, psychologically and technologically for the emerging facts. We are very much in the position of two friends of mine who recently left their home in Chicago to move to the island of Oahu and who recently wrote me that they are suffering from a syndrome very common to expatriate mainlanders. Island sickness. Every weekend they get in the car and drive clear around the island, maybe several times, hoping that some new direction will appear, but it never does.

Our struggle is toward what the black studies demonstrators have called "reeducation." Develop an island psychology in everyone on Earth and if there are any young activist SDS hippie anarchist conspirators in the audience, I would urge you to go out and get your college to institute departments of green studies at once, and, while you're at it, put away the books on traditional economics.

If we can convey that notion, somehow, in a mass way, the islandness of things, we may have to live through some mass hysteria while people drive around (or fly, perhaps) aimlessly, but once they get the idea that it's all a big circle, the race may survive. (Nature will survive in any event, of course, since it is everything. If we all go under that won't stop the regenerative process, so let's be clear that it's people that are the endangered species.)

I never thought I'd be glad about the flight to the Moon, but in spite of its absurdity, in my view, considering the other needs of the day, it may yet turn out to be the critically important thing from a conservationist's viewpoint, because *it* may accelerate the idea of Earth as an island; its finiteness.

It seems to me that if we can get enough pictures of Earth taken from space, and the further away the better, the more the context will sink in. We are isolated in all that blackness. We can never, as a race, make it across that vast sea in time to find any new home. This is the only place we have and these people on this globe are our only possible friends and lovers.

We proposed once before in a Sierra Club ad the idea of an Earth National Park; a wildlife island in space, where *we* are the wildlife. It is our only possible home and perhaps we should practice thinking and talking about it in those terms and thinking of more ways to pass it along.

40

THE ECOLOGY OF BIG BUSINESS

ROBERT O. ANDERSON

The skill of leadership seasoned by success is obvious in this industrialist's statement outlining problems and means of solving them. Mr. Anderson calls for quality rather than quantity, a demand that strikes out at our "consumer heritage."

Many people who have recently become aware of the growing crisis for man's environment—and how it has come to pass—arrive at an angry and despairing frame of mind. They see modern man stupidly condemning the soil to erosion, blindly exploiting the forest and the seas, mindlessly polluting the air and waters, recklessly fouling the countryside and the cities, while driving to extinction one species of animal life after another. Such people see man learning nothing from his own follies, crashing headlong and heedlessly to his own self-destruction.

There is certainly enough truth in this attitude to cause concern—even alarm. But it rests upon a gloomy assessment of man and what motivates him, and a sense of foreboding that anticipates doom. Perhaps anger is essential, in arousing us all to action, but it can also inhibit the constructive approach that we need for what may well be the greatest issue of contemporary society. We have witnessed a long and increasingly rapid series of scientific and technological triumphs which have made possible, in the more advanced countries, an historic evolution from an economy of scarcity to an economy of abundance. The people in advanced societies have been freed largely from manual labor, provided with the material necessities of life, and left with a reasonable amount of leisure time—thus meeting the old and commendable goal of a decent material standard of living for the general population.

Now we are suddenly aware of the irony that in the process of achievement we have created grave new problems. The migration of people freed from labor on the land, for example, has contributed to the crippling crisis of the cities. The evolution from an economy of scarcity to one of abundance has been compromised by a parallel evolution from underpopulation to overpopulation. We have failed to distinguish between the benefits of technology for the quality of life and the per capita GNP.

I once heard a prominent executive complain that he was "dying from success." I like to think of our present predicament, deplorable though it is, in that sense: as an agony of achievement. Or, as the President has said, "we are victims of our own technological genius." I also prefer to think that the opportunity ahead of us is not just that of averting disaster by the skin of our teeth, but that of responding to challenge with a burst of constructive and creative action.

The Commons

Garrett Hardin, a noted California biologist, has described the present crisis of the environment as "the tragedy of the common." He pictures a tribe of herdsmen, each owning some cattle, who pasture their animals on ground that belongs to no individual—in other words, a common. The herd grows and there is a danger of overgrazing to the detriment of all. But to each individual herdsman, the value of adding an animal to his stock outweighs the disadvantages of overgrazing because these are spread out among all the herdsmen. So each one, selfishly but rationally in his own mind, adds to his herd until the pasture is ruined.

Hardin uses this analogy to explain the present pollution of the atmosphere and waters—which he also describes as commons. Each individual, or company, or industry, or utility, or government unit generates pollutants because each is the direct beneficiary and the disadvantages are widely spread. The participants seem locked in an immediately rational but ultimately self-defeating system. This Hardin sees as the "tragedy of the common."

The solution for the herdsmen was the invention of private property. If land is grazed only by the owner's herd, then he will be the sole victim of his own abuses. He thus acquires an automatic self-interest in responsible management and the conservation of his resources.

But that solution is not available when it comes to the rivers, the lakes, the high seas, the atmosphere of this earth. There are indeed commons. They belong to no man and cannot be divided up or parceled out for responsible care by individuals. Yet if we are to avoid running into disaster, a great deal must be done about those commons—and quickly.

We all know the sobering facts: the dispersal each year in the United States of millions of tons of smoke and noxious fumes into the air; the annual dumping of trillions of gallons of hot water and unknown millions of tons of organic and chemical pollutants into our waters; the discarding yearly of 7 million cars, 20 million tons of paper, 48 billion cans, 26 billion bottles and jars. We know the results in terms of smog, pollution, and what someone has called the "uglification" of our land. We know there is a crisis of the environment.

Qualitative Social Criteria

While I do not want to soften the alarm, I do want to argue that a reaction to the environmental crisis already has set in and is fast gathering steam. Often people are not aware of a major shift in attitudes in its early stages, and I believe we are in that situation now. Let us ask, then, what are the major elements of an adequate attack on the problem, and also look at what is happening today.

For one thing, I believe there must be a general shift of values away from quantitative toward qualitative criteria for the good life and the good society, and I believe such a shift is already taking place.

The object for all mankind for countless thousands of years has been simply to escape from material want. Perhaps it was only when our basic material needs had been met that large numbers of people could see that material comfort was not enough.

Political Leadership

If we are to make an adequate response to the crisis of the environment, political leadership at various levels of government is essential. Some is present now, and is gathering force rapidly. Much more is necessary.

Local governments are becoming aroused about smog and pollution; Pittsburgh and Los Angeles are prominent examples, but there are many others. New York City plans an investment of $2 billion over 10 years for clean air, clean water, and clean streets. State governments are also awakening to the crisis. New York State voted three years ago to raise a billion dollars to clean up its rivers over a 10-year period. There is the Environmental Quality Council at the national level.

The necessary political leadership may now be on the horizon. Indeed, if I were entering politics tomorrow, I would run on an environmental platform for political reasons as well as personal convictions.

Appeal to Youth

The young people of today who will be moving into positions of influence and leadership in public and private affairs are another critical factor in an adequate response to the challenge.

I have great confidence in their response. The negative side of the present restlessness among our youth is a rejection of what they see as unmitigated materialism. The positive side is the search for new and more rewarding qualitative values. I can think of nothing that should appeal more to their constructive energies than the humanistic values inherent in a robust attack on pollution, waste, and desecration of natural resources and native beauty.

Some of the activist elements which now find their focus in opposition to the war in Vietnam may well find their next focus against projects and proposals that despoil the environment.

Technological Clean-up

Another essential part of an adequate response to the crisis is a massive concentration of scientific and technological effort.

A great deal of basic research is still needed. We do not really know the long-term effects of carbon monoxide pollution in the air on human health. Scientists are sure that air and water pollution will affect the climate, but they disagree as to whether the global temperature is going up or down.

It is not ironic to contemplate the fact that a major part of the answer to the depredation wrought by technology is technological. We have been preoccupied with the technology of production. Now we must concentrate on the technology needed to undo the damage of industrialization, urbanization, and population growth.

We may need very intensive projects, approached on a systems basis and assigned a high priority in the national scheme, to repair the worst of the damage and to manage the environment guided by a regard for the quality of human life. We shall need administrative mechanisms using the most modern techniques of research, analysis, model building, computerization, and data storage and retrieval systems. We may need, too, brand-new institutional arrangements to coordinate work in public and private sectors and at various government levels. Perhaps the first need is to pull together information on what is being done already, too much of it independently, and to coordinate existing research programs.

Industrial Statesmanship

Another essential element in an adequate response to our predicament is acceptance by private industry of an active and responsible role toward the health of the environment. This is where I come to business—big business. There is no question that industry, the products of industry, and the people who consume them are the leading polluters of the environment. This is not because any industry or company has adopted pollution as corporate policy. No responsible individual has elected consciously to follow an antisocial course of action.

Pollution of the environment is the result principally of industry's effort to exploit new technology to meet rising consumer demand, inflated by both affluence and population growth. Industry cannot be excused for a lack of foresight about the social consequences of unrestrained expansion and single-minded attention to the real or imagined whims of the consumer.

The point is that the damage has far surpassed socially acceptable limits. Private industry and the consumer must bear their full share of the burden in repairing the damage and maintaining the balance of nature. When it comes to the quality of the environment, industry must recognize the impact of its operation on society as a whole and the implications for the future of human welfare. Other branches of society have their own responsibilities; industry's responsibility is to find ways of producing without excessive pollution regardless of whether it costs more and regardless of how the increased cost is absorbed.

The implications of this are complex and far-reaching. But industry will either voluntarily or will ultimately be forced to adapt to the environmental imperatives. Fortunately, certain industries are electing the voluntary course.

What is required is a high level of industrial statesmanship. All that this entails remains to be worked out in theory and in practice. As a starter I would suggest a few foci for industry's contribution to rescuing the environment.

First, short-term research and development of antipollution technology.

Second, studies for reducing or eliminating air pollution from waste and exhaust fumes must be coordinated under some governmental agency which can review all industry. California has made a commendable start in this, and could provide a model for a long-term national program. Fossil fuels are and will continue to be the principal source of energy for the world during the balance of this century. The concept of replacing them with alternative sources of energy is intriguing, but unfortunately impracticable. We must learn to live with existing sources of energy, and to control or eliminate the pollution problem.

Third, there must be greater use of materials that will deteriorate naturally—the bio-degradable materials—rather than of hard metals or plastics.

Fourth, development of techniques for recycling waste products. Almost certainly a concentrated search for ways to dispose of automotive scrap would yield results before we all live in a continental junkyard. We may need new criteria for determining what is "economic." I have no illusions about the difficulty of this. But when the motivating force is the integrity of the environment, rather than the profitability of an isolated enterprise, then we must include more qualitative considerations in judging whether we can "afford" it or not.

Fifth, I believe that private enterprise should ration the ultimate waste materials, by avoiding unnecessary packaging for example.

Sixth, I believe that industry should take the lead in working out the thorny question of liability for damage to the environment when it does occur. We are an industrialized, urbanized, technological society whether we like it or not. Present levels of population prohibit a return to a pastoral society. With the best of will, damage to the environment will occur from time to time. I believe we should take that into account and work out an equitable solution to the question of liability so that all concerned can plan accordingly.

International Cooperation

The problems of the environment will require international cooperation on a scale never approached before. The atmosphere and the high seas are global and can be dealt with adequately only on a global basis. The awareness of the threat to the environment is an international phenomenon today. All the specialized agencies of the United Nations are in one way or another doing something about the crisis of the environment, and so are all of the UN regional economic commissions.

An indication of the level of international interest is NATO's response to the crisis. NATO embraces a large part of the industrialized, urbanized, technological societies in the world. Last spring, the United States proposed that NATO establish a Commission on the Problems of Modern Man for joint study and action. The first reaction was quite skeptical, but by fall the members agreed unanimously and enthusiastically. This has already led to a reorganization and upgrading of governmental agencies in Western Europe concerned with the problems of the environment. Joint study projects involving two or more countries had to be laid out. It seems to me to be a sign of the times that a collective security organization, long thought to be a purely military arrangement, is turning its attention to cooperative work on the problems of modern society with a view to contributing to the quality of life not only for its members but for all peoples of all nations, including the members of the rival military alliance.

This pervading international concern will surely be focused on the UN Conference on the Human Environment to be held in Sweden in 1972.

A Finite Space

New and more qualitative social criteria, courageous political leadership, massive technological projects, appeal for youth, industrial statesmanship, and international cooperation—these all seem to me to be necessary ingredients of an adequate response to the crisis of the environment. All of these elements are present today, even though they are just beginning to gather steam.

But there may be yet another essential ingredient that cannot be legislated, bought, invented, or institutionalized. This is nothing less than a change in the perspective in which man sees himself and in his relations to others who cohabit his planet.

I believe that this shift is actually taking place and that it stems from our triumphs in outer space. Only a handful of astronauts have seen the earth from outer space with their own eyes, but 500 million around the world have shared the view. I believe this will have a lasting impact on man's view of himself and on his sense of values. Man may finally see himself in his true dimension.

From outer space, the uniqueness of human life somehow takes on greater significance. We are more keenly aware that we— the human race—are the only known higher form of life in the un-measured reaches of the universe. How can this but affect the value we place on the fact that we live and breathe, and that this shared characteristic makes us unique in the cosmos?

A New Cost—Maintenance

Let me close with a general thought about the cost of an adequate response to the crisis of the human environment. Whatever it is, it will pose real budgetary problems for everyone. I would like to point out, however, that there is a precedent for the necessary public attention. In the traditional area of national security, our attitude has always been that we can afford to do whatever is re-quired for military preparedness. I submit that our national secu-rity is endangered by the crisis of the environment.

That raises two issues which I shall offer without attempting to explore here. One is the relationship between the importance of environmental quality and the cost of achieving it. To undertake the task, we must maintain a highly productive society that can mount and afford the massive effort that will be required over the next few decades. I suspect that we will be faced with a new cost, which I think of as a social cost or maintenance cost. Eventually this cost must be borne by the consumer. This social cost may be a very substantial item in terms of our GNP in the years to come, and I hope our economists appreciate its possible magnitude.

The other issue, and probably the most important of all, is the need for the scientific community to indicate clearly the most ur-gent problem area. Private and political thinking has to be guided by strong and thoughtful leadership from those who are closest to our environmental problems. Priorities must be established to prevent a scattered and ineffective attack. Reason, coupled with strong government support and scientific guidance, is the only hope of resolving the problem.

We have the people, the need is apparent, and now we need the courage to move ahead on a task that we alone have created.

41

AN ENVIRONMENTAL ETHIC

L. W. LANE, JR.

"We must make a national, if not international effort to develop a code of ethics and a body of law to govern relationships within our environment . . ."; . . . "We must evolve and accept and practice an 'environmental ethic' that provides a national code of standards similar to the golden rule and the ten commandments."

Laws and ethics on how people behave toward one another, and as groups in a socio-political-economic environment, have usually come about from absolute necessity and very often a crisis. Rarely do these codes of behavior rise to a level of wide acceptance and enforceable laws out of the simple wisdom and great foresight of a few people. The pot only begins to boil when the heat builds up under it. History will show that many of the laws which we all take for granted first saw the light of day in the writings and proclamations of crusaders and zealots, often regarded as radicals and crackpots, who were truly playing the role of David fighting the Goliath of public apathy and ignorance. With the pressures for attention and dollars in this man-on-the-moon period of our history, a great many of the 202,000,000 people in this nation will have to start hurting before the heat gets intense enough to generate a fire.

It is not my purpose to give elaborate detail to substantiate the environmental problems we live with and will eventually face in the future. I do wish to establish the premise that we are now facing scattered crises and that, as we look into the crystal ball, recognizing the rate of deterioration and the generally increasing trends causing the problems, they can only multiply. We must make a national, if not international, effort to develop a code of ethics and a body of law to govern the relationships within our environment, which are just as important to our society, system of government, and life itself as any others ever adopted.

We must develop a national "Environmental Ethic" to inspire and guide us down this very difficult road. We must, as a people and as a nation, re-identify our national values and goals to recognize perhaps the most basic and worldwide problem we face.

Our country and the free enterprise system that our constitution and democratic processes have made possible—and generally encouraged and protected by the laws of our land—have evolved from a demand for personal freedom and economic self-interest. The crisis facing our forefathers was to gain freedom on many fronts—political, economic, and religious—in order to reap the rewards of the good life in the New World. The Constitution was created to set up a workable democratic system to protect those freedoms. The Preamble of the Constitution was very precise: justice, domestic tranquillity, general welfare, common defense, and liberty were the touchstones of that day.

Survival and enjoyment of life per se, environment itself, was not in jeopardy in 1776. Environment was certainly not facing a crisis either. There was a great abundance of natural resources and a low consumption rate that gave no threat to the world of nature. Native plant and animal life seemed almost limitless; there was little to pollute the air and water. When the good land ran out and neighbors got a little too close, all that was needed was to cross a mountain range to the west to reach another valley, and there was more land with good water to settle for the asking. But now we have migrated as far west as we can, and the state by the Pacific Ocean has more people than any other state in the Union.

To launch a national program of action, we must have, on a nationwide scale, initial acceptance by the responsible opinion leaders in the fields of ecology, industry, communication, education, church, conservation, and government at all levels. We must evolve, accept, and practice an "Environmental Ethic" that provides a national code of standards similar to the Golden Rule and the Ten Commandments, to give us guideposts for our personal and moral conduct.

The acceptance of this national environmental ethic and the crusade to implement it must eventually involve every citizen of this country—and in fact, will require the cooperation of countries around the world on both sides of all curtains, whether they be made of iron or bamboo. The problem knows no limits of race, color, creed, faith, income level, political party, or boundary. Environment is the one great common denominator for all people. More than any economic, political, religious, or ethnic binder, the natural world which embodies the atmosphere that belongs to all of us, the water supply that circulates around the earth, the resources held by collective land which we all dig and drill, the animal and plant life so dependent on these common possessions, and all the social problems we must solve—no one subject can do more than this can to bring us together and unite us in common goals that also solidify the spirit and create a "oneness."

Because laws and ethics tend to limit freedom, they are resisted. The human plea, "Don't fence me in," is strong in every breast. Yet we have been forced to face the problem of preventing jungle war in other areas, to bring order and enforce proper behavior through the Pure Food and Drug Act, Robinson Patman Act, Sherman Anti-Trust Laws, Taft-Hartley Law, and many more.

In certain cases the challenge is primarily one of changing attitudes and implementing laws already on the books. This is a substantial and often readily available opportunity to protect our environment. Much painful but definite progress in civil rights is coming about in this way. Generally speaking, existing laws give planning commissions and all government bodies and individuals dealing with environmental matters far more authority to take firm action than is often exercised. In my experience in either participating in or witnessing all levels of governmental action in this field, the tough decision is often avoided, not for lack of laws, regulations, and ordinances, but for lack of sufficient information, an absence of a strong code of ethics, and, sad to say, a lack of guts.

One of man's special traits is to ask thoughtful questions about what he should do or not do. Aristotle, who put the word ethics into the common language, stressed the ethical significance of the fact that all men seek happiness. This rationale was carried further by defining the greatest happiness as coming from the contemplative use of the mind, according to Aristotle. "Peace of mind" is an increasing objective in many environmental situations today.

Perhaps most basic, as we think about the slowly emerging "Environmental Ethic" in this country, is that an obligation and sacrifice of freedom by the individual is inherent in any ethic. Aldo Leopold wrote in his farsighted book of 20 years ago, in his chapter on "The Land Ethic": "An ethic, ecologically, is a limitation of freedom of action in the struggle for existence. As an ethic, philosophically, it is a differentiation of social from anti-social conduct."

Until a few years ago there were few, if any, better illustrations of the concept of this country as a "sweet land of liberty" than man's attitudes and actions related to environment. He could cut, burn, pollute, bulldoze, dredge, fill, and foul up the environment on his plot of ground or subdivision, out of his car or smokestack, or in his well or irrigation district in just about any way he wanted to!

The laws of our land have pegged our national values to the growth and profit of our economic system of free enterprise. Land tends to be considered for zoning and tax purposes in terms of its highest economic value. In fact, our ethics governing land and other resources, including the water on and the air above the land, are strongly influenced by economic self-interest. Stewart Udall once referred to the U.S. GNP as our Holy Grail. It is true that the measures we apply to success generally emphasize quantity rather than quality, notwithstanding many examples that quality can be good business.

In a trickle of examples that are rapidly forming a stream of environmental success stories, we see more and more evidence of a public demand for correcting and preventing environmental failures and of industry and government response to environmental problems.

We are evolving an "Environmental Ethic," or at least decisions and actions that are encouraging signs of a change in thinking toward environment. It is not quite the abstract and stuffy word of a few years ago. It is more and more an "in" word. It is being increasingly accepted for its total value including physical and mental health, community values, and often values that are economically sound.

What we must believe in, as a part of our "Environmental Ethic," is a critical premise that is behind most environmental and ecological values. Any one individual, or one industry, or one local government is a member of a community of interdependent parts and must function cooperatively to determine his destiny.

A city 500 miles down the Mississippi River from another city in a different state, several days apart by stagecoach or riverboat when they were founded, is a 20th-century neighbor environmentally, just as much as adjacent communities share their environmental problems of smog, water, traffic, zoning, floods, sewage, and many more. Environmental anarchy by a homeowner, a business, a local government, or a country is becoming more and more intolerable.

Because a growing number of Americans feel this in all walks of life, we find a definite break in the logjam. The greatest progress is coming in one of the easiest but very critical areas in which to drive home the need for "oneness": air and water. Because the very cyclical pattern of air and water gives less opportunity for legal proprietary rights—and because air and water are recognized for their common value to all of us—we are finding some tough laws being passed and some voluntary efforts that we hope will correct existing problems and prevent future ones. Some situations unfortunately are perhaps beyond complete correction ecologically. If there is any silver lining in that cloudy situation, it is the fact that the Lake Eries, the Hudson Rivers, the Lake Tahoes, and the San Francisco Bays have fanned the fire of crisis to generate the heat that starts the pot boiling in public opinion, industry awareness, and government enforcement.

Recently, seven major airlines decided to equip all new planes with smokeless engines and convert 3000 existing engines. This "voluntary" step came as a result of the airlines being named as defendants in a suit by the New Jersey State Department of Health charging excessive pollution of New Jersey's air.

In Connecticut, 150 young schoolgirls waged a hard campaign from scratch called PYE—"Protect Your Environment." The result was unanimous adoption by the State Legislature of a bill calling for a master plan survey and an immediate set of protective laws for preserving the coastal and tidal areas from dumping.

In San Mateo County in California, the Regional Planning Committee brought together all local city jurisdictions to agree on an open space acquisitions program. A direct result of the educational aspect of this study was the decision to set aside 23,000 acres of the San Francisco watershed in perpetuity for open space in a joint power agreement among the County, the City of San Francisco, and the state and Federal governments.

There is a grass-roots awakening and there is lots of action going on, but we need to move faster; in comparison with the speed at which we should be moving, we are only crawling.

One of the most significant trends in our society is the emerging affluency of the blue collar segment of the population. Increasingly the blue collar worker has a boat or camper, perhaps a second home, and finds himself all too often fishing or camping by a stream or lake that is polluted by the very economy that has given him his good life. Like his union vote, his franchise as a citizen in the privacy of the voting booth is powerful.

While there are some discomforting aspects of the so-called campus revolt, young people are increasingly and very properly becoming involved in environmental issues. While they occasionally tend to be emotional and unrealistic, and tend to forget that their university is often supported by taxes and contributions that are possible only in a free enterprise and democratic system, they are coming up with some good thinking and action.

But the job has only begun—because of the magnitude of the problems and the rapid advance of many of the causes of the problems. Increased population, leisure time from longer vacations, shorter workdays and work weeks, longer active lives, more material goods and waste to dispose of, and a scarcity of virgin valleys to move on to—all of these are on the long-term upswing. There's open land, but we've reached the end of the road in terms of any mass migrations to ease the pinch of civilization. A few can escape, but the problems are of the many and not the few. For the last several years, we have seen a migration backlash, with both

Arizona and Nevada receiving their largest number of migrants from California.

In our own company, we have tried to carry a spear and to attempt to practice a code of ethics. If we consider physical health and the welfare of the family and classroom readership of *Sunset* Magazine as part of our total environmental world, our never accepting hard liquor advertising, and none for tobacco products for many years, is a dollars-and-cents reflection of how we are expressing our own code in actual business practice. The many categories of advertising not accepted by our publication comprise some 20% of the dollar volume spent in our industry. When we supported the creation of a controversial national park, we anticipated and promptly received large advertising cancellations. As an encouraging measure of progress in the last few years, I honestly feel that these advertising pages would not be canceled today. Hopefully, our ethical philosophy will be understood as we have just discontinued accepting two-wheels-off-the-road motor vehicle advertising and are applying even tough controls on real estate and land development advertising. There is no point kidding yourself—following any ethical course, including environmental, means you don't always pick up the marbles after the game is over. To think otherwise is economic myopia.

Recently we completed our investigation of DDT and several other hydrocarbons and their role in home gardening. Our August 1969 issue carried an article on "Blowing the Whistle on DDT." Because it has been our policy to adhere to similar policies or codes of ethics, for both the editorial and advertising content, we discontinued accepting DDT advertising effective with the same issue. We had heretofore carried more of this advertising category for home gardening use than any other U.S. publication and we were somewhat surprised to have the decision featured in *The Wall Street Journal* and to find the full announcement read into the Congressional Record. The decision, we have learned, has been used to strengthen arguments for tougher controls and legislation on pesticides in several states. The mail support has been very heavy in support of the position we took. These reactions only help to emphasize that there is a swell of support for "get tough" action.

The challenge for the communication media, and for any organization or individual is not to get trapped into being "all things to all people." The whole challenge of conservation is to create an orchestra of activity. Each of us has a part we can play better than some other. Some play the drum and some play the violin. We feel our role is to find successful accomplishments and give the factual "how-it-was-done" information to guide and inspire others. We accept the premise that to recognize good, we by no means have to ignore the bad.

Realistically, the worldwide recognition and strong leadership from a Secretary and a Department of Environment would be a positive way to achive many of the same goals that have been proposed as a goal for a possible Secretary of Peace. There is no better place for leadership to be exercised to develop a national "Environmental Ethic" than from the investigation and deliberations of the President's Council on Environmental Quality and its Citizens' Advisory Committee on Environmental Quality, whose chairman is Mr. Laurance Rockefeller.

In his announcement of the Council, President Nixon quoted a statement made by a former President that read: "The conservation of our natural resources and their proper use constitute the fundamental problem which underlies almost every problem of our national life. . . ."

We must all pray and work together to make the noble words and plans for action of 1969 witness for more immediate action and long-term results—more than those earlier strong words of advice given by Teddy Roosevelt in 1907 have received in the 62 years since. Time is running out, just as many of our resources are drying up—or soon will be. Noble words and occasional accomplishments are not enough. We must wage total war to win the battle to save and protect the basic physical environmental elements and social environmental values that sustain life and make it all worthwhile.

If we wait too long to develop and practice a strong "Environmental Ethic," it might well start off, "Thou shalt not kill— ourselves."

42

THE COMMITMENT OF INDUSTRY
RICHARD B. STONER

This paper, given since the Conference but included because of its relevance, is a statement from industry on the survival issue. All of us should appraise our situation as realistically as Mr. Stoner has and move forward with as much commitment. Mr. Stoner believes that we must work together on this problem to improve it. I hope the sincerity of this paper becomes the rule for industry.

Industry in America is either going to fulfill its moral obligation to lead the way in minimizing the threat of air, water, waste, and noise pollution in this decade, or the people, led by our youth, will force the government to enact legislation which requires it to do the job.

Industry is about to be caught with an inadequate response to those problems that affect the human environment—health, hunger, security. "Sociability" is about to become the planning goal of the 1970's. Sociability is making products that are not too noisy, not unhealthy, not offensive in odor, not harmful to the environment.

Sociability has real meaning to us today as we recognize that stopping pollution is the number one technological challenge to industry in this decade.

I am most concerned with the transportation industry, in which I work. Transportation vehicles are the number one contributor to air pollution, noise, and esthetic decay. Emissions from vehicles account for over half the contaminants in our air. The 100 million automobiles, trucks, and buses on America's highways spew more than 66 million tons of sulfur oxides, 6 million tons of oxides of nitrogen, 12 million tons of hydrocarbons, and one million tons of particulates annually into the air we breathe. And our factories pour even more smoke, dirty water, and wastes into our environment.

Pollution was not so great a problem until our society began to grow rapidly in population and became increasingly technological. Now we have moved into huge urban areas and have become a threat to our own survival.

The transportation industry was not concerned about engine emissions until a few years ago. Then California's smog problem was so great that the state government was forced to issue the first automobile exhaust emission standards. The response from both industry and the general public was less than enthusiastic. We protested that costs would be too high, that the time requirements were too short, and that the standards were impossible to achieve. Yet today, the industry is rushing ahead to meet the new federal restrictions.

Yet our approach has not been as direct as is necessary. The latest legal standard has been our guideline. Instead we should aim for the lowest possible level of pollution that is technologically possible. I believe that in this decade the noise and emission difficulties of the internal engine can be virtually eliminated.

The emission control effort, however, will be massively expensive. And all of us will pay. Manufacturer, equipment purchaser, and consumer will contribute their share.

What Must Be Done?

Somehow, we must find, not government pledges or industry programs, but a national commitment to improve environmental quality. As consumers, we will have to change our life style. Protection of our environment must become a personal cause of the highest magnitude in the everyday lives of tens of millions of Americans. President Nixon in his State of the Union address said, "Each individual must enlist if this fight is to be won. . . . It is time for those who make massive demands on society to make some minimal demands on themselves."

In this growing effort, government can provide guidelines, but industry must take the leadership and commit, now, today, both human and financial resources.

There is a jarring truth to Newsweek's statement that "Until a few years ago, fighting pollution ranked somewhere below giving charity on the list of corporation priorities." Industry has not led in pollution control, has not paid enough attention to the harm its manufacturing plants were doing, did not think of environmental quality.

Now, however, there is a growing feeling of responsibility. What can industry do? As a first step, it can stop air, noise, water, and waste pollution in its processes. That will be enormously costly, and some industries may need government assistance and incentives. Some enterprises will not even survive, but that is a necessary cost.

Second, sociability must become a priority design criterion in planning all new products, plants, and services.

Third, products that pollute must be modified or abandoned and replaced with those which do not pollute.

Fourth, industry-wide cooperation in reducing pollution must override competitive considerations.

Fifth, industry must fund more basic research to develop new technologies. I believe the internal combustion engine can be adapted for safe use, but if it cannot, we must be prepared to bury it and find a new system.

Government's Role

Government should make pollution a priority issue and provide incentives and requirements for industry to meet its responsibilities.

First, economic incentives should be devised that encourage all industries, large and small, to accelerate their antipollution efforts—in order to make normal economic factors provide the nation with the direction needed for this effort.

Second, there should be a federal program of penalties for those who pollute, both producers and consumers. Income from a pollution tax could finance research for new technologies.

Third, I recommend that the government reallocate funds earmarked for development of low-emission engines into more productive channels. Industry has the proper economic incentives to develop sociable products and industry will do this job. The money could fund studies to determine levels of tolerable pollution and determination of standards, or the results of interaction of emissions.

Fourth, government should make it possible for industry to exchange information freely in the public interest without fear of antitrust violation.

Much is being done about environmental degradation by industry, and a great deal remains to be done. I concur with philosopher Lewis Mumford's observation: "Any square mile of inhabited earth has more significance for man's future than all the planets in the solar system."

Media

Media—publications, the press, radio, and TV—will influence whether we survive as much as any other sector. The man voting on environmental matters, such as new laws or bond issues to pay for environmental quality, remains the ultimate decision maker. He must be made environmentally aware.

The way won't be easy. Strong, well-financed interests have their economic realms to defend. Like the cigarette advertisers who oppose health warnings in media, they are effective in influencing the public.

The universal nature of the environment offers great hope. The media can both report positive examples of improvement and challenge negative ones, and thereby bring the public into the struggle for life.

43

MEDIA FOR INVOLVEMENT

JAMES DAY

Bringing the reality of needed change to television by ". . . witnessing the event" and ". . . involving viewers" may be our best educational device. "If we can dramatize bad breath*—and make it a matter of high priority— we can do the same thing with bad air. We might even improve . . . the quality of television, itself a form of air pollution."*

How curious that we in the media should find ourselves struggling with the problem of how to attract attention and stimulate positive action on a matter no less serious nor dramatic than the death of our planet and the imminent demise of humankind.

And yet the problem is real.

The sudden death of an individual may very well be front-page news in our local newspaper. The slow, yet inevitable, death of the human species through the erosion of our life-giving environment will only rarely make the front page. More often it will be buried among the feature and entertainment items, if it is mentioned at all. The reason for the difference in treatment may lie with the ability to *comprehend* the death of an individual while the apocalyptic is beyond comprehension. We give greater prominence to that which we can grasp. News is more graspable. But the apocalyptic is rapidly becoming the norm.

Moreover, as a consequence of the communications revolution, the possibility of the apocalyptic is ever more in our consciousness. Through the miracle of instantaneous communication, every man has become every other man's neighbor. Tragedy in Africa is tragedy in San Francisco—within hours, if not minutes. Every man's problem has become our problem—if we will allow it to become our problem. But because some problems thrust into our consciousness by communications are too often beyond our individual capacity to affect, the natural reaction is to throw our hands in the air in despair and surround ourselves with a wall of indifference to close out the feelings of impotency that result from our inability to "do something about it."

The problem of the communications media is to penetrate the wall of indifference that communications itself has built. Our task is to reduce these problems to manageable, and affectable, proportions. This implies an obligation on the part of *local* radio and television stations that rarely has been met in the history of

American broadcasting. One might wish that each local station, in recognition of its obligation, would produce brilliant documentaries on the subject of man's need to recognize and act upon the imperative to stem the destruction of his environment. Local stations almost never have the capacity to produce such documentaries. And if they could, few would watch. Documentaries are akin to preaching; they convert the converted. Another method must be found.

Most stations have news programs. Why shouldn't our survival, and the events that increase or decrease our chances of survival, be included in the body of the news? Perhaps each station should have a specialist news reporter on the subject of environment. KQED, the local public television station in San Francisco, includes such a specialist on the staff of its highly acclaimed "Newsroom." His continuous (and often continuing) observations of those events affecting our environment have on occasion led to positive action. And if it seems too much to expect each local station to include a specialist reporter on the subject of environment, let us not forget that virtually all local stations have specialist reporters on sports.

But we need more than the recognition that survival of the species is news. We need to mobilize television to do what television does best: to make us witness to the event. The event may be a hearing, a meeting of concerned citizens, an act of defiance against wanton or indifferent destruction. Television's greatest gift is not its ability to *inform*, but rather its ability to *involve*.

Somehow we need to take that magnificent instrument to which millions are addicted, and without loss of the entertainment values which are its sources of income, and thus its existence, turn it to the service of man's continued existence.

If we can dramatize *bad breath*—and make it a matter of high priority—we can do the same with *bad air*. We can do it by turning television from its preoccupation with fantasy to a concern with reality. If the winning of the West can spawn a hundred television serials, why can't the potential loss of *everything* spawn at least one? I can imagine nothing with greater dramatic potential than the struggle of man to survive his own folly.

Let our most skillful writers turn their mind to this problem instead of the unrealities of such television fantasies as "Star Trek." The concept of our Earth as a spaceship has all the elements of a highly successful television serial. It might even result in an improvement in the quality of television, itself a form of air pollution.

Most importantly, it might result in an increase in the number of people who care.

For that's what it is all about: *caring*. Caring enough to make sacrifices now so that those who follow us—those anonymous millions with whom we have only the most tenuous connection—might live. Caring that the fact of a *future* is important to us. Now.

44

GETTING ENVIRONMENTAL INFORMATION TO THE PUBLIC

HAROLD GILLIAM

Much of the concern originating from the San Francisco Bay area has come from Gilliam's work as an author. His point of using facts to balance emotion is essential to winning.

Conservationists and ecologists, in informing the public about the environment and the damage that threatens it, should emphasize hard and persuasive facts. Too often they lose out because in presenting their case they rely primarily on sentiment, esthetics, or moral outrage. Yet the people who need to be convinced—editors, commentators, administrators, political office holders—are notoriously unimpressed by good intentions and noble emotions. They are usually on the lookout for hard data and well-reasoned arguments based on solid evidence.

Admittedly, individuals and citizen groups may not be able to afford professional studies to match those of well-financed government agencies and private developers. Perhaps what is needed is a publicly financed ombudsman agency to represent the long-term public interest in the environment and to assemble the data needed for decision-making.

Here, briefly, are some techniques which conservationists have used successfully.

A federal agency proposed two dams for the Grand Canyon as essential to a project providing water for desert areas in Arizona. The Sierra Club, relying on both volunteer and professional engineering experts, presented evidence to the contrary, indicating that (1) the dams would divert no water but would waste water by evaporation and that (2) the power they would produce could as well be generated by other means. This well-documented case was presented to the public in news releases and advertisements and to the decision-makers in Washington by letter and personal testimony. The arguments and the public opinion they generated helped convince Congress, which refused to approve the dams. Much of the Sierra Club Grand Canyon campaign paid for itself when the public responded to appeals for funds.

On another occasion a much smaller organization won an even more unlikely environmental battle by presenting convincing evidence. When a nuclear power plant was proposed for a scenic headland near San Francisco, the Citizens' Committee to Preserve Bodega Head and Harbor was formed in opposition. The group made little headway with esthetic arguments but was highly successful when its director, David Pesonen, presented the results of his detailed research on nuclear reactors and geologic hazards. The evidence aroused public attention in the newspapers and impressed Federal officials sufficiently for them to make further investigations. The project was subsequently abandoned.

Scientists often volunteer information essential to evaluating the environmental impact of development projects. A promising development in this direction is the formation of scientists' committees for public information throughout the U.S.—such as the New York Scientists' Committee for Public Information and the Northern California Committee for Environmental Information.

Often irreparable environmental damage has been perpetrated because the only detailed information available to officials has come from public-relations experts hired by the exploiters. Environmentalists can reverse the decline of environmental quality only by using similar techniques to tell the ecological story—the scientific data, the solid evidence, the whole truth.

45

PERSPECTIVE ON THE PRESS

WOLF VON ECKHARDT

Our survival will hinge on an informed public. The press needs to report on the environment in its actual complexity, discarding the traditional single "issue" approach, and it needs to do so on a team-reporting basis.

The press must search for better ways to inform its readers about environmental disasters before they happen. This might help avert them.

We've had this kind of soul-searching after riots. Prodded by the Kerner Commission, newspapers discovered that they had not adequately informed the public of the mood and conditions in the ghetto. News from the official renewers, poverty warriors, and civil righters proved incomplete if not misleading. It was left to the Kerner Report to state it bluntly: urban renewal has destroyed two to three times more low-cost housing than it has built.

Likewise, more newsmen should have known and reported that the negotiations for offshore oil drilling rights might lead to devastating oil spills; that those lucrative freeway systems would lead to more traffic jams; that America's home-building industry was heading toward stagnation.

Today America's newspapers are just as complacent about the environment as they were about the ghetto. We are half ignorant and half indifferent.

We are lazy and take the establishment at its word. We half believe, for instance, that the SST is essential to America's prestige, or that cleaning up the Potomac is too expensive. What's more, a newspaper's job is to report the news. Carbon monoxide in the air, like rats in the ghetto, after all, is hardly news. Not until somebody screams or dies.

Worse, we treat the environment not as an ecological, inter-related whole, but in a fragmented fashion. We report a new housing project here and a transportation crisis there. We rarely, if ever, point out that the housing project in the wrong place will make the transportation crisis worse. News affecting the environment is organized according to its source but not in terms of its impact on our place to live.

Major newspapers and news services, I suggest, should set up Environmental Teams. A team of editors, reporters, and commentators would cover all the news that affects the quality of the man-made environment, air, water, and noise pollution, city planning and housing, transportation, conservation and open space. It would not only cover these matters, but also pursue them. And it would do so not only in the halls and pressrooms of Congress, the state legislatures, and the local governments of our metropolitan area, but also out in the field where the smells are.

The team would have three missions: (1) to relate, (2) to examine, and (3) to prod.

1. News stories on matters that affect the environment would try to point out what the effects are. A report on a freeway proposal, for instance, would try to include not only the dollar cost and the estimated number of cars moved, but also the estimated amount of carbon monoxide it would generate and where the cars are to be parked. A report on a proposed new housing project would also try to report on the transportation requirements of its residents. A story on an industrial development would include not only its employment potential but also its housing needs and pollution potential.

2. The press has left it mostly to conservation groups to examine and challenge official assertions. Industry keeps claiming, for instance, that antipollution measures are unfeasible or uneconomical. The team would challenge the veracity of these claims and unjuggle some of the industrial arithmetic. Few people in this country know, for instance, that independent engineers estimate that most antipollution devices, now legally required in Germany and England, cost only from two to ten percent of industry's capital investment.

3. Much as we have theater, art, music, dance, and architecture criticism, we need sharp and articulate environmental criticism and commentary in the newspapers. It is an effective way to prod officialdom and industry and to stimulate public discussion.

The most important contribution the press can make toward greater environmental awareness is to help bring the problem into the political arena. This is why environmental news can no longer be confined to the feature pages, and to the women's and real estate sections. We must treat it as part of general, political news so that the politicians and their constituents will read it.

Space is always short, to be sure. But a newspaper ought to examine whether its front section space is always used wisely. And there are, to be sure, few newspapermen who feel qualified to report, let alone comment, on environmental relationships and design. But there are increasingly more who are interested and concerned. One of the best investments a newspaper can make to its country's future is to send some of these interested and concerned young men and women to school for a semester or two. Most universities now have courses in ecological, urban, and environmental studies.

If we are to protect our environment from irreparable damage, we must become informed, and the need for the media to be committed to that education is critical.

Education

"Detenqua"—deteriorating environmental quality—must be blamed largely on our educational system. One has only to look at the smog, the polluted waters, and our random destruction of the countryside to see that our educational system isn't working in critical areas.

Still, education is the area where results can be attained quickly. And until we are educated to cope with the seriousness of the problem, little will be accomplished.

There have been efforts to establish environmental education, but to date they haven't been widely accepted. One obstacle is the stiffness of the system. In the past, environment as an inter-disciplinary area has had a low priority in the planning of the curriculum. Now that survival is at stake, educational efforts must be and are being geared to young and old alike.

46

ENVIRONMENTAL EDUCATION

MICHAEL SCRIVEN

Dr. Scriven offers an iconoclastic dismantling of our present educational system, and a reassembly of it around a redefinition of education and survival.

Man's first education came from his natural environment, as did that of every other beast. Man the hunter, man the food gatherer, man the herdsman and farmer—these roles our ancestors learned from their environment, or else they perished. Having learned a little, enough to give him competitive superiority, man then became lear*ned*, which is the corrupt version of being knowledgeable, and the decadent phase of learning. He allowed the study of the natural environment to lapse into a rich man's pastime and began to concentrate his attention on his artifacts, both practical and puerile, from engineering to pinochle. Finally, he discovered that his artifacts were wrecking his natural environment, on which he was still dependent for survival.

That is Simple Simon's history of eco-consciousness, to date, on this planet. This history is notable for two features: (1) the inexcusability of the neglect of ecology, despite the long history of subsystem disasters such as silicosis and overcropping; and (2) the fact that so far we have been lucky. Drifting around many stars in our skies are, we may be sure, the detritus of a billion planets that were not lucky. On many of these, there was probably no ground for blame. That is, the crucial interference that led to the annihilation of the planet's life form, or of its intelligent life form, was not such that those responsible could reasonably have anticipated such a disastrous effect.

It might have occurred, for example, relatively early in the development of the intelligent race's control over its own environment, before it had had a series of examples of the possible malign effects of this control, such as we have now. Or it might have occurred in a relatively late stage, but been of a type which could not reasonably have been foreseen to have had serious consequences. There are very few possible excuses in this category for us, however, since we have now discovered that almost any interference, even those which begin by appearing to be extremely limited—like some of our insecticide activities in the early days—

may well have very far-reaching consequences, including the eventual destruction of a genuinely vital food resource or the development of a genuinely fatal counterresponse.

At this moment, on this planet, one should probably conclude that the likelihood of the human race being wiped off this planet by the use of its intentionally deadly artifacts, like the hydrogen bomb, is very much less than the likelihood of its extinction by the reaction of its natural environment to some of its intentionally benign artifacts, e.g., the antibiotics. It is surely an extremely unreliable inference, given the magnitude of the stakes, to conclude from the fact that we have always in the past been able to discover antidotes to naturally developing viruses and bacteria, and to those which have developed in response to our introduction of new antibiotics, that we shall always be able to do so. One detects in the reasoning of epidemiologists an occasional tendency to act as if it is a guarantee rather than a statistical law that epidemics are self-limiting.

Looked at in another way, the evidence is extremely frightening. The most impressive example of biological warfare known to man, the CSIRO's attack on the rabbit population of Australia, using myxomytosis, had a kill effectiveness of far over 99%. When one looks at the similar kill effectiveness of the Black Death, and several of the Plagues, and the immunity of several of the more recent flu viruses to the previously developed flu vaccines, and at the speed with which the new strains develop, then it is clear that inferences in this area can be made in two directions. One can readily argue that these periodic disasters are immensely effective almost immediately, and that it is only a matter of time before one emerges which is entirely effective, i.e., fatal to all breeding males or females—one can argue this just as readily as one can argue that in all cases a fraction of the population survives.

Of course, one cannot restrict one's discussion to biological agents. The accidental release of a chemical warfare agent, a nerve gas from the Utah proving grounds of the U.S. Army's division of chemical warfare, showed by its unbelievable lethality, in concentrations and at distances which the Army scientists were confident would prevent such an effect, that we are rapidly approaching the point where chemical agents of our own deliberate devising may do the job that may also be done by chemical agents we did not intend to have lethal effects.

In short, we have essentially reached the point on this planet where the argument that "we didn't know it was loaded" has practically no residual efficiency as an excuse for us at all. Virtually every significant activity we undertake is loaded—loaded with potential consequences of an extremely serious and possibly fatal kind for the future of mankind and other life forms on this planet.

I have now set the stage for my discussion of environmental education. I have done so by attempting to stress the fact that it is only by good fortune that we are still around—that environmental education is long overdue as part of the minimal equipment for the survival of this race on this planet. I set the stage in this way because we are about to enter a rather dangerous phase in the development of environmental education. It is about to—in fact, it has—become fashionable. We are about to see many universities introducing departments of environmental research, and special interdisciplinary programs, and all the other paraphernalia of fashion. We need to welcome this trend, but to be very carefully armed against it.

The eventual goal of environmental education is the problem of educating the *voters,* and that means the problem of getting it into the curriculum or extra-curriculum of every future citizen of this country. It is not at all a problem of achieving intellectual respectability for it. That problem is being solved, somewhat too late but nevertheless in time to give us a last chance for arming ourselves adequately against self-destruction in this dimension.

Now if we are to get "Environmental Education" into the schools we have got to solve a fundamental problem. That problem is the problem of fitting it into the rigid and already overstuffed curriculum frameworks of the state boards of education. Many prestige high schools, particularly those referred to as laboratory schools and associated with university departments of education, have already introduced extremely progressive curricula across the country, often by means of special exemptions granted them from meeting the normal state requirements. We are not interested in that level of success in the high school. We are not about to survive the problems of atmosphere and water supply contamination, the problems of lethal biological by-product threat, the problems of natural resource exhaustion, and all the other problems to which the ecologist has made us sensitive, by getting 1% or 10% of the population half-way familiar with the situation. We have got to get *every,* and that means *every,* citizen educated. In terms of the actual time scale, that really requires a program of adult education for those who cannot be reached through the school system, as well as a systematic plan for absolutely blanketing the school population of the future. No such plan has been proposed. Apart from the little gesture of one out of three alternative approaches to high school biology consisting in an ecologically oriented curriculum, we are not even in the ballpark.

It may now perhaps become more obvious why I have devoted my preamble to stressing the connection with survival. We can legitimately demand that our educational system provide students with the wherewithal for survival. That's a big stick. We are going to need the biggest stick we can get our hands on, in order to break into the curriculum. I think we should all feel that getting this change is a duty we have, with respect to our local school districts, with respect to our state departments of education, and with respect to the Congress. We have got to get changes made so that we will not have to fight uninformed or misinformed voters in the future. One might suppose that on this kind of issue it is relatively easy to inform the adult voter. And so it is, but information is not enough. His habits of mind must also be such as to make it readily apparent to him that an *extremely serious* threat is involved, one that calls for *action* and *sacrifice* on his part. The aim of environmental education in the schools should be to create that habit of mind.

One of the things going for us is the relative ease of teaching by interesting and readily understood examples in this area. We are not up against the necessity of teaching a new mathematical discipline. If we were, then the colossal difficulty of retraining the teachers in the schools as well as that of teaching the students would be added to our burden. The fact is we can use interesting, anecdote-like stories to illustrate the points that we are making. Indeed, I do not believe that a very large period of time is required in order to effectively educate the students. Nor do I believe that there is a great difficulty about a particular age level at which this can be taught. I suspect it can be taught quite well at the first grade and I am certain that it can be taught well at any grade after the fifth. Many things are going for us, but this should not blind our eyes to the fact that a very large repertoire of examples from our own past experience must be drawn upon and carefully documented in order to convey to the student, as to the citizen, the extreme seriousness of the almost unforeseeable long-term consequences of environmental manipulation in its many deliberate and accidental forms. Nor are examples of past errors enough. The real crunch is the nature and cost of the solutions. We must teach economics through eco-examples, because it is future solutions and not past errors that is our main lesson and the solutions are hard economic analyses and recommendations. And we must do the same with politics and sociology.

I am not inclined to pay a great deal of intellectual homage to what has recently been called "ecological thinking" or the "ecological way of thought" or the "ecological approach." I think there certainly is such an entity, and that it is important, and that it can be taught. But I think it comes very easily on the basis of a certain amount of well-illustrated preamble, and I do not think that we are here facing something as hard to convey as the "mathematical way of thought," or the "scientific way of thought," whatever they may be. As a matter of act I rather like the idea that ecology might be used as a way of introducing and reinforcing attempts to teach *some* aspects of scientific method, and even to some degree mathematical method.   In general, however, we have educationally a relatively simple task on our hands, but politically a tremendously difficult one. For getting changes made in our educational syatem is a problem of practical politics.

I now want to develop the claim that the educational curricula in this country are far more dangerous to our future survival than anybody has really conceived. I have so far noted only the failure to incorporate environmental education in them in any satisfactory way.   I want to stress very briefly some other major sins of commission and omission that are involved in the curriculum, so that you can see why the appeal to the concept of survival can be used to justify a very substantial reform in the curriculum, one on whose back we may find it more easy to introduce environmental education than if we had to do this as a single project.

The most significant need for our citizenry is for a generalization of the environmental education approach. What we almost wholly lack is training in the capacity to rationally discuss emotionally loaded political and social problems and materials. The way to train people to do this is by training them while they do it. It is *not* by teaching them some of the background academic materials that might well be useful in such a discussion, while failing to ever give them practice in such discussions. And yet our school systems are wholly committed to this medieval fallacy. That is, the curriculum is stuffed with the discussion of history, particularly American history, geography, and various other subjects which have an important academic relevance to the discussion of our involvement in Vietnam, our role in Greece, our task with the cities, our destruction of the forests, our educational obligations toward minority groups, etc. But this relevance is never employed. That is, these specific issues, on the adequate treatment of which our future survival depends, are never *themselves* discussed in the schools; the particular data that we need in order to handle them are never provided; and indeed we make a fetish of avoiding such "controversial" issues. We have pressure groups tooled up and ready to go, who will jump on any discussion of these matters as "partisan," and who have the power to kill them.

In the area of sex education, where the need could hardly be greater, where the symptoms of disaster are everywhere to be found and one of its causes is quite obviously ignorance, many schools have been hamstrung the moment they tried to make a reasonably appropriate educational response to this demonstrated need—by neurotic, indeed often paranoid, parental groups. I do not intend in the least to disparage a legitimate concern that hidden and dubious values, of a kind that need the most explicit discussion, might well be concealed in a sex education curriculum. I do not intend to disparage at all the desirability of home treatment of such matters. Neither of those considerations supports the conclusion that we should eliminate such issues from the curriculum, any more than we should eliminate English literature, of which the same claims can be made. It only supports the need for *more* viewpoints, *more* analysis, and *more* training. We may be grateful that environmental education is in many such respects less a matter of controversy. But we must face the fact that the number of schoolchildren receiving adequate instruction in the area of sex role and sex physiology is still pathetically small. The general problem of *response lag* is perhaps the most worrying feature of our educational system.

When we turn to the political-social area, and look at the major issue confronting the American people, as seen by the present governmental power group and most curricula, we can only be completely horrified. As seen by the current power group, the confrontatior with "World Communism" is still the major motivating factor in deciding all issues of foreign policy. Nixon's latest Vietnam speech contained very little that was both substantial and relevant to the present issue, but it did propagate the commitment to the idea of the "independent force against communism." We are not going to leave Vietnam until the South is able to survive against the North. *Why* should the South survive against the North? Because it is an anticommunist regime. Here, as in our relations with Russia and China, we find again that the crucial issue of communism is central.

What sort of education do we provide for our citizens to discuss such crucial issues? How many of them could define communism in a way that would be recognized by communists? How many of them could give the sort of justification of communism, and the sort of criticisms of capitalism that an educated communist would give? How many could show that the support of vicious fascist dictatorships produces a net gain to the peasant, the world, or—in the long run—to the United States? Surely it is an absolute prerequisite of any adequate education to handle political debate that one should be able to formulate the *position* of the opponent in a way that he would accept. Yet we do not meet this standard. In the few schools where there is any discussion of communism, it is an absurd puppet that is presented. Surely it is a necessity that we can give objectively plausible reasons for a war supporting fascism. But even our leaders cannot do this. (Compare this with the situation after Pearl Harbor.)

This point is highly relevant to environmental education. We have enemies in almost every one of the specific areas of environment legislation. If it isn't the timber companies, it is the chemical companies; if it isn't the effluent from power plants, it is the effluent from internal combustion engines. We have got to realize that effective education in this area is education for advocacy where advocacy will be controversial. The basic approach to ecology is not hard to teach. The ways to handle specific issues are much harder to teach, and they rapidly lead us into the general area of the analysis of controversy. This is something which our schools are not only failing to provide, but are to a very large extent conditioned to avoid. Education for survival is going to require it.

There are a dozen other areas in which the schools are really failing us, and failing us not from the point of view of some watcher from the ivory tower, nor from the point of view of some short-sighted would-be employer, but from the point of view of every one of us as a citizen. I'm not interested in proselytizing for particular solutions to our problems, whether political or environmental, even though it is obvious from the above examples where my sympathies lie. I am only interested in ensuring that our schools provide, and our media of public information increasingly provide, the procedures and materials for intelligent discussion of these critical areas. It is not sufficiently widely realized that the capacity to react rationally and sensibly, and not just emotionally and selfishly, to an emotionally charged issue, where one's own interests are clearly involved in a way that is not the same as that in which others' interests are involved, is a skill which needs to be learned, which needs to be practiced, and which is far more important than anything else we ever learn or practice. But it is not explicitly taught, and usually not even explicitly recognized in our schools. Training free citizens for a constrained society is a neat trick even if you focus on it. You surely cannot do it by training students, unsuccessfully, to conform to codes they don't know how to criticize rationally, don't like emotionally, and which are almost certainly inappropriate pragmatically.

I would like to go into more detail about the curriculum for environment education. But what I have said is far more important than the details of a curriculum, and it has also indicated my preferences in the curricular field. That is, I have argued for the case study approach; I have argued for emphasis on the systematic nature of ecology and the systematic nature of ecological effects in conjunction with each of the case studies; I have argued for recognition of the fact that converting scientific knowledge into practical legislation will require training in the applied social sciences and in the handling of particular controversies; I have argued for the relative ease, pedagogically, of teaching this curricular material at almost any level in the schools; I have argued for the necessity of mounting a very large-scale social effort to get it inserted, despite the ease of insertion and the flexibility of location; and I have argued for the desperate importance of doing this.

May I conclude by drawing the analogy between political and environmental education a little closer. If you define an ecosystem rather widely, with respect to man and his effects on his environment, you find yourself automatically involved in the discussion of politics and ethics. For politics and ethics are nothing more than systematic attempts to provide solutions for the problem of social interaction, i.e., the interaction of humans with their human environment. There will be little satisfaction in environmental education that teaches us how to handle our natural environment if it does not recognize the fact that part of the natural environment is ourselves. There is no natural and no logical way to draw the boundary between the unthinking and the thinking part of a man's environment. We may, for practical purposes, decide to divide our efforts in this matter. But we must recognize that in the long run our drive to achieve environmental education involves achieving adequate education for social interaction: it involves citizenship education and in fact moral education.

47

EDUCATION'S RESPONSE TO AWARENESS NEEDS

PAUL DEHART HURD

"The problem is not the goal, but the implementation. . . . The knowledge needed [to survive] is taugh within disciplines . . . without regard to its relevance for man's expectations."

Schools and colleges, being conservative institutions, respond slowly to changing biosocial conditions. There is agreement that education has a responsibility to provide people with the knowledge and skills needed for survival. The problem is not in the goal, but in its implementation. For the first time in history, man must learn how to heal the imbalances in the environment which he has made and which threaten his very existence.

Although we live in an age of science, we do so without the enlightenment necessary for a scientific age. A mismatch has developed between science, technology, education, and society—this is a condition we can no longer safely endure. This is true partly because we assume that tomorrow will differ little from yesterday.

The present orientation of education distorts the efforts of young people to understand ecological health within the framework of a humane society. The knowledge needed to deal with these problems is isolated within separate disciplines, and is taught without regard to its relevance for man's existence. The curriculum called for must link the social and natural sciences, including the humanities and engineering. Teaching will need to be interdisciplinary where the focus is on man.

An education for survival is an education for change and social action, directed toward the future we seek. To educate for change is to educate for instability, versatility, and adaptability. Individual motives must be linked with the common good. The curriculum should have a high potential for ecological integration. Skills in a wide range of logical processes and inquiry procedures are necessary as well, to make rational use of knowledge.

We will make little progress on our environmental problems unless we can reduce the present polarity within the curriculum and establish interdisciplinary courses and programs. Scholars must establish mechanisms and institutions for the study of man within a matrix of biosocial concerns. Students will need oppor tunities to investigate different aspects of environmental improvements. These opportunities are now limited by an education that is too specialized and, moreover, meaningless for contemporary times.

Some progress along these lines is evident. Environmental studies are becoming more conspicuous in university catalogs, along with courses in human behavioral biology, human ecology, and social biology; in most instances these are interdisciplinary courses. The Biological Sciences Curriculum Study is proposing a two-year life science program for the middle school built around a systematic study of man and his environmental interactions. SGAD (Students Give a Damn), a self-organized group of students from various colleges and universities, is fighting to have science taught with a concern for "the alleviation and solution of current problems now threatening the environment of man." The eco-activist is becoming increasingly conspicuous among both students and faculties. Of considerable significance is the recent establishment of an Office of Environmental Education in the Department of Health, Education, and Welfare. These efforts represent a beginning, but they are clearly not adequate for the task. They will not be until programs of general education include integrative studies focused on man and his ecological responsibilities.

48

EDUCATION FOR HUMAN SURVIVAL

STERLING BUNNELL

Man needs to return to a natural awareness through a more sensitive education. He has no choice. Limiting factors are described and an appeal is made for an understanding which will create an eco- rather than ego-centric life style.

The awesome ability of contemporary man to disrupt the world environment presents us with an unavoidable challenge: either we learn to modify our activities so that a stable relationship with the ecosystem can be maintained, or we will soon cease to exist. In the past, the checks upon us were external to our own intention—disease, hunger, and conflict with other men. Now our power to make external changes is so great that we must internalize some ethical understanding of the man-environment system. Unless we can check ourselves with wise restraint, we will push our gently cushioning ecosystem to the point where it can no longer regain its present equilibrium. It will then collapse to a simpler order which will probably not have room for us.

There seems to be something peculiar about the approaching environmental crisis which is particularly frustrating to our ordinary methods of problem-solving. Our "conquests of nature" tend to backfire and result in worse situations than those we have tried to improve. There are innumerable known instances of this type of unexpected environmental feedback, but I will cite only a few gross examples which we appear headed toward on a worldwide basis.

1. If we attempt to postpone world famine by a crash program of food production by all expedient applications of modern agricultural technology (especially synthetic fertilizers and persistent pesticides), we are apt to wreck the biosphere with chemical pollution.

2. Mechanized monocultural agriculture simplifies habitats and promotes new insect pests by eliminating their natural checks. Many of these pests can in a few years evolve strains resistant to the insecticides used against them. Large-scale monoculture is therefore very unstable ecologically and will become more so as wild lands disappear.

3. If we hope to replace fossil fuel power with nuclear power, we exchange the problems of CO_2 and hydrocarbon pollution, etc., for the equally dangerous and more insidious biologically active radioisotopes. If we try to extricate ourselves by conversion from fission to fusion power, we contaminate the world's water supply with increasing amounts of tritium. The critical mutation load above which a population is nonviable is uncertain before it is reached, and there will be strong economic pressures to exceed any arbitrary limit in an overpopulating world hungry for power.

Thus it seems that the problems of food production, power demands, industrialization, and waste disposal are not soluble in isolation but only in conjunction with stabilizing population at levels which allow us to stay within the limits of environmental tolerance. A breakthrough on one problem such as greatly increased food supply (as by synthesis of carbohydrates) could finish us off by allowing population increase to intensify other problems (pollution, thermal balance, etc.).

Our surprise at this pattern of relationships is due to our human-centered point of view. However, if we see the ecosystem as the injured host and mankind as a pathogenic agent, the situation becomes clearer. Our technological attempts to solve environmental problems usually favor the short-term goals of the pathogen. The crisis, however, is a disease of the ecosystem, and grows worse as the pathogen increases. The most successful viruses coexist rather than injure, and may even become functional components within cells. Pathogens which behave as we do would need to find a new host pronto. But ours, as the space program reminds us, is a one-host operation.

Until recently, the most advanced ethical standards were purely anthropocentric. This is no longer adequate. We now need a biocentric orientation which makes the well-being and diversity of the ecosystem a central value and sees man as a component of it instead of an entity thoroughly separate and self-contained.

If our aim is primarily human survival, we will probably fail. We will push the environmental equilibrium too far and unconsidered factors will catch up with us. A better aspiration would be to maintain and enhance the evolutionary potential of the planet. We cannot foresee which of the present life forms might contribute directly or indirectly to further evolutionary advances. From a biocentric viewpoint, the protection of the integrity and diversity of the biosphere becomes a moral necessity. Man's chances would improve as a side effect of biocentricity because only by such values can he be protected from himself.

If such a transformation occurs, we will probably see ourselves not as an isolated phenomenon called "man" but as the most conscious component in a complex natural system whose well-being is essential to our own survival. Comparable attitudes on a pre-scientific conceptual level are found in a few aboriginal hunting–food gathering cultures which have learned through long experience the consequences of environmental disregard. Our technology has allowed us to delay recognizing environmental responses (we can ignore them for generations, as on the American frontier), but has broadened and intensified their consequences so that we may not have time for trial-and-error learning.

Man probably lost psychological rapport with his environment when he developed agriculture and domesticated animals. Whereas the aboriginal hunter needed to be continually observant and appreciative to avoid starvation, agricultural man needed only to master a few methods of cultivation. A diverse and intuitive experience of nature was replaced by the abstraction of earth fertility or productivity as represented by various deities whose worship has been very costly in human life and energy. It's a long way from Ishtar and Moloch to Progress and the GNP, but the psychological lineage from agriculture to industrial man is continuous.

Certainly all modern cultures (ours included) and most primitive ones also are environmentally incompetent. Since technology will continue to innovate and spread, it is imperative that human cultures rapidly adopt those understandings which will allow us to live in a steady-state relationship with our world. How this reeducation (since it involves discarding some cherished values as well as acquiring new ones) might be accomplished is a very open question, and the best approaches are liable to vary greatly from country to country; I think that it would be most effective to concentrate primarily on our own nation and hope that others will follow our example.

On the basis of experience as a natural history educator, I would like to make some tentative and exploratory suggestions.

Any really meaningful cultural change will involve education in a much broader sense than we have usually defined it. Since the survival of all humans is at stake, environmental education should become a community goal rather than being just another subject taught in the school system (which has nevertheless the formidable task of making all intelligent citizens biologically literate). This goal is essentially twofold:

1. to instill a genuine appreciation of natural environments and processes in children who will be future voters, consumers (or nonconsumers), and practical decision-makers, and

2. to allow the development of those few highly motivated individuals who will be the field-oriented life scientists, the sense organs of our society as it moves into an uncertain future.

In order to have such educational influences, we need extensive and diverse natural areas in close proximity to urban land where most of our people will live. Thus open space is valuable not only for recreation, scenery, pollution control, reservoirs of ecosystem complexity, etc., but also as educational resources without which we will lose our ability to recognize the natural forces which shape us and our world.

Communities could take pride in the extent to which they have included unique local habitats, to be protected from disruption, in their plans for open space. Public recognition of the value of such places could contribute to their appreciation and continued existence. Other natural but not pristine areas could serve as outdoor laboratories in which children and interested adults could become actively involved in understanding natural processes.

Most naturalists seem to have had childhood opportunity to explore natural situations plus admiration for one or more older persons who shared their interests. Perhaps such relationships are necessary to make the natural environment a suitable topic to remain curious about. In some highly conformist agricultural or pastoral societies children seem to lose interest in the "nonutilitarian" environment quite early, perhaps during the period from six to ten years of age, when receptivity might be expected to be at a peak, if they were not so busy imitating their practical-minded elders.

If we assume, as I think likely, that prevailing cultural values as expressed through precepts and example by most adults tend to restrict and deaden a child's innate interest in the natural environment, it is important to begin such education during a child's "time of wonder," preferably by age six or earlier, and to start with perceptual experiences of natural phenomena, letting the sensed patterns serve as analogs for concepts which can be offered later, as the child reaches for them. (A promising program now working in this direction is the Science Curriculum Improvement Study at the University of California.) This is the reverse of traditional academic approaches, which begin with verbal systems and in which contact with phenomenal nature may be represented by the embalmed dogfish.

The natural animism of small children can serve as a vehicle for the direction of interest toward environmental phenomena. By identifying and empathizing with animals and plants living in nature, children can more easily become interested in process and relationship as their conceptual ability develops. Going into the field for direct observation of natural cycles could give them a basis for adult evaluation of the glib assumptions of technologists and promoters.

Most zoos still follow the 19th-century museum concept of exotic curiosities from faraway lands displayed in cages or boxes. A more meaningful zoo would not emphasize exotics (with whose original environments the visitors are quite unfamiliar), but would concentrate on local species or associated species supplied with enough natural habitat to allow them to function as completely as possible. You might not always be able to see a particular animal, but when you did, the chances are he would be doing something interesting. Such zoos (the most exemplary forerunner of which in this country is the Arizona-Sonora Desert Museum in Tucson) would be a positive educational resource, in contrast to the anti-ecological effect of traditional zoos.

The restoration of man-ruined natural environments could be a most educational positive conservation activity which could enlist the creative interest and enthusiasm of geographical regions and the volunteer support of many young people who are eager to work and learn in a cause they consider leading toward the regeneration of their world.

When we consider environmental education as a belated survival adaptation of our species, it seems apparent that many fashions in architecture, urban planning, industrial design, advertising, and life style act against that survival by conditioning us to accept simplified environments and personal uninvolvement.

A primary aim of education should be to encourage recognition of universal nature beyond verbal systems. We should not be content with the common human tendency to "make reality with the mouth."

The directions we take and decisions we make in the next few decades will allow or preclude the future possibilities of mankind. As we degrade or exploit the environment we do the same to ourselves, for our subjective life is largely a result of our encounter with the world and we ultimately regard our own nature as we do external nature. Consider the historic Western struggle against man's instinctive life and the diversion of its energy into the "conquest" of the environment.

If we look into the rotting depths of Lake Erie, do we see the future oceans and our own fate? The final causality of our own narrowness is likely to be ourselves. In the many millions of years available to it the earth will doubtless regenerate an intricate biota from whatever survives us. However, we can exist only so long as we avoid severely damaging the ecosystem we have now.

The supposed conflict between the survival needs of man and the protection of nature is based on an inadequate conception of both man and nature.

For our children's and grandchildren's sake, we might recall the admonition to Poe's William Wilson: "You have conquered, and I yield. Yet, henceforward art thou also dead—dead to the world, to Heaven, and to Hope! In me didst thou exist—and in my death, see by this image, which is thine own, how utterly thou hast murdered thyself."

49

THE YOUNG PROFESSIONAL

RICHARD STEARNS

"Strive after the impossible, because the possible you achieve will scarcely be worth the effort."

. . . . Unamuno

One hundred sixty-eight persons died Thanksgiving weekend 1966 in New York City because of air pollution.

No American city is unaffected by pollution of its air.

Ninety-five million Americans drink water which does not meet minimum federal health standards.

Every major river system in America is polluted.

One hundred fifty million people visited the National Parks in 1967. This was four times as many as had visited the Parks in 1950. By 1980 the figure is expected to rise another four times.

By 1975 two million new dwellings will be needed yearly, most for low-income families. One hundred thousand units of low-cost housing were built in 1968.

One hundred-fifty billions of dollars has been squandered on the war in Vietnam.

The average per person expenditure for control of air pollution in 1967 came to twenty cents.

"We are asking only for five percent."

. . . . Sierra Club

"Saving five percent" is not enough. Cities and parks share the same watersheds, the same airsheds, and the same people. Careless exploitation, if permitted, will ruin our beaches, lakes and forests as surely and as thoroughly as our cities. One hundred percent will be saved, or nothing.

In this last year conservationists fought successfully to save the Grand Canyon, to create National Parks in the Redwoods and Cascades, and to establish the national wilderness and wild rivers system. Legislation, however, is insufficient. The effectiveness of Congress and other legislative bodies has diminished steadily while that of the bureaucracy has grown. Bureaucratic planning and decision-making are the facts of life of government by and for technology.

As power flows from legislators to managers, we should ask some questions about the quality of technological leadership the new bureaucrats are fit to give. Most of our managers are still trained in the law schools, but graduate schools of public administration, engineering, and business are preparing an increasing share.

Most American graduate education is narrowly professional. How much of the curriculum of engineering schools, undergraduate or graduate, is devoted to teaching the engineer the ecological responsibility of his profession? Very little, if any. A few of our law schools have broken away from a rigid, formalistic idea of legal education. They can be numbered on one hand. "Social" medicine has only begun to make inroads in our medical schools. Our bureaucrats absorb their ecological education *ad hoc*, if at all.

Uninformed, incomplete training inevitably will mean another harvest of uninformed, incomplete public policies. Schools must begin to train professionals who are ecologists. Training professionals and ecologists is not enough.

Several years ago, Harold Taylor, the former President of Sarah Lawrence College, undertook a study for the Department of Health, Education and Welfare of the extent to which international education had penetrated our schools. Taylor's study came to a disappointing conclusion: outside of a few university departments, the cultural horizon of our schools is pretty limited. In exploring remedies, Taylor suggested that the greatest impact could be had in the shortest period of time by teaching international education to the teachers who taught teachers, i.e. by revamping the curriculum of our graduate schools of education.

I propose that we undertake something similar with respect to environmental problems.

There is a significant number of young, qualified people dissatisfied with the vision of a despoiled society. Their voices have been heard in protest against the seeming complacency of their older colleagues in the professional societies and the graduate schools. These young professionals are the lawyers, engineers, teachers, businessmen, and managers whose opportunity it will be to preserve what is left, and reclaim what can be reclaimed.

I propose that we organize four or five commissions from among these young professionals and ask them to study the ecological deficiencies of American graduate education. The Commissions should be given one to two years to prepare a thorough critique. I suggest law, medicine, engineering, and public administration as priorities.

I believe that these Commissions can profit by a working relationship with the United States National Commission for UNESCO whose membership includes many of the professional societies whose support will be indispensable if the conclusions and recommendations of the Commissions are to get a serious hearing.

I hope that the experience of the Commissions will provide the nucleus of an ongoing organization of young professionals, equivalent perhaps to the Council for a Liveable World, dedicated to constant criticism of the priorities of our technology and to the developing of ecological curriculum. It is fashionable nowadays to believe that any positive act is too insignificant to fail or too radical to succeed. Perhaps, but I prefer to believe with Renan that "the future lies in the hands of those who are not disillusioned."

Science

Scientific information, combined with unplanned technologies, has in part caused our environmental chaos. The automobile, successfully distributed by our manufacturing and marketing skills, became a problem. Fortunately, the problem is not incurable. The very forces that threaten us with a landscape of smog and cement can reverse the situation.

Concerned and knowledgeable individuals can guide us to the wise use of technology. Some of the scientists who have contributed to this volume represent those leaders who have long been willing to speak out. In doing so, they have risked their careers and invited their colleagues' criticism. Fortunately, they and other authors in this book rise above the comfort of tradition to speak of real dangers.

Results of scientific research will continue to be harnessed by technology. However, we must make better use of the research that now feeds profit technology, with its skilled public relations staff waiting for news from the laboratory.

Ethics and priorities are essential considerations. We must stop assuming that whatever we *can* do, we *ought* to do.

The many technical papers in this anthology speak eloquently of the deep social concern of their authors. The scientists who wrote them are those all-too-rare individuals who are willing to document today's ecological crisis. I have included in this section, then, only one paper, a youth delegate's appeal to the silent majority of the scientific community.

50

AN ETHIC FOR THE SCIENTIFIC COMMUNITY

NICHOLAS ROBINSON

I am not a scientist. I am a law student. And like most people, I do not understand the highly sophisticated and technical science of today. Yet daily I must rely on science in innumerable ways in this technological society. I do not believe, however, that the scientific community in this country has shared its knowledge or assessed the social impact of the mysteries of scientific research with the people.

I think of the nuclear scientists who, when they developed the awesome power of the atom and began to understand how to unleash it, were aware that they had done something awesome, and they shouldered the burden of the moral, political, and social issues themselves. And they had big worries over these burdens. The people have been excluded from the decisions on the use of nuclear power in this country. We do not know Operation Plowshare is a good thing. We do not know, although I suggest we do know, what the role of the nuclear bomb is going to be in our time. We have been excluded from the decision-making right to the ABM vote, and the ABM vote was certainly a confirmation of our exclusion. As nonscientists, we should not allow it to happen. Scientists must not preempt the normative and the philosophical and political role in our society.

The scientific community has alerted us to the problems of the environment and it has done that increasingly, and increasingly rapidly. This is magnificent. But scientists must open up all the way. A true scientific community must go beyond relating science to science, and its members' discoveries to each other. Scientists must also speak to people like you and me.

The scientific community must frame the context of our education. Scientists must translate. They must tell us what we need to know; and I suggest that this is a lifelong education process. And it is an out-of-school process. Moreover, the education has to reach all of us. The black community is not going to care about involvement until the blacks understand what they must care about.

Scientists must further frame the policy questions and marshal and present facts on both sides. Citizens—locally, nationally, and globally—must be in a position to evaluate what is invented. On any given scientific issue, even scientists perhaps cannot prove an argument to the satisfaction of their opponents. Nevertheless, we need to be exposed to this very debate in terms which we can understand. We need to come to our own conclusions on the basis of sound information.

I believe a critical concern to the scientific community is the government blacklisting of certain scientists from participation in commissions. By whose right, in a political way, is nonpolitical information denied to us as citizens? Let the information be heard, and then let the powers that be fight out the philosophies of political decisions. But let this not happen by default or exclusion.

Moreover, I think scientists have an obligation to testify for free in environmental litigation where these suits have been brought. An average environmental suit costs around $100,000 to $150,000 with volunteer help. It is perhaps the most effective way to stop environmental exploitation today. Many scientists, especially in oil and nuclear interests, are under retainer to private interests, and that clearly may conflict with the public interest. I suggest that the scientific community should decide whether its professional obligation lies with the dollar or the environment.

More important, I suggest that scientists develop a new ethic in this crisis. They must march into the committee room, into the conference, into Congress, with scientific respectability. They need an ethic which says that what they do with their science in helping society make decisions is of eminent importance if we are to remain a democracy.

If we are going to have an alert public educated by the scientists, we may survive and make value judgments with our eye toward survival. At present there is no design to our dilemma. We are but flotsam and jetsam destined like the wolf seemingly for extinction.

Law

Law is a control function of our institutions. It reflects the social mores of the people and provides a route to change problems within the system. New laws are now critically needed. Securing them is an excellent way for institutions to prepare themselves for survival.

"Our present laws arose from the need to deal with the primitive assaults of one man on another and are not designed to deal with the assaults of one system on another." (M. McClosky) New laws should protect the individual's right to a healthy life-support system.

Managing environmental resources is often a matter of balancing politically potent special interests. At times the stronger, better-financed interests gain a larger share of the power pie than is healthy. The rocket and automobile industries are examples. Through legal challenges an individual can expose the issues in the light of fact, at least partially insulated from the sphere of political or special interest influences. And by repeated challenges, a body of judge-made law can be built which recognizes the public importance of private acts.

New laws can provide the guidelines for a national survival ethic—survival not only of our environment and our race, but of our system of government.

51

THE LAW: ENFORCING QUALITY

RAYMOND A. HAIK

Says Haik: "... Our present legal system for enforcing environmental quality and dealing with our environmental injustices has failed." He lists some reasons why and makes some positive recommendations.

Once upon a time, detection and control of actions which degrade the environment were relatively simple. Today things are not so simple, nor are the answers so clear. Today we can observe the gentle stirring of a public awareness, yet what is needed is a universal public demand for change in our natural resource laws, because the laws will change only when the public demands that they be changed.

In any discussion of how the law can enforce environmental quality, we must ask:

1. What type of resource use is encouraged by present laws?
2. Who is to decide which of the many environmental injustices should be corrected by the legal enforcement action?

Today, when the industrial world is enjoying unparalleled prosperity and economic progress, we are also literally being smothered in our own filth. In our larger urban centers the air is dirty, the waters are polluted, and our open space is given over to highways and buildings. We can draw only one conclusion: that our present legal system for enforcing environmental quality and dealing with our environmental injustices has failed.

The lawsuits of today, whether they involve the filling of San Francisco Bay or a Disneyland in the federal forest, are treating the symptoms of the problem. They do not reach the real problem: namely, the continuing demands of an increasing population. The major benefit of a lawsuit is the opportunity it provides to focus public attention on environmental problems. However, the specific court decision is at best merely a holding action. If the public doesn't agree, legislative action will allow the use of the resource.

As our population grows, timber, mineral, water, land, and other resources are going to be fully utilized. They are not going to be locked up for the benefit of a few individuals, a small group, or a few countries. We should not assume that present efforts to control population will be significantly successful. Therefore, the role of law should be an attempt to regulate resource use so as to make the utilization as beneficial as possible.

It is also evident that population alone is not the only destroyer of our environment. The smaller populations residing in the industrialized nations are the primary problem causers. But, given the same technological capabilities, all people would be destroyers of the environment. Americans comprise less than 10% of the world's population and use almost two-fifths of the world's resources. Our resource appetite continues to grow. It is clear that in future years there will be few quality environmental areas if the other people of the world, in their desire to attain a small fraction of our standard of living, continue our practice of using and discarding limited resources.

I don't intend to demean the efforts of those conservationists who are starting lawsuits, but rather I mean that we should raise our sights to the difficult individual sanctions which must be universally imposed to deal with Man—the real environmental destroyer.

The earth has a maximum sustaining capacity. We must enforce the right of every man to a clean environment by applying sanctions, including lawsuits, against the destroyers of a quality environment.

It is evident that:

1. Demands on our environment will not diminish, but rather will increase at a dramatic rate as increasing numbers of people cluster in urban centers. We can only hope to develop a system for handling the environmental burden. The environment can no more remain static or be restored to some earlier condition than can man.

2. The long-range versus the short-range protection of the environment must be put into some sort of reasonable perspective. At present we are seeing a phase of specific-issue, short-range lawsuits. Because these suits are often filed by private individuals, they are vunerable to the charge that the instigators want to impose their personal environmental desires on others. These lawsuits provide clear identification of problems and problem causers and establishment of priorities of attack, but, primarily because of their specific nature, they will not be lastingly important if they do not also cause a change in our present resource laws.

3. There has been a failure of government to produce bold and thoughtful solutions to the control of human population, which is the cause of all of our environmental problems. This must guide our thinking about the lasting benefits of lawsuits seeking to preserve a specific environment.

There is a wildlife preserve in northeastern India in the Province of Assam which contains a few of the very rare and vanishing species of great Indian rhinoceros. In explaining the justification for establishing this preserve in resource-scarce India, former Prime Minister Nehru said that he reviewed the typical practical reasons and rejected them all as insufficient. But he concluded that the preserve should be established simply because it was something that had to be done. As westerners, we might be inclined to reject Nehru's justification as eastern mysticism, but I think we would be very mistaken in doing so.

Nehru was saying that the most important aspect of the preservation is not the specific site or the rare animals in it, but the act of preservation itself. Losing an entire species of wildlife would in the long run have little effect on man's environment. However, a society that is irreverent and disrespectful even to Nehru's rhinoceros is at the same time disrespectful of humanity. We dwell too often on the alleged conflict between preservation and physical progress.

But preservation is not in absolute conflict with physical progress so long as that progress is respectful and sensitive to life and to natural processes. Professor Luther P. Gerlach of the University of Minnesota writes:

> Western culture tends to see man not as part of nature, but rather as apart from and dominant over the natural environment. This view is especially marked among North Americans. The natural environment thus becomes a resource not to be interacted with but rather to be exploited for profit.
>
> Increasingly, western man is perceiving that such strategies of exploitation are maladaptive with respect to human health and general welfare. But man finds it difficult to change course and devise new strategies of adaptive resource management. For one, the sociocultural systems of the western world have been geared to exploitation and, if nothing else, inertia perpetuates the present course of action. Changes will cost money and energy and man must be persuaded to pay this cost.

The laws needed cannot be obtained unless they are preceded by a more drastic change in the attitudes of individuals toward population and resource-use controls. The goal of environmental quality is threatened by the fact that the present legal rules governing resource use are founded on the traditional doctrines of free enterprise and private property, where each person is free to use his property as he desires. This right of individual action is further complicated by the compartmentalized approach of existing resource-management laws. We treat each resource separately, with special agencies and congressional and legislative committees for each.

Conservation is basically a social problem. Our intentions are good, but it is difficult not to be self-centered. We want automobiles and highways, even though we are aware of the environmental destruction which results from them. We are not yet willing to be subject to laws that restrict our desires.

In summary, environmental decay is accelerated not only by the population pressure, but also by our attitude that resources are to be used and discarded at the least cost to the user. Since population control appears to be remote, the enforcement of whatever environmental quality we can obtain will be solely the result of how the law provides a procedure for deciding how to feed, clothe, and shelter the world's population while also anticipating the environmental result of such a decision.

One area where new laws are needed immediately is in public participation in the making of resource decisions. We need to reform the procedure by which our resource agencies make decisions. Such agencies are too often charged with being the promoter as well as policeman of the resource users. Environmental quality must be considered at the outset. The costs and controls should be determined and assigned to the user, government, and general public. By looking at the real cost of maintaining a quality environment, we can more adequately protect the environment. Such an approach requires that we remove the authority to allow the resource use from the agency charged with development of the resource.

In recent years, the public has become critical of resource agencies, especially their procedures and approach to the protection of esthetic, wildlife, and recreational interests. All too often, the agency acts only on the evidence presented by the private applicant, who naturally presents the evidence relating to his purposes, disregarding the interest of the general public. Often the agency is unable to develop the environmental effect of such use because of a lack of staff and trained personnel to match the money and talents of the private resource user.

It is in terms of the present procedures for making a resource decision that the lawsuit performs its greatest function. The lawsuit focuses public attention on the specific environmental problem and it provides a means of demonstrating that present legal and administrative procedures, whereby we rely on certain public agencies to assert broad public concerns, are inadequate. This public awareness is the most important foundation needed for changing our resource laws. It is for this reason that the conservationists are turning to legal actions to dramatize their cause.

At the same time, we must recognize that the lawsuit is merely one of the tools needed to obtain the changes in our present laws. The general public is attracted by the immediate action of a lawsuit that focuses on a single issue in a specific setting and asks for a solution. However, it is such single-purpose resource objectives which ignore the total ecology that have contributed to present environmental problems.

We must look beyond our own desires and objectives, and stop applying simplistic labels to complex social and environmental problems. Instead we must search for and create dialogue opportunities with industry and the large masses of people who populate our cities and the nations of the world. Unless they appreciate a wilderness or a Santa Barbara, the quality environment we desire will not be obtained. The forces of conservation and industry must join together to formulate new procedures for making a resource decision. A fragmented society cannot, I believe, produce bold and thoughtful solutions to complex human-resource problems. If we fail, the answers will be supplied by a population which does not value a mountain, meadow, or natural area. Under those conditions, the odds are strongly against meaningful preservation of environmental quality.

Increasingly, urban centers and corporations are "where the action is." As conservationists, we need to be concerned with city problems if we want the support of those who live in the cities. The corporate setting holds ever larger material resources—money and, more important, concentrations of human resources. The problems of poverty, housing, race, and education will not be solved within an acceptable period unless there is substantial involvement and commitment by the private sector. This conclusion is equally true about the problems of environment. While the industrialized nations and private corporations surely are environmental problem causers, they can quickly become the prime problem solvers. The emerging change in the role of the American business corporation, from a purely economic institution to a socio-economic-political institution may well prove to be one of the most important developments of the last decade.

But as historian Arnold Toynbee asks, "What is the true end of man? Is it to populate the earth with the maximum number of human beings—or is it to enable human beings to lead the best kind of life that the spiritual limitations of human nature allow?" The answer to this question can come only from a man who is aware of his nature and his environment. As Pierre Teilhard de Chardin said about a man who loses vision:

> I have often said and I repeat:
> On mounds of wheat, coal, iron, uranium—
> Under any sort of demographic pressure you like—
> The man of tomorrow will lie down and sleep . . .

The Appearance of Man

Will a world that is asleep to environmental problems enact the laws that are needed to achieve a quality environment?

52

A BILL OF ENVIRONMENTAL RIGHTS

MICHAEL MC CLOSKEY

". . . Society's interest in technical and economic progress cannot come at the cost of the individual's right to a healthy life-support system . . . we need a Bill of Environmental Rights that will make continued life possible."

Because the citizens of this country are absolutely serious about having a better environment, they are increasingly willing to go to court. The Sierra Club has about two dozen lawsuits on file right now, and more are coming. The laws we pass are only as good as our ability to see that they are enforced through the courts. But our ability to enforce public laws all too often still leaves the individual as the victim of environmental assault.

We pride ourselves on living in a society of laws, where there is no wrong without a remedy. Yet as new wrongs unfold about us, our laws give us far too few remedies. The new wrongs are the modern ones we suffer because too many people believe that technology, and the economy it serves, can bend the environment endlessly. Our laws, used to dealing with the primitive assaults of one man upon another, are not attuned to dealing with the assaults of one system upon another.

At an earlier time, a Bill of Rights was set forth to make it clear that our government's progress was not to come at the cost of certain rights of individuals. The time has now come to make it clear that society's interest in technical and economic progress cannot come at the cost of the individual's right to a healthy life-support system. We need a Bill of Environmental Rights to guarantee that the biosphere will not be poisoned.

How can we guarantee the rights to life, liberty, and property if we rupture the ecosystems on which life depends? What vitality does our old Bill of Rights have if powerless in the face of new threats?

How great is our right to life if we cannot keep smog from corrupting our lungs? If we are powerless to prevent DDT from entering our tissues?

How free are we if sonic booms can enter our homes without warrant? If we can be blasted from our repose at any hour at the instance of those who choose to fly?

How free are we if we cannot keep our population from growing to the point of pathological crowding? What point will there be to be free from unjust detention if our homes become cubicles no better than cages?

Who will want freedom of assembly if everyone lives to escape crowds?

Our old freedoms are being eroded without due process. Without any court order, any finding of fact, or any weighing of values, our health, our security, our freedom, and our privacy are being taken. These unauthorized takings of single-minded technologists are unilateral, arbitrary, and private usurpations. If society should in some instances decide that any taking is warranted, that decision should be made by open, fair, and public process.

And society should also draw lines around the nucleus of our environmental rights. Certain rights should be invulnerable, inalienable. Just as nature's law of limits fixes the tolerances needed for life, our laws also should set environmental limits beyond which society cannot intrude, no matter what the excuse.

We may be able to discover an indication of the new rights we need within the meaning of our old Bill of Rights. But the important thing is that they be set forth and established now: the right to be free from uninvited assault by noxious and annoying substances; the right to be undisturbed by uninvited sounds; the right to be unregimented and uncrowded; the right to have nature's presence accessible and to have its most vivid and vital expressions undefiled; the right to have representative biological communities survive and to have the best soils conserved; the right to live as part of a healthy ecosystem.

In short, we need a Bill of Environmental Rights that will make continued life possible.

Religion

Invocations in the Conference were shared by several faiths. Rabbi Mindick considered the Bill of Rights and environmental decay; Reverend Richard Sample, an eco-activist, appealed for church action on the environment issue—"the gut issue." Reverend Anderson summarizes the church's past and present attitudes about the environment.

53

THE CHURCH AND THE ENVIRONMENT

ROBERT C. ANDERSON

Speaking of the role of the church, and particularly the Judeo-Christian tradition, in the environmental crisis, perhaps the first proper response is a confession of the church's own sins of commission and omission. With a few lonely prophets in the wilderness, the church is late in coming to the scene of the current environmental action. To use the familiar imagery of the earth as spaceship, the church has long been concerned with the character and fate of its passengers, but has only started to turn its attention to the health of the craft as it begins to grasp the ecological fact that passengers and craft alike share a common destiny.

Apart from the need for activism on currently crucial issues (which may not be the strong suit of the church), an even more fundamental task faces the religious community and the general public, and the task is germane to the role of the church. It is a question of values. What do we want life to *be*? Dr. Paul Sears has put it this way:

> Behind the fact of life is the problem of its meaning. The creative genius of mankind is challenged in all its range to design a future not only for survival, but for a kind of survival that has meaning.

When the discussion of environmental issues enters the realm of values, it clearly becomes a religious matter. Others have said this, not always to the favor of the Christian faith. In an article in *Science* (March 10, 1967) called "The Historical Roots of Our Ecological Crisis," Professor Lynn White of UCLA points to the man-centered character of Christianity, stating that "Christianity . . . not only established a dualism of man and nature but also insisted that it is God's will that man exploit nature for his proper ends." With all things under his dominion, man too often chose to interpret this as a license to consume, rather than as a trust to keep. Content that it was "right" to exploit nature, man produced a devastating impact of exploitative practices with the possibilities offered by an increasingly efficient technology. Thus, where there was once a time when the need was for man to save himself from nature, now a time has come when the need is to save nature from man, and man from himself.

But if the historical development of western religious attitudes permitted and even encouraged the exploitation of the earth, Professor White suggests that it will also require religious attitudes to redeem the situation. "Since the roots of our trouble are so largely religious, the remedy must also be essentially religious, whether we call it that or not. We must rethink and refeel our nature and destiny."

What can the religious community do? It is imperative that some churches take corrective action on specific doctrines that violate the demands of the times and the true cause of humanity. The restriction on birth control is the obvious example. Every church can encourage its people to take their places with those agencies and groups that work for a better environment, and to learn from the persons who are doing the hardest thinking about these problems. The church (both as individuals and as an institution) can support legislation designed to heal the current afflictions. It can interpret the need to sacrifice some of the things we think of as "rights," and encourage a willingness to pay the costs of a clean environment.

However, before any of these things can be done with conviction or sincerity, the church must reassess its own values and beliefs—beginning by taking seriously the Christian teaching that this is a finite world that demands living out the Christian concept of stewardship with new sophistication and wisdom. The earth *is* a trust to keep for the sake of all men, and not a thing to destroy for personal gain or pleasure. Thus the church must help people to ponder what it means for man to be a part of the natural order, and not a creature who thinks of himself as independent of it. It can help in generating a new commitment to the earth and to the other things and creatures of creation—helping us sense, with St. Francis, what it means to say "brother wind," "sister water," "mother earth." It can foster in parishioners and citizens the development of an ecological conscience that is sensitive to the rights of other creatures, and evaluates the things of the earth in terms of ethics and esthetics, as well as economics. It can open our eyes to the fact that we are related in a profound way to the vast and complicated web of life that exists within the thin biosphere of earth, and that our own fate is tied up with the fate of other life on the planet. And in keeping with its prophetic heritage, it can proclaim the inevitable judgment of a self-wrought wrath that will befall the race if it persists in the exploitation and destruction of the Creation.

The duration of man's moment in time will depend, in part, on how well we learn the ecological lessons as to what earth is and who we are; and the meaning of each person's life can be enhanced by the same lesson. For in our growing concern for the environment and all its parts we learn something new about ourselves. In the durability of life we see strength, in its complexity there is wonder, in its fragility there is beauty. And in both the deepening mystery and the increased understanding of our place in the scheme of creation we may discover something new about humility, fraternity, and oneness.

People of the Judeo-Christian faith should be in the first ranks of those who draw wisdom from the environmental crisis, and bring creative resolution to it. For whatever the historical distortions may have been, this is a faith that is, at its heart, not exploitative, but rather the agent of healing, redemptive love—to be extended now to earth and nature, as well as to man.

Art is basic to creating a survival ethic by leading us to evaluate a meaningful existence.

In the Conference, Dr. Sears said:

> . . . We need the cooperation of the artist. I think his responsibility is much greater than we ever conceived because this is essentially a problem of design and it is the artist who can take these things and dramatize them so that they appeal to people and help to change the values and beliefs which they have.

Dr. Batisse of UNESCO in Paris said:

> . . . The artists have to contribute to the art of living. We have to design a design for life which has to be acceptable to the various groups in the world, not only to American society—it has to be acceptable also to Russian society, which is not so far away, as well as to Indian and Chinese societies, whose acceptance is indeed miles away. This definition of a sort of common goal of mankind must come; otherwise I don't think we will have any solution to any environmental problem.

A youth delegate, George Anderson, described music and its potential as a way of communicating:

> I'm a delegate for youth, especially for musicians. There is a major question as to who the real leaders of youth are. Rather than elected officials, the youth listens to people like the Beatles and Bob Dylan. I think that the leaders of youth today—and the people whom youth look up to—are the rock and roll figures of this age.
>
> I think one thing we're concerned with is getting the young people to participate in making this world a better place and not to want to drop out and run away from it. I've played in a lot of bands; I've minstreled in a lot of places; I've talked to a lot of people on college campuses; and this is a very major problem. It is very tempting for young people to want to run away from the world that they see around them into a drug haze, or just bum around the streets and

forget about it all—to do anything but get into it and participate and make this world a better place to stay.

I'm advocating getting in touch with the rock and roll people to help more on these issues. I'm saying let's get in touch with these people who sell millions of albums and work out a pamphlet that can be put into this album discussing conservation problems and solutions. This would make contact not only with the two and a half million people who buy the albums, but all their friends who are exposed to them.

54

CELEBRATION FOR A SMALL BUT IMPORTANT PLANET

HAROLD GILLIAM

We celebrate the earth.
We celebrate the seas that gave birth to life.

We celebrate the green plants that gave us breath.

We celebrate the waters that flow upon the land
and the air that envelopes the planet.

We celebrate the ocean, fount of all life.

We celebrate the microscopic diatoms
that float in the green waters
and create life-giving oxygen.

We celebrate the great whales as they rise and sound
in their hemispheric migrations,
and shoals of salmon that cruise the far seas
and come home again for the act of procreation
in the streams of their birth.

We celebrate the ground swells that rise into ridges,
curve concavely into white churning thunder,
bursting on the headlands, spreading on the beaches.

We celebrate the bays and estuaries and marshes
where the waters of the land meet those of the sea,
where life emerged into the sun
and made its first halting advance on the shore.

We celebrate the great storms
born of the impact of warm and cool air masses
far out on the moving ocean,
lashing the coasts with rain,
washing the cities, making fertile the valleys,
whitening the mountain slopes
and the high granite ridges.

We celebrate the seasons.
We shall observe the vernal and autumnal equinoxes.
We shall hold high festival at the winter solstice,
when the sun begins its long return northward,
at the summer solstice, when the sun is at climax,
the days are long and bright
and the currents of life are at the flood.

We celebrate the sunrise
    and the dew of morning on the grass,

We celebrate the coming of night
    and the rising of the constellations.

We celebrate the grassy prairies and the dry plains
    and deserts where life is thin
    and the ribs of the earth show through.

We celebrate the migrations of the flocks,
    and the rhythms that send them down the semispheres
    from arctic to tropics and back again with the sun.

We celebrate the trees,
    each wind-sculptured cypress of the ocean shore,
    each redwood of the ferny coastal canyons,
    each laurel and oak and shining-leaved eucalyptus,
    each maple and aspen and high-pointed fir.

We celebrate the rich valleys
    where grapevines grow in furrowed fields
    and peaches ripen to sweetness in the summer sun.

We celebrate the bending grasses and the grains,
    the chaparral on the hillsides,
    the acrid odors of sage and manzanita,
    the ferns of damp canyons
    and mesquite of inland deserts.

We celebrate the poetry of the earth.
    We see perfection
    in the parabolic flight of a single white egret,
    in the flock of a million shearwaters
    skimming the offshore waves,
    in the trajectory of a mountain waterfall,
    in the symmetry of an oak leaf.

We celebrate the soil, its millions living organisms,
    its microbes and minerals,
    its fungi and worms and bacteria
    that nourish the living plants,
    providing food for animals and men.

We pledge ourselves to the defense of the earth,
    of its air, of its waters,
    of the life that moves upon it.
    We shall defend it from the assaults of machinery,
    from the noxious gasses, the toxic wastes,

the subtle poisons . . .
from ourselves.

We shall come to the earth
    not with devices of destruction
    but with respect and humility,
    to guide our machines reverently upon the land.

We pledge ourselves to preserve,
    from encroaching pavement and omnivorous
    bulldozers,
    the soils of which our food is grown,
    the wild beaches of the ocean shore
    and of rivers and lakes,
    some forests where the whine of the chain saw
    will never be heard, some valleys
    where animals graze undisturbed in the sun.

We shall respect the processes of the earth,
    the long cyclic chemistry that restores the soil
    and renews the waters
    and replenishes the ambient air.

We shall abet the forces of renewal. We shall conserve the
    precious materials of the planet.
    We shall waste nothing.
    We shall return organic materials to the soil,
    recycle the metals and the paper and the water.

We shall preserve ample areas of our land,
    around our cities as well as in far places,
    not for development or exploitation,
    but for the replenishment of the species,
    that we may learn from nature
    its rich complexity and diversity,
    its checks and balances,
    its perennial search for new possibilities,
    that we may perceive supernal beauty,
    feel a sense of community with all living things,
    and create a society in harmony with the earth.

We shall take time from frenetic urban pursuits
    to contemplate a cloud, a tree, or leaves of grass,
    to behold creation
    as it takes place before us each day,
    that we may know wonder and exaltation
    and join with all men, our brothers,

in celebration of the fellow creatures
with whom we share this planet.

We cherish the hope that men may lay down their arms
and join in reverence for the earth
to build anew the habitations of the human spirit.

We invoke the prayer of the Navajo:
"that we may walk fittingly
where birds sing, where the grass is green,
our mother the earth, our father the sky."

We join with the Taoist poet:
"I shall dwell among green mountains . . .
My soul is serene."

We sing with the Psalmist:
"The heavens declare the glory of God;
and the firmament showeth His handiwork".

For all these we give thanks—
for the turning planet,
for the flowing waters,
for the moving air,
for all plants and trees,
for all creatures that move upon the land,
through the waters and the air.

We celebrate the nourishing earth,
our home and the abode of our children forever.

55

POEMS

GARY SNYDER

Snyder is committed to a life style of being part of nature rather than attempting to "subdue" it as men have done for centuries. This approach is the essence of Leopold's land ethic that all men need to follow in order for life to survive.

LONG HAIR

Hunting season

Once every year, the Deer catch human beings. They do various things which irresistibly draw men near them; each one selects a certain man. The Deer shoots the man, who is then compelled to skin it and carry its meat home and eat it. Then the Deer is inside the man. He waits and hides in there, but the man doesn't know it. When enough Deer have occupied enough men, they will strike all at once. The men who don't have Deer in them will also be taken by surprise, and everything will change some. This is called "takeover from inside."

Deer trails

Deer trails run on the side hills
    cross county access roads
    dirt ruts to bone-white
    board house ranches,
    tumbled down.

Waist high through manzanita,
Through sticky, prickly, crackling
    gold dry summer grass.

Deer trails lead to water,
Lead sidewise all ways
Narrowing down to one best path—
And split—
And fade away to nowhere.

Deer trails slide under freeways
    slip into cities
      swing back and forth in crops and orchards
      run up the sides of schools!

Deer spoor and crisscross dusty tracks
Are in the house   and coming out the walls

And deer bound through my hair

BEFORE THE STUFF COMES DOWN

Walking out of the "big E"
Dope store of the suburb,
    canned music plugging up your ears
    the wide aisles,
    miles of wares
    from nowheres,

Suddenly it's California:
Live oak, brown grasses

Butterflies over the parking lot and the freeway
A Turkey Buzzard power in the blue air.

A while longer,
Still here.

Youth's demand for survival and its challenge to our institutions may save us. Intelligent and dedicated, youth is a force capable of gaining change either within our system through votes and an activist role or outside it through violence.

The way our institutions react to youth's demands for "life" may decide the issue.

In this conference, youth played a major role, as the final paper in this chapter shows. Its enthusiastic strength moved the conference; never has there been a generation so socially concerned. Now, after six months, its weakness is visible too: a need for scholarly discipline, for its leadership to focus on a problem, become informed, and follow through. Sending the President petitions hasn't brought about major changes.

Because the young people there expressed their feelings throughout the Conference program, it is not enough to present their formal papers. Other thoughts need to be expressed too. They were always serious, and they touched extremes.

I shuddered when a youth delegate said:

> I believe that in two years people are going to be blowing up freeways in Los Angeles, that the people's park is just a beginning, that destruction in blowing up the buildings in New York is the base of the ecology movement. The government is not going to do anything to improve things.

And I was buoyed by this positive expression:

> I think that what's going on here is really fantastic in the sense that there is communication and tremendously varied groups of people and a single issue is coming out of it.

Since then the *generation gap* has been best summarized by the recent University of Houston students' losing struggle to save 225 campus trees from a construction site. Twenty-five students spent the night in the trees. Authorities were unsuccessful in getting them down. Finally one boy's mother tried to coax her son down by talking to him over a bullhorn: "Arthur, when are you coming down? Arthur, if you come down we will buy you a malt." Arthur, 60 feet up, did not respond. "Arthur, are you coming down?" "No," Arthur said. "Well, your father's goin' to drive your pickup truck home," she said, giving up. (San Francisco Chronicle, April 30, 1970)

The potential of the Conference young peoples' commitment was impressive too.

> We will stop the destruction of this planet even at the cost of our own futures, careers, and blood. The situation is simply like that. If you are not going to live for the earth, what are you going to live for? (Pennfield Jensen)

And their sincerity was summed up by their chairman, Jim Pepper. When asked by a politician what candidate or party the eco-activist youth would support, he said:

> We'll support the individual who does the job. Understand, mister, I represent or belong to no organization or special interest, only the human race. Our request is simple; we seek life, to know our grand-children can survive.

That youth will be instrumental in arousing change is certain. They will take us either to renaissance or to revolution.

56

THE YOUNG GENERALIST AND POLITICAL ACTION
PENNFIELD JENSEN

The reasoning behind a panel on the "Activism of Youth" in the context of an evaluation of the global conservation problem acknowledges the impact of "student unrest" on the realities of business, education and politics.

The phenomenon of student activism, however, is as much a barometer of a global crisis as it is a manifestation of personal frustration and organized disruption. The celebrated "generation gap" is little more than the naturally holistic consciousness of young people standing agape before a way of life that not only is ugly, irrelevant and neurotic, but which threatens to destroy us all. The agape of the natural environment, on the other hand, presents to the sensually "connected" but culturally shocked young person the clear light of moral value and societal obligation. Earth: Love it or leave it.

The impatience demonstrated with the "establishment" is the best part of today's activism. The worst part is seldom seen for what it really is: a despairing apathy that stultifies all endeavor. The activist is basically a constructivist, a creative and productive person dedicated to "making it better," at the same time demonstrating that the culture, economics, and politics of this nation are helplessly antediluvian. It's not right. It's not working. Shut it down. The healthy concerns of today are directed toward the environment and reach beyond all national boundaries. Nationalism itself is a disease of the mind that settles over a country smothering its intelligence like a blanket of rot thicker than the smog we breathe. When a young man's life becomes shattered by the blind trauma of a useless war or by the faceless sadism behind an official load of buckshot one hears windows begin to break the world over. These are dead ends. Ultimately, activism wants a big answer to a big question. We don't want merely to survive; we want to live. There is only one place in which to live and that is on this planet and we must live here together.

Elsewhere in this conference, individuals of stature and wisdom have argued for an international ecological congress to establish the laws for international use of the earth's resources. I would like to propose a corollary to this: that the ecological crisis has precipitated student activism into one of the world's most potentially constructive forces, one which could be employed and educated into great productivity. Activists do not struggle against educational systems because education is despised, but because education is *needed*. The naiveté, enthusiasm and idealism of young people is not a thing to be scorned, for it is the raw material of constructive growth.

The ecological perspective with its built-in subversifier shows all of life connected into dynamic processes with ineluctable consequences should those processes be irredeemably changed. The ecological sentence for mankind is this: "get with it or die." The consequence of genocide cannot be pardoned. The participants in that genocide cannot be excused. We do not look upon the industries, churches, developers, businessmen and politicians as being necessarily bad; we simply see them as our executioners. I am not going to befriend my executioner. I am not going to dedicate my talent and intelligence to his irresponsibility. I am going to dedicate myself to the only element that predicates our survival and the survival of our children on down to the 10^{19} power: *the stable ecology of this planet.* Whatever stands in front of that goal will be destroyed. If it is the church, we will shun its halls. If it is the school, then we will shut it down. If it is the bulldozers of profit-mad conglomerates, troop trains to corrupt wars, insane commercial gluttony or the logging trucks of our paper-tiger economy that need stopping, then we will stop them. We will stop the destruction of this planet even at the cost of our own futures, careers, and blood. The situation is simply like that. If you are not going to live for the earth, what are you going to live for?

As a species we continue to commute, pollute and salute in righteous arrogance the despoiled flag of our environment. This cannot and will not be tolerated any longer. The irony, and I hope it never becomes the tragic kind, is that never before has mankind had available the tools to self-perception and global understanding as he has today. This statement does not, however, place the argument in the hands of the technocrats of the space-race, the bomb-now-and-study-later school of scientific panaceas, for this is a pitiful travesty on the true role of science in the play called "mankind." Rather, science has brought to us an understanding of the evolutionary play in the ecological theater which has awakened us to a true and grimly challenging comprehension of Man and of Man's place on this planet. The future, in spite of its grim portent, is the greatest hope and the greatest challenge any life form has ever had or likely ever will have on this planet. Let it be clear, though, that the great blight of human overpopulation is the problem of success and let us further beware lest our epitaph read: Here lies a species who failed only because it succeeded too well.

The misapprehension of the motives and intentions of today's young activists comes from a larger misapprehension of the age in which we live. The inner yearnings of nearly all young people are for simplicy of life and for an enriching life. Coupled with the problem of global survival is the much more personal crisis of emotional survival. The cities stink. The rivers are polluted. There is no way to make an honest buck. It's all a shuck. The goal of most young people is "self realization," the riddance of neuroses, anxieties and guilt. In short, people are seeking and expressing their freedom. It is the crowning achievement of democratic culture; it is for the most part a tremendously healthy thing. The unhealthy things are catchwords in this era: alienated, freaked-out, hung-up, etc., and take their significance with respect to whichever side of the appropriate "gap" you happen to find yourself on. The role of music, performance, dancing, etc., for example, cannot be overestimated in this. The FM bands of the radio are an umbilical to a sensual vision of emotional communication. One has to give credit for that. It was created against the rules and it works, but it is not in itself the answer.

The second part of this urge to emotional wholeness and survival takes its form in an incredible exodus from the cities to the country, but this cannot last either: there simply isn't enough country. The consequence of this step-by-step introduction to the spiritual, emotional and physical nourishment of undeveloped, ecologically whole countryside will be an ever greater demand for access to our natural areas, for more natural areas and for the information, sustenance and peace they provide. The ecological perspective draws a picture of life whose germane interest is in a miracle of creation and of evolution which is wonderful, brutal and inspiring.

Where, one may ask, is the activism of youth heading? It is a certain fact that the ecological perspective and the reality of the ecological crisis will mature the destructive and volatile naiveté of the young leftist. The "hashish dreams of guerrilla warfare" based on lineal Marxist pollutionist dogma are a tunnel vision to a sign reading "no exit." The real revolution is the one already precipitated on the global food chains and on our yet unborn. Within the changing fabric of activism itself, there is a great role yet to be played and the lines belong to conservationists. It is to these people that the maturing young are going to look for help, education and leadership. It is truly to "the men of the earth," to the men of global understanding and international commitment that the reins of world leadership will be handed. This is the one area where the cooperation of all sides can be gained and is the only area where the power structure can communicate with and join forces with the great potential of the spontaneous and genuine enthusiasm of today's young activist. Without this coming together over the common goal of a quality environment and ecological stability, we will continue to suffer the ravages of confrontation and disruption only to reap the grim harvest of irredeemable waste of energy, intelligence and human life.

57
A YOUNG PHILOSOPHY
DANIEL ROSENBERG

Recently I was given a unique opportunity to work toward the solution of a pressing social issue. I say "pressing" because—though relatively small in comparison with the array of mammoth and critical social problems existing in the United States today—the recent campaign to save San Francisco Bay from brutal, piecemeal development (and destruction) may have been only a minor skirmish, but it must be looked at as part of a definitely *major* battle. I, through my employer, the Sierra Club, worked to establish the idea that our beautiful San Francisco Bay is the property of the four and a half million people living around it, who know it now as beautiful—and that it is *not* the property of investors, developers, and special financial interests who know it only as a quick road to large profits at the public's expense.

We, the people, won this battle and—yes—I am proud to say that I had a part in its winning. It is not often that a young person just out of college has the opportunity to perform meaningful service for other men and for future generations. It cost me six months of my life—day and night—but it was well worth the expenditure. I would gladly do it again, whether to prevent the spilling of more and more oil in the Santa Barbara Channel, or to preserve California's magnificent Mineral King Valley, or to prevent yet another mass killing of fish and wildlife due to pesticide poisoning in the Mississippi Delta.

I hesitate to draw the always inadequate and inaccurate generational lines, but the fact is that—through action, or more often inaction—*your* generation has willed to *my* generation a host of absolutely *critical* problems affecting the very survival of our species in a livable world, one of which is the present environmental crisis. Rare is the square inch of land on this earth which has not yet been fouled with pesticides, industrial pollution, bulldozers, strip mines, freeways, and Hamburger Palaces.

Today, and particularly in the San Francisco Bay Area, young people are developing a new life style and outlook on their world. I do not refer to rock music, hip clothes, or social mores. I'm talking about the new awareness of the social and environmental legacy willed to us by fate and man's seemingly inexhaustible capacity for stupidity through the centuries. We are just beginning; we have no real direction and no coherent leadership, but we are beginning to understand the problems and we will find solutions. We *will* provide the leadership and energy we have not yet found in the business establishment, in the political world, in the government agencies, or even in most of the colleges and universities across this land.

The generation preceding mine has willed us a system in which "more" and "better" and "greater" are the concepts by which man's supposed progress is measured. What I am questioning today is the assumption that my salvation—and my children's salvation—lies in the insensitive, largely profit-oriented notions of "progress" by which men have so long measured the quality of their life. If "more" means more of the indiscriminate dumping of increasingly larger quantities of biocides into the environment, I *don't* buy it. If "better" means the increasing devastation of our national forests and offshore shoals by "better" technology, I don't buy it. If "greater" is meant to describe the oil pipeline proposed for Alaska which would build a wall across that state impeding the annual migration of caribou herds, I don't buy that, either. I measure man's progress by the degree to which the quality of *life* —not only of people, but also of birds, deer and fish—is enhanced by an activity or a project. Judged by this standard, we seem to be *re*gressing at full speed. There is very little time left in which to change direction, and I ask you to ask yourself whether your life is contributing to progress—*real* progress toward a livable planet for my children—*or* to the general regression, according to the laws of the fastest buck, into a world environmental catastrophe. Which will it be? What are *you* doing? When will you begin?

58

ECOLOGY ACTION

MICHAEL PERELMAN

Today I am fortunate to have the opportunity to confront some people in the highest reaches of our society. I do not mean to be antagonistic when I use the word confront, but I do *not* feel that our token group of young people has had the opportunity to take part in a meaningful dialogue with the powerful people I am talking about. Further, the great majority of poor people and working people do not even have a token delegation. So it is to these powerful people that I will direct my remarks. Let me say right now that if my judgment about you is mistaken, I wish to apologize.

We have heard many pious remarks at your convention. You have great faith in the young. Yet we learned from our president's attitude toward the Mobilization how much you really value our opinion. Isn't your hope in us really that we just remain silent?

Oh, you young people are so impatient. I was impatient when I was young. Yet we learned at the Democratic Convention and at People's Park what swift and decisive action could be taken in our society. Do you crack the heads of the polluters? No, you meet with the automotive manufacturers, for instance, and settle with them out of court. Instead of the Chicago eight, I suggest the Detroit four.

Now some of you are saying, young people think they have all of the answers. We don't say that, but a few years ago when we asked about Vietnam, you were telling us that we didn't understand because we didn't have all the facts. You see, you have been short of answers too; that is why we are here talking about the disaster to which your leadership has led us. You should have bowed out long ago.

We have heard talk, but how can we believe that you are willing to act? You and your system have been the main contributors to the problem; how much would you sacrifice to become part of the solution?

We saw your dedication to the war on poverty. There were commissions. Contracts were let to major corporations. Some money even trickled down to the poor. We fear that there might be a war on pollution which will be as meaningless as the war on poverty. We cannot settle for such shams.

You tell us that our system is the best system devised by man. I agree, *for you* it is the best system devised by man. It is the system that has given you control over most of the world's resources. I merely ask whether our system has served the interests of mankind as a whole or of a select few.

You must see that nature is presenting a set of nonnegotiable demands. Either play by my rules, nature says, or I will roll over and quit like I did when I let the fertile lands become deserts or when I let Lake Erie die. To learn these rules you must completely rethink your whole set of values. I will no longer let you smother me with smog and poison me with nitrates. You must give up all hope of outwitting me with bigger and better technologies. You must abandon the automobile. Nature and the car are incompatible.

We can no longer sit back and allow you to continue in your present ways. No more business as usual. You people have misused your power. Many of us do not believe that you deserve it any longer. You people stand in the way of needed change. But please prove me wrong, please show us that you have some sensitivity for the human element. And God help us if you don't.

59

ECOLOGY: A COMMITMENT

STEPHANIE MILLS

The world that we human beings have known and loved for all our history is rapidly being destroyed. It was a nice world while it lasted, but evidently we don't want it nice, so we are eroding it assiduously. Beauty is vanishing right and left—there will be no return to paradise. This is a fact—no amount of money or good will can bring back Glen Canyon or the passenger pigeon. More and more of our natural environment is lost to us forever. It is no longer a comfort to see untouched places near the city, since it is virtually certain that someday those places will be "developed." It is hard not to see natural places and feel an impending sense of loss. The world is becoming a mangled corpse, an entity afflicted with the cancer of man. The fact that we well-intentioned souls get together and confer—assuring each other that yes, by God, the problem's still there while the mangling goes on apace outside—

is not terribly heartening. It is hard not to get together once in a while just to reassure ourselves that good souls exist, but it is certainly not enough. Most of us are out doing, yet we are inclined to feel most painfully the guilt for the things that are left undone, as though it were right that private individuals and organizations carry the total burden of salvation.

Pogo's axiom, "We have met the enemy and he is us," has gained wide currency of late, especially among conservationists. The idea is, I suppose, that all the good guys had better be simon-pure, or they aren't good at all, and that achieving that purity supersedes all other goals. The axiom that we are the enemy has, like any axiom, an element of truth. No doubt a lot of well-intentioned people have more than two children, drive cars, and consume pesticided produce. Consequently, a lot of well-intentioned people are good Germans. But the fact of the matter is that the enemy is still ninety percent without, and if we fritter away all our time cleansing the percent within, we can, but purely, kiss off the environment. Moreover, if well-intentioned people persist in dividing and thus conquering themselves, splitting up the forces they can muster for various good reasons, we can rest assured that clean or unclean, pure or impure, we will be less effective divided than in some loose but communicating coalition. Our loyalties aren't really divided but our styles are, and if we can't coexist with stylistic differences then all we are is art for art's sake.

In terms of the enemy who is not us, the Über-enemy is our exploitive way of life, and that has got to change. It is a sinful way of life, and many of us are sinners. Now perhaps it is curious that the notion of sin be introduced here, but perhaps not. The nature of the environmental crisis is such that good and evil, sin and righteousness, angels and devils do exist once more. It is a crisis which can be talked about in absolutes. When the survival of the planet is at stake, one simply does not deal with shades of gray. Back in the good old days of sin there were two main kinds: sins of omission and sins of commission. In the new era of environmental crisis, these two types of sins still exist, and both are committed on a horrendously grand scale. The committers of sins against the environment are numerous and powerful, and beyond the pale of our cosmogeny, since they are devout money followers. These are the pagans who sin by definition. They maintain that natural gifts can be singly owned and exploited, and thus become captains of industry. Their time consciousness is measured in terms of dollars and cents. They see a future that extends only as far as the next buck. Other pagans are those religious figures who indirectly advocate mass murder by ignoring the population crisis. These pagans are capable of condemning millions to a slow death. They are among the greatest of sinners, and all these exploitive pagans are doing old evil. Evil is leaving a polluted and mangled planet to your too many children because you wanted to make a buck. There is a very real schism between the ideology of the environment and the ideology of the dollar. For some people anything is all right as long as a profit is turned. Besides, it's good for the economy. The economy can perish, for all the earth cares, and in all likelihood, it will perish. The all-holy economy—and all those other tidy systems that mankind has created—are going to blow away like leaves in the storm of environmental disaster. Of this we can be assured unless we all cease to be sinners.

I mentioned earlier that there are two kinds of sin, and thus far I have only discussed sins of commission. Sins of omission are grievous also, and more damaging in some ways than sins of commission. Certainly they are prevalent. I would venture to say that ninety-nine percent of the politicians in the world today are sinning heinously against their environment by omitting to do that which they could. The time span of the environmental crisis is such that it cannot be considered in terms of dollars or the next election. The next ten years can make it or break it, yet issues of population and environment are still political hot potatoes. Any politician with a conscience knows that he is risking his career by taking a meaningful stand on population. Any politician who wishes to preserve a threatened area will be assaulted by the powerful moneyed interests and bureaucracies which are threatening it. Planetary survival is simply not a thing which one decides by pork barreling. For the most part, *it* threatens laissez-faire free enterprise. Furthermore it threatens the tenets of natalist religions. And the big question to ask is "So what?" So what if I don't get reelected or reappointed. Will my position mean anything if I'm up to my neck in bodies and sewage? More importantly, isn't it worth it to just once have the guts to take a courageous stand on a life or death issue? Well, "So what?" would be a great question for all the sinners by omission in the political arena to ask themselves, but they don't seem to be doing it. Relative to what is needed, there is no awareness of the crisis in the world political arena. There is so little action on these fronts, in fact, that a paranoiac might easily suspect a plot on his life and his children's lives. I certainly do.

You can kill a planet by omitting to save it quite as easily as you can by committing destruction. If you fail to call the cops as a murder is in progress, then you too are a murderer. Obviously, the people who omit to do the things which are in their power are an important group to reach. Certainly they must be reached. They are, in part, the earth's salvation because they have the power to force the committers of sin to stop. This is the role of the enemy who is us—to reach the omitters, and invest them with environmental conscience. Perhaps all-night vigils could be staged on Secretary Hickel's doorstep. Hopefully things have not gone so far that this cause needs a martyr, yet some brave soul may someday be chewed up by a bulldozer, or perhaps environment's first saint will die of air pollution. Let us hope that it does not take martyrdom to convince our politicians that making the earth into a habitable place once more is a worthwhile cause.

Part IV

Individuals and Activism

The independent sector is the keeper of our national conscience with regard to environmental quality.

Its strength is based on its freedom. It can provide leadership for experimentation, to seek improvement, or it can praise or criticize government and industry. Further, it can effectively arouse the public to act. Its role will be critical to survival, and basic to it is the individual and his actions.

60

THE PRIVATE SECTOR IN CONSERVATION

ELVIS J. STAHR

Dr. Stahr's broad experience as an executive in government, universities, and now in the private conservation sector is quite apparent in his statement. He underscores the importance of both a philosophy for survival and effective leadership in the private sector.

As we enter the seventies, three things impress me about the conservation situation in America.

One is the increasingly widespread concern about what man is doing to his environment. Another is the broadening of the conservation movement from a preoccupation with minerals, wildlife, and wilderness to a concern with the whole balance of nature and the total environment of man. The third is that, despite the growing awareness reflected in the first two, Earth's environment continues to deteriorate. Pollution, degradation, and even destruction of air, water, soil, natural areas, natural ecosystems, and natural beauty are still proceeding faster than are protective and corrective measures.

It is now evident that of the countless thousands of species on Earth, the most complex and dangerous is man. Man is the only one to achieve the technological capability of altering drastically the ecosystems that make life possible and thus to have the ability to destroy himself and all other life. And he is steadily engaged in doing that! He is destroying the natural environment: land, rivers, forests, wildlife, oceans, and atmosphere, and even manmade environment, the cities.

Why is this happening? It is happening because man's understanding of nature, of his own relations to it, and of what he must do about them and how, are tragically inadequate. Many men don't know what is happening—even the well-educated—and far too few are committed to learning and acting while there *may* yet be time.

What is urgently needed is a grand strategy for taking the offensive. A farseeing environmental policy, based on sound scientific research and deliberate value choices, and backed by strong political and economic decisions, is the best and probably the last hope for man to have a decent world to live in.

Unfortunately, there are three serious handicaps to the mounting of the kind of offensive that is now essential. One is the fragmented approach of our educational system; a second is the fragmented approach of our governmental structure; and the third is the fragmented approach of the conservation movement itself.

In education, the root of the failure may be the almost frenzied specialization which has virtually taken over. Even the environmental sciences are studied piecemeal; nature is broken up into little pieces—geology, botany, astronomy, zoology, bacteriology, ichthyology, climatology, etc.; but scarcely anywhere in académe are the pieces put back together.

Specialization up to a point has been useful, but the tragedy is that no one is teaching, and very few are studying, how the pieces relate to one another and to man's total environment. The typical college student and graduate student do not even realize that it is crucial to know how the pieces fit together and that it is perilous to tamper with nature's balances. In the educational community, challenging but narrow problems are solved triumphantly, while in the very process, broader, deeper, and more important problems are not only ignored but sometimes exacerbated.

In government, again there is far too much fragmentation, specialization, and lack of coordination. The need for cohesion and vision in environmental policies is glaringly acute in the federal bureaucracy, where almost unbelievable numbers of government agencies are making important environmental decisions with little administrative machinery for full exchange of information, let alone for thorough coordination of policy. And Congressional committees tend to divide up their work in the same way. But it doesn't stop there. Decisions and actions of immense collective impact on the environment are taken almost daily, mostly without serious or competent efforts at planning, by conglomerations of state agencies and by countless local authorities which have little understanding of ecology and too often don't try to get it. Then, too, private developers and chambers of commerce across the land are almost frenetically active in seeking to alter the natural environment for short-term economic objectives.

To top it all off, there is little recognition that "nature" and "nation" are very different words; that this planet, this biosphere, is really a single, unpartitionable ecosystem; that air, water, and wildlife are not divisible into separately manageable ecological compartments. A global approach to many conservation problems is ultimately necessary.

The third sector in disarray is the general public. The accepted definition of "progress" as being almost any multiplication of the works of man, has deterred people from resisting pollution, unwarranted invasions of open space, and other outrages, even when their own immediate environs are directly affected. Nearly everyone is now beginning to understand that something precious is lost when, say, a stream or lake is hopelessly polluted—but the public hasn't yet learned how to protect itself from the polluters.

Some headway is now being made toward coordinating the efforts of the numerous national and local conservation organizations on matters of nationwide or planetary import. Diversity, of course, can be and has been a source of strength. Many groups are useful, but the conservation movement must become increasingly not only evangelical but ecumenical.

It is only too clear, however, that some basic shakeups of cultural attitudes and some genuine reorientations of economic and political approaches will be the price of a habitat fit for living. They could be the price of survival. An economy based on constant and unending growth must eventually destroy itself by consuming or unbalancing its natural base. Political policies which are designed to protect the public and posterity, yet provide substantial protection to polluters, exploiters, and short-term profit seekers, can scarcely be expected to ensure a decent natural environment. The perversion of the principle of private property, to permit a property owner not only to degrade permanently what he "owns" temporarily, but even to pass pollution into the air and water on which other people depend, is a fantastic departure from the old common law of nuisance.

The problems resulting from man's appetite and his technical prowess are finally coming clear, but the solutions are not. Thus, his pressing challenge is to conceptualize and implement fresh policies, based on natural realities, which will turn him to new and sounder directions in his now rapidly degenerating relationships with the natural world. For man is making himself an endangered species, too!

Lynton K. Caldwell has suggested one of many possible new strategies, one with seven focuses:

1. the "internalized behavior" of individual people,
2. land use control,
3. population control,
4. tax policy,

5. industry and the environment,
6. domestic intergovernmental coordination, and
7. business practices, including advertising.

A global strategy would include similar elements.

Clearly the job is not one for biologists, or even for ecologists alone, or for governments alone. Every discipline and profession has some contribution to make, some in problem analysis, some in value selection and policy formulation, some in implementation, and some in all of these areas. But they must work together, and there must eventually be a management of effort.

Who is going to provide the leadership for this new offensive? Our schools and colleges can help, especially if they give an ecological perspective to the highly specialized training they give to engineers, doctors, and others.

Industry can help, but it is so specifically mission-oriented that it is unlikely to give the matter anything like the priority needed. Our vast governmental apparatus—federal, state, and local—can help, but it is scarcely the most logical choice to be leader of the strategy-planning group, at least in the beginning. Its own present organization, its susceptibility to short-term pressures, its fragmentation, layering, and inertia are some of the great problems. Those who are conservationists in government can and must, of course, continue to provide a vital part of the leadership. But they face the restrictions of funds, official policies, and public apathy, too.

I believe, therefore, that a heavy share of the responsibility of the broad-scale leadership and strategy planning is left to the private conservationists among the general public. Their work must supplement and strengthen the public sector. Private conservationists are free to criticize our government when it fails in its responsibility and to criticize a private company even on moral rather than legal grounds.

Private conservationists can work with government, and have often done so, to spur it, energize it, and support its programs. Through publications and exhortations, and a network of informed, local affiliated groups across the land, they have the means to convince the public of the reality of the ecological crisis. When people are aroused, their demands are more likely to be translated into government action.

The task is immense and the time already late. We must fight as if our lives depended on it.

And you know they do.

61

THE GRASS-ROOTS ORGANIZATION

A. J. W. SCHEFFEY

Change for survival must come from the citizenry, meaning the "grass roots." Scheffey defines our present approaches and future needs. We must harness the intangible power present in an aroused and indignant citizenry.

Citizen groups can play a paramount role in stimulating environmental awareness, in formulating policies and implementing programs, and in forging new procedures for achieving environments of quality.

The term "grass-roots" has been used in a collective sense to describe a range of organizational strategies employed to achieve substantially different objectives, with distinctive missions, constituencies, and often conflicting points of view. Three broad categories might be delineated.

1. The community-based organization charged with a general role of stewardship and oversight. These range from civic associations and garden clubs to municipal conservation commissions and regional planning advisory councils.

2. The agency or program-oriented organization, established to provide support for particular resource- or land-management schemes. These include soil conservation districts, 4-H clubs, and watershed associations.

3. Single-purpose, pressure-group operations, representing special interests and often established on an *ad hoc* basis to lobby for a specific objective. Rod and gun clubs, the Save the San Francisco Bay Association, and the Wilderness Society would fall under this category.

The community-based civic organization probably has the longest lineage. The Laurel Hill Association of Stockbridge, Massachusetts, established in 1853, is reportedly the oldest village improvement society in America. Although tied to the tradition of the town meeting and the village common, it was not a grass-roots development in our terms. It was started by a wealthy summer resident, and endowment funds came from outside the community. This kind of organization has helped generate environmental awareness throughout the land.

The term "grass-roots" emerged during the 1930's. It was recognized as an effective technique for carrying out public agency programs aimed at improved farm living, increased agricultural production, and soil erosion control. Despite its name, the idea did not grow from rural communities, but was conceived by agricultural extension and soil conservation officials as a means of gaining congressional appropriations and community sanction for implementing needed land-use programs.

The special-interest organizations developed in reaction to misguided policies of public agencies and the unenlightened resource practices of private concerns. These organizations have been responsible for some of our nation's most significant conservation landmarks, from the early concept of a national park system to recent state legislation regulating the use of estuaries and wetlands.

Needed: Grass-Root Coalitions

The positive impact of past citizen action has been profound. We must now start to consolidate these various efforts into a more focused approach to the total environment of communities and regions. In this paper I shall try to outline three major functions which the grass-roots organization is singularly qualified to perform:

1. defining quality,
2. maintaining diversity, and
3. providing a constituency for the public environment.

A model of this kind of organization is the Conservation Commission development in New England. The municipal Conservation Commission originated in Massachusetts in 1957 and has since spread beyond New England to New York, New Jersey, and Florida. Legislation is being considered in California. The Conservation Commission movement has given political stature and legal sanction to grass-roots environmental activities; and has provided the basis for a new form of resource stewardship at the community level. Legislation designated them as official agencies of local government—not to replace other government bodies, but to do a job that was frequently not done at all.

Elected members of Conservation Commissions in Massachusetts have authority to "conduct researches into local land areas . . . coordinate the activities of unofficial bodies organized for similar purposes . . . prepare and distribute maps, books, charts and plans . . . keep an index of open lands." In addition to information-gathering and education, Commissions have the power to acquire varying degrees of interest in land in addition to outright ownership, to receive gifts of land, and to manage properties for conservation and open-space purposes. Monies can be appropriated for Commission programs, and under certain conditions they can resort to the power of eminent domain for specific acquisitions.

More than two-thirds of the 350 odd communities in Massachusetts now have functioning Conservation Commissions, a body of more than 2000 officials speaking out for the environment in a variety of ways. Several thousands of acres of land have been secured, and conservation values are being incorporated into the official plans of many communities. They are focusing the energies of diversified conservation interests and giving citizens a sense of identification and purpose. Commissions are serving increasingly as a point of contact for programs of state and federal agencies, relating these efforts more effectively than ever before to local needs and regional problems. They are building a statewide "lobby" for environmental interests, and are beginning to nurture the notion of a community "conservation conscience."

Defining Quality

I link the process of defining quality—the first major function of grass-roots organizations—to that of achieving it, because this constitutes a fundamental and often neglected phase of environmental planning. Planning is a mechanism for facilitating choice, but the best choices will not be made unless the full range of alternatives are understood by the people.

The concept of quality is a slippery one to plan for, since it means different things to different people. We have to know whose quality we are talking about. It demands a profoundly popular process—strenuous, often exasperating, and always time-consuming. The role of the grass-roots coalition in initiating and nurturing this dialogue will become increasingly vital.

Policies for environmental improvement must be ecologically sound, economically feasible, and culturally acceptable. This means interaction and compromise within communities and regions. We know the positions of special interest groups at either end of the spectrum, for they have loud and articulate spokesmen. But what about the silent majority? What are their views?

Planning goals and standards have to be established by people's conception of what life ought to be like, indeed could be like.

Ecologists can provide facts, and engineers can tell us what is possible; but the tough questions about individual satisfaction and community well-being require discussion and reflection about values that have meaning for people. It involves understanding of the past, together with comprehension of what might prevail in the future. It means learning how different people perceive their environments.

Diversity

This leads to my second point, the distinction between a quality environment and environments of quality. The concept of diversity is a very important one. Like natural ecosystems, where equilibrium comes with large numbers of species and disequilibrium with monocultures, the quality of the human ecosystem will be determined in large measure by the variety and diversity of environmental conditions that can be maintained. One of the surest ways of ensuring diversity is to give full and responsive recognition to the active participation of grass-roots interests, whatever variety they might be.

Many of our most difficult environmental problems will call for sustained and powerful community intervention. If this cannot be realized within neighborhoods and communities, decisions will be made and policies established at higher levels of government, minimizing opportunities for maintaining diversity and accelerating the push toward uniformity and sameness.

The individuals who take part in local organizations know the lay of the land and are sensitive to political priorities and relationships. This fund of local knowledge and good will is a resource that must be used. Activities of municipal conservation commissions, private programs of resource inventories and open-space mapping projects, environmental defense organizations—this is what participatory planning is all about. It is a bridge between the standards of national programs and the needs of local constituencies. It provides a way to maintain diversity and regional integrity in a society that grows more monolithic and uniform each day.

A Polity for the Public Environment

The quality of environment that we are able to achieve will be determined ultimately through the political process, including trade-offs and compromise, but based increasingly upon real discussion about the goals and purposes of life. This must start with individuals, in their own communities.

In the words of Theodore White, politics ". . . is a process which should slowly bring to public concern all the private worries and hidden hopes of individuals. Generation after generation, formal politics has been disrupted by the sudden delivery, center-stage, of a concern that had once been entirely private and apart from government . . ."

I propose that we start now to deliberately build a constituency for the biosphere, a polity for the public environment. A polity is a politically organized community structured around a particular set of goals. The environment needs this kind of political spokesman organized on regional or problem-shed lines, and drawing upon the range of grass-roots energies already noted, as well as on the potential resources of the political party system as it might operate in the future.

Who's In Charge?

The basic question that more and more people are asking today is "Who's in charge? Whose landscape is it? Who is to blame? Isn't there something that can be done about it?" Response is surfacing, and it is growing, in most instances from the people. New coalitions are emerging from different grass-roots groupings; their goals are becoming broader, more comprehensive. Environmentally concerned "movements" are forming and starting to question traditional patterns of political response and the sanctity of the established economic order. This suggests a new stage of history in terms of defining the concept of public interest as it relates to environment.

It is now clear that we need a spokesman for the public environment, a political constituency for the biosphere in which man lives. If this is starting to develop, much credit must be given to past accomplishments of the grass-roots organization.

Finally, I reaffirm my belief that the quality of environment that we eventually achieve will be determined in large measure by the images of the future that we are able to create. But the formation of such images has to start in the minds of people. This is what the grass-roots organization of today should really be about.

62

MOBILIZING PEOPLE POWER

RUTH CLUSEN

The League of Women Voters has continually achieved results in their struggle to enlighten us. Its proven technique of organizing people to participate in issues is herein described.

It is no longer difficult to point to substantial evidence that achieving a quality environment depends in a large and increasing measure upon public awareness, interest, support, and participation. If the "public" (as we in the private sector are usually called) is to be more than an unthinking tool in the hands of the professionals in resource management, or the pressure groups representing single-purpose interests, or the politicians who make the final decisions, we need to become more astute about what motivates us and how to gain strength. Obviously the challenge in mobilizing people is twofold: (1) catch their interest, and (2) channel this interest into some productive action.

Capturing the interest of people in any cause has become a highly competitive and scientific discipline. In spite of this, those who desire to bring people together in behalf of environmental causes do not always demonstrate much awareness of how to go about this feat. During the last 50 years, the League of Women Voters has learned a little about this process, and during the nearly 14 years of our involvement in water-resource problems, some thoughtful attention has been given to this very problem. It seems to us that those who share environmental concern must recognize some important factors:

1. The need to reach new elements in our society, i.e. urban dwellers, young people, and minority groups. The decisions on the important environmental questions of this generation and the next are going to be made in a large measure by those who fall into one or all of these groups. If we fail to demonstrate sufficient concern for the urban environment, or to help city-dwellers to recognize their physical problems as environmental problems, or to show a renewed interest in the city and its problems, we will lose a large percentage of the population as backers for conservation causes. The money, the votes, the legislative representation, the bargaining power is becoming increasingly concentrated in cities and suburbs. Failure to recognize that we have really done very little to appeal to a large portion of our population could be disastrous in future decision-making. It is not difficult to point to selected programs involving young people and environmental awareness which could be termed successful, but we have hardly scratched the surface when it comes to making most of the next generation aware of the difficult decisions they will need to make if man is to survive on this planet. Until environmental decisions are as hotly debated as the war in Vietnam, until young people identify as closely with this spectrum of problems as they do with drugs and the draft, until they are as willing to support funds for massive protection and clean-up in our environment, we will continue to lose the battle for attention and awareness of the young.

2. The need to see the interest and involvement of more people in environmental concerns, not as winning adherents to a cause, but as involving more people in the decision-making process which should precede solutions. It would be a mistake for us to think in terms of wanting to arouse large numbers of people to concern and action on a broad range of problems as raising an army which will defend every ounce of water, every inch of ground, and every cubicle of sky against the misuse of the uninformed. If we are to involve large numbers of people in the choices to be made, then we must be prepared to give people the facts, show them how to express their wishes, and be prepared to accept the fact that the people's choices may not always coincide with those of the pure conservationist. We must not make the mistake of assuming that the "right" and "wrong" of environmental choices is so obvious that the decisions will always be what we would like them to be. What is important is that we, who because of our involvement in citizen-based organizations, have learned quite a bit about how to be politically effective, share this knowledge of technique with others without apprehension that it will be used to support unfortunate choices.

There would be little purpose in trying to bring into the decision-making process larger numbers of people from previously-unreached parts of society unless we also focus on how to channel this interest into some productive and satisfying action. To oversimplify and surely to eliminate many possibilities, I should like to suggest a few guidelines for those who seek to arouse the public to action.

1. Have well-defined goals for what you want to accomplish. Many a good idea goes floundering for lack of the ability to

see it as a part of the whole or to articulate it to laymen. People do not like to waste their time in meetings where the nature of the problem and the aims of the group are never set forth in explicit terms.

2. Include those whom you want to reach in the planning process, i.e., in the selection of goals and in the strategy sessions. Action by citizen organizations and individuals is not a commodity which can be turned on at the convenience of officials or lay leaders.

3. Be prepared to show how the doer will benefit from the action. An important principle of opinion building—the identification principle—is involved. To accept an idea or a point of view, the people we are trying to reach must see clearly that it affects them.

4. Be ready and willing to provide sufficient information and assistance to those whom you want to take action. One of the biggest blocks to more citizen action on resource problems is the feeling the average citizen has that he is incompetent to express opinions on scientific and technological matters.

5. Identify those you want to reach and tailor your plans to fit. As in any other effort to reach people, you will need to identify the audience and adapt requests for action to what they can and will do.

6. Be clear about what you want people to do. People do not buy ideas separated from action. Unless a means of action is provided, people tend to shrug off appeals for support.

7. Keep the channels of communication open. Once individuals or organizations have been enlisted it is important to keep in contact in order to maintain interest.

8. Make the doer feel he is not alone but a participant in a large effort. Don't be negative about the outlook, or the numbers of people, or the effect of citizen efforts, if you want to encourage more of the same.

9. Praise the efforts of others—and publicize their names and/or their organizations. Subjugation of one's own personality and organizational identity is often necessary.

10. Be realistic about what can be accomplished and be frank. It is better to decide to do something that has a reasonable chance of success—at least in the beginning. People become disenchanted if they never see any measurable progress.

In summary, to get action from people, they must be helped to see in the dry and often technical reports of basic data, a larger view. People must be helped to the point where they are willing to accept the inconveniences, the regulations, and the expense of the solutions to the nation's environmental problems because they are fully committed to the final goals and objectives.

63

INFORMING THE ACTIVIST

ROGER P. HANSEN

Citing quality rather than quantity as a new cultural goal, the author outlines what it takes to win environmental victories.

The history of Western civilization has revolved around three revolutions: the revolution against slavery; the revolution against poverty; and the revolution of the urbanizing society. To these I would add a fourth: the revolution for a quality of life to replace a quantitative view of existence. The environmental activists are social revolutionaries. They challenge and are trying to change a social-value system that always asks how much, how big, and how much does it affect the business climate; a value system that rarely inquires how a decision affects the bodies, the psyches, and the souls of men.

The environmental revolutionaries bring a fascinating variety of backgrounds and affiliations to their cause. They include high-school dropouts and Ph D's, labor leaders and business executives, John Birchers and members of the New Left. They belong to local groups like the Morning Glory Garden Club and the Early Bird Ornithologists, national organizations like the Sierra Club and the National Rifle Association, new state and regional conservation councils like the California Planning and Conservation League. A great many are unaffiliated.

What Are the Concerns of the Environmental Activists?

The environmental activists, some of whom would resent my label of "social revolutionary" as too extreme, have the same concerns as other Americans: poverty, race, the war in Vietnam, getting the kids into a decent college. But they have an extra dimension: a sensitivity to the physical environment and a deep concern about what's happening to it. They feel a great sense of urgency: that if man does not *survive*, then such issues as race, urban redevelopment, and academic freedom are irrelevant.

The environmental revolutionaries want the "good life" like everybody else, but they seek it in something besides bigger color television sets or a fleet of supersonic transports. They want to survive without smog, sonic booms, filthy water, poisonous pesticides, decreasing oxygen supply, and an exploding population.

How can the Environmental Activists Be Informed?

The environmental activist is already informed to some extent. It is this information that has activated him in the first place. But frequently the information he receives, perhaps from sensationalist newspaper accounts, is incomplete, inaccurate, unscientific, or so biased as to be almost worthless. If the environmentalist is to act on good information, responsible research, and thorough investigation, rather than pure emotion, what are the necessary devices? Let me suggest a few.

1. *Teams of Environmental Investigators.* Resource-management decisions with serious potential consequences—dam building, highway construction, nuclear testing, etc.—are often made by agencies which sit as both judge and jury on their own projects. It is obvious why the credibility gap between the Bureau of Reclamation, the Corps of Engineers, or the Atomic Energy Commission, for example, and the public is so enormous. We need new institutional arrangements, private or public, which would provide for *interdisciplinary* teams of environmental investigators to make objective, competent, field investigations and analyses of actual or pending environmental problems or ecological disasters. These teams would make full public disclosure of findings.

2. *Workshops and Conferences.* Too many "action programs" on environmental problems wind up as a decision to hold a workshop or conference. Often such meetings have no clearly understood purpose, are poorly organized and managed, boring and academic. But such meetings can perform a variety of functions. They can enlighten the uninformed and inspire the activists into greater performance. More importantly, they can serve as a launching pad for a continuing *action* program. In fact, if they cannot do that, if there is no follow-through, there is no reason to have a conference.

3. *Training Workshops.* A training workshop is structured to provide specific tools and know-how to activists who are all set to go out and *do* something. How do they go about it? How do they structure economic arguments? Do they know how to line up the technical and scientific expertise needed to present their case? Are there legal ramifications they haven't considered yet? What are the tools of political action and who will be using them? I observe that most environmental activists want to talk only about the "issues," the big battles—Grand Canyon dam, the Santa Barbara oil spill, *di*chloro-*di*phenyl-*tri*chloro-ethane. Their frequent ineffectiveness results from ignorance of *how* to be activists. National television spot announcements every half hour about threats to Everglades National Park will not generate effective action unless citizens know *how* to be effective. I have proposed that a National Institute for Environmental Organization Administration be established, to train a cadre of professional environmentalists equipped with the vital tools and techniques of action.

4. *Organization Coordination.* Environmental activists have been characterized by their notable lack of coordination. It has been observed that conservationists are like circus barkers, standing around on street-corners hawking their own particular brand of environmental elixir. This is changing, with the establishment of statewide councils and even regional councils of organizations concerned with environment. Since the Colorado Open-Space Council, now an information and action clearing house for 30 conservation organizations, was first established in 1964, fifteen other states have established coordinating councils. At the regional level, there is the Rocky Mountain Center on Environment, serving eight states with environmental consulting services, and the New England Conservation Services Center.

5. *Publications.* Environmental activists are buried in avalanches of newsletters, bulletins, issue papers, magazines, and reprints on conservation matters. Much of this is poorly written, overly biased, too technical, or laden with distortions, misinformation, and half truths. Succinct, well-written, factual information is in short supply; good *journalism* is missing from most environmental publications. This is due mostly to the lack of money to hire people trained and experienced in the communication arts.

6. *Mass Media.* Although mass media usually speaks to the activist rather than the activist, I can't resist commenting. The use of radio as a communications device on enviro matters is virtually nonexistent, except for one or two shows. There have been a half-dozen excellent programs on environmental problems on network television, and several on educational television; but those were confined to the pollution issue. There has as yet been no sophisticated television presentation on the total environment, and really *nothing* on population control. As for newspapers, there's the *New York Times*, the *Christian Science Monitor*—and then everybody else. Most newspaper accounts of environmental issues are still in the "big fight" context—with responsible industrial pillars of the community on one side and extremist preservationists on the other. On most counts, the mass media is still in the environmental kindergarten.

Conclusion

Training workshops and information clearing-houses do not sound very scintillating or revolutionary. But it is these basic, rather humdrum information tools that enable the activist to actually create the social revolution.

64

IMPLEMENTATION FOR GOALS

HUEY D. JOHNSON

Goals that will improve environmental qualities such as open space can be implemented with a strategy. Unfortunately, instead of being implemented, most needs are talked about or formally planned for and later shelved. The road to survival is littered with such plans. One need only visit the local city planners' office and ask to see a plan from 10 years ago and compare it to what has happened since then. The time has come to reverse that process.

Implementation is no mystery. People can have parks and ___ air, or stop unneeded dams and highways. It involves having ___ or a group combining a number of available tools ___ nd discipline to follow through.

___ ls of tools available. The first are those that ___ oven business practices, such as public rela-___ p. The other kind are social forces, such as ___ ion. Basically the tools involved are the same

___ author.

that were used by others to promote the profit-oriented, unplanned technology that led to our problems.

The scope of a specific task will dictate which tools we are to use. A local issue may be solved by one approach used by one person, while a nationwide issue, such as pollution, will require broad-base action using all tools available.

This is a working concept, based on my experience and observation. After working for several years in the field of conservation, I have come to rely on a specific series of steps when completing an action plan. I have used it often and successfully on such matters as blocking pork-barrel schemes (including dams), planning and winning an election, saving land, improving environmental management, and fund raising.

Public demand is the ultimate force for survival action. The present growing concern provides a special advantage. Because the eco-implementer is seeking improvement that is a benefit for everyone, he becomes a special interest lobbying for the public good.

Being a special interest has a major advantage. It allows you to define your goal and implement it without compromising with your opponent. This is a basic difference between negotiation (often just an early compromise) and implementation.

The following are a number of basic but elastic tools for implementation: community organization, positive community action, leadership, strategy, public relations—including education, salesmanship, publicity, legal and economic tactics, expert advice, administration, and political process.

1. *Community organization.* This is simply the ultimate strength of individuals. Since decisions on any issue will involve a tug-of-war, you must get others to join in pulling on your end of the rope. You must get "people power" on your side. Since you or a handful of you can't easily influence everyone, win the support of the opinion originators. In a town, this might be the local barber, the president of the League of Women Voters, or a Sunday school teacher. By including these people on your team, the team becomes the conscience for the community.

2. *Positive community action.* Positive community action takes many forms, including the ballot, fund raising, and the pressure manifest in group protest. For example, a group of citizens in Monterey, California, including the conservative business and political figures in town, recently marched in protest of a local power company's smoking chimneys. The chimney problem was promptly solved.

3. *Leadership*. Guiding people requires volunteer or paid leadership. General Motors has thousands of experts, yet the potential of one opposing free individual was proven by Ralph Nader. At times, pressures on a leader become intense, and anyone who is vulnerable should weigh this before accepting leadership. For instance, government employees are vulnerable and rarely can act as leaders on major issues. A chairman is a visual symbol and administrative keystone. He needs to be as immune as possible from threat or sanction.

4. *Strategy*. General Motors, in implementing its remarkable marketing success, uses strategy in its plan. Just as selling cars requires strategy, so do environmental improvement tasks.

Visually, each tool needed can be included in an action model. To get a community sewer improvement, the beginning action model might include:

$$\frac{\text{Community}}{\text{organization}} + \frac{\text{Public}}{\text{relations}} + \frac{\text{Expert}}{\text{advice}} + \text{Leadership} = \text{Goal.}$$

Strategy needs timing. On environmental issues, it is easier to make your impact in the early stages of public discussion on an issue. Once a decision is ratified by vote of, say, county commissioners, it is much harder to change it. At times, planning will require quiet preparation so that predictable opponents will not be alerted.

5. *Public relations*. We are all affected by the persuasion experts who can engineer human consent in our society. We buy the right car, agree that "growth is progress," and cheer the result of the monumental public relations coup that enlisted the hearts and dollars of millions of Americans to put a man on the moon.

Unfortunately, though, these techniques are also guilty of the promotion schemes that are responsible for much of our deteriorating environment. The exploiters of our environment hire public relations specialists to change a zoning restriction in their favor, to push a highway through a park, or to obscure local pollution ordinances. It is time those concerned with survival use public relations to improve our deteriorating environment.

Its use encompasses education and is the ongoing communication of information and philosophy. The public makes decisions, and the public must learn why something is worth doing ahead of time. School visits, television interviews, speakers' bureaus, and printed give-away materials are all familiar techniques.

Diplomacy and precise information are key aspects of public relations.

Generally, facts will decide issues, and there is a growing attitude suggesting that environmentalists and their opposition can agree on principle in a professional sense while disagreeing on specific issues. In this way, you can maintain mutual respect. Yesterday's opponent may be tomorrow's ally. More than once, information obtained from a cooperative industry or the Army Corps of Engineers has been essential in blocking exploitation.

6. *Salesmanship.* A volunteer is apt to be as effective as his knowledge of the subject. People will need to be "sold" enroute to the goal. If you don't know the subject well enough to discuss its merits, predictably you will miss securing support.

I prepare a factual position paper on an issue at an early stage. It serves to keep everyone equally informed and attuned to the goal. It allows rapid public support to grow as the information positions are distributed. Most important, it is effective in watering down any half-truths the opposing special interest may be using. This open information approach tends to keep the whole issue on a higher ethical plane.

7. *Publicity.* A press release can be based on the position paper. Interviews by reporters should emphasize that basic guideline. Otherwise, unpredictable side issues such as personality differences may be reported, rather than the issue.

8. *Legal tactics.* Legal tactics are a means of lifting an issue out of an easily influenced and confusing political sphere into the bright light of facts. Generally the threat, rather than the act of bringing suit, is effective.

9. *Economic tactics.* Economic tactics must include gathering careful facts prior to taking a position. The Grand Canyon dam issue was won on the strength of actual cost and other economic considerations, which had been carefully covered up by the exploiter's advertising. Exposing the precise and realistic public costs of a development—or, alternatively, the extent of benefits to those pushing the project—will often be sufficient to cause a bank to withdraw loans or cause taxpayers to challenge it.

10. *Expert advice.* Environmental issues can be extremely complex; part of being informed is in recognizing your limitations. Experts' advice may be needed. Because many experts are dedicated to a quality environment, they will often provide free advice.

A few moments of discussion with these experts can save you weeks of work. Sources for air pollution information, for example, are college professors, government employees, attorneys, and well-informed individuals. When necessary, hire an expert. The energy he will save you will be worth the cost.

11. *Administration.* Administration is efficiently carrying out details such as fiscal control, mailings, fund raising, and making speeches. Since detail is the Achilles' heel of volunteer endeavors and the strength of business procedures, using chairmen with business experience can strengthen administration.

12. *Political processes.* Political processes can put conservationists in a position of influence. One success with a political figure leads to others. Environmental concern is a growing political issue and thus is bound to affect elections. Shirley Temple Black's loss to California Congressman Paul McCloskey was based in part on the nonpartisan support of conservationists on behalf of McCloskey.

The first rule of implementation is to keep your goal as a target until it is accomplished. To sidetrack an implementation plan, the opposition has only to divert or divide your energies. The most important tool you have is your energy—conserve it and direct it.

The environmentalist must develop a special interest to implement the policy changes necessary for us to survive in our system. Many would argue that such hard-driving implementation is dangerous for democracy. I don't agree. Nor do I think special interest force is wrong. It is about the only way to achieve a balance in our complex system.

It would, of course, be much more comfortable to relax and allow a gentler percolation of public opinion over time decide goals, as it may have 100 years ago. But the environmental issue is too urgent to let implementation of survival action take place by chance. Instead of being manipulated by the system, we can participate in it by implementing changes.

65

CLOSING REMARKS

WILLIAM ROTH

"The population expansion, our basic personal, institutional aggressions, and the technological revolution join together in an explosive formula that may end our life on earth." Yet the phenomenon of public concern has become a "... rising tide of environmental concern.... [the politician] cannot ignore the questions."

This has been a remarkable conference. There has been not only an amazing sweep of subject matter presented with great expertise and passion, but a generational sweep as well—from youth to age. And yet with all this sweep, intellectual and human, there has been a tremendous coming together of concern. The subject, almost in spite of itself, emerges as a single entitiy. The strands weave together into one pattern—the pattern of human life on a small, rather unique planet in a vast hostile universe. And suddenly—*suddenly*—we stand here and realize that we are joined together in a gigantic enterprise—and, indeed to use a misused word, a revolutionary one.

What has created this coming together? Why has the problem of achieving a quality environment become of such overwhelming importance?

Certain recent images come to mind. Crossing the country by plane last week, I watched a movie showing an ancient train chugging across the Sonora desert. Black smoke belches out of the single stack. The smoke drifts off into the endless clear atmosphere and leaves no trace. Yet this is the same smoke that, in smaller amounts multiplied many times, you see today belching from ancient trucks crossing the San Mateo bridge. The difference is the *multiplication of effect.* What drifted into emptiness a hundred years ago, forces itself into an already polluted atmosphere today. The difference is a question of numbers. Effects that escape our notice when open spaces predominate, destroy our lives when we, the human race, predominate. The first problem, then, is people.

Population

Professor Erlich, in particular, impressively outlines the problem created by runaway population. It underlies the solution of every other environmental question. It undermines every advance, economic, social, or technological, that we have made. The backlog of malnourished, illiterate persons and of children who will never, in many less developed countries, reach adulthood, increases year by year. Erlich, Bunnell, and Borgstrom all called attention to the insidious nature of the belief that we can accommodate a steadily expanding population if we can only coax, by massive technology, more food from the ground and the sea. What Jerry Manders calls "the more, more, more kind of thinking" can create an ecological disaster.

No matter what is accomplished in food production and distribution, it will not be enough unless the fundamental issue is solved. But the mystery of birth is so burdened by the weight of tradition, religious belief, myth, and male self-regard that a critical change in our attitudes is agonizingly hard. Dr. Erlich, however, asks for some type of compulsory family regulation. Tax laws should be changed, to discourage rather than encourage reproduction. Birth-control instruction in schools should be compulsory. Ruthless pressures should be put on nations who obstruct a population solution. And, as Stephanie Mills has often pleaded, abortions—free if necessary—should be readily available.

Aggressions

The next image is all too vivid, all too present: the horrors of a Vietnam village looks at us across the breakfast table. For the second problem, a most fundamental one, lies within us—our basic aggressions. The scenes here, of course, are endless and personal. It begins with our early battles as children with our peers—half aggression, half sexual desire. It continues into our adult relationships and particularly into our marriages. It is escalated and rationalized into getting ahead; maintaining our institutions competitive; expanding our countries' influence. As Anthony Storr has said: "The sombre fact is that we are the cruellest and most ruthless species that has ever walked the earth."

Restricted Freedom

Fortunately, however, or unfortunately as it may be, part of our lives are institutional and becoming increasingly so. One challenge is the urgent need to change the direction of institutional assumptions, procedures, and goals so that they will serve the totality of human and natural good. Even as the individual's overt acts of aggression are controlled by custom, opinion, and law, so now must those organizations which direct our lives—corporate, educational, church and governmental—be controlled by laws, laws whose objectives are, indeed, the achievement of a livable and humane environment.

It is easy, however, to overlook the enormity of such an undertaking. It is not enough to insist that autombiles control their exhausts. We are also asking, in effect, for a fundamental rethinking of basic assumptions. An ethical ecology would require elimination of freedom in the struggle for existence. What, then, happens to the American way of life? The answers must strike at the entire range of values in a technological society. It is indeed an agonizing time when basic attitudes, mores, and values must of necessity be reexamined. Environmental laws require an environmental ethic that is acknowledged and accepted by individuals and institutions alike.

Technology

And last, there is the problem created by the expansion of knowledge, by the technological revolution itself. Here the images might be a medieval hamlet with wastes piled in the street becoming New York during a garbage strike; a small, meandering polluted stream in a primitive Indian town becoming the destruction of the entire ecology of our bays, rivers, and lakes by massive public and private disposal.

The immense improvements in our ability to control our environment, to dominate nature and enslave it, has brought with it pollution, the destruction of life and, finally, an intensification of the very uncertainty we had hoped to abolish.

The population expansion, our basic personal institutional aggressions, and the technological revolution join together in an explosive formula that may well end our time on earth. This is the nature of the crisis we face. And no image here can stand for this formulation so well as the atomic bomb which hangs over our environment and over us with such cruel mockery of our efforts, postures and words.

Hope

But an interesting thing is happening. It appears to me that, in a democracy, a question once asked hangs in the atmosphere. It is there, a presence. Magnified by modern communications, it grows and expands. Finally, it reaches a critical mass and maintains itself. At that point it cannot be destroyed. It will not disappear. Over our heads today circulate a host of such unanswered questions—questions that, being asked, must be dealt with.

Another important thing has happened too. The questions have been taken up not only by youth but by all ages—by the concerned citizens, the professionals, the scientists, the humanists, the politicians, and the businessmen. They sweep across wide divergencies of age, position, attitude, politics, and so forth. No politician today dares ignore the rising tide of environmental concern. They cannot ignore the questions.

Part V

Action Suggestions

Survival will be gained only from action. In addition to its major educational objective, the Conference suggested many methods of action. Action means different things to different people. Discussing solutions in a complex conference composed of politicians, planners, biologists, psychiatrists, and engineers, to name a few professions, plus an informed and intent youth, quickly demonstrated this fact.

Since action is such an elastic word, let me provide a frame of reference for the action suggestions that follow.

COMPLEXITY OF THE ENVIRONMENT

In social action concerning most issues, including solid waste disposal, pollution, or population, two things are true. First, adequate, truly interdisciplinary environmental information is not available to tell us how to cure the problem. Even with research, we may not, in our time, understand the synergistic complexities of nature. Ecology is not only more complex than we think, it may be more complex than we *can* think.* Second, social pressures affect any planned action; people will complain. For instance, people want trash removed from their homes and yards, but they are unhappy if the dump is in their neighborhood. Indeed, the public attitude toward the environment is as complicated and personalized as it is toward religion. We don't expect Baptists and Buddhists to agree, and we cannot expect to always get a consensus on environmental issues. But results require action—tough decision-making and dedicated advocates who will guide action through complex social and technical obstacles.

---

* S. Dillon Ripley and Helmut K. Buechner, "Ecosystem Science as a Point of Synthesis," *America's Changing Environment*, Daedalus, Fall 1967.

COMMUNICATION

A person trying to solve an environmental problem has to expect communication difficulties.   Thinking in terms of broad inter-related concepts of a survival ethic requires forays into many specialized areas where few have ventured and where cross communication is pioneering.   A realization of the *scope* and *complexity* of the environment can stem the frustration so often felt by an activist dealing with its problems.   Once the complexities are understood, an action implementer can subordinate details in the pursuit of the goal.

The most precious tool of an individual or an organization is informed energy. Becoming informed is essential to communication. If you understand another man's reasoning for his position or his "institutional restraints," you stand a better chance of persuading him to accept your view.   Thus personal preparation includes a scholarly effort to extend our understanding beyond our own fields, so we can communicate with one another.   The engineer and the ornithologist must appreciate each other's basis of thinking and acting.

TYPES OF ENVIRONMENTAL ACTION

Action on issues of the human environment fall into two categories: individual and sociocultural approaches.

Individual

Some have said that our system is incapable of saving the environment, that the individual is powerless against the forces degrading it. I believe the truth is that the individual is the ultimate agent of change.

Ralph Nader is an inspiring example to all of us who are a bit cowed by the overwhelming complexities of our society, for a man dedicated and informed enough to challenge General Motors is a fine example of what an individual working within the system can do.

Everything begins and ends with the individual. Each person must make his own decisions about, for example, birth control. In fact, even decisions of lasting global significance must, at times, be made by a lonely man. Thus the impact of the individual decision cannot be underestimated.   The fact that the results of Thoreau's thinking and of Theodore Roosevelt's dedicated decisions continue to be basic tools for our survival brings this point home with force.

Even individual action, as it was discussed in the Conference, meant different things to different people. In one exchange, a youth demanded more action, suggesting that individuals needed to emphasize personal acts such as picking up litter. He was refuted by another who said that seeking that kind of personal action meant that his colleague did not understand the problem, which had to be attacked on a broad political front. After reviewing the discussions and papers, I believe that both points of view are correct. The first concerns life style: personal commitment even to the point of automatic response to immediate problems in the environment. The second emphasizes that the most important thing you have is your own informed energy, multiplied by organization. By working with other individuals or supporting organizations active on such issues as population, resources, or pollution, the individual can have an increased impact.

Examples of individual action are:

Population. Population action includes deciding the size of your own family. Vocal support of the local school board in allowing sex education was described as one example of group action.

Education. Working for development of school environmental curricula and selling people on a survival ethic are individual actions in education.

Law suits. Law suits expose an issue to fact—away from special interest influences—whether the intent is to clear up a situation or focus the public's attention on the need for laws that will solve the problem. (Haik)

Freedom. The man who has not compromised his position, who is informed and dedicated, will have a greater impact. This is the basic strength of youth.

Contact with the earth (ecology action). Earth activities include actual contact with the earth, whether it is gardening or walking or voluntarily picking up litter.

Maintaining diversity. Several scientists stated that the most important action needed now is the preservation of earth's diversity of plant and animal life. (Dasmann) A number of organizations exist through which a person can join others in saving unique areas or in promoting diversity concepts.

Fund raising. Fund raising is an individual or group activity. Whether for education, public relations, law suits, or land acquisition, it has a multiple effect. First, the money collected will improve a situation, and second, the donor, upon giving, becomes informed and makes a commitment that is both financial and personal. (H. Johnson)

Chemical use. Not using DDT or other pesticides with long-term residual effects, refusing to buy products in nonreturnable/non-reusable containers, and many other consumer-oriented practices can be effective. (Commoner)

Consumption. A survival life style in matters of consumption will help reverse the bulge of our gross national product, which is, in the end, a major cost of our environmental deterioration. (Mander and Revelle) Opposition to planned obsolescence can be established by purchasing machines, including automobiles, that are built to last; personal objections to style change, including fashion changes (you wear your clothes as long as they last); purchasing products that come in biodegradable (cardboard, for example) or returnable (some aluminum) containers and refusing to buy products which are in themselves pollutants. (Perelman)

Politics. Support candidates who favor your position and oppose those who do not. Political activity may be the ultimate individual action. (Mrak, Pryor, Ehrlich, Wheeler) As panel chairman, Paul McCloskey, Jr., was challenged by two youth representatives; his response emphasized the political role.

Youth: Do you actually think that the processes that go on in Washington today, the committees, the seniority and, getting right down to what I believe is fundamental to it, do you believe seriously that we are going to be able to solve the problem—the problem that we and this political system have created—through the democratic process as it exists in this country today?

McCloskey: The answer is yes; the question is whether we can do it in time. I think we must try it within the system which, though imperfect, is still the finest system devised to attack these problems.

Youth: Let me ask a few particulars. Why is it that people should have faith in the governmental procedures that exist now to do anything about the environment when, over the last few years, the percentage of the budget, of the national budget, spent on these problems, has declined steadily? How is it, for instance, that the recent space shot took up 4 billion dollars of our national budget last year when our natural-resources program spent only 3.6 billion dollars? How is it that the federal government is going to do something about this at the same time that they lobby for the SST, at the same time that they drop the suit against the auto manufacturers, that they lobby for offshore drilling and the oil-depletion allowance, when they pursue what they're doing on the north slopes of Alaska? What is it about the government as it exists today which should lead people to become encouraged that those procedures will do anything?

McCloskey: In reasoned response to your question, which is valid, you have two alternatives: You seek to overthrow the government and seek to do this through some as-yet-undetermined structure which would attempt to accomplish the same thing, or you try to influence the government that exists to do this. Now you have your choice. If you are to get an answer to your question, I would say I would go to some area in the country in which a congressman sits who is 80 years of age, and I would run against him on exactly the program and· the platform you have just made.

Until we get more Congressmen elected who will pass laws controlling pollution in all its various forms, each incident will have to be treated separately—an impossible task.

In summarizing individual actions, we see that all are based on a

Survival ethic. A definition of survival ethic includes the recognition that the earth is finite. Each of us must be responsible for his personal acts. The same executive who voluntarily picks up litter in a park is also responsible for the decisions his corporation makes. If his firm spills oil in the ocean, he as an individual should be subject to a fine or a jail sentence, as military officers are held responsible for the actions of their units.

The individual is a symbol of commitment. Armed with a survival ethic, his feeling of responsibility toward the earth becomes a base for his activity. When the majority of people feel this commitment, the earth will be a safe place to live.

SOCIOCULTURAL CHANGE

Institutional adjustment occurs within the system through new policies. It isn't enough for a person to grow flowers to beautify the banks of a polluted river. The whole goal of environmental action must include cultural change that will result in a clean river. The shift from one widely accepted set of cultural values to another never occurs automatically or easily. Now, however, it is a matter of life or death. And time is short.

On the subject of policy making, Congressman James Scheurer said: "What we have to do is change the institutions and the laws that underpin the decision-making process in the design of automobiles, the location of power plants, the kind of antipollution devices on our power plants, and we have to remember that these decisions are made by corporation presidents and Detroit car designers. We have got to have long-term and tough administrative policies with teeth in them that count, that actually influence and control these decisions."

In the course of the Conference, the need for a realistic adjustment of our gross national product concept of unlimited growth was expressed repeatedly. (Eliassen, Bunnell, Mander, Mrak, *et al.*) Our survival is going to depend on how we readjust through change. This is a tough problem confronting the policy makers of the United States and other countries which favor increasing populations accompanied by increasing per capita income. In the United States, particularly, we are in a survival bind because of our consumption, which is roughly equivalent to our gross national product and is the accepted way of measuring the success of our society. However, this emphasis on consumption creates not only pollution problems but international tensions and even wars. As a remedy, several speakers suggested that we seek quality and not quantity in our material existence. (R. O. Anderson, Mead)

There was consensus that changes in our institutions must be the first, basic step. A few participants did not believe that the system as a whole could be made to work. But a majority felt that if institutional changes could be accomplished, it could work. However, although interested citizens will call for these changes, they must be made at the government level if they are to be more than superficial.

The participants felt that two categories of change were needed to solve environmental problems: (1) changes in the government structures, and (2) basic policy changes.

1. Structural changes

A new master agency. One structural change called for was the establishment at cabinet level of a new master agency (to be named the Department of Environmental Affairs) which would combine some existing agencies whose responsibilities overlap at present as well as take on new responsibilities. Arthur Godfrey aptly called for a Pollution Pentagon, which would set national standards for environmental quality and enforce regulations established by Congress. (Spurr)

Reorganization of Congress. An accompanying reorganization of Congress would help this agency to succeed by realigning congressional powers to encourage environmental management concepts based on wide public values rather than special interests. At present, many committees exist to guide the already overlapping management agencies. (Gill)

Regional government resource management. Regional government resource management should be based on ecological and geographical boundaries rather than on political boundaries. If one town pollutes a river, those downstream suffer. Regional control would allow the purchase of costly pollution control equipment which smaller units could not afford. (Eliassen)

Grass-roots structures. At a local level, the establishment of better municipal conservation commissions would increasingly involve grass-roots concern. The commissions could inventory resources, maintain quality inventories, map open spaces, and police the environment. (Scheffey)

Private-action citizens' efforts need to be funded to give them strength. The source might be profits made from the local resource base, such as a pollution tax on local industry.

2. Policy changes

Policy comprises the rules or guidelines of operating, and changes in government environmental policy are the most basic action needed today. I once visited a poorly run library, where the books were impossible to use because they were kept in cartons confusingly piled, one on top of another. Our present governmental policies are similarly inadequate when judged by the continuing rapid deterioration of our human environment. (Spurr)

The present lack of policy is responsible for much of the social conflict in our system. With our inadequate policy guidelines, every sector, whether industry or education, must try to safeguard its position as best it can, with whatever tools are at hand, often in a no-holds-barred fashion.

The need for a sound policy was well demonstrated in a floor discussion when the Chairman of the Board of Dow Chemical Company, Carl Gerstacker, said, "Five years ago we decided that something must be done, and so far we've done much to clean up our own communities. This has cost us a great deal of money. But we can't get our competitors to do the same thing. So when one company does something and the others do nothing, it raises the costs of the first unfairly. We found five years ago, when we made the decision to do something about pollution, that the other industries didn't join us, nor did the public get involved." Mr. Gerstacker is saying, like other industrialists, that we need some guidelines which would be standard for all industries.

We now list some policy action recommendations gathered from the participants. They are the keys to survival and the object of action implementation.

1. *Review and assessment.* Public policies, including the agencies administering them, should be carefully reviewed in terms of survival. This assessment—to be made by an independent public body—would find strengths (which would be of help to others), as well as flaws. Some areas of important environmental conflict that need to be reviewed in depth are pollution, overlap of authority, and enforced spending boundaries. Critical assessment is also imperative for funding policies, grants-in-aid to highway and water development plans, the activities of the Atomic Energy Commission, and others. (Spurr)

2. *Regulation vs. promotion.* Regulatory agencies should not have promotional functions. (Spurr, Moore) For instance, the Atomic Energy Commission both regulates and promotes research in, and use of, nuclear power. This has resulted in a lack of public discussion and review. (Pitzer)

3. *Organizational units.* The number of organizational units in the environmental sector should be kept to a minimum to eliminate the present overlap of policies and management concepts. (Spurr) Let us take pollution as an example: the Department of Health, Education, and Welfare is responsible for the control of air pollution and solid wastes, the Department of the Interior for water pollution, and the Atomic Energy Commission for radioactive discharges. But that's not all, for other departments have, or claim, authority in such areas as automobile and jet aircraft pollution and stream pollution. Overlapping occurs in other areas as well. (Roth)

4. *Individual responsibility.* We must hold individuals, including high-level administrators, personally responsible for crimes against the planet. (Spurr)

5. Social cost. Traditionally, the economic, or dollar, cost is the decisive factor in the evaluation of a potential project. We must include the social cost to determine the overall effect a project has on the environment, instead of being guided solely by immediate cost or profit. For example, automobiles not only contribute to smog but, via highway placement and noise generation, can drastically lower the quality of a community. Everyone in the community will be affected by the decline in environmental quality (including breathing in the smog) and the resultant loss in real estate values. The situation might be improved by charging the social cost to the automobile and using the money so collected to develop smog controls, possibly a substitute for the internal combustion engine, or perhaps a nonpolluting rapid transit system. Such measures would safeguard the position of each individual and treat the land and air as public resources.

Moreover, social costs must be included in all economic activities. The cost of clean water should be determined and assigned to the user, the government, and the general public. (DuBridge, Haik) Presently, the productivity and economic efficiency of many of the new technological processes depend on the avoidance of a reckoning with the important social costs represented by the ecological hazards they cause. (Commoner)

6. Sound decision-making. There are more sophisticated and economically sound bases for decision-making than we're using. (Spurr) Technologies, computers, and general systems thinking can assist in complex decision-making. (Mead) Under the present setup, two government agencies can act independently, one buying a park and the other placing a highway through it.

7. Legal teeth in planning functions. Planning functions must have legal teeth. For instance, regional planning agencies must have a legal basis, and their authority to enforce plans must be established by law. (Harrison) At present, planning is often an expensive and futile exercise: plans are prepared, presented for political discussion, and shelved after discussion—and pollution continues unabated.

8. Strong public agencies. Strong public agencies will be needed at all administrative levels, not only to manage public resources, but also to regulate the influence man has on our planet. (Foster, Spurr) Professional managers know what must be done, but without policy support to uphold decisions, we can expect Lake Erie style tragedies and worse.

9. *Resource management*. Resources must be managed on an ecologically oriented basis. Moore suggests, for instance, that at present most decisions about water use are made politically. This can only mean long-term tragedy for our cities. He outlines nine assumptions "to help us proceed toward a national and international resource management policy." His approach must be taken with other resources as well.

10. *Public participation*. We must become vitally interested in the requirements for the survival not only of our own generation but of future generations as well. Municipal conservation commissions would encourage this interest in and concern with survival. Youth was described as having great potential in this area. Skilled study teams supported by experienced experts—similar to Nader's Raiders—could quickly involve the public.

11. *An extension service and survival corps*. One of the greatest educational successes in this country was the upgrading of rural living accomplished by the Agricultural Extension Service. What we need is a new agency with a similar approach and new schools to train people in environmental issues—perhaps a new survival corps. (Spurr)

12. *Technology and the survival ethic*. From its beginning less than a century ago as a study of plant communities, ecology has expanded to include animals and human beings as inseparable parts of the total environment. It has been demonstrated that these systems are subject to the rules of experience that govern the economy of energy and material. This being the case, the extent to which all technological urban civilization violates this economy becomes clear. In nature, materials are recycled; in our economy, too much waste accumulates in useless and even dangerous form. Again, in nature, living organisms vanish or disappear, whereas people displaced from real life move to situations in which many of them have no function. (Sears)

Conference discussions were critical of technology in the context of unplanned growth. But technology's future positive role in repairing the environment was acknowledged.

Concern for past mistakes was a marked theme of the Conference. Dr. Riseborough's paper on the sea is a compendium of some of them. "Every significant activity we undertake is environmentally loaded and contains fatal danger to the planet. So far we've been lucky." (Scriven) If technology can be allowed on the basis of desirability, not possibility, we will have harnessed a necessary tool. (Sears)

The Conference discussed criticism leveled at technology in conjunction with population and consumption growth.

a) Recyclable wastes. We desperately need a global commitment to create a technology that will produce only waste materials that can be recycled. (Cole, Riseborough) Many of our products— e.g., hard metals, plastics, and pesticides—do not deteriorate naturally. The use of improved biodegradable materials could dramatically reduce the pollution of our lands and oceans. (Cole, Riseborough)

b) Managing the oceans. We need to implement new techniques developed by technology to manage resources in the oceans. (Pryor) Relatively minor efforts in technology to produce biodegradable waste products could reduce and eventually eliminate every facet of persistent pollution. (Riseborough)

c) Housing our people. New building techniques and new structural concepts could clear up many of the housing problems in our cities. (Wheaton) The geodesic dome, with its maximum enclosed space, is one example. (Sears)

d) Guiding urban development. Combining development and technology can be very productive. We could use roads, for example, to guide development and placement of new cities. (Eliassen, Owen)

e) Research. Environmental research must be undertaken with massive funding. Because of a shortage of funds, research at present is not given enough priority. To determine the needs of research, we have to find out . . . where health hazards exist and develop technologies for safer and more considerate disposal of waste products. (DuBridge) Monitoring systems are needed to study movements through the ecosystems of the world. (Riseborough) Research in computerization will help provide a total understanding of indeterminable environmental complexities. (Malone) Even now the effects of contaminants in solid wastes is not known because of the lack of adequate research. (Eliassen)

Congressman Scheurer said of research:

> If Congress is to act, they can only move with tough factual underpinning, and it is difficult to pass legislation in a field where there is so little knowledge. If we had research and development programs that made sense, based on facts, not emotions, we could get the kinds of programs passed through Congress which could get us moving on a survival course.

The lack of support may hinge on the challenge to our values that ecology presents. . . . While many of the findings of studies can be used in production for profit, those of the ecologist are mainly for the long-term, general profit, often at the cost of immediate profit. (Sears)

13. *Quality standards.* A new department of environmental affairs would establish national standards of environment quality for information and regulation. (Godfrey and others) Such an agency would work only if it supported the needs of the general public rather than regional or special interests. (Spurr)

These are some statements made about standards:

a) Standards need to be ecologically sound, economically feasible, and culturally acceptable. (Scheffey)
b) Costs and controls for standards should be assigned to the user, to the government, and to the general public. (Haik, DuBridge)
c) The definition of quality must be a basic task and must include information from the grass roots. (Clusen)
d) We need to train people to monitor environmental quality standards once they are set. (C. Johnson)
e) Open space is one way of measuring community welfare. (Harrison)
f) Food production must be commensurate with land use. (Riseborough)

14. *Tax aspects of environmental control.* Tax changes deserve top priority for a survival policy. Environmental chaos in air, water, and open-space planning is often a tax problem. Instead of taxing land, we need to tax income. (P. McCloskey) Lieutenant Governor Gill from Hawaii, where the only truly regional form of government exists in the country today, emphasized that tax reform is necessary to make regional government function.

Congressman Paul McCloskey said:

In my experience, quite often the agency that is most likely to protect development and pollution is the local government. This occurs generally because of the tax structure which makes local government dependent on the property tax for its sufficiency, upon the increasing payroll for its prosperity. Because of this, most cities, and most countries in the United States will welcome development with its payroll and its new tax base.

It may be that the solution to the problems . . . is to change the tax structure of this country, to promote the income tax, which is levied on all of us, as the source of financing the local governments. Because . . . like the Alaskan pipeline, environmentally detrimental projects occur, as one of the gentlemen here said, from a combination of economic interests and local government. Local governments, needing to increase their tax base, approve the project without regard for the overall effect it will have environmentally.

Some of the following suggestions were made:

a)   Open space and recreational opportunities would be increased by tax credits. Wildlife habitats, for example, are now being lost because of intense farming practices. If habitats were considered in government support programs, a diversity of the environment would be encouraged.

b)   We might tax families for having more than two children, instead of following the present tax reward plan (Godfrey).

c)   A pollution tax would be levied against the guilty polluter at the rate of his polluting activity. The tax revenue might be used to support the watchdog role of local citizen activists.

d)   With a tax policy change, the quality concept would supplant the quantity concept. Products that can be recycled should get a tax advantage; those that can't should be penalized.

15. *Education.* Education received emphasis from most participants regardless of their field of interest.

The permanent welfare of the world's peoples depends upon sound and widespread environmental knowledge. This in turn will require much closer communication and collaboration from among the various fields of knowledge taught in the schools; youth is beginning to understand that need better than its elders. We cannot afford to have the various disiplines carry on their teaching, learning, and research in isolation from each other. (Sears)

a)   We must have a land ethic as part of our educational system. (Harrison, Lane, and others)

b)   We must reach the voters with environmental education so that they will support laws needed for change. (Scriven)

c)   Curriculum-relevant environmental survival studies based on the concept that the earth and the environment are finite must be a basic part of school activities. Present efforts are often made by special-interest groups, such as forest-product or oil interests, who want their message emphasized. (Scriven) Furthermore we need to be trained to tolerate controversy—

not to hide from it. "To educate for change is to educate for
instability, versatility, and adaptability." (Hurd)

d)   In school we must learn that the environment is complex so
     that we don't label its various facets with simplistic terms which
     only lead to name calling (Mead).

e)   We need to build appreciation of the environment into edu-
     cation. Since we have not done this, we are trying to solve our
     problems without public understanding. (Hurd)

f)   Information and technical preparation are essential to citizen
     action. Workshops for action are effective. (Hansen) Some of
     our best pollution improvements have come from this "get
     the information and look before you proceed" approach.

g)   Open discussion and criticism in the media will move those
     responsible for the damage to remedy it. Reporters should be
     sent to school for a time so that they can familiarize themselves
     with the problems of the environment. (Von Eckhardt)

h)   There is a need for a basic and simplified vocabulary, under-
     standable to all men. (Spurr)

i)   Education must be integrated to include humanistic, social,
     and biological sciences. Schools must prepare professionals
     to be ecologists. Training ecologists in isolation from other
     professionals is not enough. (Stearns) Not only is it old-fash-
     ioned, it is fatal to modern education itself. (Hurd)

16. *Environmental planning.* Environmental planning must play
a major part in our hope for survival. At present it is much cheaper
to plan than it is to implement. (Moore) These recommendations
emerged from the papers:

a)   We need not planning for planning's sake but planning for
     action. (Richards)

b)   In order to have effective planning, we must have laws that
     support it. (Harrison) In regional planning work must be
     codified by law. (Owings)

c)   Plans must be viewed as goals and achieved through an imple-
     mentation process. (H. Johnson)

d)   A survey of our resources so that we know what we have in
     reserve, followed by better management, was one planning
     suggestion. The importance of land-zoning—that is, deciding
     in advance which lands it is logical to use for development and
     which for food production—was illustrated by Paul Sears
     when he said:

     Following World War I geographer Dudley Stamp organized a land
     use survey for England by secondary school students. When England

was barricaded by submarines during World War II and obliged to produce most of its food, this information proved invaluable. This kind of local analysis is of the greatest importance in planning.

17. *An environmental bill of rights.* To safeguard individual freedom now and for future generations, legal safeguards need to be enacted to protect men from the environmentally exploitive acts of others. (P. McCloskey)

18. *Industrial compensation.* Industry, on its own, should conceive of a financial means to correct environmental setbacks caused by its activities. (Robert O. Anderson, Stoner)

19. *Summary.* To survive we must have policy guidelines to coordinate our use of resources. This need must be a concept acceptable to men and institutions. The guidelines will support a shared system of values which will allow individuals, industries, and governments to cooperate and survive. (Mead)

Listing these suggestions is but a beginning. Many more have been made—indeed, so many suggestions, plans, and programs have been set forth that it might be worthwhile to prepare an environmental encyclopedia outlining what we already know and thus providing us with a central source of information. However, this is a secondary concern. Our primary need is to implement the suggestions we now have at our disposal.

Because the existence of every man's grandchildren is at stake, I believe that the time has come for us to establish survival as a goal and achieve it. In the past, environmental action suggestions have led to more plans, compromise, and little change. I have found that plans can be transformed into action if one adopts a predictable implementation process. In my paper in Part IV, I have described action implementation as I have used it in my work as a conservation generalist. The principal advantage of this implementation plan is that it requires the public's participation and thus brings change within, and is part of, our system.

On any nationwide scale, money is the major obstacle. One suggestion for funding was to apply the proceeds from the 10% surtax to environmental management. (Robinson) Certainly funds must be found somehow, somewhere. At present, there are no budget and no future government plans for funding that will guarantee our survival. According to statements recently released by the U.S. Bureau of the Budget, 70 billion dollars have been allocated to national defense and less than 5 billion to natural resources management. Even space-research and technology appropriations are larger than the funds provided for conservation.

However, environmental quality, since it involves all life, is an urgent priority. The money to save us must be secured at once. What we need is a combined governmental, scientific, industrial, and military approach to the problem of survival, similar to the approach NASA used in implementing its goal of reaching the moon. I feel that a similar approach to environmental management—provided we have an adequate budget, authority, and freedom to carry it through—will bring the needed changes, including clean air and clean water.

In summary: We must establish as our highest priority a broad policy based on an ethical desire to accommodate mankind in its natural environment on this earth. (Caulfield)

The above is a summary of some of the problems discussed and actions suggested at the Conference. Again the problem and its cure are complex. In the intense discussions about action Dr. Norton Ginsburg of the University of Chicago said:

> I submit to our younger colleagues in this conference that there are many complicated aspects of problem definition which have to be worked out. We are dealing with very complex ecosystems, mostly man-created, and this is not the same as looking at a neo-Rousseau conception of nature."

The discussion that followed emphasized both definition and action.

The youth-delegation response—intensely prepared in the late hours—provided a final appeal. It was a major challenge to the conference. Though not enacted, it made a major impact which we hope is just the beginning.

INTERDEPENDENCY RESOLUTION
A COMMITTEE RESOLUTION PREPARED BY
JAMES PEPPER AND CYNTHIA WAYBURN

The youth delegates reject the premise that the salvation of mankind depends on the control of land, air, and sea. We find instead that the salvation of mankind depends on the control of *man*, to the extent that natural processes can once again function in land, air, and sea; that the ecosystem, with man included, can be closed; and that life's pursuits can be predicated on equality, dignity, peace, beauty, and compassion for man and nature. We therefore propose the following resolution:

The 13th National Conference of the U.S. National Commission for UNESCO, "Man and His Environment: A View Toward Survival," does hereby adopt the following policy:

On a national scale, we urge

1. the mobilization of the national effort to attain stability of numbers, and equilibrium between man and nature, *by a specified date,* with the attainment of this goal to serve as the guide for local and national policy in the intervening years;
2. the immediate assumption of a massive, federally financed study to determine the optimum carrying capacity of our country, on the community, city, county, state, and national levels, with this carrying capacity to be predicated on the quality of life, the impact upon world resources, and the tolerance of natural systems;
3. the adoption of new measures of national well-being, incorporating indices other than the rate of growth of the GNP, the consumption of energy resources, and international credit rating;
4. the immediate rejection of international economic competition as valid grounds for the creation of national policy.

On an international scale, we endorse

1. the proposal that the leaders of all nations through the United Nations General Assembly declare that a state of environmental emergency exists on the planet Earth;
2. the creation of colleges of human ecology and survival sciences on campuses in the member nations of the United Nations;
3. the creation of national, subnational, regional, and global plans for the determination of optimum population levels and distribution patterns;
4. the creation of national, regional, and worldwide commissions on environmental deterioration and rehabilitation;
5. the proposal that the United Nations General Assembly adopt a covenant of ecological rights similar to the U.N. covenant of human rights.

Concerning the World Youth Assembly of 1970 and the United Nations Conference on the Environment of 1972:

1. We urge the use of the World Youth Assembly in July, 1970, as a platform to call for the development of an environmental ethic to guide and reshape basic attitudes toward the quality of life and development.

2. We propose that a national youth forum should be called as a precursor to the U.N. conference of 1972, to implement priorities of action necessary to reverse current trends and restore ecological balance.

3. While the 1972 U.N. conference is made up of environmental managers, they cannot meet without the presence of the heirs and beneficiaries of the environment. Therefore, as the majority of the world's population will be youth, they must be represented with full powers, as equal partners.

4. We endorse the International Ecology University, including their concepts of an Ecology Information Clearing House and an Early Warning System for all countries but particularly the so-called "underdeveloped" ones, and the setting up of leadership training courses in the fields of ecology and development.

On the political level, we recognize the need for strong organized involvement. We, therefore, pledge to work actively for political change by all available methods, including:

1. Sending lobbyists to local, state, national capitals to speak personally to elected officials.

2. Drawing up specific proposals to be offered to competing candidates in primary or general elections.

3. Supporting officials who have taken a strong stand for a healthy environment and working for their reelection.

4. Campaigning for the defeat of candidates whose positions don't make ecological sense.

5. If no candidate makes any ecological sense, we will run and support our own candidates.

6. Boycotting industries that disregard ecological common sense by irresponsibly polluting the environment.

We reflect Pogo's optimism; we are faced with insurmountable opportunity.

*   *   *

We are certain that changes will come because of youth's valid demand for a livable future. The haunting question is: Will change come from within or outside our system? Outside change would be ruinous and could mean a revolution. Change within our system could be a renaissance—a quality environment rather than our present deteriorating one. This is pragmatism, more idealistic than the old pragmatism, because society demands it.

Biographies

Biographies

ROBERT C. ANDERSON. Minister of the University Congregational Church in Missoula, Montana. Mr. Anderson was educated at the University of Chicago and the Chicago Theological Seminary. He is basically interested in the church and environment, and he is active in many conservation groups.

ROBERT O. ANDERSON. Owner and President of the Lincoln County Livestock Company in Roswell, New Mexico. Mr. Anderson is the former President and Chairman of the Board of the Atlantic Richfield Refining Company in Chicago, Chairman of the Board of the JFK Center for The Performing Arts, Chairman of the Aspen Institute for Humanistic Studies, and is active in other cultural affairs.

DIXON ARNETT. Director of Community Relations at Stanford University. A talented administrator, Mr. Arnett is concerned with the possibilities of caring for the environment through political means.

MICHEL J. BATISSE. Director of the UNESCO Natural Resources Research Division. Dr. Batisse is a former UNESCO Scientific Officer for the Middle East in Cairo. He was the initiator of the International Hydrological Decade for UNESCO and the organizer of the 1968 UNESCO Conference on the Researches of the Biosphere, and directly concerned with preparation of the UN report on the problems of the human environment. Dr. Batisse is a native of France.

JOSEPH E. BODOVITZ. Executive director of the San Francisco Bay Conservation and Development Commission. Mr. Bodovitz was an assistant executive director of the San Francisco Bay Conservation, Planning, and Urban Renewal Association, and study director of the San Francisco Bay Conservation Study. As Director of the BCDC, he oversaw one of the major conservation battles of the last decade, the struggle to save San Francisco Bay from pollution and development.

GEORG BORGSTROM. Professor of Food Science and Geography at Michigan State University. Internationally known authority on world food resources, Dr. Borgstrom has made major contributions to knowledge about food preservation and resources. His book, *The Hungry Planet,* a study of the modern world on the verge of famine, is an excellent portrayal of the present balance of population and food.

343

STERLING BUNNELL. Psychiatrist in Marin County, California. Dr. Bunnell has long combined interests in environment and education; in his private practice, he has become increasinlgy interested in conservation education. He helped originate and design field courses in natural sciences for the Biological Field Studies Association and has consulted for the Nature Conservatory on habitat preservation programs.

LYNTON K. CALDWELL. Professor of Political Science at Indiana University. Dr. Caldwell has served on the faculties of the University of Chicago, Syracuse University, and the University of California at Berkeley and has broad practical experience in public affairs. He recently finished a book entitled *Environment: Challenge for Modern Society* and has others in preparation.

HENRY CAULFIELD. Professor of Political Science at Colorado State University. Dr. Caulfield has been Executive Director of the Federal Water Resources Council, Director of the Resources Program Staff, Department of the Interior, and research associate with Resources for the Future in Washington, D.C.

RUTH CLUSEN. Second Vice-President of the League of Women Voters. Mrs. Clusen is from Wisconsin, where she has been active in both government and conservation. She has frequently testified before congressional committees on behalf of comprehensive, long-range planning for conservation and resource management.

LAMONT COLE. Professor of Biology at Cornell University. Dr. Cole is President of the American Institute of Biological Sciences and a member of the Committee on Ecology of the National Academy of Arts and Sciences. He has published several books and articles on the environment and, in recent years, has been a principal speaker at conferences on environmental problems.

BARRY COMMONER. Chairman of the Department of Botany, Washington University, St. Louis. Dr. Commoner was formerly professor of Plant Physiology and Associate Editor of *Science Illustrated*. In 1958, he was Vice-Chairman of the St. Louis Commission for Nuclear Information.

RICHARD A. COOLEY. Professor of Geography at the University of Washington at Seattle. Dr. Cooley earned his Ph.D. from the School of Natural Resources of the University of Michigan. He has been particularly active in environmental research in Alaska and was formerly with the Conservation Foundation.

RAYMOND F. DASMANN. Director of International Programs for The Conservation Foundation. Dr. Dasmann formerly served as an advisor to the national Resources Research Division of UNESCO in Paris and worked with the International Union for the Conservation of Nature. As a zoologist he taught for many years at Humboldt State College and the University of California. Two of his books are *Destruction of California* and *A Different Kind of Country*.

HENRY L. DIAMOND. Vice-President of the American Conservation Association. An attorney serving many conservation organizations, Mr. Diamond is a Counsel to Nixon's Citizens' Advisory Committee on Environmental Quality. He was recently appointed Commissioner of Environmental Conservation of New York by Gov. Rockefeller to head the single agency under which New York's conservation function will be combined.

LEE A. DUBRIDGE. Science Advisor to President Nixon. Dr. DuBridge received his Ph.D. from the University of Wisconsin and has honorary degrees from over 20 colleges and universities. He is a former President of the California Institute of Technology and has served on the Board of Directors of NET, on NASA's Advisory Committee for Manned Space Flights, and on numerous governmental and private science committees.

PAUL R. EHRLICH. Professor of Biology at Stanford University. Dr. Ehrlich is one of the vibrantly articulate young scientists concerned with population. He is the author of *The Population Bomb,* a best seller about the population explosion, and he is the inspiration of the West Coast organization Zero Population Growth. Dr. Ehrlich has been a population biologist on the faculty of Stanford University since 1959. He is co-director of the Jasper Ridge Biological Preserve at Stanford, the second oldest biological preserve in the country.

ROLF ELIASSEN. Professor of Civil Engineering at Stanford University. Dr. Eliassen was a former Director of Sedgewick Laboratory of Sanitary Science at MIT and has served as consultant to the Atomic Energy Commission, the United Nations, and the World Health Organization.

CHARLES H. W. FOSTER. Charles Bullard Research Fellow, Harvard Forest, Petersham, Massachusetts. Dr. Foster is a graduate of the University of Michigan and Johns Hopkins University. Before assuming his post as Research Fellow at Harvard Forest, Dr. Foster was a Director of Natural Resources for the State of Massachusetts and a President of the Nature Conservancy.

THOMAS P. GILL. Lieutenant Governor of the State of Hawaii. A native of California, Mr. Gill took a law degree at the University of California and practiced law and served in government for over 20 years. While serving in Congress, he was a member of committees dealing with territorial and insular affairs, Indian affairs, and irrigation.

HAROLD GILLIAM. Environmental columnist for the *San Francisco Chronicle.* Harold Gilliam is one of the best-known conservation writers in the West. He is the author of "San Francisco Bay" and *Between the Devil and the Deep Blue Bay: The Struggle to Save San Francisco Bay.* He is currently a consultant to the Department of the Interior and the President's Council on Recreation and Natural Beauty.

ARTHUR GODFREY. CBS radio and television star. Mr. Godfrey's fame as an entertainer needs no further comment. The more important fact to us is his enthusiastic commitment to the task of achieving a quality environment. His fame in this regard is growing; several times in the months since the Conference he has been called to address Congress on the subject.

RAYMOND A. HAIK. Partner in the law firm of Popham, Haik, Schnobrich, Kaufman and Doty. Mr. Haik is currently the President of the Izaak Walton League of America and has been involved in natural resources, especially water resources, affairs for many years. He has served as legal consultant, litigator, and member of study committees on water resources in the State of Minnesota.

ROGER P. HANSEN. Executive Director of the Rocky Mountain Center for the Environment. Mr. Hansen is an attorney who has done much sensitive planning work in park and recreation projects. He is also a founder and Executive Director of the Colorado Open Space Council, an umbrella structure of 29 state recreation and conservation organizations. Rocky Mountain Center for the Environment is one of several new regional organizations serving as environmental watchdogs.

GORDON HARRISON. Program Officer in Charge of Resources and Environment at the Ford Foundation. Prior to his work with the Ford Foundation, Mr. Harrison was an active journalist. At Ford since 1963, he has also been Assistant Director of Policy and Planning and Associate Director of the Science and Engineering Program.

ALFRED HELLER. President of California Tomorrow, an organization dedicated to maintaining a productive natural environment. Mr. Heller, a native Californian, heads an organization well known for its influence in protecting the environment. It publishes a magazine called *Cry California*. Mr. Heller has extensively published on environmental problems. His works include "The Phantom Cities of California" and, with Dr. Samuel Wood, "California, Going, Going . . ."

PAUL DEHART HURD. Professor of Education at Stanford University. Dr. Hurd has been on the Stanford faculty since 1951. An educationalist and botanist, he has recently written a number of major papers dealing with environmental education.

RICHARD JAHNS. Dean of the School of Earth Sciences at Stanford University since 1966. Dean Jahns is a noted author and consultant to numerous government agencies, both local and national, as well as to private industry. Formerly with the U.S. Geological Survey, Dean Jahns is considered an authority on geology in California.

PENNFIELD JENSEN. Assistant Editor of *Earth Times*. Mr. Jensen, a recent graduate of the Master's program at San Francisco State College, is Assistant Editor of a new publication concerned with environmental deterioration. He has been Executive Director of Unify, an art and ecology camp near San Francisco designed to encourage environmental appreciation in children through the medium of art.

CHARLES C. JOHNSON, JR. Administrator of the Consumer Protection and Environmental Health Service of HEW. Included in this Department are the Food and Drug Administration, the National Air Pollution Control Administration, and the Environmental Control Administration—a major portion of our federal government's care for the environment. Mr. Johnson is a professional engineer with a long career in governmental programs.

HUEY JOHNSON. Western Regional Director of The Nature Conservancy. Mr. Johnson, who served as program chairman of the UNESCO Conference on "Man and the Environment," has for the last six years overseen the 13 western states for The Nature Conservancy, a nonprofit land-conserving organization, one of whose present projects is halting the filling and development of San Francisco Bay.

L. W. LANE, JR. Publisher of *Sunset Magazine*. Mr. Lane recently completed two terms as a town councilman and Vice-Mayor of the town of Portola Valley, California. *Sunset Magazine,* which has long featured California's natural beauty, recently made the widely discussed editorial decision to refuse to advertise DDT.

THOMAS F. MALONE. Vice-President and Director of Research of the Travelers Life Insurance Company, Hartford. Mr. Malone, an engineer by training, has had a distinguished career as a consultant. He served as past President of the American Meteorological Society, as Bureau Member of the International Union of Geodesy and Geophysics, as Chairman of the National Commission for UNESCO from 1965–1967, and on innumerable committees of environmental concern, including the Advisory Committee on Traffic Safety of HEW.

JERRY MANDER. Partner in the advertising firm of Freeman, Mander, and Gossage in San Francisco. Mr. Mander is widely known for his brilliantly designed ads, including those for the Sierra's Club's campaign to save the redwoods and to keep dams out of the Grand Canyon. He is currently working on a series of ads on the environment for Friends of the Earth.

MICHAEL MCCLOSKEY. Executive Director of the Sierra Club. In lifelong work in conservation, Mr. McCloskey has been involved in studies on the West Coast and in Washington, D.C., for the establishment of the Redwoods National Forest and the North Cascades National Park. He was assistant to the President of the Sierra Club and its Conservation Director before becoming Executive Director in 1969.

MARGARET MEAD. Chairman of the Social Sciences Division and Professor of Anthropology at Fordham University. Dr. Mead is internationally known as an anthropologist, having written extensively about her findings, from *Coming of Age in Samoa,* published in 1928, to her present book, *The Small Conference: An Innovation in Communication* (with Paul Byers). She has been visiting professor at Yale, New York University, the Menninger Foundation, Columbia University, and Harvard University, to name a few.

STEPHANIE MILLS. Editor of *Earth Times*. In a widely quoted valedictorian statement made at Mills College, Miss Mills declared that she personally would not contribute to the population explosion. She subsequently worked for Planned Parenthood before starting a vibrant new biweekly on environmental deterioration.

JOSEPH G. MOORE, JR. Vice-President in Municipal Finance at Eastman, Dillon, Union Securities and Company in New York City. Mr. Moore's career with the State of Texas spanned more than 17 years, during which time he was a member of several water management boards and was responsible for developing the statewide Texas Water Plan.

FRANK E. MOSS. Senator of the State of Utah. Senator Moss is well known for his interest in the field of water resources; he has written *The Water Crisis* and authored several bills on natural resources conservation, including the bill which established Canyonlands National Park in Utah.

EMIL MRAK. Chancellor Emeritus at the University of California at Davis. Dr. Mrak joined the faculty of the University of California as a food technology specialist and chaired the David Campus' Department of Food Science and Technology for many years. He has a long-standing concern for the world's food problems, especially those of the developing nations. As Special Advisor to HEW Secretary Finch, he has played an important role in the banning of DDT.

WILFRED OWEN. A Senior Fellow at the Economics Studies Program of the Brookings Institute. Mr. Owens is one of the nation's leading authorities on transportation and urban problems. He is the author of *Cities in the Motor Age, The Metropolitan Transportation Problem*, among others. His current work on the relation of transport and communication to the environment involves a comparative study of the United States, Europe, and the developing world.

NATHANIEL A. OWINGS. Partner in the architectural firm of Skidmore, Owings, and Merrill in San Francisco. Mr. Owings is well known as an urban designer. He was appointed by former President Johnson and reappointed by President Nixon as chairman of the advisory committee that oversees planning and architecture for Washington, D.C.

JAMES PEPPER. Graduate student at the School of Landscape Architecture, University of California at Berkeley. Prior to returning to graduate school he was an instructor at the University of California. His major activities have centered on environmental affairs.

MICHAEL PERELMAN. Mr. Perelman is a doctoral candidate in agricultural economics at the University of California at Berkeley.

KENNETH S. PITZER. President of Stanford University. Dr. Pitzer became President of Stanford in 1968 after six years as President of Rice. Previously he was Professor of Chemistry and Chairman of the Faculty Senate at the University of California at Berkeley. He is a member of the Advisory Committee of the Atomic Energy Commission.

TAYLOR PRYOR. Director of the Makapuu Oceanic Center in Hawaii. Dr. Pryor is a past President of the Oceanic Foundation and the past President of Sea Life Incorporated.

ROGER REVELLE. Director of the Center for Population Studies at Harvard University. Dr. Revelle was formerly Director of Scripps Institute of Oceanography in La Jolla, California. His activities include participation in a wide range of professional societies and public organizations.

THOMAS W. RICHARDS. President of The Nature Conservancy. Mr. Richards has an impressive list of achievements in open-space programs of government agencies. He has developed open-space plans for the Arlington County Board of Supervisors, the Washington Area Open Space Project, and the Northern Virginia Regional Planning Committee's Park Committee. As President of The Nature Conservancy he directs the buying and preserving of thousands of critical acres of open space.

ROBERT W. RISEBOROUGH. Professor of Nutritional Science at the University of California at Berkeley. Dr. Riseborough is a specialist in the effects of pollutants on marine birds, particularly the pelican and cormorant along the Californian coast. For the past five years he has worked on marine pollution ecology at the Institute of Marine Resources in Berkeley.

NICHOLAS ROBINSON. Law student at Columbia University, candidate for degree in 1970. Mr. Robinson is on the U.S. National Commission for UNESCO and is active in the Collegiate Outing Association and various conservation groups, the Sierra Club in particular.

DANIEL ROSENBERG. Member of the conservation staff of the Sierra Club. A graduate of San Francisco State in Earth Sciences, Mr. Rosenberg has worked for many years for the Sierra Club, in his youth as shipping clerk, then as Conservation Organizer, and most recently as a staff member of the Club's efforts to preserve the San Francisco Bay from deterioration.

WILLIAM ROTH. Director and Chairman of the Executive Committee at Pacific Life Assurance Company. Mr. Roth is a man of many accomplishments, including present positions as a Director of Atheneum Publishers, of Norton Simon, Inc., and of Crocker-Citizens National Bank, and as a Regent of the University of California. From 1963 to 1969 he served in the Office of the Special Representative for Trade Negotiations, Executive Office of the President of the United States.

A. J. W. SCHEFFEY. Director of the Center for Environmental Studies at Williams College. Dr. Scheffey is an Associate Professor of Resource Policy. Previous to his post as Director of the Center for Environmental Studies at Williams, he taught resource policy at the University of Massachusetts and headed the federal Outdoor Recreation Resources Review Commission. He has written many studies on resources and recreation, including *Landscape and Community, A Study of Conservation Commissions in New England*.

MICHAEL SCRIVEN. Professor of Philosophy at the University of California at Berkeley. Dr. Scriven, with degrees in mathematics, philosophy, and humanities, taught philosophy at the University of Minnesota, Swarthmore College, and Indiana University, prior to his arrival at Berkeley. He has written prodigiously in the fields of philosophy, education, ethics, logic, philosphy of science, psychology, and parapsychology.

PAUL B. SEARS. Professor Emeritus of Conservation at Yale University. Dr. Sears is now living in retirement in Taos, New Mexico. He was a pioneer in this nation's conservation movement, father of Yale's first conservation school, and achieved world renown for such books as *Deserts on the March*.

GARY SNYDER. Mr. Snyder is a poet living north of San Francisco. *Wave* and *Earth Household* are among his volumes of poetry and prose.

STEPHEN H. SPURR. Dean of the Rackman School of Graduate Studies at the University of Michigan. Dean Spurr holds a co-terminus appointment as Professor in the School of Natural Resources. He was a principal figure as a consultant on the Rampart Dam Study concerning the Yukon River, and he is a noted author of texts and articles.

ELVIS J. STAHR. President of the Audubon Society. Dr. Stahr has had a long career in education, serving as Executive Director of President Eisenhower's Committee on Education and as President of West Virginia University and of Indiana University. In 1968 he became President of the Audubon Society, which has for many years played a distinguished role in educating Americans in natural values.

RICHARD STEARNS. Rhodes Scholar at Balliol College, Oxford University. Prior to his study of literature at Oxford, Mr. Stearns was a Regional Director for the McCarthy Presidential campaign and was Vice-President of the National Student Association. He is currently a U.S. Commissioner for UNESCO.

RICHARD B. STONER. Vice Chairman of the Board of Cummins Engine Company, Incorporated. Mr. Stoner is a graduate of Harvard Law School, a member of the Executive Committee of the Western Highway Institute, a Democratic National Committeeman, a member of the General Assembly of the National Council of Churches, and is very active in the fields of education and religion.

RICHARD D. TABER. Professor and Graduate Program Advisor at the University of Washington. Dr. Taber, a zoologist and specialist in wildlife ecology, taught at the University of California at Berkeley, the University of Montana, and the West Pakistan Agricultural University before coming to the College of Forest Resources at the University of Washington. He has published several articles on North American fauna.

WOLF VON ECKHARDT. Architectural critic for the *Washington Post*. Mr. Von Eckhardt is the author of several papers on the environment and of a forthcoming book. He is an outspoken proponent of increased news coverage of environmental issues.

CYNTHIA WAYBURN. Undergraduate student at the University of California at Santa Cruz. Miss Wayburn has had a lifetime interest in conservation affairs and currently serves as the conservation coordinator on the campus.

WILLIAM C. WHEATON. Dean of the College of Environmental Design at the University of California at Berkeley. The problems of the city and particularly of housing are Dr. Wheaton's area of concern. He was at one time Director of the University of Pennsylvania's Institute of Urban Studies and subsequently Director of the University of California's Institute of Urban and Regional Development. He has been a consultant to numerous governmental agencies and private firms, including the U.S. State Department, HUD, and the Ford Foundation.

HARVEY WHEELER. Fellow-in-Residence at the Center for the Study of Democratic Institutions at Santa Barbara, California. Dr. Wheeler has taught political science at Harvard, Johns Hopkins, and Washington and Lee Universities. He is a distinguished figure in political theory, having written many monographs, and he co-authored with Eugene Burdick the novel *Fail-Safe*.